MINDFULNESS

ALSO BY JOSEPH GOLDSTEIN

A Heart Full of Peace

One Dharma: The Emerging Western Buddhism

Insight Meditation: The Practice of Freedom

The Experience of Insight

Seeking the Heart of Wisdom (with Jack Kornfield)

Audio

Abiding in Mindfulness, Volume 1: The Body

Abiding in Mindfulness, Volume 2: On Feeling, the Mind, and Dhamma

Abiding in Mindfulness, Volume 3: On Dhamma

Insight Meditation Kit: A Step-by-Step Course on How to Meditate
(with Sharon Salzberg)

Mindfulness: Six Guided Practices for Awakening

MINDFULNESS

A Practical Guide
to Awakening

Joseph Goldstein

sounds true
BOULDER, COLORADO

Sounds True, Inc.
Boulder, CO 80306

Copyright © 2013 Joseph Goldstein

Sounds True is a trademark of Sounds True, Inc.

Published 2013

Cover design by Rachael Murray
Cover photo © Shooter from Shutterstock.com

Analayo Bhikku, Satipatthana Discourse from *Sattipatthana: The Direct Path to Realization*.
Copyright © 2003. Reprinted with permission from Windhorse Publications Ltd.

The Middle Length Discourses of the Buddha: A Translation of the Majjhima Nikaya, translated by
Bhikkhu Bodhi and Bhikkhu Nanamoli. Copyright © 1995. Reprinted with permission from
Wisdom Publications, wisdompubs.org.

Fernando Pessoa, excerpt from "Live, You Say, in the Present" from *Poems of Fernando Pessoa*,
translated by Edwin Honig. Copyright © 2001. Reprinted with permission from City
Lights Books.

Wislawa Szymborska, "View with a Grain of Sand" from *View with a Grain of Sand: Selected
Poems*. Copyright © 1995. Reprinted with permission from Houghton Mifflin Harcourt
Publishing Company. All rights reserved.

The Connected Discourses of the Buddha: A Translation of the Samyutta Nikaya, translated by
Bhikkhu Bodhi. Copyright © 2000. Reprinted with permission from Wisdom Publications,
wisdompubs.org.

Printed in the United States of America

Library of Congress Cataloging-in-Publication Data
Goldstein, Joseph, 1944-
  Mindfulness : a practical guide to awakening / Joseph Goldstein.
    pages cm
  Includes bibliographical references and index.
  ISBN 978-1-62203-063-7
  1. Meditation—Buddhism. 2. Tipitaka. Suttapitaka. Majjhimanikaya. Satipatthanasutta. I.
Tipitaka. Suttapitaka. Majjhimanikaya. Satipatthanasutta. English. II. Title.
  BQ5612.G642 2013
  294.3'4435--dc23
                          2013010777

Ebook ISBN: 978-1-62203-065-1

10 9 8 7 6 5 4

Dedicated to Sayadaw U Paṇḍita,
whose mastery of mindfulness and the teachings of the Buddha
has inspired and helped so many people.

Contents

Preface . . . xi

Introduction . . . xiii

The Four Qualities of Mind

1 Ardency: The Long-Enduring Mind . . . 3

2 Clearly Knowing: Cultivating Clear
Comprehension . . . 11

3 Mindfulness: The Gateway to Wisdom . . . 13

4 Concentration: The Collected Nature of Mind . . . 21

The Satipaṭṭhāna Refrain

5 Contemplating the Four Foundations . . . 27

6 Bare Knowing and Continuity of Mindfulness . . . 35

Mindfulness of the Body

7 Mindfulness of Breathing . . . 45

8 Mindfulness of Postures . . . 55

9 Mindfulness of Activities . . . 61

10 Mindfulness of Physical Characteristics . . . 67

Mindfulness of Feelings

11 Liberation through Feelings . . . 81

12 Worldly and Unworldly Feelings . . . 89

Mindfulness of Mind

13 The Wholesome and Unwholesome
    Roots of Mind . . . 101

14 The Refrain: On Feelings and Mind . . . 111

Mindfulness of Dhammas—The Five Hindrances

15 Desire . . . 121

16 Aversion . . . 131

17 Sloth and Torpor . . . 141

18 Restlessness and Worry . . . 153

19 Doubt . . . 163

Mindfulness of Dhammas—The Five Aggregates of Clinging

20 Material Elements, Feelings, and Perceptions . . . 171

21 Formations and Consciousness . . . 183

22 Contemplating the Five Aggregates . . . 195

Mindfulness of Dhammas—The Six Sense Spheres

23 How We Experience the World . . . 205

24 The Wheel of Saṃsāra . . . 211

Mindfulness of Dhammas—The Seven Factors of Awakening

25 Mindfulness . . . 225

26 Investigation of Dhammas . . . 233

27 Energy . . . 239

28 Rapture . . . 247

29 Calm . . . 257

30 Concentration . . . 265

31 Equanimity . . . 277

Mindfulness of Dhammas—The Four Noble Truths

32 The First Noble Truth: Dukkha . . . 287

33 The Second Noble Truth: The Cause of Dukkha . . . 299

34 The Third Noble Truth: The Cessation of Dukkha . . . 309

35 The Fourth Noble Truth: The Way Leading
to the Cessation of Dukkha . . . 319

Mindfulness of Dhammas—
The Noble Eightfold Path: Wisdom Factors

36 Right View: Worldly Ease . . . 327

37 Right View: Liberation . . . 337

38 Right Thought: Renunciation . . . 345

39 Right Thought: Lovingkindness . . . 353

40 Right Thought: Compassion . . . 361

Mindfulness of Dhammas—
The Noble Eightfold Path: Morality Factors

41 Right Speech . . . 371

42 Right Action and Right Livelihood . . . 379

Mindfulness of Dhammas—
The Noble Eightfold Path: Concentration Factors

43 Right Effort, Right Mindfulness,
Right Concentration . . . 391

44 The Realization of Nibbāna . . . 401

Appendix A Translation of the Satipaṭṭhāna Sutta by Anālayo . . . 405

Appendix B Glossary . . . 417

Acknowledgments . . . 423

Notes . . . 425

Index . . . 441

About the Author . . . 459

Preface

I FIRST BECAME INTERESTED IN Buddhism and meditation as a Peace Corps volunteer in Thailand. After returning home and trying to continue the practice on my own, I quickly realized that I needed a teacher. This was in 1967, and at that time there were few Buddhist teachers to be found in the West. So I returned to Asia, first stopping in India to look for someone who could guide my practice. I went to Himalayan hill stations, unfortunately in winter when all the Tibetan teachers had gone south. After visiting different ashrams, I ended up in Bodh Gaya, a small village in Northern India, where Siddhartha Gotama became the Buddha, the Awakened One.

Anagārika Munindra, my first teacher, had just returned from nine years in Burma and had begun teaching *vipassanā,* or insight meditation. When I first arrived, he said something so simple and direct that I knew I had come to my spiritual home: "If you want to understand your mind, sit down and observe it." As he explained the practice, I resonated with this direct looking at the nature of the mind and body, at how suffering is created and how we can be free.

The simple, although not always easy, practices of vipassanā are all rooted in one important discourse of the Buddha: the Satipaṭṭhāna Sutta. *Satipaṭṭhāna* is often translated as "the four foundations of mindfulness," but another, and perhaps more helpful, translation is "the four ways of establishing mindfulness." In terms of awareness of the different aspects of our experience, this slight shift of translation has important implications: it gives more emphasis to the process of awareness itself, rather than to the particular objects of our attention.

Although I had read the Satipaṭṭhāna Sutta many times over the years, I was inspired to conduct a line-by-line investigation of its meaning after reading a wonderful volume by Anālayo, *Satipaṭṭhāna: The Direct Path to Realization.* His clear analysis and deep understanding reawakened my interest in systematically presenting these teachings of the Buddha in their entirety.

Mindfulness: A Practical Guide to Awakening grew out of a series of forty-six lectures I gave at the Forest Refuge, a retreat facility for experienced practitioners at the Insight Meditation Society in Barre, Massachusetts. In the course of these lectures, besides making many references to the original words of the Buddha, I also drew on Anālayo's book, teachings from many different Buddhist teachers and traditions, and stories from my own meditation experience. Throughout the lecture series and this current work, my primary emphasis has been on how to put all these teachings into practice as a way of transforming our lives and understanding.

Introduction

MINDFULNESS IS SUCH AN ORDINARY word. It doesn't have the spiritual cachet of words like *wisdom* or *compassion* or *love,* and only in recent times has it entered the lexicon of common usage. Growing up in the fifties, I had never even heard the word. And the sixties, of course, had their own unique vocabulary. But beginning in the seventies and continuing until today, mindfulness is coming into its own. It started with meditation retreats introducing the concept—and the practice—to an ever-increasing number of people. And then, through programs like Mindfulness-Based Stress Reduction; Mindfulness-Based Cognitive Therapy; mindfulness programs in schools, universities, and businesses; and research in state-of-the-art neuroscience labs, the potential inherent in this capacity of the mind to be present, to be aware of what's happening, is gaining widespread credibility and interest.

As just one example, all patients participating in the Duke Integrative Medicine program at Duke University are introduced to the body-mind relationship and the concept of mindfulness. Jeffrey Brantley, MD, founder of the program, said, "Mindfulness is at the core of everything we do. We believe that the more mindful people can be as they face health challenges, the healthier they will be."[1]

A few years ago, a friend pioneered a program teaching mindfulness practice to second graders. Here are some of the evaluations from these young practitioners:

> "Mindfulness helps me get better grades."
>> "Mindfulness helps me calm down when I get upset. It
> also helps me with sports and to go to sleep at night."

"Thank you for teaching mindfulness. Mindfulness changed my life."

"Mindfulness really gets me calm."

"Mindfulness is the best thing I have done in my life."

"I love mindfulness."

Given the great flowering of mindfulness now taking place, it would be helpful to explore its roots. Where did this practice come from? What is the range and depth of its application? How can we understand its great transformative power to awaken us from the dreamlike patterns of our lives? Although this book is an in-depth guide to mindfulness practice and understanding, the range and depth of these teachings may open new possibilities and levels of subtlety for the application of mindfulness in our daily lives. Just as the hard science and engineering of space travel brought many new inventions to the marketplace, so too the depth of the classical understanding that comes from meditation can bring new practices and transformative insights to our lives in the world.

Over a dining-room table, someone once asked me to define mindfulness in just a few words. Phrases like "living in the moment" or "being present" give a first intimation of what mindfulness is, but asking, "What is mindfulness?" is a bit like asking, "What is art?" or "What is love?" Fully plumbing the depths of mindfulness requires time and exploration. There is a wealth of meaning and nuance in the experience of mindfulness that can enrich our lives in unimagined ways. This book is an attempt to mine these riches.

In the Satipaṭṭhāna Sutta, the Buddha's discourse on the four ways of establishing mindfulness, there is a broad range of instructions for understanding the mind-body process and different methodologies for freeing the mind from the causes of suffering. We need not attempt to put all of them into practice and certainly not all at the same time. The Buddha himself gave different instructions, depending on the temperaments and inclinations of his listeners. But once we have a simple baseline of practice that both suits our temperaments and inspires us to continue, we can deepen our understanding by expanding the field of our inquiry. At different times, particular instructions in this discourse may touch us and enliven our practice in unexpected ways.

The Buddha introduces this discourse with an amazingly bold and unambiguous statement: "This is the direct path for the purification of beings, for the surmounting of sorrow and lamentation, for the disappearance of pain and grief, for the attainment of the true way, for the realization of *nibbāna*—namely the four foundations of mindfulness."[2]

Given the magnitude and import of this declaration—this is the direct path to liberation—it will be useful to explore this discourse in detail, using the Buddha's own words to guide and deepen our understanding. And as we look at this *sutta,* we find that all of the Buddha's teachings are contained within it. With each of these four ways of establishing mindfulness, the Buddha teaches different methods and techniques that liberate the mind. By the end of the discourse, he has laid out this most amazing and complete path to awakening. Different traditions of vipassanā might emphasize one or another of these exercises, but any one of them is sufficient to bring us to the end of the path. When we open any one door of the Dharma, it leads to all the rest.

SOME NOTES ABOUT THE TEXT

A few words are needed here to explain the use of Pali and Sanskrit terms. Pali derives from the vernacular languages of Northern India at the time of the Buddha and in the following few centuries. Sanskrit was both the sacred and literary language of ancient India. Because the Buddha believed that the Dharma should be taught in ways that even the simplest people could understand, he gave his discourses in Pali.

As Buddhism evolved over the centuries, teachings and discourses from the later schools were written in Sanskrit, and many of the Buddhist terms we are most familiar with are in this language. The two languages are closely related, as you can see from these pairs of Sanskrit and Pali terms: *dharma/dhamma, sutra/sutta, bodhisattva/bodhisatta, nirvāna/nibbāna.* For ease of recognition, I sometimes use the more familiar Sanskrit forms, except when quoting or referring to Pali texts. A few times you many see both forms on the same page. In the text, most of the Pali and Sanskrit words are in italics, except for a few of the most commonly used terms.

Although the term *monk* is the usual translation for the Pali word *bhikkhu,* the commentaries have a much more expansive definition and one that empowers all of us on the path. In the context of the Satipaṭṭhāna Sutta, *bhikkhu* is a term indicating any person who earnestly endeavors to accomplish the practice of the teaching: "Whoever undertakes that practice . . . is here comprised under the term 'bhikkhu.'"[3]

In some of the translations from the suttas, I have substituted the gender-neutral term *one* for the masculine pronoun *he.* Although the Buddha originally gave many of these discourses to the order of monks, I felt that a more inclusive pronoun would be more useful for Western readers. Most of the sutta translations are from Wisdom Publications' series *Teachings of the Buddha,* although many of the excerpts from the Satipaṭṭhāna Sutta are from Anālayo's book *Satipaṭṭhāna: The Direct Path to Realization.* His translation of the complete sutta can be found in Appendix A. Also, at times I have adapted different quotations, drawing on other translations to highlight particular aspects of teachings. These adaptations have been indicated in the notes.

Although this book follows the format of the Satipaṭṭhāna Sutta and can be read through in sequence, most of the chapters are complete in themselves; it's possible to find topics of interest in the table of contents and explore those particular chapters on their own.

As we read the Buddha's words, one aspect of our cultural attention deficit disorder becomes apparent. I have found that in reading the suttas or listening to the discourses, whenever I come across a lot of repetition, my mind tends to skip over them, thinking, "Yes, I've already read or heard that," and I hurry on to the next sentence or page. Perhaps the repetitions are simply a function of the oral tradition, but there is another possibility. Maybe when the Buddha repeats certain phrases over and over again, he is trying to tell us something: that these are important qualities of mind to cultivate and strengthen in our practice and in our lives. Can we read these words of the Buddha as if he were speaking them directly to us? If we do, they have the power to open new doors of understanding and new possibilities of freedom.

THE FOUR QUALITIES OF MIND

1

Ardency

The Long-Enduring Mind

FOLLOWING THE DECLARATION THAT THE four ways of establishing mindfulness are the direct path to liberation, the Satipaṭṭhāna Sutta continues with a concise definition of the path, highlighting its essential characteristics. The Buddha first points out the four fields, or pastures, for establishing mindfulness: body, feelings, mind, and *dhammas* (categories of experience). When we establish mindfulness in them, or of them, then we abide safely. When we're not mindful, not aware, then we often get lost in unwholesome reactions, creating suffering for ourselves and others.

> What are the four? Here, bhikkhus, in regard to the body a bhikkhu abides contemplating the body, ardent, clearly knowing, and mindful, free from desires and discontent in regard to the world. In regard to feelings he abides contemplating feelings, ardent, clearly knowing, and mindful, free from desires and discontent in regard to the world. In regard to the mind he abides contemplating the mind, ardent, clearly knowing, and mindful, free from desires and discontent in regard to the world. In regard to dhammas he abides contemplating dhammas, ardent, clearly knowing,

and mindful, free from desires and discontent in regard to
the world.[1]

In this definition, the Buddha also introduces the mental qualities
necessary for walking the path: one needs to be ardent, clearly knowing, and mindful, free from desires and discontent in regard to the
world. *Ardent* implies a balanced and sustained application of effort.
But *ardent* also suggests warmth of feeling, a passionate and strong
enthusiasm or devotion because we realize the value and importance
of something. When the Buddha says that a bhikkhu (all of us on the
path) abides ardently, he is urging us to take great care, with continuity and perseverance, in what we do.

The great Chinese Ch'an master Hsu Yun attained enlightenment
at age fifty-six, and then taught for the next sixty-four years. He
died at the age of one hundred and twenty. He called this quality of
ardency "the long-enduring mind." It is what sustains and nourishes
us through all the many ups and downs of practice.

Spiritual ardency is the wellspring of a courageous heart. It gives
us the strength to continue through all the difficulties of the journey.
The question for us is how to practice and cultivate ardency, so that it
becomes a powerful and onward-leading force in our lives.

REFLECT ON THE PRECIOUSNESS OF THE DHARMA

One way to cultivate ardency is to reflect on the purpose of our practice, realizing that the Dharma is a jewel of priceless value. When
properly understood, the Dharma is the source of every happiness.
Ajahn Mun, one of the most renowned meditation masters in the
Thai Forest tradition, reminds us that understanding the mind is the
same as understanding the Dharma, and that realizing the deepest
truths of the mind is the attainment of awakening.

Another way of arousing ardency in our lives is to reflect on
how rare it is in this life to connect with teachings that liberate the
heart and mind. Dilgo Khyentse Rinpoche, one of the great Tibetan
Dzogchen masters of the last century, reminded us of this:

> Ask yourself how many of the billions of inhabitants of this
> planet have any idea of how rare it is to have been born as a
> human being. How many of those who understand the rarity

of human birth ever think of using that chance to practice the Dharma? How many of those who think of practice actually do? How many of those who start continue? . . . But once you see the unique opportunity that human life can bring, you will definitely direct all your energy into reaping its true worth by putting the Dharma into practice.[2]

These reflections generate in us tremendous respect for the Dharma, for our fellow practitioners, and for ourselves. This respect then leads us to greater caring and ardency for each moment.

REFLECT ON IMPERMANENCE

We can also strengthen the quality of ardor by reflecting on the transiency of all phenomena. Look at all the things we become attached to, whether they are people or possessions or feelings or conditions of the body. Nothing we have, no one in our lives, no state of mind is exempt from change. Nothing at all can prevent the universal process of birth, growth, decay, and death.

When we don't deeply understand the truth of impermanence, we devote ourselves, our lives, and even our meditation practice to seeking and wanting other people, possessions, experiences. We get caught up in all the appearances of *saṃsāra,* the rounds of birth and death, and solidify our sense of self in the process. There is no peace.

The following is an excerpt from *The Life of Shabkar,* a book of teachings by an eighteenth-century wandering Tibetan yogi, and is a powerful testament to the truth of change:

Another day, I went for some fresh air to a meadow covered with flowers. . . . While singing and remaining in a state of awareness of the absolute view, I noticed among the profusion of flowers spread out before me one particular flower waving gently on its long stem and giving out a sweet fragrance. As it swayed from side to side, I heard this song in the rustling of its petals. . . .

Listen to me, mountain dweller: . . .
I don't want to hurt your feelings,
But, in fact, you even lack awareness

Of impermanence and death,
Let alone any realization of emptiness.

For those with such awareness,
Outer phenomena all teach impermanence and death.
I, the flower, will now give you, the yogi,
A bit of helpful advice
On death and impermanence.

A flower born in a meadow,
I enjoy perfect happiness
With my brightly colored petals in full bloom.
Surrounded by an eager cloud of bees,
I dance gaily, swaying gently with the wind.
When a fine rain falls, my petals wrap around me;
When the sun shines I open like a smile.

Right now I look well enough,
But I won't last long.
Not at all.

Unwelcome frost will dull the vivid colors,
Till turning brown I wither.
Thinking of this, I am disturbed.
Later still, winds—
violent and merciless—
will tear me apart until I turn to dust. . . .

You, hermit, . . .
Are of the same nature.

Surrounded by a host of disciples,
You enjoy a fine complexion,
Your body of flesh and blood is full of life.
When others praise you,
you dance with joy; . . .

Right now, you look well enough.
But you won't last long.
Not at all.

Unhealthy ageing will steal away
Your healthy vigor;
Your hair will whiten
And your back will grow bent. . . .

When touched by the merciless hands
Of illness and death
You will leave this world
For the next life. . . .

Since you, mountain-roaming hermit,
And I, a mountain-born flower,
Are mountain friends,
I have offered you
These words of good advice.
Then the flower fell silent and remained still. In reply, I sang:
O brilliant, exquisite flower,
Your discourse on impermanence
Is wonderful indeed.
But what shall the two of us do?
Is there nothing that can be done? . . .
The flower replied:
. . . Among all the activities of saṃsara,
There is not one that is lasting.

Whatever is born will die;
Whatever is joined will come apart;
Whatever is gathered will disperse;
Whatever is high will fall.

Having considered this,
I resolve not to be attached

To these lush meadows,
Even now, in the full glory of my display,
Even as my petals unfold in splendor . . .

You too, while strong and fit,
Should abandon your clinging. . . .
Seek the pure field of freedom,
The great serenity.[3]

REFLECT ON KARMA

The third reflection that arouses ardor in our practice is the understanding of the law of karma. This is the fundamental and essential understanding that all of our volitional actions—of body, speech, and mind—bear fruit depending on the motivation associated with them. Actions rooted in greed, hatred, or ignorance bring unpleasant results. Actions rooted in nongreed, nonhatred, and nondelusion bring many different kinds of happiness and wellbeing.

According to the law of karma, the only things that can be said to truly belong to us are our actions and their results; the results of our actions follow us like a shadow, or, to use an ancient image, like the wheel of the oxcart following the foot of the ox. This principle is so fundamental and far-reaching that it was emphasized again and again by the Buddha and by the great enlightened beings up until the present. The very first lines of the Dhammapada highlight this understanding:

> Mind is the forerunner of all things. Speak or act with an
> impure mind, suffering follows as the wagon wheel follows
> the hoof of the ox.
> Mind is the forerunner of all things. Speak or act with
> peaceful mind, happiness follows like a shadow that never
> leaves.[4]

There is the famous statement of Padmasambhava, the great Indian adept who brought Buddhism to Tibet: "Though my view is as vast as the sky, my attention to the law of karma is as fine as a grain of barley flour." The Dalai Lama has said that if he had to choose whether to emphasize emptiness or karma in his teaching, as important as the understanding of emptiness is, he would emphasize the teachings of karma. And finally, the Korean Zen master Seung Sahn Sunim summed up the integration of emptiness and karma with this quintessential Zen statement: "There is no right and no wrong, but right is right and wrong is wrong."

But it is not enough to simply have this understanding of karma; we need to practice applying it in our lives. As we're about to act, or when thoughts or emotions are predominant, do we remember to investigate and reflect on our motivation? Do we ask ourselves, "Is this act or mind state skillful or unskillful? Is this something to cultivate or abandon? Where is this motivation leading? Do I want to go there?"

2

Clearly Knowing

Cultivating Clear Comprehension

SAMPAJAÑÑA IS THE PALI TERM for the second quality
of mind the Buddha emphasized in the opening paragraphs of the
Satipaṭṭhāna Sutta. It is usually translated as "clearly knowing," "clear
comprehension," or "fully aware." It is the ability to clearly comprehend what is taking place, and it comprises the investigation and
wisdom aspects associated with mindfulness. We will take a closer
and more detailed look at this quality of clear knowing in chapter 9:
Mindfulness of Activities.

Cultivating clear comprehension, knowing what we're doing
and why, is a profound and transforming practice. It highlights the
understanding that mindfulness is more than simply being present.
With clear comprehension, we know the purpose and appropriateness of what we're doing; we understand the motivations behind our
actions. So often we find ourselves in the middle of an action before
we quite know how we got there. Have you ever found your hand
in the refrigerator without having been clearly aware of the desire,
the decision, or the appropriateness of the act? When we act in full
awareness, of even small things, it's possible to notice the motivation
and then to consider: is this motivation, this action, skillful or not,
useful or not? In the time of the Buddha, there were a few monks

living together in a forest grove. The Buddha went to them and asked if they were all living harmoniously. Anuruddha, one of the great disciples of the Buddha, replied, "Why should I not set aside what I wish to do, and do what these venerable ones wish to do?" And each of the other monks replied in just the same way. Clearly knowing what we're doing allows us the opportunity to be living lovingkindness, rather than just practicing it on the meditation cushion.

Awareness of motivation plays a central role in the path of liberation. And as we settle into a growing awareness of ourselves, we begin to realize that our practice is not for ourselves alone, but can be for the benefit and happiness of all beings. How *does* our practice benefit others? How does feeling our breath or taking a mindful step help anyone else? It happens in several ways. The more we understand our own minds, the more we understand everyone else. We increasingly feel the commonality of our human condition, of what creates suffering and how we can be free.

Our practice also benefits others through the transformation of how we are in the world. If we're more accepting, more peaceful, less judgmental, less selfish, then the whole world is that much more loving and peaceful, that much less judgmental and selfish. Our mind-body is a vibrating, resonating energy system. Of necessity, how we are affects everyone around us. On a boat in the middle of a great storm, one wise, calm person can bring everyone to safety. The world is like that boat, tossed by the storms of greed and hatred and fear. Can we be one of those people who help to keep it safe? The Buddha gave this charge to his first sixty enlightened disciples:

> "Go forth, O Bhikkhus, for the good of the many, for the
> happiness of the many, out of compassion for the world,
> for the good, benefit and happiness of gods and men. Let
> not two go by one way. Preach, O Bhikkhus, the Dhamma,
> excellent in the beginning, excellent in the middle, excellent
> in the end. . . . Proclaim the Holy Life, altogether perfect
> and pure."[1]

We can follow, to some extent, in their footsteps.

3

Mindfulness

The Gateway to Wisdom

MINDFULNESS, THE THIRD QUALITY OF mind the Buddha refers to, is the translation of the Pali word *sati,* and it holds a central place in every Buddhist tradition. It is what makes any spiritual path possible. Mindfulness has several meanings and functions, all of which are key to the growth of wisdom. Understanding this richness of meaning opens up new potential for its power to transform our lives.

PRESENT-MOMENT AWARENESS

The most common understanding of mindfulness is that of present-moment awareness, presence of mind, wakefulness. This is the opposite of absentmindedness. Whenever we're lost or confused about what to do, we can simply come back to the present-moment experience.

After one of my public talks, a woman who had been on several retreats came up to me and said she had recently been on a cruise, and in her room was a map of the ship with an arrow and caption saying, "You are here." She said that for the rest of the voyage, wherever she was and whatever she was doing, those words became the reminder to simply be present: "You are here."

Mindfulness in this aspect is the quality of bare attention, of non-interfering awareness, which we're familiar with from our enjoyment of music. When we're listening to the music, our minds are open and attentive, not attempting to control what comes next, not reflecting on the notes just past. There is a great power when we learn how to listen; it is this quality of receptivity that allows intuitive wisdom to arise. An interviewer once asked Mother Teresa what she says to God when she prays. "I don't say anything," she replied. "I just listen." Then the interviewer asked her what God says to her. "He doesn't say anything," said Mother Teresa. "He just listens. And if you don't understand that, I can't explain it to you."[1]

THE PRACTICE OF REMEMBERING

On another level, and one which we don't often associate with mindfulness, *sati* means "remembering," and it refers to the practice of wholesome recollection that supports and energizes us on this path of awakening. In the texts, these recollections include the virtues of the Buddha, Dharma, and Sangha, as well as one's own generosity and ethical conduct.

Reflecting on the qualities of the Buddha, Dharma, and Sangha helps arouse confidence and faith in the mind, enlarging the context of our own particular struggles. We remember that all the ups and downs of practice are part of a much larger journey. On the night of the Buddha's enlightenment, he overcame the armies of Māra, the forces of desire and aversion, restlessness and conceit. And every time we confront these very same forces in our own minds, we also are sitting under the Bodhi tree of awakening. We understand that the Bodhisattva's struggle is our own.

It enlarges our perspective when we consider the magnitude of what it means to overcome the habits of seduction that keep us narrow-minded and closed-hearted. When we practice these liberation teachings of the Buddha, we are practicing a path of purification that the Buddha discovered and that so many others have accomplished. One of the most inspiring phrases to me is the traditional declaration of awakening spoken by women and men who have completed the journey: "done is what had to be done." Recollecting the Buddha, Dharma, and Sangha reminds us that awakening is possible for us as well. Mindfulness as remembering also includes reflection on our commitment to ethical conduct (*sīla,* in Pali). This may not be something we often do, but when we acknowledge our practice of sīla, it strengthens our self-confidence and self-respect. It reminds us that we can indeed train the mind, that we can discern which actions are wholesome and which are not.

Of course, sometimes our Western habit of self-judgment jumps into the mix. One time, when I was practicing in Burma and going through a long stretch of difficulty, my teacher, the Burmese meditation master Sayadaw U Paṇḍita, suggested that I contemplate my sīla. He said this as a way of encouraging me, to brighten my mind and arouse more joy. But when I heard, "contemplate your sīla," my first thought was, "What did I do wrong?"

For most of us, there may well be ethical lapses of one kind or another. But our willingness to see them and recommit to non-harming both others and ourselves keeps us moving forward. As the Buddha said, "It is growth in the Noble One's discipline when one sees one's transgressions as such and makes amends in accordance with the Dharma by undertaking restraint in the future." This is a much healthier and more beneficial approach than being weighed down by guilt over past actions.

BALANCING THE SPIRITUAL FACULTIES

Mindfulness also works to balance what the Buddha called "the five spiritual faculties": faith, energy, mindfulness, concentration, and wisdom. And one way we can understand our entire spiritual journey is as the strengthening and balancing of these faculties. Mindfulness makes us aware when any of them are deficient or in excess; for example, it balances faith and wisdom, energy and concentration. When we have too much faith, we can become dogmatic, attached to our own views. And we can see all too often how this blind belief leads to so much conflict and suffering in the world.

When faith is not balanced with wisdom, we can also become overly enthusiastic about our meditation experiences. There is a state called "pseudo-nirvāna." This is when our insight is developing, but in our enthusiasm we forget to be mindful, and then, because of our attachment to these very states, they become corruptions of insight. Sayadaw U Paṇḍita would often ask us as we described different states, "Did you note it?" Mindfulness was the true measure of our practice, not what particular experience we were having.

On the other side, we can also get attached to some understanding or insight and stay satisfied with that. In this case, we are weak in the faith that opens us to what is beyond our current level of understanding. Understanding without faith can keep us enmeshed, often unknowingly, in wrong views. In the same way, effort and concentration need to be in balance. Too much effort without enough concentration simply leads to restlessness and agitation, while an excess of concentration without enough energy leads to sloth and torpor. It is mindfulness that keeps all these factors in balance.

PROTECTOR OF THE MIND

Besides balancing the spiritual faculties, mindfulness acts as the guardian of the sense doors, because it keeps us aware of what is arising through the senses and helps us to not get lost in the proliferation of desires. When mindfulness is present, we abide more peacefully in our lives.

Mindfulness of seeing, for example, can be particularly helpful in the midst of daily life situations. I had an illuminating experience walking down Fifth Avenue in New York, looking in store windows and seeing many seductive things for sale. After some time, I noticed that my mind was continually reaching out with desire for one thing after another. Although this reaching out was enjoyable in one way, when I looked more deeply, I saw that the mind filled with wanting is not at ease; there is an ongoing edge of agitation. It happened that, some weeks later, I found myself on the same street, but this time for some reason there was more mindfulness. I was seeing everything in the store windows, but I was just seeing. It was a much happier and more peaceful way of being.

Mindfulness also serves to protect the mind from other unskillful thoughts and emotions. Without mindfulness, we simply act out all the various patterns and habits of our conditioning. Ajahn Sumedho, one of the senior Western monks of the Thai Forest tradition, quite aptly pointed out that, contrary to some popular beliefs, our aim should be not to follow the heart but to train the heart. All of us have a mix of motivations; not everything in our hearts is wise or wholesome. The great power of mindful discernment allows us to abandon what is unwholesome and to cultivate the good. This discernment is of inestimable value for our happiness and wellbeing.

In a discourse called "The Two Kinds of Thoughts," the Buddha described different aspects of this supervising and guarding function of mindfulness. These aspects can help us understand some of the nuances of mindfulness and how to guard our minds from straying into unwholesome mind states.

> "Bhikkhus, before my enlightenment, while I was still only an unenlightened Bodhisatta, it occurred to me: 'Suppose that I divide my thoughts into two classes.' Then I set on one side thoughts of sensual desire, thoughts of ill will, and thoughts of cruelty, and I set on the other side thoughts of renunciation, thoughts of non-ill will, and thoughts of non-cruelty.
>
> "As I abided thus, diligent, ardent and resolute, a thought of sensual desire arose in me. I understood thus: 'This thought of sensual desire has arisen in me. This leads to my own affliction, to other's affliction, and to the affliction of both; it obstructs wisdom, causes difficulties, and leads away from Nibbāna.' When I considered: 'This leads to my own affliction,' it subsided in me; when I considered, 'This leads to others' affliction,' it subsided in me; when I considered: 'This leads to the affliction of both,' it subsided in me; when I considered: 'This obstructs wisdom, causes difficulties, and leads away from Nibbāna,' it subsided in me. Whenever a thought of sensual desire arose in me, I abandoned it, removed it, did away with it."[2]

The Buddha applied the same application of mindfulness to thoughts of ill will and cruelty. With recurring unskillful thoughts, we need an actively engaged mindfulness, because, as the Buddha pointed out later in this discourse, whatever we frequently think of and ponder, that will become the inclination of our minds. Mindfulness has the power to show us what kinds of thoughts are arising, and in the case of unskillful ones, what we may have unknowingly been inclining our minds toward. The simple reflection that these thoughts actually do lead to one's own and others' affliction and difficulty, away from wisdom and awakening, is an effective tool to use in those times rather than being just a phrase to read.

With wholesome states of mind, mindfulness takes a different form. We don't need to be quite so actively engaged. In fact, doing so would only lead to disturbance of mind and body. The Buddha likened this aspect of mindfulness to a cowherd guarding the cows after the crops have been safely harvested, when active vigilance regarding the cows grazing is no longer necessary:

> "Just as in the last month of the hot season, when all the crops have been brought inside the villages, a cowherd would guard his cows while staying at the root of a tree or out in the open, since he needs only to be mindful that the cows are there; so too, there was need for me only to be mindful that those states were there.
>
> "Tireless energy was aroused in me and unremitting mindfulness was established, my body was tranquil and untroubled, my mind concentrated and unified."[3]

In our practice of abiding ardent, clearly knowing, and mindful, we learn to find the appropriate balance between active and receptive, doing and nondoing.

FABRICATED AND UNFABRICATED MINDFULNESS

These different skillful means can also help us understand how different Buddhist traditions speak of mindfulness, pointing to further nuances in our own practice. Each tradition uses its own language and similes, but they are all pointing to different aspects of our experience.

One aspect is mindfulness as a cultivated state, where we are making an effort to stay attentive. We need this kind of mindfulness to bring us back to the moment. Tulku Urgyen Rinpoche, one of the great Dzogchen masters of the last century, said, "There is one thing we always need, and that is the watchman named Mindfulness, the guard who is on the lookout for when we get carried away in mindlessness."

In the Dzogchen tradition, this is called *fabricated mindfulness,* and is similar, perhaps, to what in the Theravāda Abhidhamma is called *prompted consciousness.* This is when, either by reflection or determination of the will, we deliberately endeavor to generate a certain state. There is another kind of mindfulness that is unprompted. When it is well cultivated, it arises spontaneously through the force of its own momentum. No particular effort is required. It's all just happening by itself. In this state of effortless awareness, we can further discern the presence or absence of a reference point of observation, a sense of someone observing or being mindful.

Dzogchen teachings also speak of *unfabricated mindfulness,* which, in that tradition, refers to the innate wakefulness of the mind's natural state. It is called "unfabricated," because according to these teachings, this mindfulness is not something we have created. Rather, it is like the capacity of a mirror to reflect what comes before it. That capacity is in the very nature of the mirror itself. So from this perspective, it's not something we need to get or develop, but rather something we need to recognize and come back to.

Although teachings in the different traditions may have different metaphysical underpinnings, rather than get caught up in philosophical debate, we can see them all simply as skillful means to free the mind. All these different aspects of mindfulness work in harmony. It is a rare person who can simply abide uninterruptedly in unprompted or unfabricated mindfulness, without the support of appropriate effort. But as our efforts bear fruit, we do experience times of great ease, when our practice is to simply let go, relax, and surrender into the natural unfolding.

> About this mind . . . in truth it isn't really anything. It's just
> a phenomenon. Within itself it's already peaceful. That the
> mind is not peaceful these days is because it follows moods. . . .
> Sense impressions come and trick it into happiness, suffering,
> gladness and sorrow, but the mind's true nature is none of
> those things. That gladness or sadness is not the mind, but
> only a mood coming to deceive us. The untrained mind gets
> lost and follows these things, it forgets itself, then we think
> that it is we who are upset or at ease or whatever. But really
> this mind of ours is already unmoving and peaceful . . . Our
> practice is simply to see the Original Mind. So we must train
> the mind to know those sense impressions, and not get lost
> in them. To make it peaceful. Just this is the aim of all this
> difficult practice we put ourselves through.[4]

In chapter 25: Mindfulness, we will further examine mindfulness and how it functions as one of the seven factors of awakening.

4

Concentration

The Collected Nature of Mind

IN HIS DEFINITION OF *SATIPAṬṬHĀNA,* the Buddha urges us to contemplate the four fields or foundations of mindfulness—body, feelings, mind, and dhammas—"free from desires and discontent with regard to the world." "Free from desires and discontent" refers to *samādhi,* the qualities of concentration, composure, and unification of mind that occur when the mind is free of the desires and discontents that so often arise.

There are different ways of developing concentration. Ajahn Sucitto, an English monk in the Thai Forest tradition, speaks of samādhi developing naturally through enjoying embodied presence, settling back into the body, and allowing the stress and tensions to unravel through simply being aware of what presents itself. He says,

> Receiving joy is another way to say enjoyment, and samādhi
> is the act of refined enjoyment. It is based in skillfulness. It
> is the careful collecting of oneself into the joy of the present
> moment. Joyfulness means there's no fear, no tension, no
> "ought to." There isn't anything we have to do about it. It's
> just this.[1]

Samādhi is based on skillful behavior, because without this basis in nonharming, the mind is filled with worry, regret, and agitation. When my first Dharma teacher, Munindra-ji, first visited America, he was struck with how people wanted to meditate and get enlightened, but seemed less concerned with this foundation of morality. He said that it is like trying to row a boat across a river, exerting a lot of effort in the process, but never untying the rope from the dock. It doesn't go anywhere.

Those of us living in the world can cultivate this ethical conduct by training in the basic five precepts: refraining from killing, stealing, sexual misconduct, lying, and using intoxicants that make the mind heedless. On retreat, our practice of nonharming, either others or ourselves, becomes increasingly refined. Actions and their consequences are magnified in the stillness and undistractedness of the retreat, and even ordinary actions can be seen in the context of refining our sīla.

In past years at the Insight Meditation Society, we sometimes had what we called the "window wars." Especially in the winter, there could be disagreement about how much the windows should be cracked open to let in fresh air. One person would come into the hall and close all the windows because they were feeling too cold. Another person would enter and open some of them because they felt the need for fresh air. In Burma, there was a similar phenomenon with the fans—some people wanted them turned on, others wanted them turned off. In both cases, can we understand that people have different needs and desires, and let go of the idea that our own preferences should automatically take precedence?

With the foundation of sīla and a nonagitated mind, we settle more easily into a happy, relaxed state, which is itself the proximate cause of concentration. And although we often speak of the difficulties we might face in practice, it is essentially a path of increasing happiness.

CONTINUITY OF MINDFULNESS

The strengthening of concentration comes about through the continuity of mindfulness. We can practice this continuity in two ways. The first way is cultivating a directed awareness on a single object. We practice keeping the mind steady on the breath, the movements of a step, a sound. The second way develops a more choiceless awareness. Here we are cultivating one-pointedness of mind on changing objects. This is called "momentary samādhi." Our practice is the skillful interweaving of these two approaches. We can focus on a single object when the mind is sluggish or distracted, in order to develop internal joy and serenity, and then when the mind is again collected we can open to an undirected choiceless mode of awareness. After some time, we get a very intuitive feel for which is appropriate at any given time.

When I first began meditation practice, I had very little concentration. I enjoyed thinking and would spend much of the time lost in reverie. Over the years I found one particular practice that helped a lot in strengthening this samādhi factor. Both in formal walking meditation and also in just walking about, I changed the focus of my attention from simply knowing that I was stepping to feeling more precisely the particular sensations of each step—lightness, heaviness, pressure, stiffness, and so on. This is a way of practicing the embodied presence that Ajahn Sucitto mentioned.

ESTABLISHING CONCENTRATION TAKES TIME

One of the great gifts of deepening concentration is that it helps keep the various mental hindrances at bay; it is like building a fence to keep out unwanted intruders. By temporarily dampening the force of lust and craving, aversion and restlessness, it opens us to more refined pleasures of the mind. This, in turn, gives us impetus to develop concentration even more. Over time, we see the default level of concentration increase in our minds, which changes how we feel and how we are in the world. We create an inner environment of peace.

Although concentration is not the final goal of the practice, still it plays an essential role on the path to awakening. The Buddha emphasized this when he said that respect for concentration is one of the things that leads to the longevity of the Dharma, to its nondecay and nondisappearance. This is an important statement for the transmission of the Dharma to the West. We would like everything to be instant—even enlightenment—and we often don't want to put in the time or effort to develop and deepen our concentration. But as samādhi gets stronger in our daily lives, it helps us find that place where we increasingly abide free of desires and discontent in regard to the world, and this peaceful composure becomes the basis for greater happiness and freedom.

We will look at concentration in much greater detail in chapter 30: Concentration.

THE SATIPAṬṬHĀNA
REFRAIN

5

Contemplating the
Four Foundations

THERE IS AN ELEMENT OF the Satipaṭṭhāna Sutta that stands
out by virtue of the frequency of its repetition. That is a refrain that
occurs thirteen different times in the discourse, following each of the
specific meditation instructions pertaining to the four foundations
of mindfulness.

> "In this way, in regard to the body [feelings, mind, dhammas]
> one abides contemplating the body [feelings, mind,
> dhammas] internally, or one abides contemplating externally,
> or one abides contemplating both internally and externally.
> One abides contemplating the nature of arising in the body
> [feelings, mind, dhammas] . . . the nature of passing away
> in . . . or the nature of both arising and passing away in.
> Mindfulness that 'there is a body' [feelings, mind, dhammas]
> is established in one to the extent necessary for bare
> knowledge and continuous mindfulness. And one abides
> independent, not clinging to anything in the world. . . ."

Through the repetition of the refrain, the Buddha reminds us
again and again what are the essential aspects of the practice:

- Contemplating our experience internally, externally, and both;
- Contemplating the nature of impermanence—the arising, the passing away, and both the arising and passing away in regard to our experience;
- Establishing enough mindfulness to recognize simply what is unfolding moment to moment—without mental commentary—and to remain mindful of what's happening;
- Abiding without clinging to anything that enters our realm of experience.

In this chapter and in chapter 6: Bare Knowing and Continuity of Mindfulness, we will explore each of these aspects in some detail. In the sutta, the refrain first appears after the instructions on the breath. For this reason, and for the sake of efficiency, the examples in chapters 5 and 6 focus on the body. As you read, however, bear in mind that the important and explicit elements of practice outlined in the refrain apply as well to all the aspects of our experience mentioned in the other three foundations of mindfulness.

INTERNALLY AND EXTERNALLY

Contemplating the body internally seems obvious; it is mostly how we practice. It is the present-moment awareness of what arises in the body—it might be the sensations of the breath or of different sensations arising throughout the body, such as heat or cold, tightness or pressure. But what does contemplating the body externally mean? There are some interesting aspects here that meditation practitioners don't often make explicit.

Contemplating the body externally can mean being mindful of the bodily actions of others when they draw our attention. Instead of our usual tendency to judge or react when we see other people doing something, we can rest in the simple mindfulness of what the other person is doing. We can be mindful that they are walking or eating, without getting lost in our own thoughts of how fast or slow, mindful or careless they might be. An ironic and useless pattern that I've noticed on my own retreats is that my mind comments on someone not being mindful—or at least not appearing to be in my eyes—all the while being oblivious to the fact that in that very moment I'm doing exactly what it is I have a judgment about: namely, not being mindful! It usually doesn't take me long to see the absurdity of this pattern and then just to smile at these habits of mind. It's always helpful to have a sense of humor about one's own mental foibles. By practicing this simple external mindfulness, we protect our own minds from the various defilements that might arise.

Although attending to the breath is mostly internal, the instruction to be mindful of the body externally could be particularly helpful on retreat when someone else's breath may be loud and disturbing. At those times, being mindful of another's breath—whether it is in or out, long or short—can actually be part of our own path to awakening.

Being mindful of the body externally has another advantage. Have you noticed that when you're mindful of someone else moving very carefully, without distraction, that you yourself become more concentrated? This is one reason the Buddha suggested that we associate with those who are mindful and concentrated: it's contagious. In this way, our own practice becomes a real offering to our fellow practitioners.

The last part of this instruction is to contemplate both internally and externally. Anālayo suggests that this is not just a simple repetition, but rather reflects a more profound understanding that we should contemplate experience without considering it to be part of one's own experience or that of another, but just as an objective experience in itself. Being mindful internally, externally, and both reminds us of the comprehensive nature of mindfulness practice—to be aware of whatever there is, whether it is within us or without. And, in the end, to go beyond this division altogether.

ARISING AND PASSING AWAY

The second part of the refrain tells us to abide contemplating the nature of arising, the nature of passing away, and the nature of both with each object of awareness. Ledi Sayadaw, one of the great Burmese meditation masters and scholars, said that not seeing arising and passing away is ignorance, while seeing all phenomena as impermanent is the doorway to all the stages of insight and awakening. The Buddha emphasized the importance of this in many different ways.

> "Bhikkhus, when the perception of impermanence is developed and cultivated, it eliminates all sensual lust, all lust for existence, it eliminates all ignorance, it uproots the conceit, 'I am.'"[1]

> Better than one hundred years lived without seeing the arising and passing of things is one day lived seeing their arising and passing.[2]

What does this say about what we value and work for in our lives, and of the liberating effect of seeing directly—in the moment and for ourselves—the truth of change?

Ānanda, the Buddha's cousin and attendant for many years, was once recounting the many wonderful qualities of the Buddha. The Buddha, referring to himself as the Tathāgata ("one thus gone"), said in reply:

> "That being so, Ānanda, remember this too as a wonderful and marvelous quality of the Tathāgata. For the Tathāgata feelings are known as they arise, as they are present, as they disappear. Perceptions are known as they arise, are present, and disappear. Thoughts are known as they arise, are present, and disappear. Remember this too, Ānanda, as a wonderful and marvelous quality of the Tathāgata."[3]

Understanding deeply the truth of impermanence—not as a concept, but in direct experience—opens the doorway to ever-deepening insight. In the Buddha's first teaching on selflessness to the group of five ascetics, he goes through each of the five aggregates—material elements, feelings, perceptions, formations, and consciousness—pointing out the impermanence of each and how that which is impermanent is inherently unreliable and unsatisfying. And that which is unreliable and unsatisfying cannot truly be considered to be "I" or "mine." In just hearing this teaching, all five ascetics became enlightened.

How does this happen? What is the liberating power of this teaching? When we see deeply that all that is subject to arising is also subject to cessation, that whatever arises will also pass away, the mind becomes disenchanted. Becoming disenchanted, one becomes dispassionate. And through dispassion, the mind is liberated.

It's telling that in English, the words *disenchanted, disillusioned,* and *dispassionate* often have negative connotations. But looking more closely at their meaning reveals their connection to freedom. Becoming disenchanted means breaking the spell of enchantment, waking up into a fuller and greater reality. It is the happy ending of so many great myths and fairy tales. Disillusioned is not the same as being discouraged or disappointed. It is a reconnection with what is true, free of illusion. And dispassionate does not mean "indifferent" or "apathetic." Rather, it is the mind of great openness and equanimity, free of grasping.

CONTEMPLATING IMPERMANENCE

A sustained contemplation of impermanence leads to a shift in the way we experience reality. We see through the illusions of stable existence, in both what is perceived and what is perceiving. It radically reshapes our understanding of ourselves and the world. How can we practice this contemplation?

We can be mindful of impermanence on many levels. Wisdom arises when we pay attention to impermanence in ways we may already know but often overlook. There are the very obvious changes in nature: climate change, daily weather patterns, evolution and extinction of species. On the collective level, there are large-scale changes in society: the rise and fall of civilizations and cultures. On the personal level, people are born, and they die. Walking through the woods in New England, we often come across miles of stone walls and old stone foundations, with trees now growing up through them. What stories took place here? What lives as vivid as our own? What is left? We see the changing experience of our relationships or work, and most intimately, of our bodies and minds.

Given all these examples of change that are before us all the time, it is striking that we often still find the changes in our lives surprising. Somehow we count on things staying a certain way, or at least, if they are going to change, they will change to our liking.

When we pay careful attention, we see that everything is disappearing and new things are arising not only each day or hour but in every moment. When we leave our house, or simply walk from one room to another, can we notice this flow of changing experience—the flow of visual forms as we move, different sounds, changing sensations in the body, fleeting thoughts of images? What happens to each of these experiences? Do they last? The truth of their changing nature is so ordinary that we have mostly stopped noticing it at all.

As mindfulness and concentration get stronger, we more clearly and deeply see impermanence on microscopic levels. We see for ourselves that what appears solid and stable is really insubstantial and in constant flux. The perception of change becomes so rapid that in the very moment of noticing an object, it's already disappearing. At this point, people sometimes feel that their mindfulness is weak because things are not lasting long enough for our attention to land on them. But this is simply a refinement of the perception of change. We really begin to see that, on one level, there's nothing much there.

As a meditation exercise, particularly in sitting, it is sometimes helpful to notice what aspect of impermanence is most predominant. Are we seeing new things arise even before the last one has ended? Are we seeing the endings more clearly and not seeing the moment of an object arising? Or do we see both the arising and passing away of objects equally? It's not that any one of these perspectives is the right one. In the course of our practice, sometimes it is one way, sometimes another. Noticing how we perceive change is simply another way to refine our attention.

In one discourse, the Buddha makes the distinction between the establishment of mindfulness, which is the simple awareness of what is present, and the *development* of the establishment of mindfulness. In this development stage, the awareness of impermanence becomes even more predominant than the object itself. It is the beginning of movement from mindfulness of content to mindfulness of process. It is this stage of satipaṭṭhāna that leads to wisdom and awakening, because if any aspect of experience is still seen as permanent, opening to the unconditioned, nibbāna, is impossible.

This understanding is not limited to monks or nuns. Many laypeople, from the Buddha's time up until the present, have experienced profound stages of enlightenment. The Buddha addresses this possibility in a conversation with the lay disciple Mahānāma:

"Here, Mahānāma, a lay follower is wise, possessing wisdom directed to arising and passing away, which is noble, and penetrative, leading to the complete destruction of suffering. In that way a lay follower is accomplished in wisdom."[4]

6

Bare Knowing and the
Continuity of Mindfulness

THE NEXT LINE OF THE refrain says, "Mindfulness that 'there is a body' is established in one to the extent necessary for bare knowledge and continuous mindfulness." As Anālayo notes, bare knowledge here means observing objectively without getting lost in associations and reactions. It's the simple and direct knowing of what's present without making up stories about experience. This "seeing clearly" is, in fact, the meaning of the Pali word *vipassanā,* usually translated as "insight meditation."

We often miss the simplicity of bare knowledge because we look through it—or over it—for something special, or we look forward in expectation and miss what is right in front of us. There is a story of Mulla Nazruddin, a crazy-wisdom teaching figure in the Sufi tradition. It seems that the Mulla was engaged in trade between his home city and the neighboring country. The customs officials at the border suspected that he was smuggling something, but whenever they examined his saddlebags, they could never find anything of value. Finally, one day, a friend asked Mulla how he was becoming wealthy. He replied, "I'm smuggling donkeys."

Sometimes we obscure the experience of bare knowing because we are conflating simple awareness with some unnoticed attachment or aversion to what is happening. This can happen when the various hindrances are strong or when there are subtler attachments to pleasant meditative states. In following the instructions of the refrain, we need to establish mindfulness to the extent necessary for this bare knowing of what's arising and for its continuity moment to moment.

THE MOMENTUM OF MINDFULNESS

The continuity of mindfulness spoken of in the sutta is established in two ways. First, it comes about through the momentum of previous moments of mindfulness. Whatever we repeatedly practice begins to arise more and more spontaneously; at this point, the mindfulness arises by itself. From the repeated effort to be mindful in the moment, there comes a time when the flow of mindfulness happens effortlessly for longer periods of time.

There is an early insight into the nature of the mind-body process that both comes from this continuity of mindfulness and also strengthens it: it is the understanding through one's own experience that in every moment knowing and its object arise simultaneously. There is the in-breath and the simultaneous knowing of it, the out-breath and the knowing of it. A visual object arises, and in that very moment there is the knowing of it. This is true of every aspect of our experience.

This insight is the first doorway into the understanding of selflessness, and in the stages of insight, it is called *Purification of View*. We begin to see that everything that we call *self* is simply this pairwise progression of knowing and object, arising and passing moment after moment. And we also see that the knowing in each moment arises due to impersonal causes and not because there is some abiding "knower." So we can say that knowing (consciousness) arises spontaneously when the appropriate causes and conditions are present. Going even deeper, we see that the knowing faculty is not altered or affected by what is known, and this realization has liberating consequences for both our meditation practice and our lives. In meditation, as we go from painful sensations to pleasant ones, we see that the basic quality of knowing is not altered—it is simply aware of what is arising. One example of the profound consequences of this understanding is the description of Henry David Thoreau's last days. He died of tuberculosis at the early age of forty-four. In a biography of his life, his friends described his frame of mind.

Henry was never affected, never reached by [his illness]. . . .
Very often I heard him tell his visitors that he enjoyed existence
as well as ever. He remarked to me that there was as much
comfort in perfect disease as in perfect health, the mind always
conforming to the condition of the body. The thought of death,
he said, could not begin to trouble him. . . .

During his long illness, I never heard a murmur escape
him, or the slightest wish expressed to remain with us; his
perfect contentment was truly wonderful. . . .

Some of his more orthodox friends and relatives tried to
prepare him for death, but with little satisfaction to themselves. . . . [W]hen his Aunt Louisa asked him if he had
made his peace with God, he answered, "I did not know we
had ever quarreled, Aunt."[1]

We build this momentum of mindfulness very simply. We can start
with some primary object of attention, such as mindfulness of the
breath or the sitting posture. Using a particular object to focus and
calm the mind is common to many spiritual traditions. St. Frances
de Sales wrote, "If the heart wanders or is distracted, bring it back to
the point quite gently. . . . And even if you did nothing in the whole
of your hour but bring your heart back—though it went away every
time you brought it back—your hour would be very well employed."[2]

When the mind has settled a bit, we can then begin paying attention to any other object that becomes more predominant. It might be
sensations in the body, or sounds, or different thoughts and images
arising in the mind. And as the mindfulness gains strength, we sometimes let go of the primary object altogether and practice a more
choiceless awareness, simply being aware of whatever arises moment
to moment. At this point, as the awareness becomes more panoramic,
we move from emphasis on the content of the particular experience
to its more general characteristics—namely, the impermanence,
unreliability, and selflessness of all that arises. All of this strengthens
the continuity of mindfulness through mindfulness itself.

PERCEPTION

The second way we strengthen continuity is through the mental
factor of perception. In the Abhidhamma, strong perception is one

of the proximate causes for mindfulness to arise. Perception is the mental quality of recognition. It picks out the distinguishing marks of a particular object and then employs a concept—red or blue, man or woman—to store it in memory for future reference. For example, we hear a sound. Consciousness simply knows the sound; perception recognizes it, names it "bird," and then remembers this concept for the next time we hear that kind of sound. It's not that the word *bird* will always come to mind when we hear the sound, but there will still be a preverbal recognition that the sound is the call of a bird.

All this raises an interesting question regarding the use of concepts in meditation practice and understanding. On the one hand, we want to establish mindfulness to the extent necessary for bare knowing, which somehow suggests a mind free from conceptual overlay. And on the other hand, the factor of perception, with its attendant concepts, is itself a proximate cause for mindfulness to arise.

The resolution of these apparently contradictory perspectives lies in our deeper understanding of perception. Perception is a common factor, which means that it is arising in every moment of consciousness. When perception is operative without strong mindfulness—which is the usual way an untrained mind navigates the world—then we know and remember only the surface appearance of things. In the moment of recognition, we give a name or a concept to what arises, and then our experiences become limited, obscured, or colored by those very concepts.

As an example of the limiting potential of perceptions, years ago a friend told me of an incident that happened with Kevin, his six-year-old son, in school. The teacher asked a very simple question: "What color is an apple?" Different pupils answered "red," "green," or "golden." But Kevin said "white." A bit of an exchange took place, with the teacher trying to guide Kevin's response to a correct answer. But Kevin was adamant, and finally, in some frustration, he said, "When you cut open any apple, it's always white inside."

But perception can also be in the service of greater mindfulness and awareness. Instead of concepts limiting our view of what's arising, properly employed, they can frame the moment's experience, enabling a deeper and more careful observation. It is like putting a frame around a painting in order to see it more clearly. A Buddhist monk named Ñāṇananda spoke of "rallying the concepts for the higher purpose of developing wisdom, whereby concepts themselves are transcended."

MENTAL NOTING

The notion of rallying concepts for developing wisdom underlies the purpose of the meditative technique of *mental noting*. This technique uses a word—or sometimes a short phrase—to acknowledge what is arising. The mental note or label—such as "in," "out," "in," "out," "thinking," "heaviness," "in," "out," "restlessness"—supports clear recognition (perception), which itself strengthens both mindfulness in the moment and the momentum of continuity. Or, as Ajahn Sumedho, one of the first Western disciples of Ajahn Chaa, the great Thai master, expressed it: "The breath is like this," "Pain is like this," "Calm is like this."

Noting can serve the practice in other ways as well. The very tone of the note in the mind can often illuminate unconscious attitudes. We may not be aware of impatience or frustration or delight as we experience different arising objects, but we may start to notice an agitated or enthusiastic tone of voice in the mind. Noting helps cut through our identification with experience, both when the hindrances are present and when our practice has become very subtle and refined.

Mental noting also gives us important feedback: Are we really present or not, in a continuous or sustained way? Are we practicing to make our sittings—or the day—genuinely seamless? Do we understand the difference between being casual and relaxed in our application of mindfulness? We shouldn't confuse this strong intention to be aware with grimness. We can practice continuity of mindfulness with the grace of tai chi or the Japanese tea ceremony, simply taking care even with the small daily activities of our lives. This continuity is important because it builds the momentum of energy necessary to realize nibbāna.

It's important to realize that this tool of mental noting is simply a skillful means for helping us to be mindful—it is not the essence of the practice itself, which is simply to be aware. There are many Buddhist traditions that do not use this technique. But it is worth experimenting with, even for short periods of time, to see whether it is indeed helpful for your practice or not. We should also understand its limitations. Noting is not used as an intellectual reflection and should be kept to a single, silent word. David Kalupahana, a renowned Buddhist scholar, wrote, "Concepts used for Satipaṭṭhāna are to be pursued only to the point where they produce knowledge, and not beyond, for conceptions carried beyond their limits can lead to substantialist metaphysics."[3] Taking concepts too far simply solidifies our view of reality, and we get boxed in by mental constructs of our own making.

As mindfulness gets stronger, we might become aware of too many things to label, with objects changing so quickly that there's not even time to note. In this situation, we are noticing more than we note, and the labels themselves start to fall away. When awareness is well established and mindfulness is happening by itself—what we could call *effortless effort*—then we can simply rest in the continuity of bare knowing. Ryokan, a nineteenth-century Zen master, poet, and wandering monk, expressed it this way: "Know your mind just as it is."

ABIDING INDEPENDENT

The last line of the Satipaṭṭhāna Refrain unifies the practice of meditation with its goal: "And one abides independent, not clinging to anything in the world." This line encapsulates the entire path.

"Abiding independent" refers to the mind not being attached to any arising experience, either through craving or views. "Craving" or "desire" are the usual translations of the Pali word *taṇha*. But *taṇha* is also sometimes translated as "thirst," and somehow this translation conveys the more embodied urgency of this powerful state of mind. In later chapters we will examine this craving or thirst in greater detail to see how it manifests and how it keeps us in a state of dependency both in our meditation practice and in our lives.

One of the great discoveries as we proceed along the path is that, on one level, birth and death, existence and nonexistence, self and other, are the great defining themes of our lives. And on another level, we come to understand that all experience is just a show of empty appearances. This understanding points to the other aspect of "abiding independently, not clinging to anything in the world"—that is, not being attached through views and, most fundamentally, the view of self.

In our normal mode of perception, when we see, hear, smell, taste, or touch, or when we cognize things through the mind, there immediately arises a false sense of "I" and "mine": "I'm seeing." "I'm hearing." Then we elaborate further: "I'm meditating," with the corollaries "I'm a good (or bad) meditator" or "I'm a good or bad person." We build a whole superstructure of self on top of momentary, changing conditions.

THE BAHIYA SUTTA

In one short and liberating teaching, the Bahiya Sutta, or the Discourse to Bahiya, the Buddha pointed the way to freedom from this dependence through views of self. In the time of the Buddha, as the story goes, Bahiya was shipwrecked on the southern coast of India. He had lost everything, even his clothes, and so covered himself with the bark of trees. People who were passing by took him for a great ascetic and began to honor him as an *arahant,* a fully enlightened being. Bahiya soon came to believe it himself.

After some years of this, former companions who were now devas (celestial beings) appeared to him, saying that not only was he not an arahant, but not even on the path to becoming one. Bahiya, quite distressed by this news, but also very sincere in his aspirations, asked what he should do. The devas replied that there was a Buddha, a fully enlightened being, who lived in Northern India and that Bahiya should seek him out.

Bahiya finally met the Buddha while the latter was going from house to house on alms rounds. Bahiya requested teachings right then and there. The Buddha replied that it was not an appropriate time and that Bahiya should come see him at the monastery. But Bahiya requested teachings a second and then a third time: "Lord, you may die. I may die. Please teach me now." The Buddha, impressed with Bahiya's sincerity and urgency, then spoke these words:

> In the seen there is only the seen,
> in the heard, there is only the heard,
> in the sensed [smell, taste, and touch], there is only the sensed,
> in the cognized, there is only the cognized:
> This, Bahiya, is how you should train yourself.

> When, Bahiya, there is for you
> in the seen only the seen,

in the heard only the heard,
in the sensed only the sensed,
in the cognized only the cognized,
then, Bahiya, there is no "you"
in connection with all that.

When, Bahiya, there is no "you"
in connection with that,
there is no "you" there.

When, Bahiya, there is no "you" there,
then, Bahiya, you are neither here
nor there
nor in between the two.

This, just this, is the end of suffering.[4]

With this quality of bare knowing of whatever is seen, heard, felt, or cognized, we are not evaluating or proliferating different sense impressions. When we practice in this way, we understand the selfless nature of phenomena—with no "you" there—and we live abiding independent, not clinging to anything in the world.

Mindfulness
of the Body

7

Mindfulness of Breathing

WHILE THE FOUR ELEMENTS OF the refrain apply to all aspects of our experience, in the Satipaṭṭhāna Sutta the Buddha also explains in detail a wide range of specific meditation instructions. It is here that we can appreciate the great range of his skillful means, tailoring his teachings to the particular audience he was addressing.

The rest of this book is an elaboration of these teachings and instructions (each one followed by the refrain), and as we read the different approaches to practice it might be helpful to recognize which ones, in particular, resonate with our own experience and interest. As mentioned in the introduction, the door of any one of them will lead us to all the rest.

Mindfulness of the body is the first of the four ways of establishing awareness. The Buddha spoke in many different places about the benefits of using the body as an object of contemplation. He spoke of it as a source of joy that leads onward to deepening concentration. He spoke of mindfulness of the body as being the simplest and most direct way for overcoming the onslaughts of Māra, the forces of ignorance and delusion in the mind:

> "Bhikkhus, when anyone has not developed and cultivated
> mindfulness of the body, Māra finds an opportunity and
> a support. . . ."[1]

> "Bhikkhus, when anyone has developed and cultivated mind-
> fulness of the body, Māra cannot find an opportunity or a
> support. . . ."[2]

Māra finding an opportunity and support is illustrated as a heavy stone ball easily finding entry into a mound of soft clay. And the example of Māra not being able to find support is that of throwing a ball of string at a door made of solid wood. Entry is impossible.

The Buddha spoke of mindfulness of the body as being the basis for every kind of accomplishment and for leading onward to nibbāna, to awakening. This is no small claim. After the Buddha's death, Ānanda, his cousin and close attendant for many years, remarked that mindfulness of the body can truly be considered one's best friend. In the midst of endless thought proliferation, of emotional storms, of energetic ups and downs, we can always come back to just this breath, just this step. So many times in my practice I was thankful that it was that simple. We can always just come back to the simplest aspect of what's already here.

PRACTICING WITH THE BREATH

At this point in the discourse, the Buddha further clarifies this prac-tice. He asks the following question as a prelude to answering it:

> "And how, bhikkhus, does a bhikkhu abide contemplating the
> body as a body? Here a bhikkhu, gone to the forest or to the
> root of a tree or to an empty hut, sits down; having folded
> his legs crosswise, set his body erect, and established mind-
> fulness in front of him, ever mindful he breathes in, mindful
> he breathes out. . . ."[3]

With just these few lines, the Buddha gives us a fair amount of guidance.

Where to Practice

First, he is suggesting where we should practice. The forest, the roots of a tree, or an empty hut all suggest an appropriate degree of seclu-sion. It's worth considering what this might mean in the context of our lives in the world. Retiring to a physically secluded location, such as a retreat center or a cabin in the woods, would be ideal. But it could also mean establishing a place dedicated to practice right in our own home—a room, or even a corner of a room, where we create an environment of stillness and beauty.

When I first went to India, I was practicing at the Burmese Vihāra in Bodh Gaya, the place of the Buddha's enlightenment. At that time, it was difficult for Burmese pilgrims to visit India, and so the Burmese Vihāra became a favorite place to stay for Westerners interested in meditation. Even though it was right by the side of a busy road, near a village where they had loudspeakers playing Hindi film music, and right across from a public water tap, still I felt so grateful to have a place to practice. There was a sense of inner seclusion right in the midst of all that activity.

Sitting Posture

Next, the Buddha talks about the sitting posture: folding one's legs crosswise and setting the body erect. In many countries in Asia, people grow up familiar with sitting cross-legged on the floor, and it is, in fact, a good posture for sitting meditation. However, given our own Western upbringing, there's room here for some cultural adjustment, such as sitting on benches or chairs, as needed.

In the beginning of my practice, I found it impossible to sit cross-legged for even ten minutes. The pain in my knees was too intense, and I didn't have the concentration to simply be with it. I moved to a chair, which made meditating much easier. But as I'm a tall person, most chairs are not that comfortable for me either, especially when I'm sitting for long periods of time. So I put several bricks under the chair legs, a cushion or two on the seat, and then to top it all off, I draped a mosquito net over the whole arrangement. It was a cross between a throne and an airport shoeshine concession. Although it was somewhat embarrassing when my teacher would come to see me, nevertheless, it worked. I was able to sit for long periods of time, giving myself the chance to deepen the mindfulness and concentration. Slowly, then, I was able to transition to sitting cross-legged for some extended periods. The operative guideline here is to sit in a way that works for you.

Different Buddhist traditions give somewhat different emphasis to sitting posture. In Zen, for example, there is great importance given to correct posture. Here, the form becomes both the container and the expression of the awakened state. In Theravāda, there is somewhat less emphasis on maintaining a precise posture; however, as the Satipaṭṭhāna Sutta suggests, in whatever posture we take, it is helpful to keep the back straight, without being stiff or tense, as a way of staying ardent, clearly knowing, and mindful, free of desires and discontent in regard to the world.

For our own practice, it's helpful to find the balance between these two approaches. When we're sleepy or distracted, Zen-like sitting could be a big help. In both meditation and life, wise effort creates energy. We often think that we need energy to make effort. But the opposite can be just as true. Think of the times when you feel tired and sluggish and then go out for some exercise. Usually, you come back feeling alert and energized: effort creates energy.

On the other hand, if it feels like there's too much striving and over-efforting, it might be helpful to relax the posture a bit, allowing the energy to arise from within. As the mindfulness and concentration grow stronger, the back and body straighten by themselves. There's a growing energy flow from inside the body that keeps it erect effortlessly.

During one of my practice times in Burma, I was feeling a bit stuck, going over the same ground again and again. I had been sitting cross-legged with a lot of determination, but it didn't seem to be doing any good. Then I started alternating times of sitting cross-legged and sitting in a chair. It turned out that this was just enough relaxation to allow the practice to further unfold. Over time, we learn how to both use and adjust the form, seeing what is needed at any particular time.

Focusing Attention

So, we go to a secluded spot, sit in one way or another, with the back erect, and then, as the sutta says, "He establishes mindfulness in front of him." This phrase is a bit ambiguous, and Anālayo, in his book on the Satipaṭṭhāna Discourse, suggests several interpretations.

Most literally, "in front" suggests using the nostril area—the nose tip or upper lip—as the place to focus our attention. The traditional image of awareness at this point of focus is that of a gatekeeper in an ancient city keeping track of everyone who enters or leaves through the city gates. The gatekeeper doesn't follow the person into the city, nor does he exit with the person as he goes on his journey.

Different teachers suggest other ways of establishing mindfulness "in front." Two of the great Thai Forest masters, Ajahn Maha Boowa and Ajahn Dhammadaro, instruct students to first fix their attention at the nose, but then to later shift the awareness to the chest or solar plexus. And in the tradition of Mahasi Sayadaw, emphasis is given to the rising and falling of the abdomen. Strictly speaking, this is not so much mindfulness of the breath as it is the contemplation of the air element, which is another of the body contemplations.[4] For myself, I always appreciated the pragmatism of Munindra-ji, my first teacher, who said to observe the breath wherever it is easiest, wherever you feel it most clearly.

Establishing Presence of Mind

The phrase "setting mindfulness in front" also means establishing a meditative composure and attentiveness. It's setting up a presence of mind, surrounding oneself with watchfulness. This section of the Chinese version of the Satipaṭṭhāna Sutta says, "with thoughts well controlled, not going astray."[5]

In this section of the sutta, after establishing the posture, the Buddha is emphasizing the importance of setting the conscious intention to be mindful. It is a reminder to ourselves, "Yes, this is my purpose; this is what I'm doing here." It's a moment's reflection about our intention, rather than simply sitting down and settling into a perhaps familiar drift of thought and fantasy. The manner in which we begin often conditions the entire direction of the sitting.

One discourse in the Middle Length Discourses relates how the brahmin youth Brahmayu followed the Buddha like a shadow for seven months, observing his qualities and behavior. Brahmayu then describes the Buddha's way of taking his meditative seat:

> "[H]e seats himself cross-legged, sets his body erect, and
> establishes mindfulness in front of him. He does not occupy
> his mind with self-affliction, or the affliction of others, or
> the affliction of both; he sits with his mind set on his own
> welfare, on the welfare of others, and on the welfare of both,
> even on the welfare of the whole world."[6]

As we apply these words to our own practice, we can include all these aspects of setting mindfulness in front, including the specific place we direct our attention, setting the basic intention to be mindful, and developing the wish for our practice to benefit all beings.

MINDFULNESS OF BREATHING

At this point in the Satipaṭṭhāna Sutta, we have found a suitable place to practice, assumed an appropriate posture, and established mindfulness in front. The Buddha then gives a series of progressive instructions regarding the breath, which is the first of the contemplations on the body.

Here, and in many other discourses, the Buddha is pointing us to an invaluable, and often overlooked, treasure: our own breaths.

> "Bhikkhus, when mindfulness of breathing is developed and cultivated, it is of great fruit and great benefit. When mindfulness of breathing is developed and cultivated, it fulfills the four foundations of mindfulness. When the four foundations of mindfulness are developed and cultivated, they fulfill the seven enlightenment factors. When the seven enlightenment factors are developed and cultivated, they fulfill true knowledge and deliverance."[7]

This humble breath is such a good object of meditation because it is always present and it is a suitable object for all personality types. It leads to both deep concentration and penetrative insight. It is the antidote to distraction and discursive thoughts, and it is a stabilizing factor at the time of death. Not only can the last breath of our life be a mindful one, but our last breath of the day can be as well. Noticing whether we fall asleep on an in-breath or an out-breath would be a challenging, but interesting practice.

Breathing In, I Know I Am Breathing In . . .

We start the practice with the simple awareness, "I know I'm breathing in. I know I'm breathing out." We're not forcing or controlling the breath in any way. As we breathe in, we know we're breathing in; when we breathe out, we know we're breathing out. It's very simple, although perhaps not so easy at first. The mind will have a tendency to get carried away by plans and memories and judgments and comments—all kinds of mental proliferation. But each time we notice that we're not on the breath, in this part of the practice, we simply gently let go and begin again.

In the second set of instructions on mindfulness of breathing, the Buddha says, "Breathing in long, one knows, 'I breathe in long.' Breathing in short, one knows, 'I breathe in short.'" The idea here is not to control the breath in any way, but simply to notice how it is. Just this exercise can help to decondition the pattern of controlling the breath. We are just being mindful of how each breath presents itself, whether long or short. This instruction is a reminder that this is not a breathing exercise, but a training in mindfulness. Any kind of breath will do.

As with many of the instructions in this sutta, different teachers may have different interpretations and approaches. Sayadaw U Paṇḍita, one of the Burmese masters in the Mahasi tradition, talks about having the mind rush toward the object, about capturing the object forcefully, and penetrating it deeply. Other teachers emphasize a more receptive mode, as if one were listening (not literally listening to the breath, but having the attitude of receiving it).

We do not need to get into conflict, even internally, about which approach is right, but rather to see all approaches as skillful means for developing mindfulness, concentration, and insight. If the mind is over-efforting and tight, we need to soften and relax; if it is wandering a lot or very sleepy, rushing toward the object forcefully may be a big help. Ajahn Chaa, a beloved teacher in the Thai Forest tradition, used a now well-known example of this balance.

Someone came to him complaining of all the conflicting advice he gave to his students. Sometimes he would suggest one thing and then later just the opposite. Ajahn Chaa replied, "It's like this. If I see someone walking down a road and about to fall off into a ditch on the left, I'll shout, 'Go right.' Later, if the same person, or someone else, is walking on the road and about to fall into a ditch on the right, I'll say, 'Go left, go left.' It's always about staying on the path."

At times the breath can become very refined, sometimes even imperceptible. We shouldn't try to make the breath stronger in order to be able to feel it. Rather, let the breath draw the mind down to its own level of subtlety. It is like listening to someone playing a flute as they walk off into the distance. The refinement of the breath can become the vehicle for a further refinement of mind. At those times when it really does disappear, and we can't feel it at all, simply be aware of the body sitting until the breath appears again by itself.

Breathing In, I Experience the Whole Body . . .

At this point in the sutta, there's an interesting change of language. As Anālayo points out, in the first two exercises, the Buddha uses the verb "to know": breathing in, one knows one is breathing in, etc. But in the next two exercises of mindfulness of the breath, the Buddha uses the verb "to train."

> One trains thus: "I shall breathe in experiencing the whole body," one trains thus, "I shall breathe out experiencing the whole body." One trains thus: "I shall breathe in calming the bodily formations," one trains thus: "I shall breathe out calming the bodily formation."[8]

This shift of language—from knowing to training—suggests an increasing level of intentionality in our practice as we broaden our awareness from the breath to the whole body.

But here also, there are two interpretations of what it means in this context to experience the whole body. It can be taken in its literal meaning—that is, feeling the breath throughout the body or feeling the whole body as we breathe. The second interpretation of "experiencing the whole body" is found in the Buddhist commentaries, which say that this phrase refers to the whole "breath body." This means that we train experiencing the beginning, middle, and end of each breath. We go from simply knowing whether the breath is long or short to feeling the breath more intimately, experiencing the entire flow of changing sensations with each in- and out-breath.

As mentioned earlier, both interpretations can be seen as different skillful means to apply at the appropriate time. If we're too controlling of the breath, zeroing in on it may not be helpful. It might be better to be aware of the breath in the larger context of the whole body. On the other hand, if we're somewhat spaced out, lost in the wandering mind, narrowing our focus to just the stream of sensations of the breath could strengthen our mindfulness and concentration.

Calming the Formations

The last instruction in this sequence is training in calming the formations with each breath. We can do this in two ways. If we are taking the phrase "breathing in and out experiencing the whole body" to mean being aware of our entire sitting posture, calming the formations means maintaining a calm and steady posture, calming our inclinations to move. We might make determinations for certain periods of time to not make any intentional movement. When we understand "experiencing the whole body" to mean the body of the breath, then calming the formations suggests holding the intention to calm the breathing itself. Sometimes just softly repeating the words "calm, calming" is helpful in tranquilizing the breath. As the breath is calmed, the body becomes more still, and as the body posture becomes still, the breath itself is calmed. These two approaches interweave and support each other.

It's surprising that in our lives we often overlook the breath and that in our meditation practice we are sometimes bored by it. Not only is each breath sustaining our lives, but being aware and mindful of the breath was also the basis for the Buddha's own awakening. It can be for our own awakening as well.

> "Bhikkhus, if wanderers of other sects ask you: 'In what dwelling, friends, did the Blessed One generally dwell during the rains residence?'—being asked thus, you should answer those wanderers thus: 'During the rains residence, friends, the Blessed One generally dwelt in the concentration by mindfulness of breathing.' . . .
>
> "If anyone, Bhikkhus, speaking rightly could say of anything: 'It is a noble dwelling, a divine dwelling, the Tathāgata's dwelling,' it is of concentration by mindfulness of breathing that one could rightly say this.
>
> "Bhikkhus, those Bhikkhus who are trainees, who have not attained their mind's ideal, who dwell aspiring for the unsurpassed security from bondage: for them concentration by mindfulness of breathing, when developed and cultivated, leads to the destruction of the taints. Those Bhikkhus who are arahants, whose taints are destroyed, who have lived the holy life, done what had to be done, laid down the burden,

reached their own goal, utterly destroyed the fetters of existence, those completely liberated through final knowledge: for them concentration by mindfulness of breathing, when developed and cultivated, leads to a pleasant dwelling in this very life and to mindfulness and clear comprehension."[9]

8

Mindfulness of Postures

IN THE NEXT SECTION OF the sutta, the Buddha extends the scope of mindfulness of the body from the breath to bodily postures.

> Again, monks, when walking, one knows "I am walking";
> when standing, one knows "I am standing"; when sitting,
> one knows "I am sitting"; when lying down, one knows "I
> am lying down"; or one knows accordingly however one's
> body is disposed.[1]

There's a great power in the simplicity of this practice. It grounds us in the awareness of the body instead of being carried away so often by thought and ideas. My first teacher, Munindra-ji, would often say, "Sit and know you're sitting, and the whole of dhamma will be revealed." This is true for any of the four postures: sitting, standing, walking, and lying.

How exactly does this simple mindfulness practice reveal the Dhamma?

IT STRENGTHENS CONTINUITY OF AWARENESS

Mindfulness of body postures—just noticing as we move from one posture to the next throughout the day—helps strengthen the continuity of our awareness. This is not complicated; we don't need to be in some heightened state of concentration, and we can practice this as easily outside of retreat as well as in seclusion. Sit and know you're sitting; walk and know you're walking; stand and know you're standing. We don't have to be in meditation graduate school to be awake. In the Buddha's time there were many seven-year-old arahants, fully enlightened beings. I think it was because they could follow the very simplest instructions.

IT REVEALS OUR STATES OF MIND

Being mindful of how the various postures manifest during the day also reveals a lot about our states of mind. For example, as we walk, do we sometimes find ourselves rushing to go someplace or to do something? Rushing doesn't necessarily have to do with speed; it indicates some state of anticipation, wanting, energetically toppling forward, even slightly, rather than being settled back in the moment with just what there is. One of the most helpful instructions for walking meditation is, "When walking, just walk." This simple reminder can cut through the energy of rushing and the perhaps unnoticed desire for some meditative state. When walking, just walk. We settle back into the simplicity of the moment. When we're standing, are we restless or impatient, or are we standing, grounded in the present, at ease?

Mindfulness of body postures also becomes the basis for overcoming unwholesome states of mind, even quite intense ones. Before the Buddha's enlightenment, while he was still a bodhisattva, he would often go to remote jungles as a way of confronting fear in his mind.

> "And while I dwelt there, a wild animal would come up to me, or a peacock would knock off a branch, or the wind would rustle the leaves. I thought: 'What now if this is fear and dread coming?' I thought: 'Why do I dwell always expecting fear and dread? What if I subdue that fear and dread while keeping the same posture that I am in when it comes upon me?'
>
> "While I walked, the fear and dread came upon me; I neither stood nor sat nor lay down till I had subdued that fear and dread. While I stood, the fear and dread came upon me; I neither walked nor sat nor lay down till I had subdued that fear and dread. While I sat, the fear and dread came upon me; I neither walked nor stood nor lay down till I had

subdued that fear and dread. While I lay down, the fear and dread came upon me; I neither walked nor stood nor sat down till I had subdued that fear and dread."[2]

It can be encouraging for us to realize that even the Bodhisattva, intent on enlightenment, faced the same kind of difficulties that we encounter in our lives. Just the fact that small things like the rustling of leaves or a branch falling called up strong fears for the Bodhisattva connects the Buddha's journey with our own. It's clear from his description that purification of mind is not limited to sitting practice. We can face and see through these unwholesome states whenever and wherever they arise. We can plant the flag of mindfulness in whatever particular posture they arise.

Georgia O'Keeffe, the famous artist from the American Southwest, expressed this same courageous attitude toward fear in another way: "I've been absolutely terrified every moment of my life, and I've never let it keep me from doing a single thing I wanted to do."

IT SUPPORTS OUR UNDERSTANDING OF THE THREE CHARACTERISTICS

Mindfulness of postures—"when walking, I know I am walking, when standing, I know I am standing"—also opens the doorway to understanding the three characteristics of all existence.

Impermanence, or *anicca,* is obvious as we move from one posture to another. This is true not only in the big changes, such as when we go from sitting to standing or from standing to lying down, but also in all the innumerable changes that occur in the process of going from one posture to another. Especially when we slow down, we can feel the microsensations in every moment. As an experiment, simply slowly move your arm back and forth in front of you. If you do it quite slowly, you will feel so many different sensations of weight, of heaviness, of pulsing, of movement. There is so much going on in even a simple movement.

Mindfulness of the four postures illuminates the truth of *dukkha,* or unsatisfactoriness, in a very immediate way. This becomes clear when we investigate why it is that we move or change posture. When we pay close attention, we see that almost all movements are an attempt to alleviate some kind of pain or discomfort. When we're sitting, we can see this in the slight shifts of position, in order to relieve some tension; or in the larger movements of posture, when we move if the pain becomes unbearable. When we go to eat, we're relieving the suffering of hunger. When we go to the bathroom, we're alleviating a discomfort. We lie down to relieve tiredness. But even then, when we think we might finally enjoy some ease, after some time, the body needs to roll over or stretch. And after some number of hours, we need to stand up because the body is getting stiff from just lying down. All of this is summarized in the dharma statement, "Movement masks dukkha." It's worth investigating this to see for ourselves what drives the many movements we make during the day.

Mindfulness of postures also deepens insight into selflessness, or *anattā*. As we walk, we can hold in our minds the unspoken question, "Who is walking, and who is standing?" Through a sustained mindfulness of the body in different postures, we begin to see its impersonal nature.

There's an important stage of insight called Purification of View; it is the first deep realization of the selfless nature of all phenomena. This is the insight into *nāmarūpa*, often translated as "mind and matter" or "mentality and materiality." At this stage of meditation, we see that whatever is happening is simply the process of knowing and its object—the sensations of the body standing and the knowing of them, sensations of the body sitting and the knowing of them. We see that there's no one behind this process to whom it is all happening, only the pairwise progression of knowing and object rolling on.

We also deepen our understanding of selflessness by seeing the mutual causal conditioning between the mind and the material elements of the body. The body moves because of an intention in the mind, which initiates the action. This is the mind conditioning materiality. At other times, a bodily experience—of a sight, a sound, or some sensation—may condition a mind state of enjoyment or aversion. This is the body conditioning the mind.

In meditation practice, we might experience this insight into the selflessness of the process when we have the feeling of being walked, as if the movement is happening by itself. Sometimes it feels as if we're being pushed or propelled forward. This is the experience of no one there doing anything—only the play of mental and physical elements interacting in various cause-and-effect relationships.

Continuity of mindfulness of changing postures ensures the continuity of our awareness of impermanence, which in turn helps free us from identifying with the body as being a permanent self. We start living the teaching the Buddha gave to his son, Rāhula: "You should see all phenomena with proper wisdom—this is not mine, this is not I, this is not myself." Understanding that the body is "not mine" helps free the mind from desire and grasping. We no longer claim ownership of either the physical elements of the body or the mind knowing them.

The purpose of all our practice is to purify the mind of obstructive, unskillful states—in the Buddha's words, "to abandon ill will and hatred, and to abide with a mind compassionate for the welfare of all beings."

ĀNANDA'S AWAKENING

There are many stories in the discourses of monks and nuns who attained arahantship through mindfulness of the postures. Ānanda was the beloved cousin and attendant of the Buddha. Early on, Ānanda attained stream-entry, the first stage of enlightenment, but he was unable to realize full awakening. After the Buddha's death, a great council was called to recite all the teachings. There were 499 arahants and Ānanda, who was invited because of his eidetic memory and the fact that he had been present for all of the Buddha's teachings. Ānanda felt a bit ashamed that he had not yet fully realized the teachings, and so he spent the night before the council meeting doing walking meditation. Late into the night, he realized that he was making too much effort, and he decided to take some rest. Very mindfully, he walked to his bed, and fully aware, he began to lie down. Then, just in the moment of lying down, before his head hit the pillow or his feet the bed, his mind opened to full awakening, attaining all the various psychic powers as well. After lying there for some time, experiencing the bliss of his awakening, he spontaneously appeared at the council meeting, and everyone knew that Ānanda had accomplished his goal.

Even though we often privilege the sitting posture in our meditation, the path of awakening is clearly not limited to any one posture. This section of the Satipaṭṭhāna Sutta on mindfulness of postures is one of the most effective ways of bringing the insights of intensive retreat practice into the activities of our daily lives. Ajahn Chaa said, "Some people think the longer you can sit, the wiser you must be. I have seen chickens sitting on their nests for days on end. Wisdom comes from being mindful at all times."[3]

This section of mindfulness of the postures is also followed by the refrain, reminding us again of the important features of the practice. We contemplate the postures internally, externally, and both. We contemplate the arising and passing away, the impermanence of them, and stay mindful of the postures to the extent necessary for bare knowing and continuous mindfulness, abiding independent, not clinging to anything in the world.

9

Mindfulness of Activities

AWARENESS OF BODILY POSTURES LEADS quite naturally into the next aspect of satipaṭṭhāna—that is, mindfulness of activities.

> "Again, monks, when going forward and returning one acts
> clearly knowing; when looking ahead and looking away
> one acts clearly knowing; when flexing and extending one's
> limbs one acts clearly knowing . . . when eating, drinking,
> consuming food, and tasting one acts clearly knowing; when
> defecating and urinating one acts clearly knowing; when
> walking, standing, sitting, falling asleep, waking up, talking,
> and keeping silent one acts clearly knowing."[1]

"Clearly knowing," the translation of the Pali word *sampajañña,* is sometimes translated as "clear comprehension." Clearly knowing means seeing precisely or seeing thoroughly, with all of the five spiritual faculties (confidence, energy, mindfulness, concentration, and wisdom) in balance.

TRAININGS IN CLEAR COMPREHENSION

There are four ways of training in this quality of mind that the Buddha spoke of with such frequency.

Recognize the Motivation Behind an Action

The first way of training is clearly knowing the purpose of doing an action before we do it, understanding whether or not it is of benefit to ourselves and others. This practice takes our meditation a step further than simply knowing the posture of the body. Here we need to see and reflect on our motivation for doing something. Is it skillful? Is it unskillful? Practicing this discernment has tremendous implications for our lives in the world. Because our motivations are often subtle and hard to see—they are often mixed or are a series of conflicting motivations—it takes a lot of honesty, clarity, and mindfulness to see them clearly, to know the inner purpose behind our actions.

One incident that helps to illustrate the complexity of our motivations occurred when I was on a long self-retreat. I had been doing some Dharma reading and had come across a story that I thought would be useful for my colleague, Sharon Salzberg, who was writing a book at the time. For Dharma teachers, a good story is like gold, so I was glad to see that my first impulse was to share this story with her. But immediately following came the thought, "No, I'll keep this story for myself." Then other thoughts came in quick succession: "That's just being selfish. I should share this with her. But maybe I'll also tell her what I'm going through so that she feels a little indebted to me. No, that's just more ego." And on and on. Finally, I began wondering where in this whole sequence was there a pure motivation. In looking back, I saw that there was a moment of purity, and it was in that very first impulse to share. So clearly knowing, or clear comprehension, doesn't automatically purify our minds of all unskillful thoughts. Rather, it allows us to see what is going on in our minds and, on the basis of that clear seeing, to make wiser choices. Clear comprehension is a great ally in our daily encounters with Māra.

Māra is the embodiment of delusion, and unlike the devil or Satan in some Western religions, who is considered lord of the underworld, in the Buddhist tradition, Māra is seen to be king of the highest heaven realm. His mission is to keep us all ensnared in his realm of saṃsāric attachments, and he uses many seductive and confusing ploys to accomplish this.

Māra might manifest as the simple enticement of desire and greed. We can see this enticement frequently around food, at those times when we overeat or excessively indulge in foods that are unhealthy.

On a subtler level, mind states that are hindrances to our practice can masquerade as friends. For example, sloth and torpor, the dullness and sluggishness of mind, can appear to us as compassion. We might be feeling tired or frustrated, and then this kindly voice arises in the mind: "I've done enough. I've been working really hard. Let me take a little rest." Sometimes we do need rest, but sometimes the kindly voice is just that aspect of sloth and torpor that retreats from difficulties. I've found it helpful at times to use a phrase found in different suttas, "Māra, I see you," as a way of disentangling from the seductions of unskillful states. Of course, seeing all these aspects of Māra and freeing ourselves from them depend on our ability to know clearly what is going on.

This aspect of clear comprehension—seeing the purpose of our actions and whether they are of benefit or not—rests on our understanding the ethical dimensions of mindfulness. This is the discernment of wholesome or unwholesome mind states and actions, which lead respectively to happiness or suffering. There is a Tibetan prayer and aspiration that expresses this understanding: "May you have happiness and the causes of happiness. May you be free of suffering and the causes of suffering." This section of the Satipaṭṭhāna Sutta, on being mindful of and clearly knowing all our daily activities, is the beginning of actualizing this prayer in our lives.

When we clearly comprehend the purpose and benefit of our actions, we open the possibility of making wiser choices. "Where is this action leading? Do I want to go there?" Thich Nhat Hanh, the well-known Vietnamese Buddhist master, poet, and peace activist, expressed it very simply: "Buddhism is a clever way to enjoy life. Happiness is available. Please help yourselves to it."

Know the Suitability of an Action

The second training involves knowing the suitability of an action. Even when something is wholesome, we need to look further to see if it is the appropriate time and place. The Buddha highlights this particular aspect in his teachings on right speech, which are summarized in two questions: Is it true? Is it useful? Something might be true, and yet now may not be the suitable time to express it. Clearly knowing the suitability of action puts our activities into a larger context, one which takes into account the effect of our actions on others.

This wise reflection also helps free us from getting caught up in spiritual self-images. I had a striking lesson in this in Bodh Gaya, India, when I saw my teacher Anagārika Munindra intensely bargaining with a peanut vendor in the bazaar. To my Western eye, it seemed a little unseemly—a great meditation master haggling over a few cents' worth of peanuts. When I asked him about this, he simply replied, "The path of the Dhamma is to be simple, not a simpleton." He didn't have any self-image problems; he was doing what was appropriate for that time and place.

Know the Fields of Practice

The third training in clear comprehension is knowing the proper pastures for our meditation practice. The Buddha outlined this very succinctly in the Satipaṭṭhāna Sutta when he spoke of the four fields of mindfulness—the body, feelings, mind, and different categories of experience (dhammas)—as being the proper domains for those practicing for awakening.

There is a story of one monk who every time he did something unmindfully would go back and do the action again. And after practicing this way for twenty years, he became an arahant. I like this story both for its suggestive practice and also because it speaks to a dedicated commitment to awakening.

Knowing clearly the proper domain of practice also points to the importance of sense restraint, so that the mind doesn't wander mindlessly in the alluring realm of sense objects. Restraint is not something that is highly valued in our culture. We often see renunciation as a burdensome activity, something we think might be good for us, but which we really don't like. Another way of understanding its value, though, would be to see renunciation as the practice of nonaddiction. In this way of understanding, we can more easily experience its true flavor of freedom.

Understand Nondelusion

The last aspect of clear comprehension is nondelusion—that is, seeing clearly the three universal characteristics mentioned earlier. We clearly know the impermanent, unreliable, and selfless nature of all phenomena. Nondelusion understands that with all of the bodily actions mentioned, there's no *one* there doing anything; there's doing without a doer. It's all just empty phenomena rolling on according to the great law of cause and effect. The famous thirteenth-century Japanese Zen master Dogen expressed it this way in the Genjo Koan: "What is the way of the Buddha? It is to study the self. What is the study of the self? It is to forget the self. To forget the self is to be Enlightened by all things."

This section of the sutta—mindfulness of activities—also highlights the emphasis the Buddha placed on monks and nuns deporting themselves in a quiet and dignified manner. This doesn't mean being stiff or contrived, but rather, as Tsoknyi Rinpoche, a Tibetan Dzogchen master, called it, having a "carefree dignity." Although in the West the very notion of deportment and dignity seems a little old fashioned, in Asia it is a very noticeable and beautiful aspect of Buddhist cultures. Especially in those who are practicing mindfulness, either as a monastic or a layperson, there is a certain sense of respect and grace in the way people move and relate to one another. This is not to say that the same defilements are not at play in Asia as in the West. They are. It's simply that embedded in the cultural norm is a support and reminder to act and move with awareness, clearly knowing, being embodied rather than distracted.

After this section on mindfulness of activities, the Buddha repeats the refrain that follows each of the sections, reminding us to contemplate all these activities internally and externally, seeing their nature to arise and pass away, and establishing mindfulness to the extent necessary for bare knowing and continuous mindfulness, abiding independent, not clinging to anything in the world.

10

Mindfulness of Physical Characteristics

IN THIS CHAPTER, WE WILL discuss the various components of the body and the ways of meditating that take us beyond the very concept of "body." In this section of the Satipaṭṭhāna Sutta, the Buddha is analyzing more closely what it is we call "body" in terms of anatomical parts, the elements, and its nature to die and then decay. These are powerful meditations that begin to decondition our strong identification with the body and the suffering that results from that identification.

THE ANATOMICAL PARTS

The next instructions the Buddha gives in this first foundation of Mindfulness of the Body direct our attention to an analysis of what constitutes the body through a contemplation of its anatomical parts.

> "Again, monks, one reviews this same body up from the soles
> of the feet and down from the top of the hair, enclosed by
> skin, as full of many kinds of impurity thus: 'in this body
> there are head-hairs, body-hairs, nails, teeth, skin, flesh,
> sinews, bones, bone-marrow, kidneys, heart, liver, diaphragm,
> spleen, lungs, bowels, mesentery, contents of the stomach,

feces, bile, phlegm, pus, blood, sweat, fat, tears, grease, spittle, snot, oil of the joints, and urine.'"[1]

In this sutta, thirty-one parts are mentioned; in other lists, thirty-two or thirty-six are given. And some discourses simply end with the phrase "and whatever other parts there may be."

The question is, why did the Buddha teach—and why would we want to contemplate—what are called in Pali the *asubha*, or non-beautiful or unattractive aspects of the body? What we call "the body," and what seems so attractive and delightful from one perspective, is really just a collection of interrelated parts, none of which, in themselves, is particularly lust inspiring. And so this contemplation serves to diminish the power of that strong conditioning in the mind.

As we contemplate the body—our own bodies and those of others—from this perspective, both internally and externally, we also see the impermanent, contingent nature of all these anatomical parts. We understand that what we call body, that which we so often take to be self, is an interdependent system of organs, bones, blood, neural pathways, and other components. In contemplating this way, when some of these parts or systems wear out or stop working properly, we don't take it to be some failure of self or some defeat of the body; rather, we understand it to simply be the nature of all conditioned things. It is precisely summed up in the second law of thermodynamics—the law of entropy, which says that all systems tend to disorder.

What is surprising is how hard it can be for us to accept this basic truth of how things are, even in the face of such overwhelming and universal evidence. This particular contemplation in the Satipaṭṭhāna Sutta is a powerful reminder of the impersonal and unreliable nature of the body. It helps free us from pride and lust, disparagement and fear, as we see with greater clarity just what this body is.

The Potential for Wrong Attitude

Some caution is needed, however, as we undertake this practice. If it is undertaken with the wrong attitude, instead of leading to the calming of desires, to equanimity and freedom, it can unintentionally strengthen unwholesome disgust and aversion. Years ago, the well-known Cambodian monk Maha Ghosananda came to the Insight Meditation Society during one of the annual three-month retreats.

During one sitting period, he led the meditators in an unusual guided eating meditation. He had people visualize having some food in front of them, reaching for it, placing it in the mouth, and then visualizing what happens to the food as we chew. Not all that appealing. He then continued guiding people to see what happens as we swallow, as the food is being digested in the stomach, and finally as it is eliminated as waste.

What was so interesting was the reaction to this contemplation on the part of the meditators. One of them asked Maha Ghosananda, "Why do you have so much aversion to food?" In fact, he didn't have any aversion to it at all; all he was doing was guiding us through the process of what actually happens. But some people were projecting their own repugnance and distaste for visualizing the unattractive aspects of eating.

We can learn to see things as they actually are, without lust for the pleasant or aversion to the unpleasant. In this section of the sutta, the Buddha points to the appropriate attitude:

> "Just as though there were a bag with an opening at both ends
> full of many sorts of grain, such as hill rice, red rice, beans,
> peas, millet, and white rice, and a man with good eyes were
> to open it and review it thus: 'this is hill rice, this is red rice,
> there are beans, these are peas, this is millet, this is white
> rice'; so too he reviews this same body. . . ."[2]

This balanced contemplation of the nonbeautiful qualities of the body has the power to lead us all to full awakening, because we see that there's nothing in or of the body to hold on to, to claim as "I" or "mine." In a moment, or gradually over time, the mind can relinquish all grasping and be free. As the Buddha said, "Bhikkhus, in clinging one is bound by Māra; by not clinging, one is freed."

THE ELEMENTS

The next instructions the Buddha gives for contemplating the body draw the mind down to a further level of subtlety and refinement:

> "Again, monks, one reviews this same body, however it is
> placed, however disposed, as consisting of elements thus: 'in

this body there are the earth element, the water element, the fire element and the air element.'"[3]

Here the Buddha is using the ancient Indian scheme of the four basic qualities of matter. An interesting question arises regarding the use of this framework in the light of current scientific understanding. We might translate these four elements into the more familiar terms of solid, liquid, plasma, and gas. It is also possible through the attainment of *jhāna,* a high degree of concentrated absorption, to experience the body on extremely subtle levels far beyond our usual level of perception. These four elements do correspond to particular experiences on this level. It would be interesting if a modern scientist were able to compare our contemporary way of describing the smallest particles of matter with these meditative perceptions. But even in our more ordinary way of perceiving things, the four material states are a useful way of describing our subjective felt sense of the body and the physical world.

The earth element refers to the common experience of solidity, the qualities of stiffness, hardness, or softness.

Next, the water element refers to the qualities of cohesion and fluidity. Imagine dry flour; on their own, its particles do not hold together. When we add water, the particles all adhere to one another, creating dough. According to the commentaries, the water element is not perceived separately from the other elements, but it is what holds them all together.

The fire element refers to temperature—heat and cold. It is also the feeling of lightness in the body. The fire element functions in different ways. It is how something is warmed. It is that by which things age. It is excessive heat that burns things up. And there is digestive heat. In Burma, this is called "stomach fire"—when it is strong, food gets well digested; when it is weak, there is stomach trouble. This understanding helps explain the Burmese fondness for very hot chili peppers. Although eating them creates a burning sensation, people enjoy it for its health benefit.

The air element causes movement in the body, the feeling of extension, expanding, distending. It is also the feeling of pressure. In meditation, when we're being mindful of the rise and fall of the abdomen, we're really being mindful of the air element.

Contemplation of the Elements

Although the suttas and commentaries go into great detail about each of these elements, we don't particularly have to know which sensation is what element. It's fine to use the common words for the sensations we feel, knowing that it is one or another of the elements becoming predominant.

We can undertake the contemplation of the elements in different ways, each one leading us to direct insight into the three characteristics, which in turn leads to freeing the mind from clinging. In walking meditation, for example, we can experience these different elements at work. When we lift the foot, the lightness that we feel in the foot and leg is the fire element. When we're pushing the foot forward and feeling movement and pressure, we are feeling the air element. When we're placing the foot on the ground and feel the hardness or softness, we are feeling the earth element.

Experiencing the familiar activity of walking in this way effects an important shift in our meditation practice. In our everyday notion of the body, we might say, "I feel my leg." But there is no sensation called "leg." Rather, what we feel are certain sensations, like pressure, heaviness, and lightness, and then we create an image or concept: "leg." In meditation, we move from the concept of body to the awareness of the body as a changing energy field. On this level, the sense of the body as being something solid and substantial disappears.

When we were reporting to Sayadaw U Paṇḍita, he would ask us to describe, as accurately as possible, what we actually felt in taking a step, and then to notice what happened to each of those sensations. This mindful precision helped illuminate the body as the interplay of these four elements. As we free ourselves from the concept of "body" and increasingly experience the direct felt sense of it, the mind becomes less prone to attachment and to the desire, aversion, and conceit that come from it.

Working with the Sense of "I Am"

The contemplation of the elements is also a powerful remedy for the deeply conditioned pattern of conceit. "Conceit," in its Buddhist usage, refers to the deeply rooted sense of "I am," "I was," "I will be." This is one of the last defilements to be uprooted and is one of the final veils of ignorance that needs to be removed before full awakening.

Notice how often this sense of "I am" arises in relation to our bodies, particularly when we are comparing our bodies, in one way or another, to other people's. Notice, then, how many different thoughts and emotional patterns get triggered through these comparisons, how many projections we get lost in: "If we buy this product, we will be like, or look like, the perfectly beautiful beings advertising it." Because the comparison is such an obvious ruse, the fact that it often conditions our behavior points to its appeal to some deeply rooted pattern in our psyche.

In seeing the body as a collection of parts, none of which by themselves are particularly alluring, and then experiencing the body simply as an interplay of elements, the conceit of "I am" falls away. Feelings of either pride or unworthiness with regard to the body no longer make sense. Bhikkhu Ñāṇananda spoke to this when he referred to the conceit of taking the elements to be self as "the misappropriation of public property." Sāriputta, the chief disciple of the Buddha, spoke to this point:

> "[T]here comes a time when the waters in the great oceans
> are not enough to wet even the joint of a finger. When
> even this external water element, great as it is, is seen to be
> impermanent, subject to destruction, disappearance, and
> change, what of this body, which is clung to by craving and
> lasts but a while? There can be no considering that as 'I' or
> 'mine' or 'I am.'"[4]

This is a powerful reminder of the inherent instability of the elements, and it is strikingly similar to the description of the changes that will take place as our sun comes to the end of its life as a star. What does this mean for what we rely on, for where we take refuge in the world? Contemplation of the elements leads to a radically different vision, where we go beyond even the concept of "being."

In the second part of the instruction on the elements, the Buddha uses a graphic image to help effect this change of perception:

> "Just as though a skilled butcher or his apprentice had killed a
> cow and was seated at a crossroads with it cut up into pieces,
> so too, one reviews this same body, however it is placed,

however disposed, as consisting of elements thus: 'in this body there are the earth element, the water element, the fire element and the air element.'"[5]

Although our sensibilities may be offended by the images of butchering cows (it doesn't really seem very Buddhist!), the Buddha was just using the ordinary experiences of daily agrarian life to point to profound Dharma truths. Even today in India, all the cycles of birth and life and death are out on the streets. They are not hidden or prettified as often happens in the West.

Why does the Buddha use this example? While the cow is still whole, whether alive or dead, we would still refer to it as a cow; but once it is cut up into pieces to sell as meat, at that point, the notion of cow is no longer there. This image, unpleasant though it may be, is used as an example of what happens when we experience the body as just the elements. We begin to lose the concept of a being or a person. An example of this occurs when we're doing walking meditation, and we simply feel the sensations of the different elements arising and passing. At that time, there's no sense of a solid body, only the feeling of sensations in space and the knowing of them.

The Path of Purification, one of the great Buddhist commentaries from the fifth century AD, explained the power of this contemplation of the elements.

> This bhikkhu who is devoted to the defining of the four elements is immersed in voidness and eliminates the perception of living beings. . . . [B]ecause he has abolished the perception of living beings, he conquers fear and dread, and conquers delight and aversion (boredom), he is not exhilarated or depressed by agreeable or disagreeable things, and as one of great understanding, he either ends in the deathless realm or he is bound for a happy destiny.[6]

Relative and Ultimate Truth

Through our practice of contemplating the four elements, we open a doorway to understanding two overarching principles that frame twenty-six hundred years of Buddhist wisdom. These are the principles of relative and ultimate truth. Although the Satipaṭṭhāna Sutta does not refer to these truths per se, the various instructions given in the discourse directly imply these two levels of understanding.

Relative truth is the conventional world of subject and object, self and other, birth and death. All the familiar experiences of our lives are contained in this truth. Ultimate truth sees this same world quite differently. On the level of ultimate truth, there is no subject-object separation—in fact, no "things" at all. And its very deepest aspect is the unmanifest, the uncreated, the unborn, the undying.

As a way of understanding how these two truths relate to one another, think for a moment of being in a movie theater, completely engrossed in the story. We might feel happy, sad, excited, or terrified, all depending on the movie being shown. Now imagine looking up and seeing the movie being projected on to the screen. We realize that nothing is really happening on the screen except for the play of light and color. There's no one there actually falling in love or dying. Yet when we're absorbed in the story, it all feels very real. Going further, what happens to our experience of even the light if there's no place for it to land—no screen, not even particles of dust in the air? The light is unmanifest if there's no object on which it can land.

On the relative level, we live and act and relate as individuals, one with another, with all our personal stories and histories. On the ultimate level, there's no self, no "I," no one there at all. Everything is a play of momentary, changing elements. In the Sutta Nipāta, one of the oldest of the collections of the Buddha's teachings, the Buddha again directly points out the practice of freedom:

> Dry out that which is past, let there be nothing for you in
> the future. If you do not grasp at anything in the present
> you will go about at peace. One who, in regard to this entire
> mind/body complex, has no cherishing of it as "mine," and
> who does not grieve for what is non-existent truly suffers
> no loss in the world. For that person there is no thought of
> anything as "this is mine" or "this is another's"; not finding
> any state of ownership, and realizing, "nothing is mine," he
> does not grieve.[7]

"Don't grieve for what is non-existent." The contemplation of the elements illuminates the level on which "I" and "self" simply do not exist. On that level we really are free from drowning in the dramas of our lives. One story illustrates this so beautifully. His Holiness the Sixteenth Gyalwa Karmapa, one of the great Tibetan masters of the last century, was dying of cancer in a hospital in Zion, Illinois. During his last days, his students and disciples gathered around, grieving the imminent loss of their great teacher. At one point, it's said that the Karmapa turned to them all and said, "Don't worry, nothing happens." For awakened beings, there is no one there to be born or die. All of that is the movie on the screen.

There is also a certain caution here: It's possible to become attached to this ultimate perspective before we are truly free. We can get caught in the perspective that it's all empty, that nothing really matters, and remain stuck in a limited understanding, dismissing the need to practice and losing our connection to what the ancient Taoists called "the ten thousand joys and the ten thousand sorrows."

Nārgārjuna, who lived in the second century and was one of the greatest Indian adepts, highlighted this danger: "It is sad to see those who mistakenly believe in material, concrete reality, but far more pitiful are those who are attached to emptiness."[8] Nyoshul Khen Rinpoche, a renowned Dzogchen master and teacher of many Western practitioners, further elaborated on this potential pitfall of attachment to emptiness:

> Those who believe in *things* can be helped through various kinds of practice, through skillful means—but those who fall into the abyss of emptiness find it almost impossible to re-emerge, since there seem to be no handholds, no steps, no gradual progression, nothing to do.[9]

A mature spiritual practice sees the union of the relative and ultimate levels, with each informing and expressing the other. The development of what are called "the four divine abodes"—lovingkindness, compassion, sympathetic joy, and equanimity—are all based on the conceptual level of beings: "May all beings be happy. May all beings be free of suffering." At the same time, the deeper our understanding of selflessness, the freer and more spontaneous are these beautiful mind states. On the relative level, love and compassion are states we cultivate; on the ultimate level, they are the responsive nature of the mind itself. Dilgo Khyentse Rinpoche taught that when we recognize the empty nature of phenomena, the energy to bring about the good of others dawns uncontrived and effortless.

This understanding gives rise to the rare flower of *bodhichitta,* the awakened heart, which is the motivation that our practice and our lives are not for ourselves alone, but for the welfare and benefit of all. We need to start in a very humble way, simply planting the seed of this aspiration within ourselves, without pretension, without grandiose expectations. Manifesting *bodhichitta* is a lifetime practice. His Holiness the Dalai Lama acknowledged this even for himself: "I cannot pretend that I am really able to practice *bodhichitta,* but it does give me tremendous inspiration. Deep inside me I realize how valuable and beneficial it is, that is all."[10]

THE CORPSE IN DECAY

The last set of instructions the Buddha gives on mindfulness of the body is the contemplation of corpses in various states of decay. For most of us, there is limited opportunity to undertake this practice, and so I will just include here the bare instructions, and leave it to the reader to contemplate them in the most appropriate way.

> "Again, monks, as though he were to see a corpse thrown aside in a charnel ground—one, two, or three days dead, bloated, livid, and oozing matter . . . being devoured by crows, hawks, vultures, dogs, jackals, or various kinds of worms . . . a skeleton with flesh and blood, held together with sinews . . . a skeleton without flesh and blood, held together with sinews . . . disconnected bones scattered in all directions . . . bones bleached white, the color of shells . . . bones heaped up, more than a year old . . . bones rotten and crumbling to dust—he compares this same body with it thus: 'this body too is of the same nature, it will be like that, it is not exempt from that fate.'"[11]

Although we might not have access to charnel grounds, the last sentence of the instruction can be a powerful reminder for us to reflect deeply on the decaying nature of the body and what happens to it after death. We can visualize a corpse in these various stages of decay, remembering that our own bodies are of exactly the same nature. We can become so identified with the body that we might find it difficult to look at or visualize the decomposition of a corpse. And yet decomposition is just nature at work. This is what is true for all living things. The more we can open to this truth, the less attached we can be to the idea of these bodies staying unchanged and the evident impossibility of that, and the less we suffer when they do change.

A compelling practice might be to look carefully at animals killed on the road by passing cars. Sometimes it looks like they are just resting peacefully, but more often, they have been squashed in some way or scavengers have begun to pick them apart. It's not a very pleasant sight. Yet it reveals the nature of the body—of our bodies—and it helps us open to the universal truth of death and decay. The point here is not to become morbidly obsessed, but rather to use and care for the body without the underlying attachment to it. This contemplation itself could lead us to full awakening.

Mindfulness
of Feelings

11

Liberation through Feelings

AS WE CONTINUE EXPLORING THE teachings of the Satipaṭṭhāna Sutta, it is important to remember that the Buddha gave these teachings for the purpose of freeing the mind from suffering. He is talking about liberation, not about simply getting more comfortable in our lives or sorting out our personal histories. Although these may be helpful by-products of the practice, the teachings in this discourse address the very largest questions of birth, aging, disease, and death, and how we can be free in this great cyclical wheel of existence.

Although most of us are living engaged lives in the world, with all the responsibilities, difficulties, and pleasures therein, it's still possible to practice with the highest aspirations, whether we call these aspirations the highest happiness, peace, or awakening. And whether we just get glimpses of this possibility or fully realize it, these understandings transform how we live in the world.

The Buddha begins this next section of the sutta with a rhetorical question: "And how, bhikkhus, does one in regard to feelings, abide contemplating feelings?" What is meant by the word *feelings,* which is the English translation of the Pali word *vedanā?*

In English we use this word in a wide variety of ways. Webster's dictionary lists fourteen different meanings for this one word. Sometimes it refers to emotions: "I feel happy, sad, peaceful, or angry."

Sometimes it refers to physical sensations: "I feel hot or cold, pressure or tightness." It can also refer to an opinion or attitude: "The general feeling of the group was to act."

In Buddhism, vedanā, or feeling, is more narrowly defined, and it is precisely this very specific meaning that makes it such a powerful element of our practice. Mindfulness of feeling is one of the master keys that both reveals and unlocks the deepest patterns of our conditioning. *Vedanā* refers specifically to that quality of pleasantness, unpleasantness, or neutrality that arises with the contact of each moment's experience. These feelings arise with both physical and mental phenomena. There's a sensation in the body or we hear a sound, and we feel it as being pleasant, unpleasant, or neutral. Likewise with a thought or an emotion—we feel it as having one of these three feeling tones.

FEELINGS AND CONDITIONED RESPONSE

Why is this important? Why does the Buddha single out feeling as one of the four foundations of mindfulness, as one of the five aggregates of existence, as a key link in the teaching of dependent origination? The feeling tone of experience is so vitally important because it conditions our various reactions in the mind and actions in the world.

When we're not mindful, pleasant feelings habitually condition desire and clinging, unpleasant feelings condition dislike and aversion, and neutral feelings condition delusion—that is, not really knowing what is going on. Yet when we are mindful, these very same feelings become the vehicle of our freedom.

The Buddha elaborates on this when he talks of two kinds of people: the uninstructed worldling and the instructed noble disciple. When the uninstructed worldling is contacted by a painful feeling, he/she feels aversion to it, feels sorrow and grief, and becomes distraught. The Buddha uses the example of being struck by two kinds of darts. The painful feeling itself is the first dart, and when we're not mindful, the unpleasant mental reaction to it is the second. Two darts, striking twice, with the second causing more suffering than the first.

And the suffering doesn't stop there. The Buddha goes on to say:

"Being contacted by painful feeling one seeks delight in sensual pleasure. For what reason? Because the uninstructed worldling does not know of any escape from painful feeling other than sensual pleasure . . .

"This, bhikkhus, is called an uninstructed worldling who is attached to birth, ageing and death; who is attached to sorrow, lamentation, pain, displeasure and despair; who is attached to suffering. . . ."[1]

All of this follows as habituated tendencies when we're not mindful of the original feeling tone. It would be interesting to notice how many of our actions through the day—even small changes of posture—come about through an effort to avoid unpleasant feelings.

We might wonder what is the difficulty in avoiding unpleasant feelings through the enjoyment of different sense pleasures. This is the usual way of the world. We will explore this in much greater detail in later chapters as we investigate what the Buddha called the "gratification, the danger, and the escape from sense pleasures." For the moment, though, simply reflecting on the transitory nature of pleasant feelings gives us an indication that they are not a final refuge from suffering.

The Buddha also spoke of the instructed noble disciples—that is, us in our more mindful moments:

"Being contacted by that same painful feeling, one harbors no aversion to it. . . . Being contacted by painful feeling, one does not seek delight in sensual pleasures. . . .

If one feels a pleasant feeling, one feels it detached. If one feels a painful feeling, one feels it detached. If one feels a neither-painful-nor-pleasant feeling, one feels it detached. This, bhikkhus, is called a noble disciple who is detached from birth, ageing and death; who is detached from sorrow, pain, displeasure and despair, who is detached from suffering. . . .

"This, bhikkhus, is the distinction, the disparity, the difference between the instructed noble disciple and the uninstructed worldling."[2]

The Buddha then summed up this wisdom of nonreactivity in two lines from the verse that followed these teachings:

Desirable things do not provoke one's mind,
Towards the undesired one has no aversion.[3]

So mindfulness of feeling is no little thing. The teaching is clear, but what is striking is how powerfully conditioned are these tendencies of like and dislike. Once, during a two-month self-retreat, I was going through a very difficult time, with many uncomfortable sensations in the body and lots of very unpleasant mind states—feelings of despair, hopelessness, and anguish. As I continued with my sitting and walking practice, it became clear that when I didn't catch the trigger point, when I wasn't mindful of the first dart, I would get lost in the reactivity of the mind. Then, at certain points, the mindfulness would reemerge, and there would be a spacious, open awareness, in which I was simply mindful of all the intensely unpleasant physical sensations, without them leading to aversive mind states. The difference between being mindful of the unpleasant sensations and lost in reactivity was clear, and I kept wondering why, in seeing the possibilities of either suffering or ease, the mind would repeatedly fall into the patterns of fear and hope: fear that the painful feelings would go on forever, and hope that they would finally go away. Why didn't the mind just naturally rest in the ease of mindful awareness?

This whole experience was an important lesson in the power and depth of habituated responses, and also an affirmation that it is possible to retrain the mind. In any moment—in the midst of painful experience or even right in the midst of our reactivity—we can apply this training of mindfulness of feeling. The Buddha highlighted the importance of this training in one very pointed statement:

> "Bhikkhus, that one shall here and now make an end to suffering without abandoning the underlying tendency to lust for pleasant feeling, without abolishing the underlying tendency to aversion towards painful feeling, without extirpating the underlying tendency to ignorance in regard to neither-painful-nor-pleasant feeling . . . this is impossible."[4]

He went on to say that it *is* possible to make an end to suffering by abandoning these tendencies.

MOMENT-TO-MOMENT AWARENESS OF FEELINGS

We may feel that abandoning the tendencies the Buddha refers to is an impossible task: "How could I ever free myself completely from desire and aversion?" But the Buddha is saying that this is something we can do, and that we do it in the moment. The question, then, is how to put this teaching into practice. In the words of the sutta,

> When feeling a pleasant feeling, one knows, "I feel a pleasant feeling." When feeling an unpleasant feeling, one knows, "I feel an unpleasant feeling." When feeling a neutral feeling, one knows, "I feel a neutral feeling."[5]

It's the simple, direct, and clear recognition of the feeling aspect of experience. We don't need to analyze, judge, compare, or even particularly understand why these feelings are happening. It's simply to know that pleasant feeling is like this, unpleasant feeling is like this, neutral feeling is like this.

In formal meditation sessions, we might spend some time focusing just on the feeling tone of our moment-to-moment experience: "pleasant, pleasant, unpleasant, pleasant, unpleasant," and so on. The key is not to do this mechanically but to refine our awareness of this feeling aspect of either physical sensations or mental events. Even doing this for short periods illuminates the very transitory nature of feelings. In our more active times in the world, we can use the more obvious reactions of likes and dislikes as a reminder to turn our attention to the feelings that prompt those reactions. These reactions can be the signal that we overlooked the feeling that preceded them.

As a way of attuning to vedanā, or feelings, we might first pay attention to those feelings that are strikingly pleasant or unpleasant. I have found New England winters to be particularly helpful in this regard. In walking outside on a frigid winter day with strong winds blowing, we can clearly recognize the unpleasant feeling. And then, by simply turning toward the sun with our backs to the wind, we experience pleasant feelings of contrasting warmth. Or we might notice the different feelings that arise around mealtimes, perhaps the pleasant feeling in smelling or tasting delicious food, or the unpleasant feelings when we overeat.

Seeing the Changing Nature of Feelings

This practice of recognition and mindful awareness of feelings leads us to a deeper and more direct insight into their impermanent nature. As we see the transitory nature of whatever feelings arise, we become less identified with them, less attached to the pleasant ones, less fearful of the unpleasant ones.

We all have some experience of this in the ordinary process of growing up. Think back to when you were a child, or if you can't remember that far back, think of a child who you know. Emotionally labile, children can go from laughter to tears and back again in just a few moments as the mind reacts to pleasure or discomfort. But as we grow older, we understand more clearly the passing nature of what is pleasant and unpleasant. We don't have quite the rapidity of a child's emotional swings. There's somewhat more equanimity and ease.

In one passage, the Buddha compares the play of feelings arising and passing away to the changing winds in the sky.

> Just as many diverse winds
> Blow back and forth across the sky,
> Easterly winds and westerly winds,
> Northerly winds and southerly winds,
> Dusty winds and dustless winds,
> Sometimes cold, sometimes hot,
> Those that are strong and others mild—
> Winds of many kinds that blow;
>
> So in the very body here,
> Various kinds of feelings arise,
> Pleasant ones and painful ones,
> And those neither painful nor pleasant.
>
> But when a bhikkhu who is ardent
> Does not neglect clear comprehension,
> Then that wise one fully understands
> Feelings in their entirety.
>
> Having fully understood feelings,
> One is taintless in this very life.

Standing in Dhamma, with the body's breakup,
The knowledge-master cannot be reckoned.[6]

Although this is easy to understand—that all feelings, pleasant, unpleasant, and neutral are impermanent—it is not always easy to sustain this awareness. We find our minds reactive to these feelings, caught up in some attachment or aversion. We might be doing walking meditation and the thought comes, "Let's have a cup of tea." If we're mindful of the pleasant feeling associated with that thought, then we go on walking. If we miss noticing this feeling, then we may be seduced by the idea that the cup of tea will make us happy, and not see that it's just another quickly passing feeling in the mind.

TRAINING THE MIND

Meditation provides us an opportunity to observe the mind's reactions to different kinds of feelings. How does the mind respond when pleasant sexual feelings arise in the body or pleasant fantasies in the mind? Do we indulge or resist? Are we mindful and nonreactive, seeing clearly their impermanent nature? How does the mind respond to unpleasant feelings of pain or discomfort? How does the mind respond when we're ill? The Buddha gives some direct instruction here: "You should train like this: my body may be sick yet my mind will remain unafflicted."

So often, we put certain situations outside of our practice—when they are either particularly pleasant or particularly unpleasant. I found that especially with the latter, it's helpful to see them as being training for dying. We would all like to die with a peaceful state of mind, but it is likely that as we're dying, there will be some amount of pain or discomfort of one kind or another. If we have trained ourselves to be mindful of these kinds of feelings, both physical and mental, during the ordinary experiences of our lives, then at the time of death, our minds and hearts will abide in a place of greater ease.

We can also train in mindfulness of feelings with external situations. There is a story of Ajahn Chaa going on retreat by himself in a little hut in the forest, but not far from a village. One night, the villagers were having a celebration with loud music playing on loudspeakers. At first, Ajahn Chaa became annoyed, thinking, "Don't they know I'm here on retreat?" But after a few moments of consideration, he realized the problem was in his own mind, not in the sound. He thought, "Well, they're just having a good time down there. I'm making myself miserable up here. No matter how upset I get, my anger is just making more noise internally." And then he had this insight: "Oh, the sound is just the sound. It's me who is going out to annoy it. If I leave the sound alone, it won't annoy me. It's just doing what it has to do. That's what sound does. It makes sound. This is its job. So if I don't go out and bother the sound, it's not going to bother me."[7]

We often don't see that it is the feeling we're attached or averse to, and not the object itself. We might think we're attached to the fantasy or averse to the sound or certain sensations in the body, but on closer looking, we see that all this movement of mind revolves around the feeling tone. It's the pleasant feeling we like and want to hold on to, the unpleasant feeling we want to push away, and the neutral feeling we don't even know we're feeling.

But as we practice being mindful of these feelings as they arise, and see with greater immediacy their impermanent nature, we become less entranced by them, less reactive. The Buddha gave direct and explicit instructions regarding mindfulness of feelings, which point the way to ultimate freedom:

> Whatever feeling one feels, whether pleasant, unpleasant
> or neither-painful-nor pleasant, one abides contemplating
> impermanence in those feelings, contemplating fading away,
> . . . contemplating relinquishment. Contemplating thus, one
> does not cling to anything in this world. When one does
> not cling, one is not agitated. When one is not agitated, one
> personally attains Nibbāna.[8]

12

Worldly and Unworldly Feelings

AS THE TEACHINGS ON MINDFULNESS of feelings continue, the Buddha opens us to a deeper understanding of happiness and suffering in our lives. He goes on to divide the pleasant, unpleasant, and neutral feelings into worldly ones and unworldly ones. Here, mindfulness of feelings goes deeper than simply recognizing its effect—that is, whether the feeling is pleasant, unpleasant, or neutral. Mindfulness at this deeper level recognizes the genesis of these feelings—what they are based on—and this distinction has profound implications.

DISTINGUISHING BETWEEN WORLDLY AND UNWORLDLY FEELINGS

Worldly feelings arise from contact with the senses: these are feelings dependent on sights and sounds, smells and tastes, touch sensations, and also thoughts connected with these objects. We enjoy a good meal or a soft touch, and we experience a pleasant worldly feeling. Or if there is a bad smell or a painful sensation, then we experience an unpleasant worldly feeling. Or there might be an ordinary sight, neither pleasant nor unpleasant, which leads us to experience a neutral worldly feeling. All of these worldly feelings arise simply from the play of our daily lives.

Unworldly feelings refer to something quite different. These are the feelings associated with renunciation. In our Western cultures, the idea of renunciation doesn't always inspire us. We tend to think of it as deprivation, something that might be good for us in the end, but is not that much fun now. But another way of understanding renunciation is as nonaddictiveness to sense pleasures. From this perspective, renunciation holds out the possibility of happiness now. The less addicted we are to the seduction of sense pleasures, the less commotion there is in the mind. We experience greater ease and simplicity of living.

Imagine what it would be like if the mind wanted everything that was advertised on television. We would be in a constant state of dis-ease, wanting this, wanting that. I think this is why we all prefer commercial-free programming. In the words of one Tibetan teacher, we learn to rest our weary minds. The Buddha highlighted this understanding when he said, "What the world calls happiness, I call suffering; what the world calls suffering, I call happiness."

The Hidden Dangers of Worldly Pleasures

The distinction between worldly and unworldly feelings—that is, feelings associated with sense objects and feelings associated with renunciation—opens up greater subtleties in our meditation and dramatically different ways of understanding pleasure and happiness. Almost every message we get throughout our lives is that happiness comes through enjoyable, pleasant sense experience. And for most of us it does, temporarily. But these pleasures also contain within them hidden dangers.

What are these dangers? Sometimes the pleasure itself is ultimately harmful, as in many kinds of addiction. There was an advertisement for a certain brand of cigarettes that showed a beautiful woman and handsome man in an idyllic setting, standing with cigarettes in hand. The caption read: "I don't let anything stand in the way of my pleasure." The danger inherent in this ad speaks for itself. Another potential drawback in the happiness of sense pleasures is that if we become attached to the pleasant experience, then we feel sorrow and loss when it changes. And when we're not mindful of pleasant worldly feelings when they arise, we're unknowingly strengthening our habit of desire:

> "When one is touched by a pleasant feeling, if one delights in
> it, welcomes it, and remains holding to it, then the underlying tendency to lust lies within one."[1]

UNWORLDLY FEELINGS: THE
PATH TO ENLIGHTENMENT

In the teaching about unworldly feelings, the Buddha is pointing out a different kind of pleasure and a deeper kind of happiness, one without hidden dangers. These pleasant unworldly feelings become the very basis of our awakening. But this understanding was not obvious, at first, to the Bodhisattva on his path to enlightenment. After he left home at the age of twenty-nine, Siddhartha Gotama, the Buddha-to-be, spent six years practicing the great austerities of his times. There are vivid descriptions of these practices, which aimed to subdue the ego through self-mortification. But at the end of these six years, the Bodhisattva found himself no closer to the goal.

> "I thought, 'Whatever recluses or brahmins in the past, present or future have experienced painful, racking, piercing feelings due to exertion, this is the utmost, there is none beyond this. But by this racking practice of austerities I have not attained any distinction in knowledge and vision worthy of the noble ones. Could there be another path to enlightenment?'
>
> "I considered, 'I recall that when my father the Sakyan was occupied, while I was sitting in the cool shade of a rose-apple tree, quite secluded from sensual pleasures, secluded from unwholesome states, I entered upon and abided in the first absorption, which accompanied by applied and sustained thought, with rapture and pleasure born of seclusion. Could that be the path to enlightenment?' Then following on that memory, came the realization: 'That is the path to enlightenment.'
>
> "I thought, 'Why am I afraid of that pleasure that has nothing to do with sensual pleasures and unwholesome states?' I thought: 'I am not afraid of that pleasure since it has nothing to do with sensual pleasures and unwholesome states.'"[2]

Indeed, after his enlightenment, the Buddha declared himself to be one who lived in happiness.

There is an important message here about the role of joy and happiness in our path of practice. With the emphasis on the great truth of suffering and its causes, on the need for right effort, on the dangers of continually indulging sense desire, it is sometimes easy to overlook that this is a path of happiness, leading onward to happiness. One discourse tells of King Pasenadi, one of the rulers in the Buddha's time, coming to visit the Buddha and then describing what he sees:

> "But here I see bhikkhus smiling and cheerful, sincerely
> joyful, plainly delighting, their faculties fresh, living at ease,
> unruffled, subsisting on what others give, abiding with mind
> [as aloof] as a wild deer's."[3]

Beneficial and Unbeneficial Types of Pleasure

In the Satipaṭṭhāna Sutta, it is the instruction on mindfulness of feelings, distinguishing between the worldly ones and unworldly ones, that highlights the difference between beneficial and unbeneficial types of pleasure. In the time of the Buddha there was a wealthy merchant named Visākha living in the ancient city of Rajāgaha. Both he and his wife had attained the third stage of enlightenment, called "nonreturner." Later, his wife was ordained as the nun Dhammadinnā, and she soon finished the spiritual journey, becoming an arahant.

At one point, Visākha goes to the nun Dhammadinnā with a series of questions. Visākha asks, "What habitual tendencies underlie pleasant, unpleasant, and neutral feelings?" She responds as we might expect: "Desire or lust is the conditioned tendency underlying pleasant feeling, aversion is the conditioned tendency underlying unpleasant feeling, delusion is the conditioned tendency underlying neutral feeling."[4] And, as mentioned previously, without abandoning these underlying tendencies, liberation is impossible.

But then Visākha goes on to ask a further probing question, one that has great implications for our understanding of the path. "Lady Dhammadinnā, do these habitual tendencies of desire, aversion, and delusion underlie all pleasant, unpleasant, and neutral feelings?" She replies, "These habitual tendencies do not underlie all feelings; they do not have to be abandoned in regard to all feelings."[5]

She is saying there are some pleasant feelings, secluded from unwholesome states, that lead onward to enlightenment. And there are also some unpleasant feelings that arise from renunciation and do not condition aversion, and they too can lead to awakening.

Unworldy Unpleasant and Neutral Feelings

What are these unpleasant feelings not associated with aversion? Often in practice, we go through stages of meditation that are difficult. There are stages of practice where unpleasant physical sensations predominate. Or we might feel fear, misery, or despair about our practice or about the world, and we feel that enlightenment seems very far away. This is what St. John of the Cross called "the dark night of the soul." All of these are unworldly unpleasant feelings coming out of a deeper place of practice.

Likewise, there are neutral feelings that are not associated with delusion or forgetfulness. Worldly neutral feelings are conditioned by the blandness of the object; nothing stands out, and so they go unnoticed. Unworldly neutral feelings are born of equanimity, and they become very strong in the fourth absorption and in the insight stage called "equanimity about formations." At these times of great refinement of mind, the neutral feelings actually bring more pleasure than pleasant ones.

Dhammadinnā's reply, that the habitual tendencies of desire, aversion, and delusion do not underlie all feelings, and so do not have to be abandoned with regard to all feelings, points out the different kinds of feelings that arise, both worldly and unworldly. She highlights a different understanding of happiness and the role that this kind of joy plays on the meditative path. The Buddha approved her replies, saying to Visākha, "Dhammadinnā is wise. If you had asked me the meaning of this, I would have explained it to you in just the same way."

UNWORLDY FEELINGS OF JOY IN OUR OWN EXPERIENCE

By beginning to discern the difference between the two kinds of feelings, worldly and unworldly, we can slowly open to possibilities of a happiness not mixed with the taints of various defilements. But even though we might understand this possibility, as beings living in this world, we often don't fully trust it or live this understanding. Much of our lives is spent seeking and enjoying different sense pleasures, even though we know and understand their limitations. Could we really be happy without delighting in all the pleasant worldly feelings? The Buddha addresses this concern directly:

[Y]ou might think: "Perhaps these defiling states [desire, aversion, and ignorance] might disappear. . . , and one might still be unhappy." That is not how it should be regarded. If defiling states disappear . . . , nothing but happiness and delight develops, with tranquility, mindfulness and clear awareness—and that is a happy state.[6]

Generosity

We may not yet know the happiness of full enlightenment, but all along the path, we do experience clear times of nonsensual joy, the unworldly pleasant feelings. We experience them in times of generosity, when we are renouncing mind states of greed and stinginess. Think of times when you were generous with someone, giving something out of love or compassion, respect or gratitude. Practicing generosity is an easily accessible gateway to the happy, unworldly feelings based on renunciation, and it is the reason the Buddha usually begins his progressive teachings speaking of generosity.

Love and Compassion

We feel nonsensual joy when we practice qualities like love and compassion. The great Zen master and poet Ryokan summed up the expression of this feeling when he wrote, "Oh that my monk's robes were wide enough to gather up all the people in this floating world." Sometimes we see the best qualities of humanity emerge in times of great disasters, where there is an outpouring of generosity from people all over the world. We can feel the purity of those mind states. People aren't giving in order to get anything back for themselves, and they are often moved to give more than they might have under more normal circumstances. In this response to suffering, there is the purity of a spontaneous, compassionate response, which brings its own kind of happiness.

Renunciation

We feel a nonsensual joy when we practice the renunciation involved with following the precepts. We renounce harmful actions, and this renunciation brings the unworldly pleasant feeling of nonremorse. And even if we've done unskillful actions in the past—as we all have—there is a certain strength and confidence and happiness from the moment we make the commitment to nonharming.

We feel pleasant unworldly feelings on retreat, in the renunciation of our familiar comforts. We begin to enjoy the beauty of simplicity. We get a taste of what King Pasenadi was describing when he saw the monks and nuns gathered around the Buddha. When I go on retreat, it is so clear that everything I need is right in my small room, and when I think of my regular life, it seems so cluttered by comparison. Sometimes at home I'll be meditating at night in my study, where the room is dark except for all the little lights on the computer, the modem, the surge protectors, the printer, the phone. It's like a control center for my life in the world.

Concentration

We experience nonsensual joy of unworldly pleasant feelings in states of concentration, where the mind is secluded from unskillful states. At first our minds are often restless and agitated, jumping from one thing to another, reacting to the various pleasant and unpleasant feelings that arise. At a certain point, whether for short periods or sustained ones, the mind settles down, resting easily on the object of attention, carried on the current of mindfulness. There is an ease and pleasure here much greater than that of our usual sense delights. There's a greater sense of unification.

One of our teachers, Dipa Ma, once sat in meditation for three days in a jhanic state of absorption. And it's said that the Buddha could remain in such concentrated states for up to seven days at a time. What sense pleasure offers that possibility? Can you imagine three days of nonstop eating, of nonstop music listening, of nonstop sexual pleasures? At a certain point, they would all become exhausting and even undesirable. This points to the difference between worldly and unworldly pleasant feelings.

Clear Seeing

We experience an even higher nonsensual joy in the various stages of insight and awakening. Here it is not the absorption in the unworldly pleasant feelings of concentration, but the special happiness of clear seeing—that is, seeing deeply and vividly the changing, selfless nature of all that arises. And as insight practice matures in various ways, there is an even more refined kind of happiness. Mahasi Sayadaw, one of the great Burmese masters of the last century, describes it this way: "At times the different objects to note may shrink to one or two or all may even disappear. However, at this time, the knowing consciousness is still present. In this very clear open space of the sky, there remains only one very clear, blissful consciousness, which is very clear beyond comparison and very blissful."

HOW TO PRACTICE WITH PLEASANT UNWORLDLY FEELINGS

How do we practice with these different kinds of pleasant unworldly feelings? We can go back to the instructions of the Satipaṭṭhāna Sutta, which remind us that the path to realization is simply being mindful of all the different feelings as they arise. When a pleasant feeling arises, know it as worldly or unworldly; when an unpleasant feeling arises, know it as worldly or unworldly; and the same with neutral feelings.

The caution here is not to make all this too complicated or the source of doubt and confusion. We shouldn't spend an hour just trying to figure out exactly what kind of feeling it is. Rather, we should simply use this as a framework of understanding, and begin to notice and explore the difference between the experience of sense pleasures and what we might call dharma pleasures. Likewise with unpleasant or neutral feelings.

In these instructions, the Buddha is not saying that we should strive to have only unworldly feelings. Both kinds will arise naturally in the course of our lives. But by noticing and being mindful of what kind of feeling it is, we learn to recognize more clearly the underlying tendencies of the worldly feelings—desire, aversion, and delusion—and through mindfulness practice, abandon those tendencies. We can rest in the simple awareness, "This is a pleasant (or unpleasant or neutral) worldly feeling connected to the senses," and we can appreciate the potential of the unworldly feelings as being part of the stream leading to liberation.

APPLYING THE REFRAIN

Just as after every other section of this discourse, the Buddha repeats the refrain. We are reminded to contemplate feelings internally, externally, and both, to contemplate the nature of arising and passing away and both the arising and passing away of feelings. The Buddha then completes this instruction by saying:

"Mindfulness that 'there is feeling' is established to the extent necessary for bare knowledge and continuous mindfulness. And one abides independent, not clinging to anything in the world. That is how in regard to feelings, one abides contemplating feelings."[7]

Mindfulness of feelings externally means that we are aware of feelings arising in others; mindfulness fosters empathetic joy when others experience pleasant feelings, and it fosters compassion when others are in pain. When we're not mindful of feelings—pleasant, unpleasant, and neutral; worldly and unworldly—and we don't contemplate them internally, externally, and both, then we easily become identified with these feelings, taking them to be self.

In one discourse, the Buddha asks Ānanda, his faithful attendant, a rhetorical question about how people regard the self. The Buddha goes on to say that people might believe that feeling is "myself," or "my self feels," or even "my self is without feeling." This identification then feeds the conditioned tendencies of desire for the pleasant, aversion to the unpleasant, and ignorance of the neutral, and so keeps us caught on the wheel of saṃsāra. Through contemplating feelings as impersonal processes, arising out of contact with the six sense objects (mind is included as the sixth sense), we no longer take these feelings to be self. And in those moments we are practicing the Buddha's essential teaching, "Nothing whatsoever is to be clung to as I or mine."

MINDFULNESS
OF MIND

13

The Wholesome and Unwholesome Roots of Mind

IN THIS SECTION OF THE Satipaṭṭhāna Sutta, the Buddha gives instructions for the third of the four foundations of mindfulness—namely, mindfulness of mind. He begins this teaching with a question, "And how, bhikkhus, does one in regard to the mind, contemplate the mind?" He then goes on to explain:

> "Here one knows a lustful mind to be 'lustful,' and a mind without lust to be 'without lust.' One knows an angry mind to be 'angry,' and a mind without anger to be 'without anger.' One knows a deluded mind to be 'deluded,' and a mind without delusion to be 'without delusion'; one knows a contracted mind to be 'contracted,' and a distracted mind to be 'distracted.'"[1]

In this list of mind states, the Buddha emphasizes knowing the presence or absence of the three unwholesome roots of mind and how they color or condition our minds. These three roots are greed or lust; hatred, which includes ill will and anger; and delusion or ignorance, which encompasses bewilderment and confusion.

Although the Buddha is emphasizing the simple recognition of these unwholesome states or their absence, it is worth paying attention to the quality of the mind when it *is* free from different forms of greed, hatred, or delusion. At those times, even though we may not be experiencing their positive counterparts in a direct way (in the absence of anger or ill will, we may not necessarily feel strong lovingkindness), we can still recognize the ease and peace and openness of mind that are present. In later chapters, we will be exploring the wholesome states of the factors of awakening in more detail.

What Is Skillful and What Is Not

By emphasizing the recognition and knowing of the unwholesome roots, and the wholesome ones in their absence, the Buddha is highlighting the wise discernment of what is skillful and what is unskillful—that is, discerning what leads to happiness and liberation and what leads to suffering. Although this discernment is basic to the Buddha's teaching, in our Western culture it is a very delicate process. For many people, it is an easy step from recognizing a particular mind state like greed or hatred as being unwholesome to the feeling that you're a bad person for having it, or that somehow it's wrong for the mind state to even arise. This pattern of reaction simply leads to more self-judgment, more aversion, and more suffering. It's not a helpful cycle.

It's important to understand which mind states are skillful and which are unskillful, not in order to judge ourselves or be reactive to them, but in order to see which lead to happiness and should be cultivated in our lives, and which lead to suffering and should be abandoned. The distinction between wholesome and unwholesome mind states brings a moral dimension into psychology. This is particularly important because these different states are not only arising in our minds, but they are also what motivate our actions.

Why is there so much avoidable suffering in the world—violence, war, hunger, injustice—or in the difficulties of our personal relationships? That suffering is just these unwholesome mind states being acted out. For our own happiness and for greater peace in the world, we first need to know what is skillful and what is not and then to recognize all these states when they arise in the mind. The Dalai Lama emphasized the importance of this when he said that actions should not ultimately be measured by their success or failure, but by the motivations behind them. We can't always, or even often, control outcomes, but we can train our minds and hearts. This is the training of the third foundation of mindfulness: mindfulness of mind.

How can we put this training into practice and, in the words of the sutta, know for ourselves the lustful mind as lustful and the mind without lust as being without lust? Similarly, how can we know for ourselves an angry mind or a deluded one? There is a verse in the Dhammapada that succinctly describes how these unwholesome states manifest: "There is no fire like lust, no grip like anger, and no net like delusion." In practicing mindfulness of mind, we need to see for ourselves how we experience each of these states. We might feel that fevered excitability of wanting or greed; we might experience the tightness, contraction, and alienation of anger and hatred; we might feel the confused entanglement of delusion. The Thai master Buddhadasa describes these tendencies yet another way: "pulling in, pushing away, and running around in circles."

As a simple experiment in meditation, when you're sitting, you might ask the question, "What's the attitude in the mind right now?" This question often illuminates whether the mind is holding on in some way or wanting some other state to occur, and is a direct application of mindfulness of mind. Often, just in asking the question, we can feel the mind relax from a clinging or aversion we hadn't even realized was there.

Know When Unwholesome Mind States Are Absent

In some way, a more difficult aspect of the practice is to notice when these states are absent. For some reason, we are more likely to dwell on the difficulties, and we often overlook the presence of the wholesome states of mind. This has a major effect on how we view ourselves. In this section of the Satipaṭṭhāna Sutta, the Buddha is giving equal importance to being mindful of each. We notice the ease of the mind not caught in the grip of the unwholesome states and also the presence of their positive counterparts when they arise. As an experiment, pay attention to the next time you experience a strong wanting in the mind. Stay as mindful as possible of how it manifests in the mind and body. And then notice as the wanting disappears, either in a moment or gradually over time. Instead of rushing back to the breath or some other object of meditation, pay attention to the mind free of wanting, experiencing the coolness and peace of that state.

A clear recognition of what is what—this is lust, this is its absence—then becomes the frame for the deeper direct experience of the mind state itself, free of any words or concepts. Michael Cunningham, in his novel *The Hours*, writes, "Everything in the world has its own secret name—a name that cannot be conveyed in language but is simply the sight and feel of the thing itself." This is mindfulness sinking into the object and knowing it fully.

In these instructions to know whether the unwholesome roots are present or not, the Buddha is pointing out something quite essential for our freedom. Since the *kilesas,* defilements, are not always present, they are therefore adventitious, which means they are not inherent or innate to the mind; they are not the nature of the mind itself, but are visitors that come at different times due to conditions. The Buddha makes this point quite directly:

> "Luminous, bhikkhus, is this mind, but it is defiled by adventitious defilements. The uninstructed worldling does not understand this as it really is; therefore I say that for the uninstructed worldling there is no development of the mind.
> "Luminous, bhikkhus, is this mind, and it is freed from adventitious defilements. The instructed noble disciple understands this as it really is; therefore I say that for the instructed noble disciple there is development of the mind."[2]

Simple, but Not Easy

This understanding and the explicit instructions in the text suggest a very different attitude for working with unwholesome states than the ones we usually bring to practice. Instead of drowning in the defilements through identification with them, or judging them, or denying them, the Buddha reminds us to simply be mindful both when they are present and when they are not, remembering that they are visitors. Although this is very simple, it is not always easy to do.

For so many years I would struggle with the difficulties in my practice, thinking I was a bad meditator when different defilements arose or my mind was wandering a lot. Or at times the self-judgment would get worse, and I would think that I was a hopeless, psychological mess. At one particular time, when I was struggling with a lot of intense fear, instead of applying the instructions to simply be mindful of it, I found thoughts proliferated wildly: "I'm such a fearful person. It will take thirty years of therapy to unwind all this conditioning," and so on.

It took a while to actually follow the Buddha's instructions and see that the difficult mind states were not in themselves a problem or a mistake. They were simply part of the path, impermanent and selfless, just like everything else. Fear is just a mind state. At this point of understanding, there was a certain kind of joy in becoming aware of the defilements, because I would rather see and explore them than not see them and simply act them out.

CONTRACTED AND DISTRACTED MIND

The next instructions in this contemplation of mind are to know the contracted mind as contracted and the distracted mind as distracted. *Contracted* here refers to the inner withdrawal of the mind due to sloth and torpor. There's little or no energy to meet the object; we experience dullness and heaviness, collapsing inward. This state is contrasted with the mind distracted by externals and pursuing different sense objects due to restlessness.

There is an interesting progression of instructions in this section of the sutta on mindfulness of mind. First we develop awareness of the three wholesome and unwholesome roots, becoming mindful of them so that the mind remains free and unattached. Next, the Buddha says to be mindful both of the contraction of mind in sloth and the distraction of mind in restlessness. By not getting lost in or becoming identified with either of these states, the mind then finds the balance necessary for deeper concentration and the higher states of mind that follow.

What is reassuring about all of these instructions is that they fully acknowledge the difficulties that arise in practice. It's not that somehow we need to be free of all the hindrances and defilements in order to proceed. Here the Buddha is saying that mindfulness of all these states when they arise is itself the path to freedom: through bare attention and mirrorlike wisdom, we see their ephemeral, impermanent, and selfless nature. That itself is sufficient for liberation.

Later in the text, there is a further and more complete investigation of the various hindrances and enlightenment factors, where they themselves become the specific objects of meditation. But in this third foundation of mindfulness, mindfulness of mind, the emphasis is on simply noticing the general quality of the mind as it is influenced by different mind states, moods, or emotions.

Ask Yourself, "What Is Happening?"

I have found that noticing the quality of mind in this way is of particular value in two ways. First, during times of struggle, where for one reason or another we don't quite know what is going on and there is a lack of ease or connection, where we have the feeling of efforting, striving, struggling, but without much success, then, at these times, it is helpful to sit back, open up the awareness, and simply ask the question, "What is happening?" Very often there's a mind state present that we're simply not acknowledging. Maybe it is a dullness we're trying to fight our way through, or it might be a distracted, restless energy with a lot of thinking. Or it might be the angry mind caught up in a story. In each case, when we acknowledge and accept just what it is, the mind no longer struggles. We simply know with bare attention that this is what's present. To repeat the Buddha's words:

> "Here one knows a lustful mind to be 'lustful,' and a mind without lust to be 'without lust.' One knows an angry mind to be 'angry,' and a mind without anger to be 'without anger.' One knows a deluded mind to be 'deluded,' and a mind without delusion to be 'without delusion'; one knows a contracted mind to be 'contracted,' and a distracted mind to be 'distracted.'"[3]

Feelings of struggle can become very useful feedback. They are always telling us that something is going on that we're not accepting, not opening to. Because if we were accepting it, we wouldn't be struggling.

Be Aware of Moods and Emotions

The second way I have found especially useful in applying this mindfulness of mind is in the awareness of our daily background moods or emotions. So often we go through a day, or part of one, influenced by a certain mood. It might be sadness or boredom or excitement; it might be some irritation or a feeling of clarity, or depression or happiness. Because these moods and mind states are so amorphous and generalized, we often sink into them and become identified with them, and they become the unconscious filter on experience. At these times, we're looking at the world through colored glasses.

Emotions and moods are often what we most personalize. When we identify with them, we build a superstructure of self on top of the shifting landscape of experience: "I'm angry," "I'm sad," "I'm happy." But as we practice this mindfulness of mind, we notice more clearly what mood or emotion is present and how it is coloring or conditioning the mind, without adding the idea or sense of self. We simply know the angry mind is like this, the sad mind is like this, the happy mind is like this. Experiencing the mind in this way opens us to what Ajahn Chaa called "a taste of freedom":

> Within itself, the mind is already peaceful. That the mind is
> not peaceful these days is because it follows moods. It becomes
> agitated because moods deceive it. The untrained mind is
> stupid. Sense impressions come and trick it into unhappiness,
> suffering, gladness and sorrow, but the mind's true nature is
> none of these things. Gladness or sadness is not the mind, but
> only a mood coming to deceive us. The untrained mind gets
> lost and follows these things, it forgets itself, then we think
> that it is we who are upset or at ease or whatever. But really
> this mind of ours is already unmoving and peaceful, really
> peaceful. So we must train the mind to know these sense
> impressions and not get lost in them. Just this is the aim of all
> this difficult practice we put ourselves through.[4]

GREAT AND NARROW, SURPASSABLE AND UNSURPASSABLE

In the last part of the instructions on mind, the Buddha says to know the great mind as great, and the narrow mind as narrow; a surpassable mind as surpassable, and an unsurpassable mind as unsurpassable; a concentrated mind as concentrated, and an unconcentrated mind as unconcentrated; and finally, a liberated mind as liberated, and an unliberated one as unliberated.

The Qualities of Concentration

According to the commentaries, the first three pairs refer to different qualities of concentration. *Great* and *narrow* refer to how far the concentration pervades. For example, in the *brahmavihāra* practices of love and compassion, they refer to whether we are radiating these feelings toward all beings or just one person. *Surpassable* and *unsurpassable* refer to the level of absorption and whether the higher levels are attainable or not. (As an interesting footnote, *unsurpassable* refers here to the fourth *jhāna,* because the higher formless absorptions have the same degree of concentration, simply more refined objects.[5]) The third pair, *concentrated* and *unconcentrated,* emphasizes being mindful of whether stable one-pointedness in both *samatha* (concentration) and vipassanā (insight) meditation is present or not.

In this part of mindfulness of mind, the Buddha is pointing out two things. First, even deeper states of concentration and absorption need to be contemplated with wisdom, because as pleasant and satisfying as they might be, such states are still constructed, conditional states, subject to arising and passing away. They are not the final refuge. Second, we can and should be mindful both at times when we're concentrated and at times when we're not. Instead of judging ourselves when our mind wanders, we can simply notice, "unconcentrated." In this way, the practice of mindfulness is all-inclusive; no state is left out.

Noticing the Liberated Mind

In the last line of these teachings, the Buddha says to know the liberated mind as liberated and the unliberated one as unliberated. *Liberated* here means both full awakening, when all the unwholesome tendencies have been uprooted, and also the mind temporarily free of defilements, a state we often experience in vipassanā practice. Given the propensity to focus on the hindrances and defilements and difficulties, this is a good reminder to notice those times when the mind *is* free of greed and lust, free of aversion and ill will, free of bewilderment and delusion. We can notice the ease and purity of mind in these moments of simple bare attention, when we're aware without clinging, without condemning, without judging. As one Tibetan teacher described the practice of liberation, "Short moments many times."

The importance of mindfulness of mind, and, indeed, all the foundations of mindfulness, is summed up in a teaching of Sayadaw U Tejaniya clearly expressing the importance of monitoring our minds:

One thing you need to remember and understand is that you cannot leave the mind alone. It needs to be watched constantly. If you do not look after your garden it will overgrow with weeds. If you do not watch your mind, defilements will grow and multiply. The mind does not belong to you, but you are responsible for it.[6]

14

The Refrain

On Feelings and Mind

IN CHAPTERS 5 AND 6, we discussed the Satipaṭṭhāna Refrain in detail, using mindfulness of the body, and mindfulness of breathing in particular, to exemplify the essential aspects of meditation practice. To review, the refrain follows each section of meditation instructions in the Satipaṭṭhāna Sutta. It seems safe to assume that by stating the refrain so often—thirteen different times—the Buddha is emphasizing the most crucial components of the path to awakening. In this chapter, we will apply the refrain to mindfulness of feelings and mindfulness of mind, the second and third foundations of mindfulness.

PRACTICING MINDFULNESS INTERNALLY AND EXTERNALLY

First, we contemplate feelings and mind internally, externally, and both. Although there are different interpretations of what *internal* and *external* mean in this context, there is one common interpretation that clearly applies to all four foundations of mindfulness: *internal* refers to one's own experience, and *external* refers to the experience of others. This is a reminder of the comprehensive nature of mindfulness. Our practice is to be aware of whatever there is, whether within or without, and in the end go beyond this division altogether.

The last few chapters have been an in-depth discussion of contemplating feelings and the mind internally. This contemplation means becoming aware of pleasant, unpleasant, and neutral feelings, both worldly and unworldly, as they arise in our minds. It also means becoming aware of our minds as they are influenced by the wholesome or unwholesome roots, and knowing the mind as concentrated or not, surpassed or not, liberated or not.

But *how* does one contemplate these aspects externally? The Buddha talks of the development of insight in various ways. One is through our own direct experience; another is through inference and induction. If we put our hand in fire and it burns us, we don't need to keep rediscovering this result by repeatedly touching the flames. Hopefully, after one or two times, we learn by inference that next time we touch the fire, it will again burn us.

We can experience this same kind of insight with regard to feelings. It is often obvious, either through a person's bodily expressions or words, when they are feeling something as either pleasant or painful. Then, by inference, from our own experience of pleasure and pain, we can know, at least to some extent, what the other person is feeling. The same is true of various mind states. When we're mindful of mind externally, and we see someone angry or loving, greedy or generous, distracted or concentrated, then by inference, based on our own experience of these states, we can open to and become aware of the other person's mental state—just as it is, free from our own unmindful reactivity.

Why is this important? Why did the Buddha include this external awareness of feelings and mind states?

Just as pleasant feelings condition desire, unpleasant ones condition aversion, and neutral feelings condition ignorance when we're unmindful internally, so too might seeing painful feelings in others trigger grief, sorrow, or denial in ourselves when we're unmindful externally. In some circumstances, painful feelings in others can trigger cruelty. I saw some of these reactions play out in the various responses to the mangy dogs in India. These dogs have no home and scrounge around in the marketplace for scraps to eat. Often people would just ignore them or shoo them away. But sometimes people would throw rocks at the dogs to scare them off because they didn't want to confront the dogs' painful feelings of hunger and desperation.

Likewise, when we're unmindful externally, the pleasant feelings in others could trigger jealousy or envy. The writer Anne Lamott expressed this possibility very clearly when she described how difficult it is for writers to accept the triumphs of other writers, especially a friend: "It can wreak just the tiniest bit of havoc with your self-esteem to find that you are hoping for small, bad things to happen to this friend, for, say, her head to blow up."[1]

Arousing Wholesome Mind States

When we are mindful of the feelings of others (mindful externally), as well as our own, we open up possibilities for wholesome states to arise either spontaneously or prompted by reflection. We might feel joy for the pleasant feelings of others, rather than envy, and compassion for their painful feelings, rather than fear or apathy.

There are many examples of how we can develop wholesome mind states through practicing mindfulness externally. On one of my stays at a meditation center in Burma, I met a friend from America who had already been living there as a monk for several years. It took some time for my mind to settle down, and when I observed how calm and concentrated my friend was, the comparing mind sprang to the fore, tinged with envy and self-judgment. But after noticing this pattern with its attendant suffering, I started doing the meditation on *muditā*, or empathetic joy. This is the practice of wishing the happiness and success of others to continually grow and increase. It was surprising to me how quickly the mind shifted from the suffering of envy to the happiness of joy in my friend's success. It was another lesson in the power of the practice to choose and cultivate what is skillful. It's possible to change the channels of our minds.

At a Buddhist-Christian conference at the Abbey of Gethsemani in Kentucky, the monastery where Thomas Merton lived and wrote, I had another illuminating experience of how being mindful of the mind states of others can have important consequences. We had been meeting for several days in the chapter room of the monastery, and one day I happened to be behind the Dalai Lama as he was walking down the corridor after the meeting. There was a statue of the Virgin Mary at the end of the hallway, and as His Holiness passed it, he paused, bowed, and then moved on. This is something that would never have occurred to me to do, and yet it was so clear that the Dalai

Lama was deeply respectful of all that the statue represented. So being mindful externally revealed certain limitations I had created in my own mind. Moreover, at the end of the conference, the abbot of Gethsemani, in his concluding remarks, commented on how moved he was by seeing the Dalai Lama bow to the statue of the Virgin Mary and how that act of respect said more about interreligious dialogue than any of the many words spoken at the conference.

Reactivity in the Mind

We can also learn from times when at first we're not being mindful externally, but then, through our own reactivity, we become aware of what's happening. There is a common psychological understanding that those qualities that we're most reactive to in others are often the ones we have least accepted in ourselves. How do we react when we're with someone who is angry or greedy? Are we simply noticing that those mind states have arisen in others, or is there some reactive charge in our own minds?

Reactions to others can be a powerful mindfulness bell, reminding us to pay attention. There is a lot to observe at those times. We can become mindful of our own reactive mind states, such as impatience, anger, or fear. We can then become mindful of the bodily actions, feelings, or mind states of others that have triggered our reactions, noticing if we're also reactive to those same qualities in ourselves. And then we can pay attention to what happens as we settle into a mindful awareness of all these things.

The emphasis on mindfulness both internally and externally keeps things in balance. We don't become overly self-centered or self-absorbed, forgetting the context in which we're living, nor do we become so caught up in the externals that we miss what is happening in our own bodies and minds.

In practicing mindfulness internally, externally, and both internally and externally, we begin opening to the understanding of *anattā*, the empty, selfless nature of feelings and all experience. We shift our understanding from "I'm having a pleasant feeling" or "She is having a pleasant feeling" to "There is a pleasant feeling." As Anālayo points out, in this contemplation, the boundaries of "I" and "others," of separate selves, are left behind. It is the experience of phenomena independent of any ownership.

ARISING AND PASSING AWAY

The second part of the refrain, as mentioned earlier with respect to the body and feelings, tells us to contemplate the nature of arising, of passing away, and both arising and passing away of the mind as it is conditioned by different states. The Pali word *saṃsāra* means "wandering on," "continuing on," or "revolving." It traditionally refers to our wandering through the different realms of existence over many lifetimes. But we can also see this same process at work within a single lifetime, and even a single day.

How many different mind worlds do we inhabit from one hour to the next? We're happy, sad, bored, excited, fearful, calm—the list goes on and on. As we contemplate the arising, passing, and both arising and passing away of the various mind states, we begin to free ourselves from both identification with and reaction to them.

We can contemplate the impermanence of these states in several ways. When we focus on their arising nature, we emphasize awareness of the moments when they first appear: anger arises, desire arises, calm arises. We can further understand the impermanent, conditioned arising nature of mind states by seeing what triggers them. We can notice the relationship of thought to emotion and emotion to thought, and how each can powerfully condition the other. For example, when people are on an intensive meditation retreat, many "time thoughts" will come to mind. If we're calm or concentrated, the thought "another week of practice" might arouse the feeling of ardency or joy. Or if we're struggling with some hindrance, the very same thought could trigger restlessness or loneliness. By noticing both the trigger thought and the resultant mind state, we are contemplating the arising nature of these states and stay free in the current of changing experience.

We can also be mindful of the passing away of mind states, emphasizing awareness of the moment when they fall away or disappear. I have found this contemplation of the departing moment particularly useful when desire is present in the mind. So often, in the throes of the wanting mind, we feel an urgency to fulfill the desire, that somehow we have to gratify it in order to feel fulfilled. We forget that it is the desire itself that desires, and that the great law of impermanence will resolve it all by itself. So we notice desire, desire, and then its end, its passing away. When we do so, we are let out of the grip of desire's grasping nature.

The more often we see this passing-away nature of mind states and emotions, the less driven we are by them. Direct insight—that is, seeing into their passing away—brings about the space to be with mind states and emotions without fear, without identification, and without reaction.

Arising and passing away, on their deepest levels, lead to wisdom and awakening. This is expressed most simply in words often found in the suttas: "Whatever has the nature to arise has the nature to cease." Sometimes people would just hear this one teaching and attain stages of realization. Although on one level it seems very obvious, this statement has profound implications. If we could fully open to the truth of it, we would be free of attachment and clinging to anything at all.

The importance of this insight is summed up in one verse of the Dhammapada: "Better than one hundred years lived without seeing the arising and passing of things / Is one day lived seeing their arising and passing."[2] What does this say about what we value and work for in our lives, and about the liberating effect of seeing directly, in the moment, the truth of change? The refrain reminds us, with regard to body, feelings, and mind, to be mindful of them internally, externally, and both, and to contemplate their arising and passing away.

BARE KNOWING

The next line of the refrain answers the unspoken question, "Just how much mindfulness is needed?" It says, "Mindfulness that 'there is a feeling' or 'there is mind' is established in one to the extent necessary for bare knowledge and continuous mindfulness." "Bare knowledge" here means observing or knowing objectively what is arising, without getting lost in associations, reactions, judgments or evaluations, or, if we do get lost, to then become aware of those states themselves.

As an example, imagine having a painful sensation in the jaw. We might notice the unpleasantness, but then add the commentary, "I'm such an uptight person." Or we might have the pleasant feeling of a concentrated and spacious mind and then experience the proliferation of thoughts about what a good meditator we are. But instead of these proliferating thoughts about a pleasant or unpleasant feeling, we can simply have bare knowledge that a pleasant or unpleasant feeling is present. Or instead of analyzing why certain emotions arise and then diving into our entire psychological history, we can simply know that there is lust or absence of lust, ill will or the absence of ill will. Here we're mindful just to the extent necessary for bare awareness.

This bare awareness reveals a lot about the nature of the knowing mind. We begin to observe that bare knowing is effortless; it is the very nature of the mind itself. We can see this so clearly with sounds. When we're undistracted and a sound arises, that sound is known spontaneously, effortlessly, and exactly. We don't need to make an effort to hear it. This is the mirrorlike quality of the mind. We can also experience the same spontaneous knowing in movement. When we're undistracted, the sensations of the movements are being known effortlessly. This bare knowing is not something we try to do or create; rather, it is something to come back to. A little mantra that has helped me a lot in my practice is a reminder of this aware nature: "It's already here."

In these instructions in the refrain, the Buddha is first saying we should establish mindfulness to the extent necessary for bare knowledge. That means simplifying, which can be a challenge, especially for us here in the West. It means letting the mind settle back into noninterfering awareness, just knowing what presents itself. Bare knowledge is the simple and direct experience of knowing what is present, without making up stories about experience.

CONTINUITY OF MINDFULNESS

Continuity of mindfulness comes from repeatedly coming back to bare attention every time we're distracted. Continuity implies a certain kind of right effort. It is not the effort to know, but the effort to repeatedly come back to bare knowing. From this practice of coming back from our wanderings to what is present in the moment, we build a momentum of mindfulness, and at a certain point it begins to flow on by itself. Think of the time of learning to ride a bicycle. At first, we're struggling to find the balance, falling off, beginning again. But at a certain point, we build enough momentum of forward movement that keeping the balance becomes effortless. We can see this same process at work in learning to play a musical instrument, becoming proficient in a sport, or developing skill in almost any discipline. In meditation, when a certain momentum of mindfulness is developed, we find less struggle and greater ease.

By including all the four foundations of mindfulness in the practice, the Buddha is giving the method for accomplishing bare knowing and continuous mindfulness, because no experience is left out. If pleasant, unpleasant, or neutral feelings are predominant, we're mindful of them. If either wholesome or unwholesome mind states arise, we're mindful of them.

As the continuity of bare knowing becomes stronger, awareness becomes more panoramic. The emphasis moves from mindfulness of the content of the experience to mindfulness of the process of change itself. At this time, there is simply a flow of experience, and the three universal characteristics—impermanence, unsatisfactoriness, and selflessness—become increasingly vivid.

ABIDING INDEPENDENT

This leads to the last line of the refrain, which summarizes the result of our practice: "And one abides independent, not clinging to anything in the world." "Abiding independent" means not being dependent on objects of experience through desire or through the view of self, not identifying with anything as being "I" or "mine." In one discourse, the Buddha said that whoever hears this, has heard all the teachings; whoever practices this, has practiced all the teachings; whoever realizes this, has realized all the teachings. We abide independent, not clinging to anything in the world.

MINDFULNESS OF DHAMMAS

The Five Hindrances

15

Desire

THE FOURTH AND LAST FOUNDATION of mindfulness is called "mindfulness of dhammas." The Pali word *dhamma* (*dharma* in Sanskrit) has a wide range of meanings, depending on the context. It can mean "truth," "the law," or "the teachings of the Buddha," as well as referring to the specific elements of the mind and body. Each of the mental and physical elements is called a "dhamma."

In the Satipaṭṭhāna Sutta, this last foundation of mindfulness is often translated as mindfulness of mental objects. But this can be somewhat confusing because objects of mind have already been included in the second and third foundations. So what is the Buddha singling out as being distinct in this fourth way of establishing mindfulness? Anālayo, in his book *Satipaṭṭhāna: The Direct Path to Realization,* offers a clear and cogent analysis of how the term *dhamma* is used here. He suggests that in this context *dhamma* means "categories of phenomena," highlighting how different dhammas, or elements of experience, function. The Buddha includes in this part of the sutta a comprehensive list of the basic organizing principles of his teachings: the hindrances, the aggregates, the sense spheres, the factors of awakening, and the four noble truths.

Michael Carrithers, who wrote about the forest monks of Sri Lanka, said that in this foundation of mindfulness "the propositions of doctrine are transmuted into immediate perception, here and now."[1] It is this transmutation of doctrine into direct perceptions that brings the teachings alive for us. Instead of a philosophical analysis or discussion, the Buddha is showing us how to investigate these truths, these dhammas, for ourselves.

For me, this was a transforming possibility. I had studied philosophy in college, but found it ultimately frustrating because there was no exploration of how to apply the various philosophies to life, to our moment-to-moment experience. In this fourth foundation of mindfulness—mindfulness of categories, of general principles—the Buddha gives detailed instruction on how to do just this:

> "And how, bhikkhus, does one in regard to dhammas abide
> contemplating dhammas? Here, in regard to dhammas,
> one abides contemplating dhammas in terms of the five
> hindrances."[2]

Why does the Buddha begin here with the hindrances? When we're not mindful of them, the hindrances envelop the mind and obstruct it from developing wise discernment regarding skillful and unskillful actions. They hinder the mind's developing concentration and other awakening factors, and they prevent the realization of the four noble truths. In order to proceed on the path, we first need to know how to work skillfully with what impedes our journey.

HOW THE HINDRANCES IMPACT THE MIND

There are two well-known similes that the Buddha uses to describe how the hindrances impact the mind. The first simile describes how, in different ways, the hindrances obscure our perception. The Buddha uses the example of a pool of clear water that reflects our image. When sense desire is present in the mind, it is as if the pool were suffused with a colored dye. Desires color our perceptions. When aversion is present, it is like boiling water. We can't see clearly. When we're heated up by anger, we're in a state of turbulence. Sloth and torpor are like the pool overgrown with algae. There is a stagnation of mind that prevents us from seeing clearly. Restlessness and worry are like water when it is stirred up by the wind. The mind is tossed about by agitation. And doubt is like muddy water, where we can't see to the bottom, and everything is obscured.

The second simile the Buddha uses suggests the underlying emotional tone of being caught up in the hindrances and what it is like when we're free of them.

> "Bhikkhus, suppose a man were to take a loan and undertake business, and his business were to succeed so that he could repay all the money of the old loan, and there would remain enough extra to maintain a wife; then, on considering this, he would be glad and full of joy. Or suppose a man were afflicted, suffering and gravely ill, and his food would not agree with him and his body had not strength, but later he would recover from the affliction and his food would agree with him, and his body would regain strength; then, on considering this, he would be glad and full of joy. Or suppose a man were imprisoned in a prison house, but later he would be released from prison, safe and secure, with no loss to his property; then on considering this, he would be glad and full of joy. Or suppose a man were a slave, not self-independent but dependent on others, unable to go where he wants, but later on he would be released from slavery, self-dependent, independent of others, a freed man able to go where he wants; then, on considering this, he would be glad and full of joy. Or suppose a man with wealth and property were to enter a road across a desert, but later on he would cross over the desert, safe and secure, with no loss to his property; then, on considering this, he would be glad and full of joy. So too, bhikkhus, when these five hindrances are unabandoned in himself, a bhikkhu sees them respectively as a debt, a disease, a prison house, slavery, and a road across a desert. But when these five hindrances have been abandoned in himself, he sees that as freedom from debt, healthiness, release from prison, freedom from slavery, and a land of safety."[3]

It's helpful to reflect on these similes not as literary images, but as pointers to how our minds are actually affected by the presence or absence of these mind states. Pay particular attention to moments of transition, when we go from being lost in one of the hindrances to being mindful of them. We can then notice more clearly and directly how they influence and condition our minds. Often they have become such familiar parts of our inner landscape that we overlook, or don't realize, the impact they have on our lives. And because of this, we might lack a sense of urgency or ardency about working with them.

Here, in this fourth foundation of mindfulness, the Buddha reminds us that abandoning these hindrances is a necessary step on the path of awakening. He said that when attended to carelessly, "these five hindrances are makers of blindness, causing lack of vision, causing lack of knowledge, detrimental to wisdom, tending to vexation, leading away from nibbāna."[4] But when we attend to these states carefully, we learn to see into their empty, transparent nature and no longer get so caught up in their seductive power. They then become the focus of our mindfulness and the very vehicle of our awakening.

FIVE STEPS TO WORKING WITH THE HINDRANCES

The question is, how can we practice working with and abandoning the hindrances without suppression, without aversion, without self-judgment? In these instructions, the Buddha speaks of five steps in finding the middle way between indulgence and suppression. In this chapter, we will apply the five steps to sense desire, the first of the hindrances, though the five steps outlined in the sutta are the same for all of them:

> "Here in regard to dhammas one abides contemplating dhammas in terms of the five hindrances. And how does one in regard to dhammas abide contemplating dhammas in terms of the five hindrances?
>
> "If sensual desire [aversion, sloth and torpor, restlessness and worry, doubt] is present, one knows, 'there is sensual desire [etc.] in me'; if sensual desire [aversion, sloth and torpor, restlessness and worry, doubt] is not present, one knows 'there is no sensual desire [etc.] in me'; and one knows how unarisen sensual desire [etc.] can arise, how arisen sensual desire [etc.] can be removed, and how a future arising of the removed sensual desire [etc.] can be avoided."[5]

Step 1: Recognize Desire When It Is Present

The first step is the simple recognition of desire when it is present in the mind. We can experience this wanting mind in many ways.

Sometimes we are overwhelmed by obsessive passions. So much of great literature, going as far back as Homer's *The Iliad,* illuminates this theme. There is the wanting and desire of addictive cravings, both big and small. We can get lost in recurrent fantasies or even just passing whims of the moment. In meditation, desire can take the form of indulging our internal dramas or stories, or it can come in the form of expectations—desiring for something else to happen. I sometimes call this the "in-order-to" mind—that is, we are aware of something *in order* for something different to arise. Maybe we're noticing a pain in order for it to go away or a pleasant feeling in order for it to continue. When we don't recognize when desire is present, we're simply lost in its distorting energy; when we are aware of it, it becomes part of the path of awakening.

Step 2: Know When Desire Is Absent

The second step in the instructions is to know when sensual desire is absent: "If sensual desire is not present, one knows, 'there is no sensual desire in me.'" This is the conscious act of recognizing the absence of the hindrances—here, desire in particular. This is what the Buddha called "the luminous mind," free of desire, which is the basis for delight, joy, tranquility, happiness, concentration, and insight.

It's important not to gloss over these instructions with a simple pro forma recognition that the hindrances seem to be absent. When we actually contemplate—that is, are mindful of—the experience of the mind free of desire and the other hindrances, we develop confidence and faith in the practice based on our own experience rather than on belief and hope. We understand then, for ourselves, the similes of being out of debt, in good health, out of prison, free of slavery, and abiding in a safe place.

The next three steps in the instructions emphasize the understanding of conditionality.

Step 3: Know What Conditions Underlie the Presence or Absence of Desire

There are many things that lead to the arising of sense desire. Most obviously, when we're not mindful of an arising sense object or the pleasant feeling associated with it, then the habitual conditioning of desire and craving easily gets activated. I've often noticed this in the lunch line at retreats, where the sight or smell of food can easily feed our desires. Or perhaps we see someone who is attractive to us, and if we're not mindful simply of seeing, we might get lost in what is called the "vipassanā romance," carried away by our fantasies for many moments, hours, or even days.

The Buddha points out the danger of this lack of attention:

> "Bhikkhus, whatever a bhikkhu frequently thinks and ponders upon, that will become the inclination of the mind. If one frequently thinks and ponders upon thoughts of sensual desire, one has abandoned the thought of renunciation to cultivate thoughts of sensual desire, and then the mind inclines to thoughts of sensual desire."[6]

In this regard, we see the importance of knowing what kinds of thoughts are arising in our mind, because the more often they are repeated, the more probable they become. We begin to be conscious of what patterns have been established, but often go unnoticed.

Sensual desires also arise from the fundamental misperception that they will actually bring about a lasting happiness—something that, given their impermanence, is not possible. In Tolstoy's *Anna Karenina,* Anna's lover comes to this realization: "Vronsky, meanwhile, in spite of the complete realization of what he had so long desired, was not perfectly happy. He soon felt that the realization of his desires gave him no more than a grain of sand out of the mountain of happiness he had expected. It showed him the mistake men make in picturing to themselves happiness as the realization of their desires."

Most of us have had some realization of this truth; it is usually what brings us to the Dharma. But actualizing this understanding in our lives can be challenging, particularly in the lay life. On retreat, we live quite simply, close to a monastic lifestyle. But in our lives in the world, we are bombarded with images and sounds urging us to seek delight in the vast array of sensual pleasures. I have seen so many advertisements in newspapers and magazines and on the Internet telling us to "increase your desire," as if somehow that were a good thing to do. It makes all the more important the practice of understanding how sensual desire does arise, so that we can balance the prevailing norm.

It might be reassuring to know that this is not simply a problem of our times. The Buddha, before his enlightenment, faced the same temptations and tendencies.

> "[F]ormerly, when I lived the household life, I enjoyed myself, provided and endowed with the five cords of sensual pleasure . . . that are wished for, desired, agreeable, and likeable, connected with sensual desire and provocative of lust. I had three palaces, one for the rainy season, one for the winter, and one for the summer. I lived in the rains' palace for the four months of the rainy season, enjoying myself with musicians . . . and I did not go down to the lower palace.
> "On a later occasion, having understood as they really are the gratification, the defects, the disadvantages, and the release in the case of sensual pleasures, I abandoned craving for sensual pleasures, I removed the fever of sensual pleasures, and I dwell without thirst, with a mind inwardly at peace. . . . There is a delight apart from sensual pleasures, apart from unwholesome states, which surpasses even divine bliss. Since I take delight in that, I do not envy what is inferior, nor do I delight therein."[7]

Step 4: Know What Conditions Underlie the Removal of Desire

The next instruction in this section of the sutta says, "[O]ne knows . . . how arisen sensual desire can be removed." Given that these desires will certainly arise, how do we work with them once they are already present? There are many texts in which Māra, the embodiment of sensual-realm desires, appears and then loses all power in the moment of being recognized. "Māra, I see you" is the recurring phrase of recognition, and it is one that I have found very helpful in the practice. In the moment of being mindful of sensual desire when it has already arisen, we are no longer lost in it, feeding it, or identified with it. When we're mindful of desire in the mind, we begin to see desire's impermanent, impersonal nature.

It's important not to underestimate the power of mindfulness. Although the word *mindfulness* in English is a bit prosaic, when we look past the word to the quality of mind itself, we see its enormous power. Mindfulness is the root of all that is wholesome. If mindfulness, though, is not yet strong enough to immediately disentangle us from desire, we can also use wise reflection to weaken its hold. I call this mindful reflection our internal Dharma coach, which helps us reflect on the Buddha's teachings in the very moment they are applicable. Often, remembering our basic intention for practice—is it to be lost in desire or to be free?—is enough to slip out of Māra's grip.

Step 5: Avoid Future Arisings of Desire

The last of the instructions of mindfulness of dhammas in regard to the hindrance of sensual desire is knowing how a future arising of sense desire can be avoided. By knowing how it arises, we can practice taking some wise preventative measures—that is, taking care of our mental health and wellbeing in the same way we take care of our physical health.

We can sometimes reflect on the unattractive aspects of the body. Of course, this is a very un-Western approach to life. It flies in the face of so much of our cultural conditioning, which focuses on beauty, obsesses on beauty, and avoids anything that might indicate that we're ageing, that the body does get sick and die. Reflecting on those aspects of the body that are not attractive can be a strong counterbalance to all the other images that beguile us.

The Buddha also spoke of guarding the sense doors—that is, being mindful right at the moment of contact with each of the senses. He spoke of moderation in food and association with wise friends, both as ways of avoiding the arising of unarisen sense desires. The beauty of this entire section of the sutta is that, like any good physician, the Buddha leads us from diagnosis to cure to prevention. And as it repeats in the refrain after each instruction, "And one abides independent, not clinging to anything in the world."

Together, the five steps outlined in this chapter further our understanding of the conditioned, selfless nature of all phenomena. All things arise when the appropriate conditions are present, and all things pass away as conditions change. Behind the process, there is no "self" who is running the show.

In general, the five steps can be grouped into three broader categories or aspects:

- Know when a hindrance is present and when it is absent,
- Know the conditions leading to the arising and removal of a hindrance, and
- Know the conditions that prevent future arisings of a hindrance.

In chapters 16 through 19, we will discuss the remaining hindrances—aversion, sloth and torpor, restlessness and worry, and doubt—in the context of these broader perspectives.

16

Aversion

THE SECOND HINDRANCE THE BUDDHA highlights for our investigation is aversion. What is this mental state and how do we recognize it? The Pali word for aversion is *paṭigha,* which literally means "striking against." Bhikkhu Bodhi explains it as the attitudes of resistance, rejection, or destruction. They are all different aspects of the condemning mind and include a wide range of aversive states: violent rage and hatred, anger, ill will, animosity, annoyance, irritation, fear, and in very subtle ways, sorrow and grief.

There is something of interest here as we contemplate the English usage of some of these words. According to the Abhidhamma, all of these mental states are rooted in hatred (*dosa* in Pali). Although in English, we usually reserve the word *hatred* for an intense hostility or extreme dislike, there can be an insightful and perhaps not obvious understanding of the mind when we consider that even the milder forms of aversion we're more familiar with are deeply rooted in the more powerful underground force of hatred. We can see the force of this mind state when it erupts in times of war; in racial, ethnic, or gender violence; or in intense interpersonal conflicts.

But as powerful as hatred is as an often-hidden current in the mind, the power of mindfulness lets us look clearly and deeply into our own minds and begin to weaken and finally uproot even the deepest tendencies. The Swiss psychologist C. G. Jung expressed both the potential and difficulty of this process: "One does not become enlightened by imagining figures of light, but by making the darkness conscious. The latter procedure, however, is disagreeable and therefore not popular."[1]

KNOW THE CAUSES OF AVERSION

In the first two steps of this contemplation of dhammas, we acknowledge whether aversion, in any of its forms, is present or absent. We then become mindful of the conditions that lead to its arising. All the various states of aversion are conditioned reactions to what we find unpleasant. Just as an untrained mind becomes entranced by pleasurable experiences, it also becomes dissatisfied or angry or fearful of unpleasant ones.

Physical Pain

It is easy to see this conditioning in our relationship to physical pain. We usually react to pain with dislike, fear, discouragement, contraction, frustration, or impatience. We just don't like it. And on subtler levels, we might think we're being quite open to and mindful of the pain, yet the very language we might use to describe it in a way we consider objective is really just further conditioning aversion.

I had a striking example of this during one of my retreats in Burma. I had been sitting for some time, and my body felt quite open with a free flow of energy, except for one particular place of tightness in my neck. When I went for my interview with Sayadaw U Paṇḍita, I described my practice and the energy block I was experiencing. He pointed out that calling it "a block" was not only just a concept that I was overlaying on the experience of tightness, but also that in this context, the very concept of "block" contained within it seeds of desire and aversion. "Block"—something I want to get rid of. Being directed back to the simple experience of tightness and hardness, I could let go of the subtle aversion that was in my mind and the wanting of the tension to be different. And as my mind relaxed, I began to see what I had been calling a "block" and feeling as something solid was instead a small field of changing sensations.

Unpleasant Thoughts

Aversion also arises when we think of some painful or unpleasant situation. We can think of someone or some event and then get angry just thinking about it. And we can have these same aversive reactions to anticipated future situations, even though they have not yet happened. But in these moments, we're really just getting angry at a thought.

A Zen story illustrates this point. There was a hermit monk living in a cave in the mountains of Japan. He was a talented artist, and over time he painted a picture of a tiger on the wall of the cave. He was extremely meticulous in his work, and it took him several years to finish. When it was finally done, the tiger was so realistic that when he looked at it he became frightened. I have found the note "painted tiger" a good reminder that when we get angry at something we are remembering or anticipating, in that moment we're simply getting angry at a thought in the mind—a painted tiger.

It is revealing to notice the intimate relationship of thought and emotion. One often sparks the other, causing a chain reaction of mental proliferation. A certain thought arises, and if we're not mindful of it as a thought, an emotion might quickly follow. The reverse can be true as well, with various emotions, including the hindrances, sometimes causing a flood of thoughts. But seeing this conditioned interrelationship over and over again helps to weaken our identification with what is arising, and we understand on deeper levels the conditioned nature of the hindrances and other mind states. We no longer take them so personally.

The Buddha gave some specific examples of this conditioning. In one sutta, he talked of how ill will and malice are stirred by thinking that someone in the past (or present or future) has done us an injury, or has injured a loved one, or has done favors for an enemy (someone we don't like).

We should examine our own minds to see if, indeed, these are the types of thoughts that lead to ill will.

Unpleasant Situations

On retreat, there are some specific situations that can give rise to aversion. We might get impatient or frustrated with unpleasant conditions. There is also the phenomenon called the "vipassanā vendetta." This happens when we're going through some difficulties in our own practice, and we project this dissatisfaction onto others. If we're feeling tired or grumpy, small things can provoke aversion or irritation.

Usually it is a particular person on the retreat who begins to irritate us. We don't like how they move, what they wear, how they eat, and so on. Very often we have never even spoken to this person, but the judging, aversive mind latches on and colors our experience of them.

Personalizing Difficulties

In ordinary life situations, aversion arises when we personalize difficulties that are essentially impersonal. When we get to the airport two hours early and then find that our flight has been cancelled, do we get annoyed or remain equanimous? What happens when we're stuck in traffic or are in unpleasant weather? These are situations that are not directed at us personally and are due to causes clearly beyond our control, yet we often act as if they are a personal affront.

The Buddha summed up all these causes of aversion in one of his descriptions of the suffering mind: aversion arises when we don't get what we want or we do get what we don't want. Mindfulness of dhammas—in this case, the hindrance of aversion—can free us from this conditioned habit of ill will.

KNOW WHAT CONDITIONS THE REMOVAL OF AVERSION

The Buddha's next instruction tells us to know the conditions for the removal of aversion once it has already arisen.

Practice Mindfulness When Aversion Is Present

The first and most direct approach is simply being mindful of it, without judging the aversion or ourselves for having it. We simply open to it as an arisen mind state. The practice of noting can be helpful here. We can make the soft mental note, "ill will," "anger," or "discouragement" as soon as it arises and keep noting softly until it disappears. It would be interesting to notice how many notes it takes until the aversive mind state passes away. Is it five or twenty or a hundred? At a certain point, the mind state will change, and noticing its passing away offers a deepening and important insight into its impermanent nature.

Sometimes, though, even if we are noting the aversion, this mind state seems to persist. If we feel really caught by it, we can then bring some further investigation to these aversive states. First, check the accuracy of the note. Instead of making a general note of aversion, look more carefully at the specific form the aversion is taking. For example, at one point in my practice in Burma, I was feeling a general mental malaise at the noisy surroundings, but I wasn't seeing precisely what my mind was doing. As the unease persisted, I looked more carefully, and I saw that my mind was caught in a cycle of grumpy, internal complaining. As soon as I was able to note "complaining, complaining," its power over the mind began to diminish.

Note the Relationship of Mind to Emotion

Another investigative technique for removing hindrances once they have arisen is to look at the relationship of the mind to the emotion. We may feel we're being mindful, but often are actually feeding the aversion by our reaction to it. Quite a few years ago, I was involved in a situation that provoked a lot of self-righteous anger. Someone had done something that in my view created a lot of harm. The more I thought about what happened, the angrier I became. It became so strong that the energy of the anger actually woke me up from sleep at four o'clock in the morning. At that point, the intensity of my response aroused a tremendous interest: "What exactly is going on? How am I getting so hooked by this anger?"

As soon as I asked these questions and began to look at my relationship to the anger, rather than harking back to the situation again and again, the anger itself started to dissolve. I understood, in a deeper and more immediate way, that no one *makes* us feel things in a particular way. Although different conditions may prompt different emotions to arise, how we relate to those feelings is up to us.

There is a range of skillful relationships to anger, ill will, and other forms of aversion, and we need to find the one that is appropriate to our own particular conditioning. For example, if we tend toward patterns of self-judgment and unworthiness, we can emphasize a gentle approach to anger, as suggested by the Vietnamese master Thich Nhat Hanh:

> The Buddhist attitude is to take care of anger. We don't suppress it. We don't run away from it. We just breathe and hold our anger in our arms with utmost tenderness. . . . Then the anger is no longer alone, it is with your mindfulness. Anger

is like a closed flower in the morning. As the sun shines on the flower, the flower will bloom, because the sunlight penetrated deep into the flower.

Mindfulness is like that. If you keep breathing . . . , mindfulness particles will infiltrate the anger. When sunshine penetrates a flower, the flower cannot resist. It is bound to open itself and reveal its heart to the sun. If you keep breathing on your anger, shining your compassion and understanding on it, your anger will soon crack and you will be able to look into its depths and see its roots.[2]

On the other side, if we tend to self-indulgence or self-pity, the warrior mode suggested by Sayadaw U Paṇḍita might be more appropriate: "Pulverize the defilements, show them no mercy." Here we take the sword of wisdom and forcefully cut through our attachments and identification with them. Two simple notes that I have found helpful in loosening the grip of repetitive patterns of the hindrances are "dead end" and "enough." The former is a reminder that these repetitive patterns of thought don't go anywhere; they simply cycle back again and again. And the latter is a way of wielding the sword of wisdom, albeit lovingly, and not indulging ourselves in the aversive thoughts.

We can also use the power of investigation to see if there are associated emotions that might be feeding the aversive mind states like a hidden, underground spring. Maybe feelings of hurt or self-righteousness or fear are underneath the anger and feeding it. Becoming mindful of those feelings often unlocks the pattern.

Use Wise Reflection to Weaken Aversion

Besides following the basic instruction of being mindful of hindrances already arisen and then using further investigative techniques if they persist, we can also use wise reflection to help weaken the grip of the aversive mind states. Anger or annoyance is very seductive—"I have good reason to feel this way." The Buddha described this pattern very succinctly: "anger with its poisoned root and honeyed tip." When we're being seduced by the honeyed tip, either by enjoying the energetic rush of anger or by justifying it to ourselves, different reflections might be helpful.

When the Buddha spoke of the kinds of thoughts provoking malice and ill will, he ended with the reflection, "What good will it do to hold on to malice, anger, or resentment?" When these states are predominant in the mind, we can remind ourselves of this question and realize that we're the ones who are suffering. Being lost in aversive mind states is like holding onto a hot, burning coal. There really is no reason that justifies our continuing to hold on rather than letting it go. There is a well-known verse in the Dhammapada that highlights this point: "He abused me, he beat me, he defeated me, he robbed me. Those who harbor such thoughts do not still their hatred."

A second helpful reflection reminds us of the ultimate reference point of our practice: is our main concern being right or being free? This question presents an interesting challenge in life situations where anger seems justified. In the discourses, there is a story of a woman named Videhika, who lived in the ancient Indian city of Savatti. She had a reputation for being very kind and gentle, but her maid, Kali, wanted to test her to see if she truly was that way. So Kali began to sleep late and not do her job very well. At first, Videhika was simply displeased, but over time, as Kali continued in her errant ways, Videhika became increasingly annoyed and angry, finally striking her maid in anger.

When I first read this story, I had an unexpected response. Although not at all condoning the physical abuse, I did feel some sympathetic resonance with Videhika's situation. If we're counting on someone to fulfill an agreed-upon responsibility, isn't it quite normal and even justified to become annoyed and angry when they fail to do so simply out of laziness or disregard—and not just once, but many times?

The Buddha, in telling this story, is making quite another point. On a deeper level, the story reminds us of the radical, uncompromising freedom of nibbāna, of liberation. This is a freedom that's not simply about feeling good and, therefore, depending on conditions being a certain way. This freedom of mind remains untouched by the changing winds of circumstance. The difficulties that we face in our lives can become a truth-reflecting mirror of our minds. Do we get angry or upset when things don't happen the way we would like them to? Or do we respond from a place of wisdom? For most of us, it is probably both. But if we're mindful when the aversive reactions arise, and then we see if there is some important message about the situation contained within them—"This is wrong. I should do something about it."—we can reflect on the nature of freedom and not hold on to the anger or hatred, even as we take appropriate action.

A third reflection that can help when the mind is caught up in some form of aversion and the mindfulness is not quite strong enough to free ourselves from identification with it, is the reflection on the value and importance of patience. In *A Guide to the Bodhisattva's Way of Life,* Shāntideva writes, "Why be unhappy about something if it can be remedied? And what is the use of being unhappy about something if it cannot be remedied?"[3]

The Dalai Lama often speaks about honoring one's enemies because they teach us patience. This may be easy to agree with theoretically, but it is hard to do in practice. Notice the next time you're having difficulty with a person or with a certain situation. Can you genuinely feel grateful to him or it for the opportunity to practice patience? Do we even remember to try? It's easy enough to be patient when everything is going well. It's precisely the times of difficulty that challenge us to strengthen this important factor. Remembering to make patience a practice helps loosen our attachment to our own views, our attachment to being right.

Think About Something Else

The Buddha's last suggestion for dealing with aversive states, after trying all these other possibilities, is very simple and pragmatic: "Think about something else." Often we chew on something endlessly, even when it's clear the proliferation of thoughts about it is not productive. At this point, distracting or diverting our minds can be skillful.

PREVENT THE FUTURE ARISING OF AVERSION

The last of the instructions in this section of the sutta is to know the conditions that prevent the future arising of aversion. The most far-reaching of these conditions is the development of lovingkindness, *mettā* in Pali. This is the generosity of the heart that simply wishes all beings to be well and happy. Metta helps prevent the arising of aversion because it focuses on the good in people, rather than on their faults.

Sometimes people think that if we have too much lovingkindness, always focusing on the good in others, it will make us stupid in some way, that we'll no longer see the truth of what is going on or be able to take appropriate action. But it is precisely the mind not clouded by anger or hatred that allows us to see situations clearly and to chart the right course of action, even in very difficult situations.

It's important to realize that all aversion does not fall away with our first loving wish. The Bodhisattva spent years, and whole lifetimes, cultivating and purifying this quality. But as we practice it, recognize it, and become more familiar with it, mettā begins to arise more and more spontaneously in our lives. It becomes the way we are, rather than something we do. As lovingkindness grows stronger, both for ourselves and others, we feel more tolerance, are a little less judgmental, and slowly and gradually start to live in a growing field of benevolence and goodwill. Here is where mettā as a dissolver of aversion also becomes the ground for wisdom. The more loving and patient we are with difficulties and disturbances, the less lost we are in reactivity. Our choices and actions become wiser, which in turn leads to more happiness, more mettā, and greater freedom.

17

Sloth and Torpor

ALTHOUGH SLOTH AND TORPOR ARE two different mental factors, they are closely related and always occur in conjunction with one another. We can briefly discuss the distinction, but for the most part, we will consider them as a pair, examining their presence or absence and the conditions for their arising, removal, and prevention.

Sloth is a sluggishness of mind, of consciousness, which dispels energy. It is a lack of driving power, and we feel it as a kind of sinking state. Torpor is the dull or weakened state of the mental factors, making them unwieldy. In this state there is no mental agility or pliability. Torpor is like a heavy blanket smothering the various mental factors, and we experience it as drooping, nodding, or sleepiness. So sloth has to do with dullness of consciousness, and torpor with dullness or heaviness of the mental factors.

When sloth and torpor are strong, the mind is described as "inert as a bat hanging on to a tree, as molasses cleaving to a stick, or as butter too hard to spread." This sleepiness or dullness is very common for people at the beginning of a retreat, especially when they are coming from busy, hectic lives. In our lives, we largely run on the energy of stimulation—from interactions with other people, cups of coffee, or the interface with the Internet. When people enter the silence and undistractedness of a retreat, there are often the withdrawal symptoms of dullness and sleepiness. But slowly we connect with a deeper source of energy within us, and the mind becomes increasingly wakeful and alert without the need for external stimulation. The sleepiness and dullness of sloth and torpor may continue to arise from time to time, perhaps at particular times in the day, but over time it becomes easier to work with them as passing mental states, rather than as some defining characteristic of our minds.

SLOTH AND TORPOR IN MEDITATION PRACTICE

There is, however, a subtler aspect of these hindrances, one that is much harder to recognize. This is not merely the feeling of sleepiness, but rather the deeper pattern or tendency of withdrawing from difficulties. This is the habit of retreating from challenges rather than arousing the energy and effort to engage with them. In these situations, sloth and torpor are like the reverse gear in a car, never going forward to meet experience but always pulling back.

This pattern of retreating from difficulties strengthens the tendencies toward laziness and inactivity, passivity and lethargy. At these times, there is no energy or power to do or accomplish anything. Here, the factors of sloth and torpor keep us from drawing on the strength that we actually have.

Sometimes this complacency happens on obvious levels, and sometimes it happens on very subtle levels. Our meditation may be going well, with everything flowing along effortlessly, and then because no obvious effort is required, sloth and torpor creep in. We experience a sense of coasting, like we've put our minds on cruise control, rather than an alert, but tranquil vibrancy.

Once sloth and torpor take over the mind, in whatever form, this hindrance likes to hold on tight and not let go. It's something like a three-toed sloth, which hangs from a tree and doesn't move even if a gun goes off right next to it. This state is seductive because it is very cozy and comfortable. It's the mind that loves the snooze button on the alarm clock. Instead of waking up alert and ready to go, it's the mind that says, "Oh, just a few more minutes of this warm and comfy state."

Sloth and torpor also don't care much for energetic people. I was once on a retreat in Australia with Sayadaw U Paṇḍita. The person living in the room across the hall from me had a lot of energy. He always stayed up later at night than I did and was up earlier in the morning. At first, I had a lot of comparing, self-judging thoughts, but after a while, I found myself projecting all my self-judgments on to him, seeing all his faults. Then, in a moment of clarity, I saw it all as impersonal, as different mental factors playing themselves out. It was really sloth and torpor's response to energy—not mine. When I realized this, the whole situation became lighter, freer, more harmonious, and, in the end, more inspiring.

KNOW THE CAUSES OF SLOTH AND TORPOR

When the mind is contracted under the influence of sloth and torpor, there is not much joy or pleasure in the practice, not much delight in our lives. We're always pulling back or holding back. The practice of mindfulness of dhammas with regard to this hindrance is a powerful way of freeing the mind from its influence. The first steps are simply to notice when sloth and torpor are present and when they are absent, so that we can recognize the difference. We get to know our minds very clearly.

Discontent, Boredom, Laziness, and Drowsiness

After becoming familiar with their presence or absence, we then contemplate the conditions for their arising. Surprisingly, the main condition given in the texts for the arising of sloth and torpor has to do with the wisdom factor—namely, giving unwise or careless attention to certain mental states like discontent, boredom, laziness, and drowsiness.

> "There are, bhikkhus, discontent, lethargy, lazy stretching, drowsiness after meals, sluggishness of mind: frequently giving careless attention to them is the nutriment for arising of unarisen sloth and torpor and for the increase and expansion of arisen sloth and torpor."[1]

This unwise or careless attention might mean thinking that there is no harm in these states or in indulging thoughts that further them: "I'm really tired" or "This is so boring." Just as thoughts often trigger the emotions of desire and anger, so too can thoughts powerfully condition the arising of sloth and torpor. Sometimes we're fooled into unwise attention because sloth and torpor can come masquerading as compassion for oneself. We might feel tired or bored or restless, and then sloth and torpor come in and with a very kindly voice say, "If I work too hard I'll probably get sick. Let me take care of myself. A little nap will be just the thing." Of course, at times we do need rest, but often we don't; instead, the retreating mode of this hindrance is simply coming into play.

In the early years of my practice, I would often be on retreats where we would wake up at four in the morning and then sit for two hours before breakfast. I was motivated to get to the hall early in order to find a place against the back wall. I would begin my sitting and then, after not too long, would lean back against the wall and soon be drifting off into sleep. This pattern continued for many days. At some point, I began thinking, "This is stupid. I'm just wasting time. I should probably sleep until breakfast and then at least be awake for the rest of the day." Although these thoughts were persistent, I didn't give in, but kept coming to the hall for the early morning sit. Remarkably, after four or five days of my dozing off, one day I went into the hall and stayed awake and alert for the whole time.

This was an important lesson for me. Even when we think that nothing much is happening in our practice and we're just falling asleep, if we keep on going, the intention and energy of perseverance eventually bear fruit.

Difficult Emotions

Another aspect of unwise attention is not acknowledging difficult emotions. There might be a strong, and even traumatic, emotion arising, and sometimes sloth and torpor arise as a defense against feeling it. Care is needed here, because sloth and torpor sometimes act as appropriate regulators for how much and how quickly powerful repressed feelings come up. But for our more usual, run-of-the-mill unpleasant feelings, the arising of sloth and torpor can be a signal that perhaps something else is going on that we should look at. This doesn't mean that we should overanalyze or search for some hidden emotion. Rather, we can hold this understanding lightly and simply take a look to see what's there.

Overeating

A third cause for the arising of sloth and torpor is overeating. Notice how you feel just after taking food, and see if there is some relationship of the state of mind to the amount of food you eat. The Buddha suggested stopping five mouthfuls short of feeling full. It is a challenge to know exactly when this is, but keeping this suggestion in mind makes us more mindful of the condition of our stomachs and keeps us from indulging the desires and cravings of our minds.

Occasionally, sloth and torpor can also arise from not eating enough. One time in Burma, through a combination of the diet and being very slow and mindful while eating, I wasn't taking enough food, and I lost twenty pounds. I was becoming weaker and weaker, and sometimes actually fell over from my sitting position. It was the only time that Sayadaw U Paṇḍita told me to lighten up a bit on the mindfulness while eating so that I could take enough food to sustain the body in a healthy way.

An Imbalance of Concentration and Energy

The fourth condition for the arising of this hindrance is the imbalance of concentration and energy. If the concentration is much stronger than the energy, we sometimes fall into what is called "sinking mind." It is a very pleasant, dreamlike state, in which there is a calm, floating feeling, but not much alertness. We might stay in the state for extended periods of time, enjoying a mind that is not agitated, but is nevertheless not truly awake. You might recognize this condition from those times when you're riding in a car or on a train for a long journey and the mind seems to slip into an in-between place of waking and sleep. It's relaxed and somewhat enjoyable, but lacking in the energy that makes mindfulness possible.

KNOW WHAT CONDITIONS THE REMOVAL OF SLOTH AND TORPOR

Once sloth and torpor have already arisen, and we have investigated to some extent the conditions for their arising, contemplation of dhammas then explores how to work with and overcome this hindrance, how we can heat up this congealed mind state with interest, energy, and awareness.

Practice Mindfulness

As with the other hindrances, the first strategy is simply to be mindful of it, making sloth and torpor the very objects of our attention.

We try to note them as soon as they arise and investigate how exactly we are experiencing them. Rather than just sinking into them, we ask ourselves, "What *is* this experience I'm calling sleepiness or dullness?" We can notice the particular sensations in the body, the feelings in the mind. We can notice the contracting, withdrawing, sinking nature of sleepiness. At that time, although there is not much energy or alertness, the mind is not restless. So if we can bring some mindfulness and interest to bear, it's possible to find the threads of concentration and calm within the sleepy state itself.

Sometimes our attachment to clarity can keep us from being deeply mindful of the sleepiness or dullness. We might be struggling with it so much that we don't actually see these states clearly for what they are. On one retreat, our teacher, Dipa Ma, suggested that we sleep only three hours a night and not lie down at all during the day. This went considerably beyond my usual mode of practice, and I found myself very tired during the day. But Dipa Ma had added one other instruction: "If you fall asleep when you're sitting, never mind." This last reminder was the crucial piece. As I found myself nodding off when sitting, I remembered Dipa Ma's words and just relaxed into the experience, instead of struggling to stay awake as I usually did. Something quite striking occurred: I sometimes did nod off for a few moments, but because the struggle was absent, I would often come back into awareness with a sudden jerk, and then I'd be wide awake and alert for the rest of the sitting.

The great power of mindfulness here, as with desire or anger, is that we can be with all these states when they arise, and we can stay aware of them until they disappear. Mindfulness and bare attention reinforce our insight into their impermanence, as we realize that we don't have to fulfill desire or act on anger or indulge the sleepiness in order for it to pass away. We see that these states all come and go by themselves.

Develop Mental Clarity

But at times, simple mindfulness is not strong enough to stay aware in the midst of sloth and torpor. The Buddha, pragmatic as always, suggested other remedies as well. He said that as an antidote to this hindrance, we should develop clarity of cognition. What does this mean? Developing mental clarity, or clarity of knowing, happens in several ways.

First, it develops through a careful noting of a greater number of objects as a way of brightening awareness. For example, if we have been noting or noticing the breath as our main object of attention, we can add several touch points to the cycle. We might notice the place where the buttocks touch the cushion or chair, or the sensations of the hands resting on the thighs or on each other. The noting of experience would then be, "In, out, touching, touching. In, out, touching, touching." Or we can add the experience of feeling the whole body: "In, out, sitting, touching." It's also helpful, at times, to add hearing to the mix of objects. Sound is a good object because we're usually quite effortlessly aware of it arising. When we include more objects in our field of awareness, the mind becomes more active and alert, counteracting the influence of sloth and torpor. Another way clarity of cognition develops is through an emphasis on two particular factors of mind. The first is called *vitakka* in Pali, sometimes translated as "initial application," the aiming of the mind toward the object. The second factor is called *vicāra,* which is "sustained application," the sustaining of the attention on the object. *Vitakka* is a bee first being attracted to a flower, and then *vicāra* is the bee buzzing around it. Initial and sustained application are factors of the first jhāna, or concentrated absorption, and they oppose the forces of sloth and torpor. We can emphasize these factors by consciously remembering to aim and connect with the arising of each object of awareness, and then sustain the attention for its duration.

Clarity of cognition also means developing a radiant mind. In Tibetan, the words for "radiant" and "knowing" are the same. So in developing the radiant mind, we focus more on the knowing aspect than on what is being known. Doing this with sloth and torpor is somewhat like seeing fog reflected in a mirror. Even though fog as an object is not very distinct, the mirror still reflects it perfectly. Here, we want to be more aware of the mirror than what is reflected in it. Similarly, even though dullness and sleepiness may be diffuse states, the knowing mind can know them perfectly, and we can become aware of the knowing itself.

Lastly, we can develop clarity of cognition by focusing on light. We can do this simply by directing our attention to the perception of light either from an external source, be it natural or artificial, or from some internal vision of light in the mind.

Open Your Eyes or Change Posture

It's possible that even with our attempts to be mindful of sloth and torpor in the ways suggested, and with all our efforts to develop clarity of cognition, this hindrance might still prove formidable. But there are some other reserve reinforcements that we can call upon to engage with this state of mind. If we are feeling very sleepy, it can be helpful to open our eyes and sit with the gaze slightly raised; it may take some effort, but we are less likely to doze off.

I had one interesting experience of this during a time when sloth and torpor were particularly strong in my practice. After repeatedly nodding off, I decided to sit with my eyes open in a very exaggerated way, almost like a cartoon character. As I sat up very straight, with my eyes propped open, I could feel waves of sleepiness descend. Everything in me just wanted to close my eyes and doze off. But I kept them open, and I felt the wave of sleepiness pass through my head, past my eyes, into my body, and then disappear. About a minute later, another wave would pass through. This happened five or six times, after which I was completely awake. This was an important lesson in realizing that sleepiness is not some monolithic, unchanging state requiring us to go to sleep, but rather a changing energy pattern that we can be with and allow to pass through.

Some of the other suggestions for working with it include changing postures, standing or walking, going outdoors, splashing water on one's face, and even pulling one's earlobes.

Practice Wise Reflection

Another powerful remedy for sloth and torpor is wise reflection that engages interest and tends to ardency. One such reflection is considering this precious human birth and the profound transiency of our lives. At the time of our death, our minds may well be in a weakened state, our bodies enfeebled, and our senses dull. How will we want to be in this condition? It's easy to say that we want to die with awareness, seeing the whole process clearly, conscious of our dying moments. But how do we train for this? Each time sloth and torpor arise and we're mindful of them, can we take it as a practice opportunity for dying?

This is the attitude of seeing difficulties as challenges, rather than withdrawing from an engagement with what is arising. There is a story in the novel *Zorba the Greek,* by Nikos Kazantzakis, about someone who saw a cocoon, and, thinking to help the struggling butterfly emerge, opened the fibers. But in doing so, the person removed the very struggle that was necessary for the butterfly to strengthen its wings and fly. The adage "The way out is through" can inspire our own efforts in challenging times.

Engage with Good Friends and Profitable Talk

The last two remedies for sloth and torpor are good friends and profitable talk. Even in a silent retreat environment, we can inspire each other. When we're feeling sluggish—and not too caught up in aversion—seeing others practicing can encourage us. And when we're feeling energetic, we can recognize that we may be inspiring others. This is a very practical application of the understanding that our practice is not for ourselves alone.

In the first few years of my meditative journey, I was living at the Burmese Vihāra in Bodh Gaya, India. A Danish friend, an ardent practitioner, lived just across the hall. Often, late at night, as I was ready to go to bed, I would see the light still on in his room. Inspired by his diligence, I just kept on sitting and walking, and I would usually overcome the feelings of drowsiness.

Profitable talk, in addition to conversations with dharma friends or teachers, in the context of a retreat might mean reading dharma books and texts for fifteen or twenty minutes as a way of raising energy and again arousing the motivation to practice. Likewise, for those inclined, chanting can also inspire the mind, increasing our faith and confidence in the practice.

Take Rest

It's helpful to remember that sloth and torpor are not fully uprooted from the mind until one is an arahant. We might take some comfort in knowing that even the greatest disciples of the Buddha struggled with them at different times in their practice. It's said that Mogallāna, one of the two chief disciples, even though he became fully enlightened in just one week, had to deal with this hindrance. During that week, while he was meditating in the forest, his mind shrank and withered and became unworkable. The Buddha, through his power of mind, came to know of this and appeared to Mogallāna.

He said, "Mogallāna, are you drowsy?"

"Yes sir, I am nodding."

"Listen, and I will teach you ways for overcoming it."

The Buddha then spoke of all these various ways of arousing energy. He concluded by saying that if none of these remedies work, then we should take rest.

But even as we can take rest, we can bring mindfulness to the fore. When we're tired and feel we need a nap, I have found that lying down until everything lets go and we're about to fall asleep, and then getting up at just that moment, is usually sufficient to rejuvenate us. Getting up at that point of letting go shows that what we actually needed was a moment of deep relaxation rather than some time asleep. We can also lie down with a specific intention to get up at a certain time, and we can make the intention to be mindful in the sleeping state itself.

PREVENTING THE FUTURE ARISING
OF SLOTH AND TORPOR

The last step in the contemplation of sloth and torpor is knowing how the future arising of this state can be avoided.

> "And what, bhikkhus, . . . prevents unarisen sloth and torpor
> from arising and arisen sloth and torpor from increasing and
> expanding? There are, bhikkhus, the element of arousal, the
> element of endeavor, the element of exertion; frequently
> giving careful attention to them . . . prevents unarisen sloth
> and torpor from arising and arisen sloth and torpor from
> increasing and expanding."[2]

Arousal, endeavor, and exertion: as these qualities of energy are developed and strengthened, not only sloth and torpor, but also all the other hindrances, are weakened and avoided.

But as a useful reminder, Anālayo points out that in working with the hindrances, the first step of satipaṭṭhāna is not in actively opposing the hindrance or struggling with it, but in clearly recognizing and being mindful of it, and in recognizing the conditions related to its presence or absence. It is when more active measures are needed that we then call on our other Dharma resources to free the mind from their hindering effects. As the Thai Forest monk Ajahn Chaa tells us:

> In ending, I wish that you continue your journeys and practice with much wisdom. Use the wisdom that you have already developed to persevere in practice. This can become the ground for your growth, for the deepening of yet greater understanding and love. Understand that you can deepen your practice in many ways. Don't be lazy. If you find yourself lazy, then work to strengthen those qualities which overcome it. Don't be fearful or timid. If you are timid in practice, then work with your mind so that you can overcome that. With the proper effort and with time, understanding will unfold by itself. But in all cases, use your own natural wisdom. This that we've spoken of today is what I feel is helpful to you, and if you really do it, you can come to the end of all doubt. You come to where you have no more questions, to that place of silence, to the place in which there is oneness with the Buddha, with the Dhamma, with the universe. And only you can do that. So do it, already. From now on it's up to you.[3]

18

Restlessness and Worry

THE FOURTH OF THE HINDRANCES the Buddha mentions in the Satipaṭṭhāna Sutta are the mind states of restlessness and worry. The Pali word for restlessness is *uddacca,* which means agitation, excitement, or distraction. It is sometimes translated as "shaking above," where the mind is not settled into the object but hovering around it. "Restlessness"—literally, without rest—expresses all these aspects. The Pali word for worry is *kukkucca,* which is the mind state of regret or anxiety. This refers to how we feel about not having done things that we should have done and about having done things that we shouldn't have. Although restlessness almost always accompanies worry, it is possible to have restlessness present without worry or regret.

HOW RESTLESSNESS AND WORRY MANIFEST

In the first instructions that we practice with each of the hindrances, we simply notice whether the hindrance is present or absent in the mind. And as with the other hindrances—desire, aversion, and sloth and torpor—there are both obvious and subtle manifestations to restlessness and worry. We're very familiar with the obvious expressions of restlessness and worry. We can feel a physical restlessness, where there is an agitated energy in the body and we can't sit still. The expression "jumping out of one's skin" describes this experience. There are also obvious restless states in the mind. We can repeatedly get lost in various kinds of thoughts and feel them as a kind of inner turmoil or whirlwind.

Yogi Mind

There is often an obsessive quality to mental restlessness. One manifestation of it is something we call "yogi mind." *Yogi* is the term we use for anyone who is meditating, and in intensive retreats we sometimes go through times when our thoughts are completely out of proportion to their importance or even their connection to reality. On one self-retreat at the Insight Meditation Society, I started hearing the sounds of the water in the heating pipes as people talking in the kitchen, which was quite far away. I was so convinced of the reality of these conversations that I had to go down to the kitchen to make sure everything was okay. On another retreat, one yogi asked the managers to please write the airlines to reroute the flights overhead because they were disturbing his practice. Sometimes, in the throes of the restless mind, we get so lost in our own obsessive thoughts that we lose touch with the reality of what is really going on.

Subtle Kinds of Restlessness

There are also subtler kinds of restlessness. Sometimes our practice is going very well, the mindfulness effortless and the concentration reasonably strong. Yet even at these times, and maybe just for a few seconds, the mind can slip in and out of quickly passing thoughts. The current of mindfulness may be strong enough for us not to be too sidetracked by them, but it is interesting to recognize this as a kind of restlessness of mind.

Restlessness and worry, as well as other defilements, can appear in other very subtle ways. There is a story of Anuruddha, one of the great disciples of the Buddha, going to see Sāriputta, who was second only to the Buddha in his wisdom:

> When Anuruddha had perfected himself more and more
> in the jhānas and in those refined meditative perceptions,
> he one day went to see the Venerable Sāriputta and said:
> "Friend Sāriputta, with the divine eye that is purified, transcending human sight, I can see the thousandfold world
> system. Firm is my energy, unremitting; my mindfulness is

alert and unconfused; the body is tranquil and unperturbed; my mind is concentrated and one-pointed. And yet my mind is not freed from the cankers, not freed from clinging."

Thereupon Sāriputta replied: "Friend Anuruddha, that you think thus of your divine eye, this is conceit in you. That you think thus of your firm energy, your alert mindfulness, your unperturbed body, and your concentrated mind: this is restlessness in you. That you think of your mind not being freed from the cankers: this is worrying in you. It would be good, indeed, if you would abandon these three states of mind and, paying no attention to them, direct your mind to the deathless element, Nibbāna."[1]

Like sloth and torpor, the mental factor of restlessness is not fully uprooted until full enlightenment, so even when we've seen through the illusion of self and are free of desire and aversion, this subtle restlessness and clinging of mind is still there. Reflecting on this may help us be more patient with our own times of restlessness, realizing that this mind state has deep roots.

General Anxiety

Worry, too, manifests in different ways. Sometimes it is a form of remorse or regret about past unskillful actions or about skillful actions left undone. Sometimes we worry about some imagined future, about things that have not even happened. One friend spoke to me of obsessive worry about loved ones, about what might happen, even though everything was fine in the moment. We often worry about anticipated problems. I've noticed this come up in travel. The flight I'm on may be a little late, and I'm worrying about whether I'll make the connection. Feeling some anxiety and tension, I find myself sitting in the seat, urging the plane to go faster. In situations like this, it's helpful to reflect that the worry has absolutely no bearing on the outcome. We are simply making ourselves tense and miserable. To whatever inconvenience there may or may not be, we're saying, in effect, "Let's add a little suffering to the mix."

Comparing Mind

Sometimes we worry about our practice. While goals and aspirations are key elements in our spiritual journeys, the mind can easily be overconcerned about our progress, about how we think we're doing, obsessing about our enlightenment or lack of it. With this kind of worry, it's very easy to fall into self-judgment, a certain kind of spiritual self-absorption. We start comparing ourselves to other meditators—the length of our sits, the amount of food we take, how slowly we're moving—and our minds can easily get agitated by this worry about our practice. We lose the simplicity of easeful resting in the moment, mindful of whatever is arising.

KNOW THE CAUSES OF RESTLESSNESS AND WORRY

So the first instructions about this hindrance are simply to notice whether these mental states are present or not. As the Buddha said in the sutta,

> "If restlessness and worry is present . . . one knows 'there is restlessness-and-worry . . .'; if restlessness and worry is not present . . . , one knows 'there is no restlessness-and-worry . . .'"[2]

Then, as with the other hindrances, we recognize and investigate what causes these states to arise.

An Imbalance of Concentration and Energy

A basic framework for understanding the causes for the arising of restlessness is seeing it as an imbalance of concentration and energy. Restlessness often comes from an excess of energy and not enough concentration or steadiness of mind to hold it. It's as if the energy is spilling over the edges of a container.

This imbalance can arise from different causes. It can come from unwise attention to our thoughts or to mental states of disquietude. We get drawn into the content of our minds. This is particularly true for people with a predilection for thinking—which is almost all of us. We need to see this tendency clearly. Sāriputta, one of the two chief disciples of the Buddha, was of this tribe. His great analytic powers slowed his progress a bit, which is why, after hearing the teachings, it took him two weeks to become fully enlightened, while it took Mogallāna only one.

We're sometimes pulled into restless thought activity because of the deeply ingrained idea that thinking leads to wisdom. Of course, thoughts can be creative and lead to deeper understanding, but there is a whole domain of insight and wisdom that is beyond the realm of discursive thinking. It is a realm that can never come through the thought process, but only through direct experience. No matter how much we read about or think about a good meal, it will never give us the experience of actually eating it.

Unwise Attention

Restlessness and worry also come about through unwise attention to situations in the world. This doesn't mean that we should be apathetic or nonresponsive; rather, it means that we should examine things with the eye of wisdom and see what the appropriate response might be. Mental agitation contributes nothing but more confusion. St. John of the Cross explicitly expressed this when he said, "Disquietude is always vanity, because it serves no good. Yes, even if the whole world were thrown into confusion, and all things in it, disquietude on that account would still be vanity."

Too Much Talk

One of the conditions for the arising of restlessness mentioned in Buddhist texts has particular relevance in our age of instant communication—that is, provocative talk and prolonged discussion. Although on a silent retreat actual conversations might be minimal, the ease and availability of electronic devices often seduce us into different kinds of communication. We might think that a quick email or text message is inconsequential, forgetting how energetically open we might be. What we consider a small thing can turn out to have huge ripple effects, agitating the mind and making concentration difficult to sustain.

Dwelling on Past Unskillful Actions

Another cause for the arising of worry and regret is remembering past unskillful actions, either of commission or omission. These thoughts and memories can become very vivid in the stillness of our meditation practice. On one level, becoming conscious of these memories is part of the purifying process—seeing clearly what is unwholesome, learning from it, and then letting go. But often the mind obsesses about these past actions and simply gets mired in self-judgment and self-recrimination.

To see and understand this cause of restlessness, worry, and regret more clearly and specifically, it is helpful to examine what the Buddha called the "ten unwholesome actions." These are actions that cause harm to others, lead to remorse in ourselves, and bring unwanted karmic results. There are three unwholesome actions of body: killing, stealing, and sexual misconduct. There are four unwholesome actions of speech: lying, harsh talk, backbiting, and useless talk. And there are three unwholesome actions of mind: covetousness, ill will, and wrong view of self. We can reflect on these and become mindful of how each one becomes the cause for mental disturbance.

Judging One's Own Progress on the Path

Worry and restlessness also arise from an excess of striving in our practice and an overconcern with one's progress or level of insight. We can get caught up in what I call "practice assessment tapes," continually judging and assessing how we are doing. When I was a young boy, I planted my first garden. Then, as the carrot tops began to emerge from the ground, I became so excited that I pulled them out to see how much they had grown. Not a very good strategy for growing vegetables—or indeed, anything else. Years later, at those times in my meditation practice when there was a lot of self-judgment about how I was doing, I began to remind myself, "Joseph, just sit and walk. Let the Dharma do the rest." The Korean Zen master Seung Sahn Sunim expressed it well: "Don't check. Just go straight."

KNOW WHAT CONDITIONS THE REMOVAL OF RESTLESSNESS AND WORRY

After contemplating and understanding the causes for the arising of restlessness and worry, the next step is knowing how to work with them once they have arisen.

Practice Mindfulness

As with all the other hindrances, mindfulness of the states themselves is the first approach: "Desire is like this," "Restlessness is like this." And then bringing the wisdom eye to bear, you practice seeing them as not "mine," not "I," not "myself." I have found it sometimes helps to use the Pali words to note the hindrances, as these words can help to depersonalize them, to see them free from all the associations and connotations of the English words.

Whenever we feel the mind is not settled on the object, not at rest, we can become mindful of the restlessness itself. Notice the physical energies in the body. Notice the difference in the emotional tone between restlessness and worry, so that you can distinguish one from the other. Restlessness feels more scattered; worry feels more anxious.

As we become mindful of these states of mind, rather than being lost in them, the mindfulness itself starts to bring the factors of concentration and energy into balance. This can happen in two ways. First, we can become mindful as if with a wide-angle lens. We settle back, aware of the whole body, just feeling and noticing the whole whirlwind of physical and mental energy. Sometimes I picture this hindrance as a Jackson Pollock painting, and mindfulness is the frame we put around it. The point of the frame is to help us see the picture more clearly.

Be Precise with Your Attention

The second approach in balancing energy and concentration is to use the mental zoom lens. In this instance, we focus the mind more precisely on a particular object like the breath, or we become quite precise in moving about, strengthening the quality of composure in our movements. Both of these actions help to calm all the obsessive thinking in the mind.

On one retreat in Nepal, we were all living in quite difficult conditions. There were five of us sharing a cement floor, right next to the toilets, with a lot of city noise filling the monastery. My mind was grumbling quite a bit about what I was taking to be all these distractions. When I went to report my experience to Sayadaw U Paṇḍita, he had just a few words of advice: "Be more mindful." My very first inner reaction was somewhat dismissive; I thought that he wasn't taking my concerns very seriously. But then, as I began the walking meditation outside, I thought to actually put his words into practice. I became more mindful, carefully attending to even the subtlest sensations of the movement. And much to my surprise, in the very moment of this more careful attention, all the mental grumbling disappeared. With more precise mindfulness, there was no room for this hindrance to arise.

There are three mental factors at work here, strengthening concentration relative to the energy. We discussed the first two, initial and sustained application, in the previous chapter on working with sloth and torpor. The third factor that strengthens the concentration is mindfulness—that is, staying aware of what the experience is.

Open Your Eyes

Another simple approach for working with the restless mind is opening the eyes when we're lost in streams of discursive thought. Sometimes just having a physical point of reference for where we actually are helps connect us with the reality of the moment rather than be swept away in the momentum of the thought process.

Practice Wise Reflection

If we're trying to be mindful in all these various ways, but are still getting lost in a flurry of mental activity, wise reflection can help bring things to balance. We can reflect on our purpose for practicing. Why are we doing this? We can remember that the fundamental purpose behind all our efforts is the purification of our minds, freeing ourselves from the forces of greed, hatred, and ignorance. And we can remember that we're doing this not only for ourselves, but also for the welfare of all. In this reflection, we reconnect with our respect for the practice and respect for ourselves in doing it.

When we remember our sense of purpose, it is easier to connect again with the object of awareness, to be mindful of just what there is. And as the scattered, dispersed mind begins to settle on the present-moment experience, we go from restlessness to restfulness, and our practice continues to deepen.

Reflecting on our present commitment to sīla, ethical conduct, can ease the mind from excessive worry, regret, or guilt about past actions. All of us, the Buddha included, have done unskillful acts in the past. Rather than forget, or suppress, or wallow in self-recrimination, we can see these past unskillful actions with wisdom, learn from the mistakes, and draw strength and confidence from our commitment to nonharming. A wonderful line from the poem "St. Francis and the Sow," by Galway Kinnell, expresses this understanding: "[S]ometimes it is necessary to reteach a thing its loveliness . . . until it flowers from within, of self-blessing."

Flowering from within of self-blessing requires distinguishing between guilt and remorse. Guilt is an unwholesome factor of mind that simply reinforces the sense of self with negative self-judgment: "I'm so bad," with an emphasis on the "I." Guilt is simply an ego trip of the mind. Remorse, on the other hand, acknowledges the action, understands its unwholesomeness, makes amends when possible, and then moves on. This is an act of self-forgiveness, which is honest in its assessment and wise in its understanding of impermanence and selflessness.

Although it's difficult in the moment of self-judgment, it's helpful to keep a sense of humor about our minds when we're seeing these patterns: "Yes, this is what my mind does. Self-judgment is like this." One technique that I've used to good effect when I'm noticing a lot of self-judgment or judgment of others is to start counting the number of times judgments appear in the mind: "self-judgment one, self-judgment two, . . . self-judgment five hundred and thirty eight." At a certain point, I simply start to smile at my mind, seeing how ridiculous it was to believe the judgments, or even to condemn them, which would in turn simply be another judgment. As soon as I can smile at these workings of the mind, this particular pattern loses a good deal of its power.

Know That Awareness Is Already Present

Lastly, when we're caught up in excessive worry about our practice and our progress on the path, we can balance the linear-stage model of the path with the perspective emphasized more in the Thai or Tibetan Dzogchen traditions: understanding that the mind's empty, aware nature is already here. From this perspective, it's not something we need to get or develop, but rather something we need to recognize and come back to. I've used two reminders to great benefit in my practice: "Already aware" and "It's already here."

We can prevent the future arising of restlessness and worry in a variety of ways. From the moment we recommit to the sīla of non-harming, our mind settles into freedom from nonremorse. Even if we have done unskillful things in the past, as we all have, we know that from this point onward, we are taking care with our actions of body, speech, and mind. This, of course, is nothing more than following the eightfold path of practice, which we will explore in much greater detail in later chapters. Reading dharma books, conversing with good friends, associating with wise teachers—all help the mind to stay free from restlessness and agitation that have not yet arisen.

19

Doubt

AS WITH EACH OF THE other hindrances, the Buddha outlines five steps for contemplating doubt:

> "If doubt is present, one knows 'there is doubt in me'; if doubt is not present, one knows 'there is no doubt in me.' And one knows how unarisen doubt can arise, how arisen doubt can be removed, and how a future arising of doubt can be prevented."[1]

As a side note, it is interesting to highlight the Buddha's use of language. Although from the ultimate perspective, there's no self, no "I," still, in conventional, everyday usage, he is saying, "Is doubt present in me or not?" Right here is an integration of relative and ultimate truths. On the conventional level, we speak of "I," "me," and "self" even as we understand on a more ultimate level the selfless nature of all phenomena.

Before exploring how to recognize doubt, we need to distinguish two general usages of the word. The first kind of doubt is helpful. It is an aspect of inquiry and investigation, and it motivates us to examine things carefully. Just as we don't want to dogmatically believe everything we hear, we don't want to automatically disbelieve something simply because it doesn't fit our current view. The beauty and power of the

Buddha's message is his reminder that we shouldn't believe something because we read it in books or because some teacher said it. There is a need to investigate all the teachings for ourselves to see whether they are of benefit or not. It is the second kind of doubt that is considered a hindrance. This is the mind state of uncertainty, wavering, and indecision. It is like coming to a crossroad and not knowing which way to go. The mind simply wavers back and forth between alternatives, and we end up not going anywhere.

Unnoticed, doubt is the most dangerous of the hindrances because it can bring our practice to a standstill. When doubt is strong and paralyzes us with indecision, it doesn't even give us an opportunity to take a wrong turn and then to learn from our mistakes. With doubt, we're always checking ourselves, vacillating, trying to decide. Yann Martel, in his wonderful book *Life of Pi,* expresses the effect of doubt very well: "To choose doubt as a philosophy of life is akin to choosing immobility as a means of transportation."

MANIFESTATIONS OF DOUBT

In the context of satipaṭṭhāna, doubt refers specifically to doubt about the Buddha, Dharma, and Sangha. These terms have broad implications, and in meditation practice, doubts about these implications take some very particular forms. Even if we have great confidence in the Buddha and his teachings, certain doubts can still arise.

Doubt in the Relevance of the Teachings

The Buddha lived thousands of years ago. We may wonder if what he said is really applicable now or whether he even said it. These kinds of doubts have a useful role when they lead to investigation; they're not useful when they lead to indecision and confusion or when they trigger an automatic rejection of things we would rather not hear, that we find unpalatable for one reason or another. We might have doubt about karma or rebirth or about the contemplations on the nonbeautiful aspects of the body. But rather than investigating and seeing for ourselves whether they have meaning for us, we often use doubt as a way of simply dismissing what is beyond our current level of understanding. Another approach to countering doubts is expressed in a phrase by the poet Samuel Taylor Coleridge: "the willing suspension of disbelief."

Doubt in the Path of Practice

At different times we might start to doubt the practice. "What does sitting here watching my breath have to do with anything? It's really useless!" This might lead to comparing different practices or wondering about the value of meditation in a world filled with suffering.

One of the strongest examples of doubt in my practice came as I was just beginning to learn about Tibetan Dzogchen teachings. Having practiced for so many years in the Burmese tradition of vipassanā, my mind was tormented by the question, "Which tradition is right?" I would go back and forth, playing the lawyer for both sides. Finally, after a month of this relentless doubting mind, I realized that I was asking the wrong question. It was not a matter of which tradition was right, but rather, coming to the understanding that all the teachings were skillful means for liberation. If we take teachings as statements of some absolute metaphysical truth, then different and often contradictory teachings become a big obstacle. If, though, we see metaphysics as skillful means, then the only relevant question is: Does this teaching help to free the mind? With this perspective, it's quite possible to find different teachings helpful at different times.

Doubt in Our Ability to Practice

Perhaps an even stronger manifestation of doubt has less to do with our confidence in particular teachings and more to do with our own ability to put them into practice. This is the deeply ingrained pattern of self-doubt. We hear these voices in the mind, saying, "Am I doing this right?", "I can't do it," "It's too hard," "It's not the right time. I should have waited." When this pattern of self-doubt is strong, it is not only a hindrance to our practice, but it also becomes a debilitating force in our lives. We get into the habit of frequently undermining ourselves, holding ourselves back.

There is a revealing phrase in English regarding this mind state: we say someone is "plagued by doubt." Doubt *is* like a plague that weakens us. When doubt is strong, instead of making the experiment, whether in meditation or anything else, and engaging fully in the experience so that we can see for ourselves whether it is beneficial or not, the mind simply gets lost in endless speculation. Then doubt becomes self-fulfilling, because staying lost in doubt really is useless.

It doesn't allow for the opportunity to investigate for ourselves. This endless conjecture is exhausting. Doubt is likened to a thorny mind. It keeps jabbing us, and we feel irritable, dissatisfied, and discouraged.

Doubt Disguised as Wisdom

Given all these downsides of doubt, why is it such a powerful force in the mind? The great seduction of doubt is that it comes masquerading as wisdom. We hear these very wise-sounding voices in our minds, questioning our ability, questioning the practices we are doing, questioning the teachers, and they all seem so reasonable and wise that we get caught up in believing these endlessly engaging thought loops. At these times, we are not recognizing these thoughts as simply being the hindrance of doubt.

Know When Doubt Is Present and Not Present

So the first step is learning to see through the masquerade and recognize doubt when it arises. As the sutta says, "[O]ne knows 'there is doubt in me.'" Through a careful mindfulness of our thoughts, we become more familiar with our own particular tapes and note them accurately: "I can't do it"—doubting tape. "I'm not doing it right"—doubting tape. "What's the point?"—doubting tape.

The next part of the instruction, noticing when doubt is not present, is equally important yet often overlooked. We can notice the absence of doubt in two ways. First, when things are moving along easily, when mindfulness and concentration are relatively strong and steady, it would be helpful to actually notice the quality of the mind at that time. We can notice that all of the hindrances, including doubt, are not present. What is the experience of the mind at that time?

A second way of noticing when doubt is not present (and this is true for the other hindrances as well) is to be particularly mindful in times of transition from one mind state to another. For example, suppose you are lost in a storm of doubt. At a certain point, you recognize it and begin to be mindful of it. Then, either quickly or gradually, under the light of mindfulness, the doubt will disappear. Nothing lasts forever. In the moment doubt passes away, notice the difference in your experience. What does it feel like to be free of doubt, even for a few moments?

KNOW THE CAUSE OF DOUBT
AND HOW TO REMOVE IT

The next instructions of the sutta say that we should investigate the cause of an arisen doubt and how to remove it once it has arisen.

More-or-Less Mindful

The Buddha pointed out that unwise attention is the proximate cause for doubt to arise:

> "There are, bhikkhus, things that are the basis for doubt: frequently giving careless attention to them is the nutriment for the arising of unarisen doubt and for the increase and expansion of arisen doubt."[2]

We experience unwise attention in different ways. One way is by not paying careful attention in the moment *to* the moment, not seeing and recognizing what the particular thoughts and feelings are that give rise to doubt. This can happen when we're being what I call "more-or-less mindful." We're going along, somewhat aware of what is happening, but not in a precise and accurate way. In this situation, unnoticed thought tapes gather momentum and begin to dominate the mind stream.

When we bring a close attention to the moment, we can be aware of thoughts closer to their beginning and not be seduced by their convincing tone. We see that each of these doubts is itself just another passing thought, and we don't give them any power. We can then come back to the simplicity of the moment—to the breath, to a step, to just what is arising. In these moments, the power of doubt no longer holds sway.

Wholesome vs. Unwholesome

Another far-reaching aspect of unwise attention that gives rise to doubt is not knowing what is wholesome and what is unwholesome. Without this understanding and wise discernment, we're not able to overcome the forces of greed and aversion and delusion in the mind. Not knowing what brings happiness and what brings suffering, we stay stuck in the quagmire of many wrong actions, all of which are a further breeding ground for doubt.

As just one example of this lack of discernment, many people live with the belief that the accumulation of more and more sense pleasures is the key to happiness. This is akin to the belief that drinking salt water will quench our thirst; the more we drink, the thirstier we get. Without an understanding of what is skillful and what is unskillful, we end up doing a lot of things that either don't bring their promised results or actually bring harm to others and ourselves. This, in turn, leads to doubt and confusion about what we're doing in our practice and our lives.

For this reason, there is the counterintuitive teaching that it is better to do an unskillful act knowing that it's unskillful than to do it without that knowledge. If we go ahead and do that act, even as we know that it's unskillful, there are still the seeds of wisdom that can lead to future restraint.

Just as unwise attention gives rise to doubt, we can overcome this hindrance and prevent its arising by cultivating wise attention, not only in our meditation practice but also in our lives. It's interesting to note that the very opposite of doubt is the beautiful mental factor of faith. Bhikkhu Bodhi describes the function of faith as clarifying the mind, in the same way a water-clearing gem causes muddy water to clear. Through hearing and studying the teachings, and then through our own investigation of them, we develop a growing confidence in the Buddha, in the Dharma, in the Sangha, and in ourselves. At a certain point, we're no longer beset by the wavering of doubt, and even when we face difficulties and challenges, this confidence gives us the strength and determination to persevere. The gradual overcoming of doubt gives greater meaning and power to the taking of refuge, because, at least to some extent, it is verified in our own experience, leading onward through all the stages of awakening.

MINDFULNESS OF DHAMMAS

The Five Aggregates of Clinging

20

Material Elements,
Feelings, and Perceptions

IN THE NEXT SECTION OF mindfulness of dhammas, the
Buddha outlines the contemplation of what are called "the five aggregates" (*khandhas,* in Pali) of experience: material elements, feelings,
perceptions, formations, and consciousness. The Buddha uses this
contemplation to analyze our subjective experience and, through this
experiential analysis, to deconstruct the deeply held concept of self.

There are many instances in the discourses where people would
hear these teachings and either become fully enlightened or, if not
ripe for that final awakening, have the "cloudless, stainless vision of
the Dhamma" arise in the mind, "turning upright what had been
overthrown, revealing what was hidden, showing the way to one
who was lost, or holding up a lamp in the dark for those with eyes
to see."[1]

When we bring the teachings on the five aggregates into the
realm of direct experience, they lead us into a profound investigation of what it is we call "life." These teachings open up new levels
of understanding, similar to, and even more transformative than, the
great discoveries of the atom or the quantum realities that underlie our conventional perceptions of the world. The teachings on the
aggregates directly point to those realities underneath the surface

appearance of "self" or "I" or "being." Through this investigation, we begin to discover what we really are.

In the Satipaṭṭhāna Sutta, the Buddha begins this section with the basic question of our practice: "How does one abide contemplating dhammas in terms of the five aggregates of clinging?" But before examining this question, it might be helpful to note a few things about this teaching.

What does the Buddha mean by the term *khandha?* It is a Pali word (*skandha,* in Sanskrit) that is usually translated as "aggregate." We can understand this on two levels. On the general level, it means a collection or a heap of things, including all the elements that make up the substance or groupings of something. For example, the term *dukkhakhandha* means all that is included under the term *dukkha,* or all that makes up the idea of suffering or ill. More specifically, *khandha* refers to the elements of substrata of existence that give rise to the appearance of various forms of life. As the Buddha puts it:

> "Just as, with an assemblage of parts,
> The word chariot is used,
> So when the aggregates exist,
> There is the convention 'a being.'"[2]

In this light, what we call the birth and death of a person, of a being, of self, are seen as just the arising and passing of different aggregates. The power of the teachings lies in their directions for us to experience this for ourselves.

In the Satipaṭṭhāna Sutta, and in many other discourses as well, the Buddha doesn't refer to just the five aggregates, but often uses the expanded phrase "the five aggregates of clinging." This refers to our identification with, desire for, or clinging to these aggregates, either individually or collectively. These tendencies result in our attachment to the concept of self or being, and it is this clinging to the aggregates that is the underlying cause of suffering. When the Buddha summarizes the first noble truth, he says, "In short, the five aggregates of clinging are dukkha."

How then do we contemplate these five aggregates? Although they all arise together, it is helpful to explore them one by one, so that we get a clearer understanding of what each of them is and how we directly experience them. In this chapter, we will explore the first three aggregates of clinging.

MATERIAL ELEMENTS

The teaching begins with what is most tangible and obvious: the first aggregate of material form or materiality (*rūpa,* in Pali). In the earlier section of mindfulness of the body, we discussed in some detail the nature of these material elements. Whenever we are mindful of a physical sensation—hardness, softness, pressure, vibration, heat, cold, lightness, heaviness—we are contemplating the first aggregate. And in the instructions of the sutta, the Buddha is saying to know each of these basic elements, each of these sensations, as being *rūpa.*

This is a more profound instruction than we might at first realize, because it leads us from the level of concept—body, head, chest, arm, leg, foot—to the level of direct experience. We may think that we're feeling the foot or leg, but there are no sensations called "foot." It is only when we go past the concept to what we're actually feeling that we can apply the next instruction: "Here one knows, 'such is material form, such its arising, such its passing away.'"

One of the most deluding aspects of concepts is that the concepts themselves don't change. We use the same words—*head, body, man, woman*—whether it's today, yesterday, or tomorrow. The words remain the same, which reinforces the illusion that there is something permanent that these words refer to. Yet when we contemplate the first aggregate of material elements, we clearly experience their changing nature. All of these sensations are in constant flux and change.

This is very obvious in walking, whether in slow walking meditation or moving around at a more normal pace. When we're undistracted, we become aware simply of sensations in space. There's no body, no foot, no leg—nothing solid or permanent at all. Likewise, when we hear a bell or some other sounds, the concept of what we're hearing stays the same—bell, bird—but our experience in the contemplation of *rūpa* is one of a flow of changing vibrations.

FEELINGS

As we stabilize our attention and mindfulness on this first tangible aspect of experience, the aggregate of material form, it leads naturally into the contemplation of the second aggregate, that of feeling (or *vedanā*, in Pali). We've already discussed in some detail mindfulness of feelings, but now we'll look at the key role this aggregate of feeling plays in the journey of awakening.

The feeling tone is so important because it is the conditioning factor of our reactions. When we experience something as pleasant, we like it, and we want to hold on to it and have it continue. So we can see how pleasant feelings condition desire, craving, and grasping. When we experience something as unpleasant, we don't like it, and we try to push it away and have it end. These unpleasant feelings thus condition aversion, anger, irritation, and fear. When we apply the Buddha's teaching, "one knows, such is feeling, such is its arising, such is its passing away," we learn both to recognize this feeling aspect more quickly and to see its changing nature.

Although this sounds very simple, how often do we remember in the midst of some strong feeling of pleasantness or unpleasantness that it too will soon change and pass away? We can pay attention to the impermanence of feelings both in our meditation practice and in our daily lives. Perhaps you're sitting and the mind has settled into a more concentrated state where there is stillness, calm, and ease of body. Watch the tendency of the mind to like this state, to cling to it, to want it to continue. This would be a good time to notice and note the feeling aggregate: "pleasant, pleasant." But even as we recognize the pleasant feelings and note them, our minds may drift into a subtle identification with them: "Pleasant, pleasant, I'm feeling pleasure." We recognize what is going on, but can still be identified with the enjoyment of it.

A technique that I've used to help cut through this identification is to make a more comprehensive note of what is happening. For example, at one point in my practice, a lot of sexual fantasies were arising in the mind. I started noting, "pleasant, pleasant," but somehow this was not strong enough to cut through the attachment. Then I became a little more precise, noting "contact, pleasant," and seeing more clearly that contact with the visual image was the condition for pleasant feeling to arise. This helped me to see the pleasant feeling more impersonally. By noting "contact, pleasant," I felt like I hit the right acupuncture point. The identification with the feeling fell away, and the alluring images disappeared much more quickly.

We can also do the same thing when we're getting caught in identifying with unpleasant feelings. As we practice in this way with the aggregate of feeling, we are applying the Buddha's profound instruction to his son, Rāhula: "See everything with perfect wisdom. This is not mine, not I, not myself."

PERCEPTION

The third of the five aggregates is perception. Perception, like feeling, is singled out from all the other mental factors as one of the aggregates because of its prominent role in the process both of our conditioning and our liberation. As mentioned earlier, perception is the factor that picks out the distinguishing marks of an object, names it, then remembers this word or concept and applies it the next time we experience that particular object. For example, we hear a sound. The sound waves and the ear are physical phenomena. Its being pleasant or unpleasant is the feeling tone. It is perception that recognizes the particular sound, names it "bird," and then applies the same name the next time that kind of sound is heard again. When perception and mindfulness are balanced, they work together in the service of insight. But when they are out of balance, perception can keep us imprisoned in the world of concepts, imprisoned in the conventional idea of self.

The particular perceptions we have, the concepts we use to describe things, often condition the way we feel about different experiences. Unfortunately, in many situations our perceptions are inaccurate. On one retreat, a meditator told me the story of his building a new home out in the country. As he was watching the building go up over a period of months, he began to notice two great blue herons flying around the area. They are majestic birds, and he was delighted to see them. Then, a short time after the house was finished and he had moved in, he began to hear a chirping sound from the basement. Thinking that the blue herons had made a nest while the house was being built and had just had chicks, he was delighted every time he heard the sound. Sometime later, when repairs were being done in the basement, the workman came up and commented that there was a faulty smoke detector making a kind of chirping sound. As soon as the sound went from being a delightful blue heron to an annoying smoke detector, it had to be fixed immediately. In this situation, nothing had changed but the concept, and yet the attitude of mind was very different.

The Perception of Solidity

When we don't observe the five aggregates carefully, there's one deeply habituated perception that we have about the world and ourselves that becomes the origin of many inaccurate conclusions. It's a perception that keeps us from understanding what is true. This is the perception we have of the solidity of things. We believe in the solidity of material phenomena, in the solidity or stability of relationships, of societies. But as long as this perception of solidity and stability is fixed, we don't deeply understand the impermanent and insubstantial nature of all phenomena.

Why is this perception of solidity so strongly conditioned in our view of reality? One reason is the rapidity of the changes taking place. Things are moving so quickly that we don't see the discontinuities. For example, when we go to a movie, we don't see separate frames of film. They are moving quickly enough across the screen that all the images flow seamlessly into one another. Or when we see an electric light, we see the light as continuous rather than as a flow of electrons through a filament.

Another reason we don't see the insubstantial nature of phenomena is because we are usually observing things from a distance and so not seeing their composite nature. If we look at a hillside from a distance, all we will see is a mass of color. As we come closer, we begin to see individual trees, then parts of trees, and then, on a cellular or molecular level, no trees at all. On this level, the perception of solidity, and even of a tree, has disappeared. This is the same with all objects of experience. They seem solid only from one limited perspective. For this reason, the view of solidity is called a hallucination of perception.

Kalu Rinpoche, one of the great Tibetan masters of the last century, clearly expressed this understanding: "You live in confusion and the illusion of things. There is a reality. You are that reality. When you know that, you will know that you are nothing and, in being nothing, are everything. That is all."

Concepts

When there is perception without mindfulness, which is our usual way of being in the world, we recognize just the surface appearance of things; we have not entered deeply into the experience and do not see its impermanent, insubstantial nature. We can see this tendency to solidify our view of the world through superficial perceptions and concepts in many areas of life, sometimes with very harmful consequences.

Place and Ownership

We create concepts of place and then take them to be real. How many wars have been fought and people killed over boundaries? When the astronauts viewed our planet from space, many commented on the beauty of seeing it whole and undivided. We create concepts of ownership and possessiveness, with the idea that we can fundamentally "own" things. Sometimes this is on a global scale, as in the eras of colonialism, when one country claimed ownership of another. Sometimes it is on a local scale, as we claim our own personal space. If you were on retreat, how would you feel upon walking into the meditation hall and finding someone sitting in "your" place? Most likely, there would be at least a few moments of disturbance. The Buddha taught that we cannot be said to truly own even these minds and bodies, much less anything else.

Time

A powerful concept that often rules our lives is the concept of time, of past and future. But when we look carefully at how we experience what we call "time," what do we find? Perception recognizes certain kinds of thoughts—memories, recollections, plans—creates the concepts of past and future, and then takes these concepts to have some intrinsic reality. But what is actually happening is simply different thoughts arising and passing in the moment. When we begin to see that our experience of past and future is just a thought in the moment, a huge burden is lifted from our lives. It doesn't mean that we don't use these thoughts skillfully; rather, that we're not lost in our mind-created worlds.

And on an even subtler level, we can also see that the notion of "present" itself is a concept, and one that we can become attached to. The Portuguese poet Fernando Pessoa, expressed it well:

> Live, you say, in the present;
> Live only in the present.

But I don't want the present. I want reality;

. . .

I only want reality, things without time present.[3]

And the Buddha connected this insight with the very process of awakening when he taught,

> Let go of the past, let go of the future, let go of the present, and cross over to the farther shore of existence. With the mind wholly liberated, you shall come no more to birth and death.[4]

Self

Besides the constructs of place and time, we also live in the mind-created world of self-image or role. This is the idea of ourselves that we present to others, that we believe of ourselves. As soon as we identify with any role or image, it is already a limitation. It is like a mold that we pour ourselves into, and then wonder why we feel contracted. We can also create limiting spiritual self-images. This is when we get caught in practice-assessment tapes in our minds, identifying with the ideas that our meditation is going well or badly—what I call the "good yogi, bad yogi syndrome." We also project these assessments onto others and then suffer with the comparing mind.

When we're not caught up in concepts of self-image, the mind is more open and relaxed, more spontaneous in the moment. Christine Cox, a writer and editor, wrote about a wonderful moment with His Holiness the Dalai Lama.

> My friend Sid once placed a Groucho Marx mask in a hotel room where the Dalai Lama would be staying during a visit to an Ivy League university. It was a gesture of karmic abandon because, really, who could gauge the terrestrial and spiritual consequences of such an act? . . .
>
> So imagine this: a cascade of university bureaucrats arrayed in the Dalai Lama's suite, waiting for their guest to appear. They sit erect in armchairs designed for slouching. . . .
>
> Minutes pass and then a door flings open. Unaccountably, Groucho Marx—wearing long maroon robes and serious

lace-up shoes—emerges, chuckling loudly, laughing so hard that tears come to his bespectacled eyes. . . .

How do people react when a dignitary—especially of the spiritual kind—does something so, well, undignified? Intrigued, I call up the university official in charge of the visits of the accomplished and the famous and the presidential. She clearly is not a woman easily impressed. How did she feel, I asked, at the Groucho Moment? At first, she tells me, she didn't know how to react. And then she and everyone started to laugh at the wonderful absurdity of the situation, laughed with a joy and incaution uncharacteristic of people in their position. . . .

The Dalai Lama didn't care about maintaining his image. He saw a chance for fun, for deflating others' expectations, and he took it. And he just somehow knew whom to thank. Wagging his finger at Sid, he took off the mask, still laughing. Even His Holiness needs a little Groucho in his life.[5]

We create concepts about things that may seem even more fundamental, such as age, gender, race, and culture. How old is your breath? Is the pain in your knee male or female? What color is your mind? It's not to say that these concepts don't point to certain differences of experience. They do. But we often become so identified with and attached to the concept that we solidify and fix the sense of who we are. The Nobel Prize–winning poet Wislawa Symborska illuminates the limitation of this conventional world of perception in her poem "View with a Grain of Sand":

> We call it a grain of sand,
> but it calls itself neither grain nor sand.
> It does just fine, without a name,
> whether general, particular,
> permanent, passing,
> incorrect, or apt.
>
> Our glance, our touch means nothing to it.
> It doesn't feel itself seen and touched.
> And that it fell on the windowsill

is only our experience, not its.
For it, it is not different from falling on anything else
with no assurance that it has finished falling
or that it is falling still.

The window has a wonderful view of a lake,
but the view doesn't view itself.
It exists in this world
colorless, shapeless,
soundless, odorless, and painless.

The lake's floor exists floorlessly,
and its shore exists shorelessly.
The water feels itself neither wet nor dry
and its waves to themselves are neither singular nor plural.
They splash deaf to their own noise
on pebbles neither large nor small.

And all this beneath a sky by nature skyless
in which the sun sets without setting at all
and hides without hiding behind an unminding cloud.
The wind ruffles it, its only reason being
that it blows.

A second passes.
A second second.
A third.
But they're three seconds only for us.

Time has passed like a courier with urgent news.
But that's just our simile.
The character is invented, his haste is make believe,
his news inhuman.[6]

One of our deepest conditionings and the source of so much suffering in our lives comes from one basic misguided perception, which is the mind-created concept of self. This is the idea that there is someone behind experience to whom it is all happening. We recognize a pattern of physical and mental elements, call it "Joseph" or "self," and then fail to look past the perceived pattern, not seeing that these concepts are only a designation for an arising appearance of complex interactions.

Imagine for a moment a great summer storm. There is wind and rain, thunder and lightning; but there is no storm apart from these elements. "Storm" is simply the concept or designation for this interrelated mix of phenomena. In the same way, when we look more closely at what we are calling "self," we see a constellation of rapidly changing elements, each one of which is itself momentary and insubstantial. Understanding our experience through the lens of the five aggregates helps us realize for ourselves the fundamental selfless nature of all phenomena.

Formations and Consciousness

FORMATIONS

The fourth aggregate is called *saṅkārā* in Pali. This is a very important term in the Buddha's teaching, and like the Pali word *dhamma* (*dharma,* in Sanskrit), *saṅkārā* has a wide range of meanings. It can refer to all formations or conditioned things, as in the frequently repeated phrase "all formations are impermanent, all formations are unsatisfactory, all formations are selfless." It can refer particularly to mental volitions as the determining karmic force in the mind. And in the context of the five aggregates, *saṅkārā* refers specifically to all the mental factors that arise in different combinations with each moment of consciousness, except feeling and perception, which were singled out as aggregates because of their unique importance.

The Four Categories of Mental Factors

In the Buddhist psychology, mental factors are the building blocks of all mental activity, including thoughts, emotions, moods, and mind states. They arise in different combinations and color each moment of consciousness according to their own characteristics. The Abhidhamma delineates these factors into four basic categories. These teachings have a very practical relevance for a deeper understanding of our lives. By being mindful of all these different factors as they become predominant, we begin to see their impermanent, impersonal nature.

The first category of mental factors is called "the universals," because they are common to all moments of consciousness. Among these seven universals are some of the qualities of mind already discussed. The seven common mental factors are contact, feeling, perception, attention (which is different and more superficial than mindfulness), one-pointedness, volition, and something called "life faculty." Each of these arises in every moment, with varying degrees of strength.

The second category is called "the occasionals," because they are sometimes present and sometimes not. They include such factors as initial and sustained application of mind, decision, energy, rapture, and "desire to do." The last is a motivating factor that urges us to perform an action. An interesting aspect of this desire to do is that it is ethically neutral. It can be associated with either wholesome or unwholesome actions.

The third category are the fourteen unwholesome factors of mind: greed, hatred, delusion, shamelessness, fearlessness of wrongdoing, restlessness, worry, wrong view, conceit, envy, avarice, sloth, torpor, and doubt. Of all these unwholesome mind states—those that bring suffering to others or ourselves—four of them are always present in every unwholesome consciousness: delusion, shamelessness, fearlessness of wrongdoing, and restlessness.

It is helpful to highlight these four unwholesome factors in our awareness, because doing so can help us understand what fuels the impetus for unskillful actions. Sometimes when we're about to do something we know is not quite wholesome—perhaps the second helping of dessert when we're already full, or some moment of wrong speech—we might look at these particular factors present in the mind to see how they are conditioning the action. Bringing an actively engaged interest to what is happening can help us free ourselves from their grip.

The fourth category of mental factors is comprised of what are called "the beautiful factors of mind." Although I have been unable to discover the reason for this asymmetrical use of terms, *unwholesome* and *beautiful* rather than *unwholesome* and *wholesome,* in some way it inspires a certain delight to consider the mind and heart made beautiful by the cultivation of these factors. Of the twenty-five beautiful mental factors, nineteen are common to every skillful state.

Some are familiar to us, such as the factors of faith, mindfulness, nongreed, nonhatred, tranquility, conscience (fear of wrongdoing), pliability, and lightness of mind. Others we might not immediately recognize—for example, wieldiness, proficiency, and rectitude of consciousness. When we recognize beautiful qualities as being present, especially the more obvious ones, we can nurture them, knowing that we are cultivating wholesome states in the moment and happy results in the future.

Contemplating the Mental Factors

The contemplation of the fourth of the aggregates, *saṅkārās,* is an essential part of our practice, because whenever we identify with any of these factors, whether wholesome or unwholesome, we reinforce both the concept and felt sense of self. Identification with mental factors creates the perspective of "I'm thinking," "I'm angry," "I'm sad," "I'm happy," "I'm making effort," "I feel rapture," "I'm restless." We build this superstructure of "I," of "self," on top of what are actually momentary, changing conditions. When we observe them more carefully, we see that each of these mental factors arises out of conditions in the moment, expresses its own nature, and passes away as conditions change. One Tibetan text describes this phenomenon as clouds passing through the sky, without roots, without a home. More useful and freeing perspectives than identifying with these factors would be language such as "the thought is the thinker," "love loves," "anger angers," "joy enjoys." These mental factors are not "self," not "I," not "mine"; they don't belong to anyone.

What helps us contemplate all these mental factors with wisdom and insight is seeing what conditions the arising of different emotions and mind states. We can notice how often a mood or emotion is triggered by a particular thought. We might think of a person and feel delight or longing or anger. Although the thought or image of the person may be very quick, the triggered emotion can linger on in the mind and body. Or sometimes our moods trigger certain patterns of thoughts. We might feel tired, discouraged, or grumpy and then begin to notice a lot of critical, judgmental thoughts.

We can also see how thoughts and emotions, the whole array of mental factors, are also conditioned by our backgrounds and levels of understanding. What makes one person happy may leave another quite ill at ease. For many laypeople, the enjoyment of sense pleasures brings a kind of happiness, while for a monk, the indulgence of the worldly life might seem burdensome.

The Factor of Volition

In this fourth aggregate of mental formations, there is one particular factor of fundamental importance. This is the factor of volition (*cetanā,* in Pali), and one of the specific meanings of *saṅkārā* refers to just this particular quality in the mind. Bhikkhu Bodhi describes volition as being the factor that is concerned with the actualization of a goal. It's like the chief of staff of the mind, coordinating all the other factors to accomplish a purpose. It is common to every moment of consciousness, and its function is to organize, gather, and direct all the other mental factors for a particular end.

What makes volition (sometimes referred to as *intention*) so important in the understanding of our lives and in the possibility for happiness is that it carries the karmic force of the action. What this means is that all intentional, volitional actions, whether of body, speech, or mind, have the power to bring about results both in the present and the future. The energy of intention is like the potential of a seed. A seed is so small, yet a small seed can become a huge tree. Moreover, just as each seed can bear many fruits, so too each of our volitional actions can produce myriad results.

Intention itself is ethically neutral. It is the motivation associated with the intention behind an action that determines the particular karmic fruit of the action, whether pleasant or unpleasant. Although there can be many different motives underlying our actions, they can all be traced back to one of three wholesome or three unwholesome roots; the wholesome ones are nongreed, nonhatred, and nondelusion, and the unwholesome ones are greed, hatred, and delusion. Because motive plays such a determining role in how our lives unfold, one teaching says that "everything rests on the tip of motivation."

Although motivation determines the result, it is the volitional nature of the act that provides the karmic energy. The practice of seeing and understanding this factor of volition is important not only because of its karmic potential, but also because we often unknowingly identify with it. Even as we become mindful of different mental factors like desire or calm, anger or joy, and see them as not-self, we can easily identify with the volition underlying actions, the felt sense that in the midst of all the activities of our lives: "*I'm* the one willing them." In this way, intention or volition can become a subtle hideout of self.

How can we begin seeing directly this crucial factor of volition? Although it is a common factor, arising in each moment, it is not always the predominant one. So it is best to begin noticing it before obvious physical movements. The body doesn't move by itself; it moves because of a volition in the mind. We can see this every time we change posture or reach for something or turn as we're moving about. These are movements that are not happening on their own. There is some energetic factor in the mind that wills the action.

We can notice this in various ways. We might get a forewarning of intention in the mind through being aware of a thought to do something. The thought, itself, is not the intention, but it can alert us that an intentional action may follow. As we observe this process carefully, we sometimes feel a certain gathering of energy in the mind—the impulse or command moment—that results in the hand reaching or the body turning. Sometimes we might not feel anything so tangible; rather we simply know, in the moment before acting, that we're about to move—I call this the "about-to moment." All of these processes connect us with the factor of volition.

We can also notice that volitions keep arising throughout the action, not only in the initiation of the action. Intention is analogous to an electric current that keeps an appliance running or a light bulb shining. If the current stops, then the appliance also stops or the light goes out. In the same way, even within one step, there needs to be a continuous flow of intentions to keep the foot moving through the air. If the intention stops, the foot will stop moving. We can have a direct experience of the impersonal nature of intention at those times when we're moving about with a certain momentum. We might notice that to stop the forward movement would require a decision in the mind. And we see that in the absence of that decision, the flow of intentions keeps us moving along all by itself, as if it had a mind of its own.

Take some time to explore how you experience the factor of volition in the mind. This is not thinking about volition; rather, it is taking an investigative interest in what it is that moves us throughout the day. On one self-retreat in the mountains of India, I experimented with this investigation. Standing on the side of a road, I kept waiting to see the actual intention to move. Over time, many different thoughts arose to move, but they didn't initiate the action. Finally, perhaps conditioned by impatience, I noticed the command moment, the impulse, that started the movement.

Although intentions are very quick and small, each one contains a huge power—that is, the power to bring about results, the power to bear fruit. In the contemplation of this aggregate of mental formations, we understand both the experience and import of intention and also all the different associated mental factors, wholesome or unwholesome, that determine its result.

CONSCIOUSNESS

The last of the five aggregates is consciousness (*viññāna*, in Pali). This is the cognizing function of the mind, that which simply knows. Although consciousness is often delineated as it relates to each of the sense doors—for example, seeing or hearing consciousness—it has one basic characteristic, which is knowing or cognizing. This characteristic has a powerful implication for our lives—that is, this basic cognizing activity does not change in different circumstances. Although it is colored by different mental factors, when we recognize the bare knowing nature of consciousness, we see that it manifests in just the same way regardless of what is arising. In this sense, we could call it a mirrorlike awareness, as the nature of a mirror is simply to reflect what comes before it.

The Conditioned Nature of Consciousness

In the teachings of the aggregates, the Buddha gives special emphasis to understanding the impermanent, conditioned nature of consciousness. As an example, a moment of seeing consciousness arises from the conjunction of four causes: the working organ of the eye, a visible form, light, and attention. If any of these conditions are absent, then seeing consciousness cannot arise. It's helpful to explore this conditioned nature of consciousness directly in our own experience, as a way of freeing ourselves from identification with even this activity of knowing. As you're reading this book, seeing the words on the page, what would happen if you had no eyes, or there was no light at all, or no attention on the object? Would any seeing occur? We have spontaneous insights into this conditioned nature of consciousness at those times when we are completely absorbed in some activity and don't hear what is going on around us. If there is an absence of attention to the sound, hearing consciousness doesn't arise.

The Buddha emphasized this contingent nature of consciousness in his response to a monk named Sati, who had the view that there was just one consciousness that went from life to life. The Buddha then asked Sati,

> "What is that consciousness?"
>
> "Venerable sir, it is that which speaks and feels and experiences here and there the result of good and bad actions."
>
> "Misguided man, to whom have you ever known me to teach the Dhamma in that way? Misguided man, in many discourses have I not stated consciousness to be dependently arisen, since without a condition there is no origination of consciousness?"[1]

Here we see that consciousness is not something permanent, always present, waiting for some object to be known; rather, it is a process continually arising and passing away many times a moment. We have the illusion of continuity because the process is happening so quickly. Bhikkhu Bodhi, in his book on the Abhidhamma, writes,

> Within the breadth of a mind moment, a *citta* [consciousness] arises, performs its momentary function, and then dissolves, conditioning the next citta in immediate succession. Thus, through the sequence of mind moments, the flow of consciousness continues, uninterrupted like the waters in a stream.[2]

One of the great implications of this impermanence is that consciousness, as with all the other aggregates, is insubstantial and empty, like a mirage or magical display.

> "Suppose, bhikkhus, that a magician or a magician's apprentice would display a magical illusion at a crossroads. A man

with good sight would inspect it, ponder it, and carefully investigate it, and it would appear to him to be void, hollow, insubstantial. For what substance could there be in a magical illusion? So too, bhikkhus, whatever kind of consciousness there is, whether past, future, or present, internal or external, gross or subtle, inferior or superior, far or near: a bhikkhu inspect it, ponders it, and carefully investigates it, and it would appear to him to be void, hollow, insubstantial. For what substance could there be in consciousness?"[3]

The great challenge here is both to understand consciousness as a magical display and at the same time to live a life of wisdom and compassion, engaged with the world. An intriguing description of how these two levels inform one another, of how the mind creates the reality we experience, was written by Victor S. Johnston in his book, *Why We Feel: The Science of Human Emotions.*

Consider a world without consciousness. The darkness is a bubbling cauldron of energy and vibrating matter, locked in the dance of thermal agitation. Through shared electrons, or the strange attraction of unlike charges, quivering molecules, not free to roam, absorb and emit their characteristic quanta packages of energy with the surrounding fog. Free gas molecules, almost oblivious to gravity but buffeted in all directions by their neighbors, form swirling turbulent flows or march in zones of compression and expansion. . . . A massive solar flux and cosmic radiation from events long past crisscross space with their radiant energy and silently mix with the thermal glow of living creatures. . . . [W]ithin the warmth of their sticky protein bodies, the dim glow of consciousness is emerging to impose its own brand of organization on this turbulent mix of energy/matter. The active filter of consciousness illuminates the darkness, discards all irrelevant radiation, and in a grand transmutation converts and amplifies the relevant. Dead molecules erupt into flavors of bitterness or sweetness, electromagnetic frequencies burst with color, hapless air pressure waves become the laughter of children, and the impact of a passing molecule fills a conscious mind with the aroma of roses on a warm summer afternoon.[4]

Investigating Consciousness

There are different perspectives we can bring to the investigation of consciousness. One comes from the understanding that the more mindful we are of the arising object, the clearer the consciousness of it becomes. When we bring a close attention to the breath, or sensations, to sights and sounds and thoughts, over time, we experience the knowing itself becoming increasingly clear and lucid.

Another approach I have found helpful in experiencing directly this fifth aggregate is reframing our experience in the passive voice. The language that we use to describe experience (even to ourselves) has a conditioning effect on how we experience things. Our usual linguistic construction is the active voice: "I'm hearing," "I'm seeing," "I'm thinking." The very language we use, whether spoken or not, reinforces the sense of the knower, the witness, the observer who is standing behind experience and receiving it all.

Instead of noting our experience from the viewpoint of an observer, we can shift from an active voice to a passive voice: "a sound being known," "a thought being known," "a sensation being known." It's not that we need to continually repeat these phrases, but rather to just be directly in the experience of things appearing and being known moment after moment.

Reframing in this way is helpful because it takes the "I" out of the description. The philosopher Ludwig Wittgenstein expresses this succinctly when he says, "The sense of a separate self is only a shadow cast by grammar." We can experience this passive-voice perspective very clearly in walking meditation. When a step is taken, different sensations appear and are known in the very moment of their arising. This simplicity of movement and sensations being known reveals different things about the nature of consciousness. First, we see that each moment of knowing, of consciousness, is arising simultaneously with the sensation—not a moment before, not a moment after. Second, we notice that the knowing arises spontaneously. There's no one commanding consciousness to arise. When the conditions are there, consciousness appears automatically.

Purification of View

Whether we're attending to each object of experience actively—that is, sending the mind to the object—or passively, reframing our experience as things being known, as the mind settles for sustained periods of time, continued mindfulness and investigation lead through different insight experiences. One is called Purification of View, in which we experience each moment as the paired progression of consciousness and its object, understanding that there is no one lurking behind the process. We see that everything we are calling "self" and "I" is simply the interplay of mental and physical phenomena, knowing and object arising and passing away moment after moment.

At this time we can clearly distinguish mind and materiality. Imagine, for a moment, a corpse. Somehow you manage to pump air into its lungs. The physical movement of the lungs expanding would be there, but there is no mind, no knowing. Yet when we are breathing, something else is going on. We can see both the mental and physical processes happening.

While we can distinguish mind and matter, they are nonetheless inseparable. It's like looking at a visible object and seeing both its color and its form. We can't separate the two; the color has a shape, and the shape or form has a certain color. Yet these two characteristics, while inseparable, are quite distinct.

This insight into the pairwise progression of knowing and object is the first deep, experiential understanding of *anattā*, or selflessness. Although this insight is not yet complete—in many situations, we still identify with thoughts or feelings or consciousness—still it is a radical departure from our usual way of perceiving the world and ourselves. As we continue the practice and our perception of impermanence becomes more refined, we see the rapid arising and passing away of not only the object, but also the knowing mind. There are times when we see consciousness itself continually dissolving. At those times, there is nothing to hold on to, there is no place to take a stand; it's as if we're on the shifting sands of a very steep slope.

This is a time in practice of great insecurity, because we see so deeply there is nothing substantial to call "I" or "mine." It even seems as if we've lost all ability to meditate; neither the object nor the knowing last long enough for us to be mindful of them, and so we think that mindfulness has fled. With the dissolving aspect so strong, the mind begins to experience various stages of fear and even disgust at the instability of phenomena. Here, a teacher can be very helpful to remind us to be patient and to keep practicing.

If we can stay steady through this difficult time, we experience various perspectives on the process of mind and materiality, and we come to a place of great equanimity, where we have an even fuller understanding of the nature of consciousness. Some of the great masters of the Theravāda tradition describe these experiences very clearly. Ajahn Jumnien, a contemporary Thai meditation master, wrote:

> At some point the mind becomes so clear and balanced that whatever arises is seen and left untouched, with no interference. One ceases to focus on any particular content and all is seen as simply mind and matter, an empty process arising and passing away of its own . . . a perfect balance of mind, with no reactions. . . . There is no longer any doing . . .[5]

But this refined state presents its own challenges. It is important to be mindful of the knowing mind because it is easy to become subtly identified with this very pure and refined consciousness. The great Burmese master Mahāsi Sayadaw reminds us of this:

> [At times there is] nothing to note, with the body disappearing and the sense of touch lost. However at this moment, knowing consciousness is still apparent. In the very clear open space of the sky there remains only one very clear, blissful consciousness, which is very clear beyond comparison and very blissful. The yogi tends to delight in such clear, blissful consciousness. But, the consciousness is not going to stay permanent. . . . It has to be noted as "knowing, knowing."[6]

Here, great care is needed in our practice. It is easy to mistake wonderful and subtle states of mind for the mind released. As the twelfth-century Ch'an master Ta Hui said, "As soon as there's something considered important, it becomes a nest." If freedom is our aspiration, we don't want to make even consciousness our nest. As long as there is identification with anything, any sense of the knower, the one knowing, then we are still bound by the conventional, conditioned mind.

22

Contemplating
the Five Aggregates

THE GREAT IMPORT OF THESE teachings of the five aggregates is that they provide a framework for our experiential analysis of what we call "self." And as the Buddha pointed out, when they are not properly understood, they become the source of agitation, stress, and suffering in our lives. This inquiry is not an abstract exercise in Buddhist philosophy, but rather a way of seeing directly and precisely into the nature of our experience.

In the great collection of suttas called the "Connected Discourses" (Samyutta Nikāya, in Pali), there are 159 short discourses on the aggregates. The Buddha here goes into some detail about how we habitually take the aggregates as objects of clinging, and how we can free ourselves from this clinging by seeing their impermanent, unsatisfying, and selfless nature.

INSIGHT INTO IMPERMANENCE

In the classical progression of these three characteristics, the Buddha almost always begins with impermanence, and we find this in the very instructions of the Satipaṭṭhāna Sutta:

> "Again, monks, in regard to dhammas, one abides contemplating dhammas in terms of the five aggregates of clinging.

> And how does one in regard to dhammas abide contemplating dhammas in terms of the five aggregates of clinging?
>
> "Here one knows, 'such is material form, such its arising, such its passing away; such is feeling . . . perception . . . volitions . . . consciousness, such its arising, such its passing away.'"[1]

Beginning with the insight into impermanence, whenever we notice the arising and passing away of phenomena—whether a physical sensation, a feeling tone, a perception at the sense doors or concepts in the mind, intentions and other mental states, or consciousness—we are practicing mindfulness of the aggregates in the way the Buddha instructed.

Although the truth of impermanence reveals itself naturally as we pay attention to each arising object, we can also set our intention to specifically key into this truth of change. When I was practicing with Sayadaw U Paṇḍita, he would ask us to report not only on what objects were arising in our meditation, but also on what happened to each object as we observed it. It requires a precise and sustained interest to investigate in this way.

> Sitting to one side, that bhikkhu said to the Blessed One: "Is there, venerable sir, any form that is permanent, stable, eternal, not subject to change, and that will remain the same just like eternity itself? Is there any feeling . . . perception . . . volitional formations. . . . any consciousness that is permanent, stable, eternal, not subject to change, and that will remain the same just like eternity itself?"
>
> "Bhikkhu, there is no form . . . no feeling . . . no perception . . . no volitional formation . . . no consciousness that is permanent, stable, eternal, not subject to change, and that will remain the same just like eternity itself."[2]

THE UNSATISFYING NATURE OF EXPERIENCE

Contemplating the impermanence of the aggregates reminds us that they are all part of an endlessly passing show, and for this reason, they are, in the end, unsatisfying. Munindra-ji, my first teacher, would often ask, "Where is the end of seeing, of hearing, of thinking, of knowing?" There is nothing wrong in these experiences; they simply don't have the capacity to satisfy our deepest aspirations for happiness and peace. Because of their unstable, changing nature, we are always waiting for the next hit of experience.

We can see this anticipation play itself out in our worldly desires and also in our meditation practice. How often are we waiting for the next concentrated walking or the next easeful, "good" sit? The paradox of the spiritual life is that, as objects of clinging, all of these changing phenomena, whether sense objects or meditative states, leave us unfulfilled, precisely because they don't last. Yet as objects of mindfulness, any arising experience becomes the vehicle of our awakening. We don't have to wait for some good or special experience in order to be mindful. Any object will do; nothing is outside the range of mindfulness.

VIEWING THE AGGREGATES AS NON-SELF

From contemplating the impermanent, unsatisfying nature of the aggregates, we open to the deepest experience of them as non-self. As this insight deepens, we no longer claim ownership of them as being "I" or "mine," and so no longer suffer when inevitable change happens. This is a radically different way of viewing this body and mind.

> "Bhikkhus, whatever is not yours, abandon it. When you have abandoned it, that will lead to your welfare and happiness. . . .
>
> "Suppose, bhikkhus, people were to carry off the grass, sticks, branches, and foliage in this Jeta's Grove, or to burn them, or to do with them as they wish. Would you think: 'People are carrying us off, or burning us, or doing with us as they wish?'"
>
> "No, venerable sir. . . . Because, venerable sir, that is neither our self nor what belongs to our self."
>
> "So too, bhikkhus, form is not yours, [feeling is not yours, perception is not yours, volitional formations are not yours,] consciousness is not yours. Abandon it. When you have abandoned it, that will lead to your welfare and happiness."[3]

Abandon here means abandoning the sense of ownership, of identifying with the aggregates as being "I" or "mine."

The question for us, then, is how have we become so attached to the aggregates as being self? Our claim of ownership has been long established in the cosmic registry of deeds. And we defend our claim with great tenacity. As mentioned earlier, we become attached to and identified with the idea of self because we are satisfied with superficial perceptions and with the concepts we use to describe experience. This complacency of observation keeps us from seeing clearly the impermanent, insubstantial nature of what we're calling "self."

The Composite Nature of the Body

We can see clearly how this superficial observation creates the sense of self in relationship to the body. We get up in the morning, look in the mirror, see certain colors and forms, recognize a pattern, and then create a concept designating what we see—a reflection of Joseph, of self, of me, as if Joseph or self is some substantial being.

We rely on these perceptions, not only regarding reflections in a mirror, but also in our experience of the body and other physical phenomena. How much of our sense of self comes from the superficial perception we have of the body? It seems so solid, so me. There was a tee shirt, advertised in *The New York Times,* that had imprinted on the front, "Me Me Me." Perhaps we should create our own that says, "Not Me Not Me Not Me."

When we observe the body more closely, contemplating the first aggregate of the physical elements, we cut through the illusion of solidity and see the body's composite nature. We can see it in terms of the many interrelated elements of the skeletal, muscular, and circulatory systems, of all the different organs. Yet when we wrap it all up very nicely in skin, we get so easily attached to it, claiming it as "my" body. Or we get attached to other people's bodies. How attached would we be if we had x-ray vision? This attachment to the body also deeply conditions our fear of death. The more we cling, the harder it is to let go.

And in looking even deeper, on the cellular or atomic level, we see mostly empty space. One science article remarked that if we took all the space away from what constitutes the body, what would be left would be smaller than a particle of dust. In meditation, we go from the perception of the solidity of the body to understanding it as a changing, fluid, insubstantial energy system.

Identification with Thoughts and Emotions

We also condition a strong sense of self when we identify with the mental aggregates, with particular feelings or thoughts, emotions or meditative states. Notice the felt sense of self when we're lost in or identified with thoughts: "I'm thinking," "I'm planning," "I'm judging." The *I* is quite extra. Notice our claim of ownership of the many stories we make up about ourselves or others. By paying careful attention to all these elements of mind, we see how much of the time we're living in the world of mental projections.

One of the most freeing insights of meditation practice is realizing that the only power thoughts have is the power we give them. Yet they are tremendously seductive, particularly when they are intertwined with different emotions. Unnoticed thoughts have a compelling power in our lives; yet when we are aware of them, we understand them to simply be the play of the aggregates, impermanent and empty of self. Notice carefully the difference in experience between being lost in a thought and being aware of it. However long you may be carried away on the thought train, in those moments of waking up from being lost, open to that experience of wakefulness, that moment of recognition, without hurrying back to the breath or the body. This moment can reveal both the empty nature of thought and the illuminating power of awareness.

In teaching about the nature of mind, Dilgo Khyentse Rinpoche reminds us of this empty nature:

> Normally we operate under the deluded assumption that everything has some sort of true, substantial reality. But when we look more carefully, we find that the phenomenal world is like a rainbow—vivid and colorful, but without any tangible existence.
>
> When a rainbow appears, we see many beautiful colors—yet a rainbow is not something we can clothe ourselves with, or wear as an ornament; it simply appears through the conjunction of various conditions. Thoughts arise in the mind in just the same way. They have no tangible reality or intrinsic existence at all. There is therefore no logical reason why thoughts should have so much power over us, nor any reason why we should be enslaved by them. . . .

Once we recognize that thoughts are empty, the mind will no longer have the power to deceive us. But as long as we take our deluded thoughts as real, they will continue to torment us mercilessly, as they have been doing throughout countless past lives.[4]

In the same way, we become identified with certain moods or mind states, not only creating and feeling deeply a sense of self, but also often building a whole life story of self around the emotion: "I'm this way," "It's such a deep pattern," "It will take so long to be free of this." We build the story of our lives and then live in that story. But all that is actually happening is the rise and fall of momentary mind states.

It is our practice of mindfulness, as outlined in detail in the Satipaṭṭhāna Sutta, that shows us the impermanent, selfless nature of the aggregates. This is what the Buddha called "true knowledge."

> "Here, bhikkhus, the instructed noble disciple understands form is subject to arising, subject to vanishing, subject to arising and vanishing. He understands feelings, perceptions, volitional formations, consciousness is subject to arising, subject to vanishing, subject to arising and vanishing. This, bhikkhus, is called true knowledge."[5]

DECONSTRUCTING THE CONCEPT OF SELF

With this foundation of understanding the aggregates, the Buddha gave a series of discourses in which he deconstructed the concept of self with incisive clarity. We see that "self" or "I" is not something we need to get rid of or demolish. Rather, we understand that it was never there in the first place. Although these discourses were spoken in the context of the Indian philosophical tradition of the time, following the thread of the dialogue can result in a startling and radical transformation of understanding.

One particular discourse begins with a conversation between the monk Anurādha, and some wandering ascetics, in which the wanderers posited that at the time of death, a Tathāgata (the term used for a Buddha) describes himself in one of these four ways: as either existing after death or not existing; as both existing and not existing; or as neither existing nor not existing.

When Anurādha replied that a Tathāgata describes himself apart from these four cases, the ascetics reviled him, saying, "This monk must be newly ordained, not long gone forth; or, if he is an elder, he must be an incompetent fool." After going to the Buddha and recounting the story, Anurādha asked, "If those wanderers should question me further, how should I explain in accordance with the Dhamma, so that no reasonable consequence of my assertion would give ground for criticism?" The Buddha then asked Anurādha a series of questions, which culminated in a very different framework of understanding. As we read this dialogue, rather than skimming over the repetitions or thinking that it is simply a philosophical exercise, we might imagine that the Buddha is asking these questions of us and reflect on their depth of meaning.

> "What do you think, Anurādha, is form [feeling, perception,
> volitional formations, and consciousness] permanent or
> impermanent?"
> "Impermanent, venerable sir."[6]

The Buddha then asks whether what is impermanent should be seen as satisfying or unsatisfying, reliable or unreliable, and whether what is impermanent and unreliable can be considered as "this is mine, this is I, this is myself." When Anurādha answers, "No, venerable sir" to each of these questions, the Buddha continues:

> "What do you think, Anurādha, do you regard form as the
> Tathāgata?"
> "No, venerable sir."
> "What do you think, Anurādha, do you regard the
> Tathāgata as in form?"
> "No, venerable sir."
> "Do you regard the Tathāgata as apart from form?"
> "No, venerable sir. . . ."
> "What do you think, Anurādha, do you regard form, feel-
> ing, perception, volitional formations, and consciousness
> [taken together] as the Tathāgata?"
> "No, venerable sir."
> "What do you think, Anurādha, do you regard the
> Tathāgata as one who is without form, without feeling,

without perception, without volitional activities, without consciousness?"

"No, venerable sir."[7]

Now the Buddha strikes the vital point when he says that since in this very life *the Tathāgata is not to be found,* is not to be met with in reality, and it is therefore not proper to say of him that he can be spoken of in some other way after death.

The Buddha concludes the dialogue reiterating the essential point of his teaching:

"Formerly, Anurādha, and also now, I make known just suffering and the cessation of suffering."[8]

This understanding that the self is not to be found either within or apart from the aggregates provides a profound reference point for a deeper understanding of our lives. What is it that we are actually attached to? What is it that we crave? We begin to understand that this path of practice is not about getting some new experience of one or more of the aggregates, but rather to be free from clinging to any of them as "I" or "mine."

Dilgo Khyentse Rinpoche expresses the importance of this realization:

> The idea of an enduring self has kept you wandering helplessly . . . for countless past lifetimes. It is the very thing that now prevents you from liberating yourself and others from conditioned existence. If you could simply let go of that one thought of "I," you would find it easy to be free, and to free others, too. If you overcome the belief in a truly existing self today, you will be enlightened tomorrow. But if you never overcome it, you will never gain enlightenment. . . .
>
> Use any practice you do to dissolve this idea of "I" and the self-oriented motivations that accompany it. Even if you do not succeed in the beginning, keep trying.[9]

MINDFULNESS OF DHAMMAS

The Six Sense Spheres

23

How We Experience the World

THE NEXT SECTION OF THE discourse focuses on teachings regarding the six internal and external sense spheres. The internal spheres are the six sense bases, namely, the eye, ear, nose, tongue, body, and mind; the external spheres are their respective sense objects: visible forms, sounds, odors, tastes, tactile sensations, and mind objects. When we turn our attention to the direct experience of these six internal and external sense spheres, we find they are a subtle, profound, and far-reaching part of the practice. They are the basis for everything we know, for the arising of the entire world of our unfolding experience.

> "Bhikkhus, I will teach you the all. . . . And what, bhikkhus, is the all? It is the eye and forms, the ear and sounds, the nose and odours, the tongue and tastes, the body and tactile objects, the mind and mental phenomena. This is called the all."[1]

Ledi Sayadaw, one of the great Burmese meditation masters and scholars of the late nineteenth and early twentieth centuries, likened the sense bases to six train stations from which trains travel to various destinations. Either they take us to situations of suffering, or they take us to realms of happiness or to freedom and full awakening. Consider how all the wholesome and unwholesome actions we do, with their respective karmic consequences, originate at one of the sense doors. Here it is important to remember that mind and mind objects—thoughts, reasoning, memory, reflection, moods, emotions—are simply treated as the sixth sense. These experiences of mind are seen as impersonally as any other sense object.

These are the Buddha's instructions in the Satipaṭṭhāna Sutta for working with the sense spheres:

> "[I]n regard to dhammas, one abides contemplating dhammas in terms of the six internal and external sense-spheres. And how does one . . . abide contemplating dhammas in terms of the six internal and external sense-spheres?
>
> "Here, one knows the eye, one knows forms, and one knows the fetter that arises dependent on both, and one also knows how an unarisen fetter can arise, how an arisen fetter can be removed, and how a future arising of the removed fetter can be prevented."[2]

The instructions go on to say that we should know, in the same way, each of the other sense bases (ear, nose, tongue, body, and mind), their respective objects, and the fetter that arises dependent on them. And we should know, as well, how those fetters that have not yet arisen can arise, how once arisen they can be removed, and how a future arising of them can be prevented.

THE CONDITIONED ARISING OF CONSCIOUSNESS

We might think that the first part of the instruction—one knows the eye and form, ear and sound, etc.—is unremarkable. But there is an important difference between our commonplace understanding and what the Buddha is pointing to. In our usual mode of experiencing the world, we habitually reference all these experiences to someone, a self, behind them all: "I'm seeing," "I'm hearing," "I'm thinking." While it is not hard to see the play of impermanence in the different sense *objects,* it's more difficult to see and understand the conditioned, selfless nature of the sense bases (eye, ear, nose, tongue, body, and mind) and the consciousness that arises dependent on them.

As an experiment, the next time you're eating, pay attention to the sense base of the tongue and the taste consciousness that arises. What is the experience of that rather strange organ, which moves around the mouth, turning food over, seeking out the touch sensations of the food and the various tastes and flavors that arise? As we are mindful of this little drama, it can sometimes seem as if the tongue has a mind of its own, with its own particular agenda. With a more careful attention, we see that all of its movements are being directed by intentions in the mind.

Investigating further, we can also see how every moment of taste consciousness, the knowing of taste, arises from a conjunction of causes: when food, tongue, moisture, and attention all come together, then consciousness of taste arises. Now, imagine for a moment, what would happen to this consciousness if either tongue or food were absent. It becomes obvious that there would be no knowing of taste at all; no taste consciousness would arise. It is this kind of investigation that helps illuminate the conditioned, selfless nature of consciousness, which, when unexamined, is often the last hideout of the sense of self.

We can explore each of the sense spheres in this way, giving us a direct, intuitive experience of the contingent nature of each sense-door consciousness. On this level of experience, we become much less identified with any of the play of phenomena that is endlessly rolling on. We see that each experience is simply just what it is, and that the "I" and "mine" are extra.

All of this is succinctly summed up in one sutta of the Connected Discourses of the Buddha. A bhikkhu named Udāyi came to Ānanda and asked,

> "Friend Ānanda, in many ways [the nature of] this body has
> been declared, disclosed, and revealed by the Blessed One thus:
> 'For such a reason this body is nonself.' Is it possible to explain
> [the nature of] this consciousness in a similar way . . . : 'For
> such a reason, this consciousness is nonself?'"
>
> "It is possible, friend Udāyi. Doesn't eye-consciousness
> arise in dependence on the eye and forms?"
>
> "Yes, friend."
>
> "If the cause and condition for the arising of eye-
> consciousness [eyes and forms] would cease completely

and totally without remainder, could eye-consciousness
be discerned?"

"No, friend."

"In this way, friend, this has been declared . . . by the Blessed
One thus: 'For such a reason this consciousness is nonself.'"[3]

We can investigate this understanding in the same way with each of
the sense spheres—how consciousness itself is a conditioned arising,
not "I," not "self," not "mine."

Teijitsu, the abbess of a Zen nunnery in Japan, had this same
realization:

> And then she saw that arising arose, abided, and fell away. . . .
> She saw that knowing this arose, abided, and fell away. Then she
> knew there was nothing more than this, no ground, nothing to
> lean on stronger than the cane she held, nothing to lean upon at
> all, and no one leaning, and she opened the clenched fist in her
> mind and let go and fell into the midst of everything.[4]

THE DEPENDENT ARISING OF DEFILEMENTS

What keeps us, then, from opening the clenched fist of our minds
and falling into the midst of everything? The Buddha points the way
in the next part of the instructions in the Satipaṭṭhāna Sutta. He says
not only to know the sense base and its object, eye and form, ear and
sound, etc., but also to know the fetter, or defilement, that arises
dependent on both of them: how it arises, how it can be removed,
and how it can be prevented.

In our practice we can watch for the arising of the fetters at any
of the six sense doors. This is not an academic exercise. What the
Buddha is talking about here is the arising and ending of suffering
in our lives. This is made vividly clear in the third discourse the
Buddha gave after his enlightenment, called "the Fire Sermon." He
was talking to a group of one thousand monks who had formerly
been fire-worshipping ascetics, and so he used this theme because it
corresponded with their own particular background.

> "Monks, all is burning. And what, monks, is the
> all that is burning? The eye is burning, forms are

burning, eye-consciousness is burning, eye-contact is burning, and whatever feeling arises with eye-contact as condition—whether pleasant or painful or neither-painful-nor-pleasant—that too is burning. Burning with what? Burning with the fire of lust, with the fire of hatred, with the fire of delusion; burning with birth, ageing, and death; with sorrow, lamentation, pain, dejection and despair. . . .

"The ear is burning. . . . The mind is burning. . . .

"Seeing thus, monks, the instructed noble disciple becomes disenchanted with the eye, with forms, with eye-consciousness, with eye-contact, with whatever feeling arises with eye-contact as condition—whether pleasant or painful or neither-painful-nor-pleasant; becomes disenchanted with the ear . . . with the mind. . . . Becoming disenchanted, one becomes dispassionate. Through dispassion, [one's mind] is liberated."[5]

Since it is unlikely that any of us have been worshipping fire, at least in this life, it would be useful to investigate how it is that we do experience the defilements as they arise. Is it as a burning, or a contraction, or a feeling of stress and unease? In these times, perhaps the Buddha would have called this talk "the Stress-Reduction Sermon."

Practicing with the Defilements

If we can recognize not only what the fetter is that arises with sense contact—that is, whether it is a form of greed or wanting, aversion or dislike, or a dull not-knowing—but also how we feel it energetically, this can help us notice the arising defilements more quickly. Feeling them directly in this way can motivate and inspire us to let them go, because we are actually experiencing the suffering of them. It is like holding on to a hot coal: once we're aware of the burning sensation, we don't need much prompting to drop it.

We can bring these instructions of the Buddha into our practice at whatever sense door is predominant. For example, when we're sitting and feeling the tactile sensations of the breath as it passes the nostrils, or the sensations of movement in the chest or abdomen, do we notice any resistance or any wanting? Sometimes the defilements, the fetters, are very obvious, and sometimes they are extremely subtle. There might be a slight holding or fixation of mind or a feeling of trying to push things along. There is an apt Taoist phrase: "Don't push the river." The breath, like the river, is flowing on fine by itself. But we are often trying to fix things, wanting to make things a little better.

There is a world of difference between the wanting mind, when there is a leaning into experience, and the true openness of nonpreference. This is not to say we suddenly stop making choices in our lives; rather, when we're mindful at the different sense doors, we can practice relaxing into a mind not conditioned by wanting, even if just for a few moments at a time.

In addition to investigating the arising of the fetters at the sense doors during sitting meditation, we can also notice them as they become predominant at different times during the day. There might be disturbing sounds or sights that stimulate desire or aversion, or the aromas of food as we're about to eat, or thoughts or fantasies that carry us away. Sometimes I imagine the different objects of the senses as having little hooks, and then I watch how often we get caught by them as they arise and pass away.

> "Forms, sounds, tastes, odours,
> Tactiles, and all mental objects:
> This is the terrible bait of the world
> With which the world is infatuated.
>
> "But when one has transcended this,
> The mindful disciple of the Buddha
> Shines radiantly like the sun,
> Having surmounted Mara's realm."[6]

So we know the eye, the visible forms, and the fetter that arises dependent on both; we know the ear and sounds, nose and smells, tongue and tastes, body and sensations, mind and mind objects and the fetters that arise dependent on them. It is exactly in these six sense spheres that we either get caught by desire or aversion or delusion, or remain free. This is why the Buddha gave such importance to understanding and being mindful of them.

24

The Wheel of Saṃsāra

WE WILL CONTINUE THIS EXPLORATION of the sense spheres with a focus on the last part of the instructions:

> "[A]nd one also knows how an unarisen fetter can arise, how an arisen fetter can be removed, and how a future arising of the removed fetter can be prevented."[1]

Here, we're not simply knowing the fetters that can arise, but also *how* they arise and how we can free ourselves from their influence. This requires a more careful look at the process unfolding in our bodies and minds and at the causes and conditions giving rise to the defilements.

This exploration is analogous to all scientific investigation. Some time ago, there was an article in *The New York Times* about the great advances in genetic research. It highlighted how the more precise the understanding of fundamental genetic processes, the more precise and pinpointed can be the cure for many diseases. In Buddhist texts, the Buddha is often referred to as "the Great Physician" because of his detailed understanding of the causes of suffering and its cure. This is the great gift of the teaching: although we all have to do the work, we don't have to figure it all out by ourselves. One well-known Buddhist chant reminds us of the various qualities of the Dharma: to be realized here and now, timeless, inviting us to come and see, onward leading, to be practiced by the wise.

DEPENDENT ORIGINATION

The teaching that most precisely pinpoints the origin and release from suffering is the profound analysis of what is called "dependent origination." This is sometimes referred to as the arising and passing away of the world. The usual description of dependent origination contains twelve links, beginning with ignorance and volitional activities, traditionally thought of as the past-life causes for our present rebirth. Here, though, the Buddha describes the links of conditioning in just this life that keep the defilements arising and thus keep the wheel of samsaric existence rolling along:

> "And what, monks, is the origin of the world? In dependence on the eye and forms, eye-consciousness arises. The meeting of the three is contact. With contact as condition, feeling [comes to be]; with feeling as condition, craving: with craving as condition, clinging; with clinging as condition, existence; with existence as condition, birth; with birth as condition, ageing-and-death, sorrow, lamentation, pain, dejection and despair come to be. This, monks, is the origin of the world."[2]

The links of dependent origination describe both the large cycles of birth, death, and rebirth through different realms of existence and, perhaps of more immediate applicability, the process governing our unfolding lives here and now. Since we have already taken birth, the sense spheres are a given. Then, dependent on the sense spheres, contact (the conjunction of the sense base, sense object, and consciousness) inevitably follows. With contact comes feeling, that "taste" of the object as being pleasant, unpleasant, or neutral.

Breaking the Chain of Dependent Arisings

Right here we are at the critical juncture. It is just at these links of sense spheres, contact, and feeling that the Buddha shows us the way out of suffering, shows us the door to freedom. When there is unwise attention given to contact and feeling, then our conditioned response to pleasant experience is desire; to unpleasant experience, aversion; and to neutral experience, dullness or delusion. But if we are mindful of contact and feeling, then we cut the chain of dependent arisings right there, and it doesn't lead on to the further links of desire, clinging, becoming, and the cycle of birth and death.

The question for us is how to put this into meaningful practice, so that it doesn't remain just an interesting idea. It's easy to forget that the Buddha is always pointing us back to our own direct experience of what creates suffering and how we can be free. We can be mindful of the sense spheres, contact, and feeling in different ways. We might simply notice the different sense objects as they arise: sights and sounds, smells and tastes, sensations and thoughts. Or we might emphasize the process of contact: seeing, hearing, smelling, tasting, touching, and thinking. This is the moment of sense base, sense object, and consciousness all coming together.

Sometimes we emphasize the knowing aspect and rest in the knowing. Here, there is less effortful directing of the mind to the object; rather, there is the practicing of a more receptive awareness, the ease of simply knowing whatever appears. Remember that in all situations, there are only six things happening—that is "the All" that was mentioned in the last chapter. To repeatedly notice the arisings in this way takes us out of the complexities of our life stories and into the simplicity of the moment's experience. Mindfulness here doesn't imply cutting off sense impressions and feelings, which in any event would be impossible, or trying to avoid them. Rather, mindfulness means simply being aware of what arises moment to moment.

If, as we're noticing the sense objects or the contact or just resting in the knowing, we find ourselves still getting caught up in reactions and the various fetters and defilements that keep arising, then it could be helpful to make a note of the feeling tone—"pleasant, pleasant," "unpleasant." The note could be either a soft mental label or just a precise noticing of these feelings.

Sometimes a double note—"contact, pleasant" or "contact, unpleasant"—helps to unhook the mind from its entanglement with the object. Including the note "contact" brings us directly in touch with the particular sense object, while the note "pleasant" or "unpleasant" reminds us to be mindful of the feeling, rather than unconsciously reactive to it.

Mindfulness of Desire

It all seems so simple: be mindful of the sense spheres, of contact, of feeling, and come to the end of suffering. But we all know that the long-established habits and tendencies of mind often speed us past these doorways of liberation. Many times we find ourselves already in the grip of desire before we awaken to what is happening. Fortunately, understanding the next links in this chain provide some back-up possibilities for freeing the mind.

Conditioned by feeling, desire arises. At this point, we can become mindful of the desire itself. This part of the practice is tremendously illuminating because here we are investigating one of the primal forces of life itself. "Desire" is the usual translation of the Pali word *taṇhā*, although we can also understand it as craving, hungering, or thirst. Its central importance is highlighted in the Buddha's song of enlightenment, which arose in his mind just after his awakening under the Bodhi tree. The last lines of this verse, which proclaims the liberated state, say, "Realized is the unconditioned, achieved is the end of craving."

We may not be at the point of proclaiming this for ourselves, but we can begin understanding the force of *taṇhā*, of desire, more clearly and experience the freedom of its end, even if only for a few moments at a time. One way to explore this in your practice is to notice when some simple desire arises in the mind. It might be a desire for a cup of tea, a piece of chocolate, or your next vacation. We can try to be mindful of the desire without getting lost in it, without pushing it away. We can feel the energy of wanting in the body. As we're being mindful of this desire, we may notice that, at some point, the desire disappears. Highlight that moment, because right there is an important insight into the impermanent nature of desire itself. We see that desires do not need to be gratified in order to be resolved. Like everything else, they arise and pass away by themselves.

Sometimes desire disappears and doesn't come back. At that time, at least for those moments, we have cut the chain of dependent arising. But at other times, it's as if the desire is lurking, just waiting for some moments of unwise attention to arise, and then it strengthens into the next link in the chain, which is clinging. At this point, things are getting more serious. This is our last chance before we are moved to act. But it is also a very interesting juncture in the mind.

We can notice the difference between desire and clinging. Desire is the wanting, the thirst for something. Clinging is the holding on to, grasping at either the object of desire or sometimes even the desire itself. I find I'm often less entranced by the actual object and more attached to the energy of wanting. I may be holding on to the thought of wanting something out of fear of not getting. At these times, it feels as if the object is secondary and that what is really happening is I'm trying to avoid a feeling of deprivation. So many seductive thoughts come into play here: "Why not have the second (or third) cookie? It will give me more energy," "Be good to yourself." These are ways by which we rationalize clinging rather than observing it.

Becoming familiar, experientially, in different ways with these links in the chain of dependent origination—sense spheres, contact, feeling, desire, and clinging—puts into practice the Buddha's instruction in the Satipaṭṭhāna Sutta: "[O]ne knows how an unarisen fetter can arise, how an arisen one can be removed, how an unarisen one can be prevented." Keep in mind that when the Buddha speaks about fetters or defilements, he is speaking about suffering, and so this practice is not something removed from our everyday life, but the key to peace and happiness.

THE CONDITIONED NATURE OF PERCEPTION

Anālayo, in his book *Satipaṭṭhāna: The Direct Path to Realization,* also points to another powerfully conditioned progression, beginning with the sense spheres and ending with all the complex entanglements of our mental projections. Understanding this progression is another way of applying the Buddha's instructions to know the arising, removal, and prevention of the fetters. In this sequence, contact at the sense spheres is the basis for feeling and perception. And it is the factor of perception that can then lead to conceptual proliferation. It is helpful to examine how all this happens and what it means for how we live our lives.

As discussed earlier, perception is the mental factor that interprets experience by recognizing and remembering the distinguishing features of an object. In the simplest examples, perception recognizes the differences between red and blue, hot and cold, man and woman. But there is one understanding here that is critical to our freedom:

perceptions are not absolutes; they are conditioned on many different levels. One of the great misconceptions we often carry throughout our lives is that our perceptions of ourselves and the world are basically accurate and true, that they reflect some stable, ultimate reality. This misconception leads to tremendous suffering, both globally and in our personal life situations.

What are some examples of the relative conditioned nature of perception? On one level, the way we see things is based on our karmic predispositions. What a vulture might see as a delectable meal, we would see as very unappetizing rotting flesh; same object, different perceptions. Cultural conditioning also influences how we perceive things. Think of all the violence in the Middle East. From one set of cultural values, suicide bombers are perceived as violent terrorists; from another set, as martyrs for a holy cause. The Buddhist scholar Rune Johansson wrote, "Things are seen through the lenses of our desires, prejudices, and resentments and are transformed accordingly."[3]

We can see the bias of our perceptions in more ordinary circumstances of our lives. Some years ago, I was involved in a highly charged organizational conflict. It seemed so obvious to me that I was seeing the situation clearly. Of course, those with opposing views thought the same thing. Communications were getting very heated, with feelings of anger and defensiveness running high. At a certain point, feeling my own suffering and that of others, I stepped back and asked myself a question that proved very freeing: *Why* do others feel the way they do? How are they perceiving the situation?

As soon as I was no longer caught in attachment to my own perception of things, I became less caught in judging and blaming, and it became much easier to understand other people's strong feelings. Bankei, a sixteenth-century Japanese Zen master, summed up this willingness to let go of *attachment* to our perceptions, knowing them to be relative and limited, when he said, "Don't side with yourself." Obviously, this doesn't mean that we simply let go of all our viewpoints, always surrendering to the ideas of others. Rather, that we see how all sides are conditioned and then bring as much wisdom as we can to determine the best course of action.

Our perceptions are also conditioned by the latent tendencies in the mind, the habitual projections that color how we view ourselves and the world. For example, a common perception in meditation is that a pleasant sitting is good and that a painful one is bad. Although we may know intellectually that this isn't true, this felt assessment comes from perceptions conditioned by the latent tendencies of desire and aversion. What makes the Buddha's understanding of the mind so powerful is the recognition that because perceptions are conditioned by our mental habits, we can also train our perceptions in a way that supports happiness and freedom.

The Four Hallucinations of Perception

The Buddha spoke of four great hallucinations of perceptions that keep us bound to the wheel of saṃsāra, the wheel of conditioned existence. He called them "hallucinations" because with respect to happiness and freedom, we perceive things erroneously, all the while thinking we are seeing them correctly. As a simple example of mistaken perceptions, during one retreat I was doing walking meditation outside in the parking lot of the center. There was a bird standing near the back bumper of a car, and seeing its reflection in the chrome bumper, it repeatedly flew into the bumper, thinking there was another bird there. How often do we fly into the mistaken perceptions of our lives?

What are the four important distortions of perception that the Buddha pointed to?

Taking What Is Impermanent to Be Permanent

First, we take what is impermanent to be permanent. Although our immediate reaction to this might be one of denial—"Of course I know things are impermanent"—knowing it intellectually, and even, at times, experientially is quite different from living and manifesting that understanding moment to moment.

A good feedback for when we're hallucinating in this way is the presence of attachment or clinging. When they are present, we are not seeing clearly and deeply the impermanent nature of what is arising. We're deluded into thinking a particular experience is worth holding on to. This is not to suggest that we close off to experience; rather, that we don't cling to it.

Taking What Is Unattractive to Be Attractive

The second hallucination of perception is taking what is unattractive to be attractive, the nonbeautiful to be beautiful. There are many examples of how we are beguiled by superficial appearances leading to erroneous perceptions. The basic mission of the immense cosmetic and advertising industries is to get us to perceive our human bodies as being more beautiful and perfect than they really are.

Understanding this hallucination of perception frees us to see things from various perspectives, using different skillful means to let go of clinging. This understanding does not mean that we dismiss the experience of beauty in our lives. There are many poems in the Pali suttas extolling the beauty of nature and the peace that can be found there. And the Buddha's teachings call all of the wholesome mind states beautiful, reflecting a deep appreciation of where true beauty resides. Rather, understanding this hallucination is a reminder to look more deeply when we find ourselves caught in attachment and lust for a beautiful form. The nonbeautiful aspect in these situations becomes more apparent when we take a closer look at the object or call to mind its changing nature and inevitable decay.

Taking What Is Unsatisfactory to Be Happiness

The third hallucination of perception is taking what is suffering or unsatisfying to be happiness. Most of what the world calls happiness is the enjoyment of sense pleasures. We spend so much time seeking the next hit of pleasant experience or working hard for some future pleasure. But since all pleasures are all impermanent, there is no end to the seeking. As the Sufi teaching figure Nazruddin said of eating burning hot chili peppers, "I keep waiting for a sweet one."

Sometimes we're enticed by a minor pleasure that hides a much greater suffering. We see this clearly with various harmful addictions, but in more ordinary ways as well. I recently saw some statistics about how much harm attending loud rock concerts or playing one's MP3s at too high a volume does to our hearing. For some reason, we take the damaging volume to be happiness.

In this hallucination of perception, we're often deluded into thinking that wanting itself is happiness. Have you experienced the idea that there is something you must have or must do, and then experienced an almost obsessive quality in the mind that ceases only when you either get it or the desire goes away? And all the while we think this is happiness, until that moment when we finally stop wanting and feel the relief and ease of that. And somewhat ironically, what the world calls suffering—renunciation, restraint at the sense doors, silence, simplicity, environments with few entertaining distractions—the Buddha calls happiness, because of the ease, open-heartedness, and peace of mind that they bring.

Seeing through this hallucination of perception, taking what is ultimately unsatisfying to be satisfying, is the basis for a great compassion to arise. It's said that after the Buddha's enlightenment, he was moved to teach by compassion, because he saw all beings seeking happiness, wanting happiness, yet doing the very things that caused suffering. And cutting through our own hallucinations can become the fuel for *bodhichitta,* the wish to awaken in order to help beings find a truer happiness.

Taking What Is Non-Self to Be Self

The last hallucination of perception is taking what is non-self to be self. We can see this happening many times a day. Notice how often we identify with sensations in the body or thoughts or emotions as being "I," as being "self." Or we identify with the knowing of all these experiences, creating the sense of self as the observer.

One of the most liberating aspects of the teachings is the reminder that because perceptions are the results of mental habits, they are also amenable to training. That teachings have the power to liberate should not be overlooked. The Buddha talked of two kinds of super-normal powers. There are the ones that we may have read about, such as flying through the air, seeing other realms of existence through the divine eye, and knowing the minds of others. Although for most of us these are beyond the range of our experience, there are personal accounts of them from some of our teachers. Although they may fascinate us, the Buddha did not give importance to such accomplishments. For those who are not enlightened, he said, these worldly powers are bound up with attachment and taints.

The second kind of supernormal powers are called "noble" ones, because they are not bound up with such defilements. The Buddha described these powers as mastery over one's perceptions. And this mastery comes through the power of mindfulness. As Anālayo writes:

> The presence of *sati* [mindfulness] directly counteracts automatic and unconscious ways of reacting that are so typical

of habits. By directing *sati* to the early stages of the perceptual process, one can train cognition and thereby reshape habitual patterns.[4]

TRAINING OUR PERCEPTIONS

As countermeasures to the hallucinations of perceptions, the Buddha recommended cultivating other ways of perceiving. And it is in this section of the Satipaṭṭhāna Sutta on mindfulness of the sense spheres that we can practice training our perception in more beneficial ways.

Anālayo points out that this training does not refer to a process of reflection or consideration, but only to awareness of a particular feature of an object, the experience of different objects from a particular point of view. For example, we can train ourselves to see the general characteristics of all experience—that is, their impermanent, unsatisfying, and selfless nature. Or we might train our perceptions in ways tailored to our own particular conditioning.

One monk in the Buddha's time was contemplating the nonbeautiful aspects of the body. He was diligent in his practice for many months, but wasn't making any progress in his meditation. The Buddha came to know of this, and through his divine eye, he saw that for many previous lifetimes this monk had been a goldsmith, highly attuned to beautiful things. So through his psychic powers, the Buddha created a beautiful golden lotus, which slowly underwent change and disintegration. And as the monk contemplated the impermanence of beauty, he soon became enlightened.

We can train our perceptions to see those characteristics of experience that balance our own particular unwholesome tendencies of mind. If, for example, there is a lot of aversion in the mind, if our tendency is toward annoyance, irritation, and ill will, we can train ourselves to perceive the good and beautiful qualities in others, which becomes the basis for mettā and loving feelings. Or if we're often lost in lust, then contemplating the unattractive aspects of the body will serve us. As noted previously, one whole section of the Satipaṭṭhāna Sutta is devoted to contemplating different stages of decaying corpses. The final training in this noble supernormal power of mastery over one's perceptions is abiding in equanimity, mindful and fully aware of whatever arises. In all of these ways of training perception, we are making choices out of wisdom rather than out of habitual reactivity.

REVISITING THE REFRAIN

As with all the other instructions in the sutta, the Buddha follows this section on the sense spheres with the refrain, emphasizing particular ways of developing this contemplation.

> "In this way, in regard to dhammas, one abides contemplating
> dhammas internally . . . externally . . . internally and externally.
> One abides contemplating the nature of arising . . . of passing
> away . . . of both arising and passing away in dhammas."

Contemplating internally, externally, and both internally and externally means that we notice how the sense spheres, and all the conditioning that follows from them, operate in ourselves, in others, and in both ourselves and others. The more we understand our own process of conditioning, how our perceptions are influenced and colored by deeply rooted habits of mind that are often unconsciously activated, the more we can understand how other people come to their own points of view. This is very different than being overly attached to our own opinions and way of seeing things. Meditation retreats are almost always humbling experiences because we get such a direct look at the range and depth of conditioning in our minds. As we open to this, there's a growing humility and generosity of heart.

So we pay attention to the sense spheres internally, externally, and both. We also contemplate the arising and passing away of experience in the six sense spheres. The easiest place to observe this is in the impermanence of the sense objects: sights and sounds, smells and tastes, sensations and thoughts. It takes a somewhat more refined attention to notice the impermanence of the sense bases themselves. Contemplating the arising and passing away of phenomena is the doorway to realizing the other characteristics as well. When we experience the impermanence of phenomena, internally or externally, we also understand their unsatisfying and selfless nature.

The Buddha then concludes the refrain:

> "Mindfulness that 'there are dhammas' is established in one
> to the extent necessary for bare knowledge and continuous
> mindfulness. And one abides independent, not clinging to
> anything in the world.

"That is how in regard to dhammas one abides contemplating dhammas in terms of the six internal and external sense-spheres."[5]

Mindfulness of Dhammas

The Seven Factors of Awakening

25

Mindfulness

THE NEXT SECTION OF THE Satipaṭṭhāna Sutta describes mindfulness of the seven factors of awakening. These qualities of mind are referred to as the seven treasures of a Tathāgata, the term used by Buddhas when speaking of themselves, and they are said to be unique to the teachings of a Buddha.

> "All those Arahant Buddhas of the past attained to supreme enlightenment by abandoning the five hindrances, defilements of mind which weaken understanding, having firmly established the four foundations of mindfulness in their minds, and realized the seven factors of awakening as they really are."[1]

The Buddha called these seven factors "antihindrances" because they counteract those forces in the mind that keep us in delusion. They are called "factors of awakening" because they incline the mind toward nibbāna, toward freedom. What are these seven factors? They are mindfulness, discrimination of states, energy, rapture, calm, concentration, and equanimity.

There is an entire section of the Samyutta Nikāya, the Connected Discourses, devoted to these seven links of awakening. A few excerpts from these texts will give some sense of the importance the Buddha placed on them:

"Bhikkhus, I do not see even one thing that, when developed and cultivated, leads to the abandoning of the things that fetter, so effectively as this: the seven factors of enlightenment."[2]

"Bhikkhus, the seven factors of enlightenment, when developed and cultivated, are noble and emancipating; they lead the one who acts upon them to the complete destruction of suffering."[3]

Then a certain bhikkhu approached the Blessed One . . . and said to him: "Venerable sir, it is said, 'an unwise dolt, an unwise dolt.' In what way, venerable sir, is one called 'an unwise dolt?'"

"Bhikkhus, it is because one has not developed and cultivated the seven factors of enlightenment that one is called 'an unwise dolt.'"

"Venerable sir, it is said, 'wise and alert, wise and alert.' In what way, venerable sir, is one called 'wise and alert?'"

"Bhikkhus, it is because one has developed and cultivated the seven factors of enlightenment that one is called 'wise and alert.'"[4]

The instructions in the Satipaṭṭhāna Sutta for contemplating these factors follow a format analogous to the one for contemplating the hindrances, except instead of abandoning them, one cultivates them.

"Again, monks, in regard to dhammas one abides contemplating dhammas in terms of the seven awakening factors. And how does one in regard to dhammas abide contemplating dhammas in terms of the seven awakening factors?

"Here, if the mindfulness [and all the others in turn] awakening factor is present, one knows 'there is the mindfulness awakening factor present in me'; if the mindfulness awakening factor is not present, one knows, 'there is no mindfulness awakening factor in me'; one knows how the unarisen mindfulness awakening factor can arise, and how the arisen mindfulness awakening factor can be perfected by development."[5]

How do we put these instructions into practice? The Buddha said that just as the dawn is the forerunner and precursor of the arising of the sun, so too, good friendship, association with the wise, and careful attention are the forerunners and precursors of the arising of the factors of enlightenment. This is where we start: hearing the teachings and paying attention. Many discourses teach that the four foundations of mindfulness, when developed and pursued, bring the factors of awakening to perfection. And, as we will see, these seven factors form a progression, each one leading to the next. So if we prime the pump of the enlightened mind and practice the first of the awakening factors, all the rest follow along.

Not surprisingly, the first of the factors of enlightenment, and the one that starts the wheel of awakening rolling, is mindfulness. In order to know whether, as the instructions of the sutta indicate, mindfulness is present or not, we first need to know what mindfulness actually is. As mentioned earlier, mindfulness is the translation of the Pali word *sati,* a word profoundly rich in meaning and application. *Sati* is derived from the root meaning "to remember," but its meaning goes far beyond our usual notion of memory.

THE FOUR QUALITIES OF MINDFULNESS

R. M. L. Gethin, a highly regarded contemporary Buddhist and Pali scholar, carefully analyzed all the ways *sati* is used in the suttas and the Abhidhamma, and he summed up the various expressions and manifestations of mindfulness in four basic applications. Although in its most general sense, mindfulness signifies attentiveness to the present, this attentiveness expresses itself in some very specific ways. And as we look at each one of these aspects of mindfulness, we can understand why it is the one factor of mind that is useful in every situation. While the other factors of enlightenment can be out of balance with one another, there can never be too much mindfulness. In fact, it serves to both bring about and balance all the other factors.

Not Forgetting

The first application of mindfulness is the quality of not forgetting, not losing what is before the mind in the present moment. Mindfulness stays firmly with the object without wobbling or drifting off. We could call this aspect "the stability of awareness" because it stays as steady as a post set firmly in the ground. It also serves to bring us back to the object each time we get lost, like a signpost. When the momentum of mindfulness is well developed, it works like a boomerang; even if we want to distract ourselves, the mind naturally rebounds to a state of awareness.

Presence of Mind

The second aspect of mindfulness is its quality of standing near the mind, which manifests as being face-to-face with whatever is arising, rather than giving it only sidelong glances. Directly facing what is arising guards the gates of the sense doors. In street parlance, we might say that by standing near, mindfulness is watching our backs—or perhaps more accurately, watching our fronts—so that we're not seduced by the show of passing phenomena. The Genjo Koan, a well-known teaching in the Zen tradition, says, "To carry yourself forward and experience myriad things is delusion. That myriad things come forth and experience themselves is awakening."

Remembering

The third aspect of *sati* is one that we don't often associate with mindfulness, but, in fact, it hearkens back to its root meaning of remembering. Here, mindfulness calls to mind, or remembers, what is skillful and what is not, what is inferior and what is refined, what is beneficial and what is harmful. It is this aspect of mindfulness that makes it possible to follow the Buddha's instruction to let go of and abandon what is unskillful and to develop and cultivate what is skillful.

Mindfulness thus becomes a key factor in strengthening our inner moral compass. If we don't remember and call to mind what is wholesome and what is not, then we simply toss about on the waves of habitual mind states, often acting out the latent tendencies of different defilements. This particular facet of mindfulness is closely related to the arising of two mental states the Buddha called "the guardians of the world." In Pali, they are called *hiri* and *ottappa*, often respectively translated as "moral shame" and "fear of wrongdoing," or sometimes as "self-respect" and "conscience."

These two factors are easily misinterpreted and therefore often ignored in our culture. But in so doing, we are discarding qualities that provide the basis for great beauty and strength in our lives. It's interesting to reflect on the English meanings of these two terms. In our complex cultural conditioning of race, class, and religion, shame and fear have often been used as vehicles and expressions of oppression. In these instances, we don't see shame or fear as particularly wise or compassionate mind states.

What, then, is the Buddha talking about when he calls *hiri* and *ottappa* the "guardians of the world"? In the Abhidhamma, these two states are universal beautiful factors of mind, meaning that they arise in every wholesome consciousness. Moral shame is the feeling of repugnance at bodily and verbal misconduct. We feel remorse and are ashamed of it. Fear of wrongdoing is a wise fear with respect to future consequences and to the opprobrium of the wise. They both manifest as a pulling back from the unwholesome.

A certain care is needed to appreciate the importance of the Buddha's teaching about these guardians of the world. It can be illuminating to notice what reactions we might have to them. We might have the notion that being free of what others think puts us in a greater place of openness or freedom. Or we might think that feeling shame about one's unskillful actions, either contemplated or already done, is not a psychologically healthy state.

Indeed, if we do not properly understand them, we could use some approximation of these qualities to bludgeon ourselves with guilt, recrimination, and feelings of unworthiness. On the other hand, we can hold them in the light of wisdom. In this beautiful manifestation, they arise out of mindfulness and a deep caring and respect for ourselves and others. This understanding manifests as holding a standard of behavior that can inspire restraint at critical moments or renewal in the many times we fall short. In all of these situations, it is the power of mindfulness that calls to mind, that remembers, whether an action is indeed beneficial or not.

On one retreat, I had a vivid experience of the power of *hiri* and *ottappa*. I had been sitting for some time, and my mind started getting seduced by a very enjoyable but somewhat unwholesome fantasy. I was mindful enough to know that it was happening and to know that it was unwholesome, but even noting it wasn't enough for me to abandon the grasping and simply let the fantasy dissolve into the flow of empty phenomena. After seeing it come up repeatedly over quite a few days, I wondered what would finally unhook my mind.

Suddenly, *hiri* and *ottappa* came to the rescue, like reinforcements from the rear that turn the tide of battle. I began imagining having actually done the action of the fantasy and began envisioning it then coming to the attention of friends, colleagues, and teachers. Like magic, a feeling of wise shame immediately arose and the desirability factor of the fantasy completely disappeared. It was like waking up from a dream. My mind again felt clear and open and balanced, much freer than when I was caught by the enchantment of the desire.

How much suffering arises for ourselves and others when we don't understand the wise practice of these two guardians? Verse 67 from the Dhammapada encapsulates this understanding: "No deed is good that one regrets having done."

It is important to remember that very few of us have totally perfected our actions. We will get seduced many times. But having a reference point of understanding can inspire us to simply begin again. A counterintuitive but very helpful teaching is that it is better to do an unwholesome deed knowing it is unwholesome than to do it without that knowing. If we don't even know that something is unwholesome, then there is no motivation to change. But in knowing that something is unwholesome, even as we might be doing it, then the seeds of wisdom and future restraint are there.

Close Association with Wisdom

The last aspect of mindfulness is its close association with wisdom. This comes about through bare attention and clear comprehension. The quality of bare attention can manifest on different levels and is called different things in the various Buddhist traditions: mindfulness, naked awareness, innate wakefulness. It is naked and bare because it is simple, direct, noninterfering, and nonjudging. It's not making up stories about experience; it's just the simple awareness of things as they are. A wonderful haiku by Basho captures this quality of mind: "The old pond / A frog jumps in / Plop."

We can bring this simplicity to our meditation practice. Munindra-ji would often say, "Sit and know you're sitting, and the whole of the Dharma will be revealed." But sometimes in our practice we're looking for something special, and so we miss this simplicity and overlook what is right in front of us. The power and strength of bare attention come not from special experiences but from a sustained continuity of awareness. We're not looking for any particular experience, for the breath or the body to be a special way. Rather, we're simply listening to, being aware of, and receiving the contact of whatever presents itself. It's like listening to a new piece of music when we're relaxed and attentive at the same time. It's not hard to be mindful; it just takes training to remember to be mindful.

The other aspect of mindfulness, closely associated with wisdom and conducive to its arising, is called "clear comprehension." This means seeing something precisely, thoroughly, from all sides. Clear comprehension broadens the practice of bare attention from a narrow focus to one that sees things in context.

Chapter 9: Mindfulness of Activities discussed in some detail the four aspects of clear comprehension: knowing the purpose or motivation of an action, knowing the suitability of the action, knowing the proper domain for mindfulness, and understanding nondelusion. This last aspect reveals an essential element of our practice: while mindfulness is present in every wholesome mind state, the wisdom factor of mind (nondelusion) is not always present. And this salient understanding highlights the importance of using the power of mindfulness in the service of wisdom. As Sayadaw U Tejaniya has emphasized, "awareness alone is not enough." For mindfulness to function as a factor of awakening, it has to be the springboard for investigation. When mindfulness brings us face-to-face with the object, what do we learn?

It is this investigative aspect of nondelusion that is the direct link to the next of the factors of awakening, the wisdom factor of mind called "discrimination of states."

26

Investigation of Dhammas

THE PALI TERM FOR THE second factor of awakening is *dhammavicaya,* which is the wisdom factor of mind. *Dhammavicaya* has been translated in various ways: "discrimination of states," "investigation of truth," or "discerning the Dhamma." We might think of this awakening factor of mind as that which discerns and illuminates the truth by means of discriminating wisdom. As one teacher expressed it, it is "knowing what's what."

> When a bhikkhu, dwelling mindful in this way, discriminates, inspects, applies investigation by means of wisdom . . . , then the awakening factor of dhamma-discrimination is instigated for that bhikkhu.[1]

And it is precisely this investigating factor or activity of mind that awakens us from ignorance.

There is a wonderful commentary on the Buddha's teachings called *The Questions of King Milinda.* Milinda was a Greek king of ancient Bactria, a land in what is now Afghanistan and that was a legacy of Alexander the Great's Asian empire. Like other educated Greeks of his time, Milinda was well versed in philosophical debate, and it was said that as a disputant, the king was hard to overcome. The Buddhist monks in his realm complained that the king constantly harassed them with questions and counterquestions, with arguments and counterarguments. So they finally went to the arahant monk Nagasena and requested that he go to the king and subdue him. Nagasena replied:

> Never mind just this one king. If all the kings of India would come to see me with their questions, I could well dispose of them and they would give no more trouble after that. You may return to the capital without any fear whatever.[2]

The Questions of King Milinda is an account of the dialogues between Nagasena and the king, and many of the questions raised in the book are the same ones that we might ask today. Nagasena's replies are always illuminating. In one of the dialogues, the king asks by how many of the factors of enlightenment does one actually awaken. Nagasena replies that awakening is by means of just one, this factor of investigation of dhammas. So why then, the king asks, does the Buddha speak of seven factors of awakening? Answers Nagasena:

> "Does a sword placed in its sheath and not grasped in the hand succeed in cutting what needs to be cut? In exactly the same way, Your Majesty, one cannot awaken by means of the awakening-factor of dhamma-discrimination without the [other] six awakening factors."[3]

Although the other six factors of awakening are needed to unsheathe and wield the sword of wisdom, it is this factor of discrimination of states that cuts through ignorance and delusion and liberates the mind. As Krishnamurti said, "It is the truth that liberates, not your efforts to be free." As with all the factors of enlightenment, the instructions in the sutta are to know whether this quality of discernment is present or not, and how it can be developed and cultivated. In fact, the entire Satipaṭṭhāna Sutta is a map guiding us in this investigation. But in all cases, our investigation is in the service of wisdom, comprehending things as they really are.

CULTIVATING INVESTIGATION

There are many ways to cultivate and develop this factor of discernment, and different Buddhist traditions may emphasize one method or another for awakening wisdom within us. But, as Bhikkhu Bodhi points out, "the initial function of wisdom as an enlightenment factor is to discriminate between the wholesome and unwholesome mental states that become apparent with the deepening of mindfulness."[4]

Discerning What Is Skillful and What Is Not

The last chapter described one function of mindfulness as remembering and calling to mind what is skillful and what is not. Mindfulness brings us face-to-face with these arising states; the wisdom factor of investigation then illuminates the states themselves and discerns the difference between the two. This is not an academic exercise. The wisdom factor in our minds is like an investigative reporter who digs deep to get to the bottom of things—in this case, understanding the very causes of our suffering and their end.

The Buddha helps us with this discernment when he points out that unwholesome actions of body, speech, and mind are all rooted in greed, hatred, or delusion, and that all wholesome states are rooted in their opposites. It takes honesty and openness to cultivate this factor of investigation in our lives, to see clearly the different motivations that arise in the course of a day. As a simple example, notice your mind state as you're about to sit down for a meal. Are you as settled back as when you're doing walking meditation or listening to a sound, or is there a slight toppling forward in desire and anticipation? You can check to see what the attitude of the mind is at that moment. Or you might investigate your motivations before speaking. Are they coming from a mind state of lovingkindness, of self-reference, or of anger and ill will? It's important not to bring reactive judgments to these discernments, or if we do, to be aware of them. We are practicing in order to see things as they are and to make wise decisions based on that understanding.

Sometimes there is a rapid alternation of motivations. We need to be watchful both to see what is going on and to distinguish what is wholesome from what is not. On one retreat, I was reflecting on the awakened qualities of the Buddha, particularly the aspect of a mind free of any grasping or clinging. I started imagining what it would be like to simply abide in that state, and then I thought, "Why not just do it?" It clearly feels better to not want than to be lost in desire and craving. We all know this from our own experience, even if it is a short-lived realization.

As I was inspiring myself with these wholesome reflections on the Buddha and the possibility of living in greater freedom, my mind suddenly went to thoughts about my favorite meditation sweatshirt—so comfy—and then wishing I had a few of them in different colors. In a flash, I'd gone from an inspiring and motivating reflection on the free and nongrasping mind of the Buddha to being seduced by, and momentarily believing, that several colored sweatshirts were the key to happiness.

In the above scenario, we can see the importance of the first two factors of enlightenment come into play. At some point, the watchman named "mindfulness" became aware of all the sweatshirt thoughts. And then the factor of investigation looked to see what defilements of mind were feeding them. The first was the simple desire for that comfy, cozy sweatshirt feeling. But in addition, I could also see the defilement of conceit, which in Buddhism has a very specific meaning. Conceit is that factor of "I was this, I am this, I will be this," and then, at times, compares this sense of self with others—better than, worse than, equal to. In this case, even though I was already on a meditation retreat, I was projecting a sense of self, and what that self would be wearing, into future retreats. At this point, I made the conceit factor into a little cartoon character named Was-Am Will-Be, which became an effective note every time I saw conceit arise. Then the liberating power of this awakening factor of discerning the Dhamma revealed itself in seeing the selfless nature of all these self-related thoughts.

Recognizing Habit Patterns of Suffering

Truth-discerning wisdom also comes into play when we find ourselves caught in major storms of afflictive emotions or simply acting out basic personality tendencies. In these situations, Ajahn Chaa's reminder that there are two kinds of suffering—one that leads to more suffering and one that leads to its end—can prompt the arising of discernment of dhamma. Instead of getting lost in and acting out habitual patterns of suffering, in times of emotional turbulence, we can first investigate what is actually going on—that is, the nature of the emotion itself—and then see how we are relating to that emotion. Are we claiming it as being "I" or "mine"?

Sometimes the simple act of clear recognition is enough to come to a place of acceptance and letting go. Instead of being tossed about in a storm of undifferentiated emotions, we can begin to discern whether our emotion is fear or loneliness, boredom or unhappiness. Clarity of discernment through investigation of dhammas can bring acceptance because we are aligning ourselves accurately with the present-moment experience. It is a way of acknowledging, "Yes, this is what's here." From this place of acceptance, we can then see more clearly the impermanent, selfless nature of the emotion and free ourselves from identifying with it: letting go by letting be.

Seeing Personality as Not Self

Investigation of the Dhamma also reveals a lot about our basic personality structure. The Buddhist commentaries describe three basic personality types, each with a positive and negative aspect. The greedy or desirous type mostly sees what it likes, what it wants. Through wisdom, this quality is transformed into faith and devotion, where there is a movement toward the wholesome. Aversive types typically see what is wrong with their world and with everyone in it. In its positive transformation, aversion becomes discriminating intelligence. And deluded types generally don't notice much of anything. But in its enlightened aspect, delusion transforms into great equanimity.

The value of such a personality template is that by recognizing our own patterns and those of others, we begin to understand them all as being impersonal, simply as the playing out of habitual tendencies, rather than as the expression of some reified sense of self. They become less of an unconscious prison and more the playground of transformation.

Understanding the Nature of Thought

One of the most freeing aspects of investigating the mind comes from examining our thoughts. Mostly we are lost in the movies of our minds and not even aware of the fact that we're thinking. But as we become more mindful of thought as an object of awareness, we begin to notice *what* we're thinking, and then, on a deeper level, wisdom sees the very ephemeral, impermanent nature of thought itself. Dilgo Khyentse Rinpoche points to the freedom that's possible with this understanding:

> When a rainbow appears we see many beautiful colors—yet
> a rainbow is not something we can clothe ourselves with, or

wear as an ornament; it simply appears through the conjunction of various conditions. Thoughts arise in the mind in just the same way. They have no tangible reality or intrinsic existence at all. There is therefore no logical reason why thoughts should have so much power over us, nor any reason why we should be enslaved by them. . . .

Once we recognize that thoughts are empty, the mind will no longer have the power to deceive us. But as long as we take our deluded thoughts as real, they will continue to torment us mercilessly, as they have been doing throughout countless past lives.[5]

Exploring the Processes of Mind and Body

With strong mindfulness as the foundation, the enlightenment factor of investigation also explores the basic nature of this mind and body, focusing more on the momentary process than on any particular content. The Buddha spoke often of how seeing this process clearly is the doorway to freedom:

"When one perceives impermanence, the perception of non-self is stabilized. One who perceives non-self eradicates the conceit 'I am,' [which is] nibbāna in this very life."[6]

As mentioned in earlier chapters, we see that what we call "self" is simply the pairwise progression of knowing and object. And at different stages of practice we have increasingly refined perceptions of this progression, seeing the rapid rising and passing away of all phenomena. Direct experience of impermanence on this level reveals the inherently unsatisfying and selfless nature of all conditioned arisings. This is beautifully expressed in a famous verse from the Diamond Sutra, one of the great teachings in the Mahayana tradition, capturing in just a few words the essence of this factor of awakening: "Thus you should think of this fleeting world: A star at dawn, a bubble in a stream; a flash of lightning in a summer cloud, a flickering lamp, a phantom and a dream."

Through the wisdom arising from investigation, we become inspired to make efforts to fully actualize it. And this inspiration becomes the basis for the cultivation of *viriya,* or energy, the next awakening factor.

27

Energy

THE THIRD FACTOR OF ENLIGHTENMENT is energy. We can understand the progression of these factors, with one leading to the next, through these words of the Buddha:

> Abiding thus mindful [of body, feelings, mind, and categories of experience—the four satipaṭṭhānas], one investigates and examines that state with wisdom, and embarks upon a full inquiry into it.
>
> In one who investigates and examines that state with wisdom and embarks upon a full inquiry into it, tireless energy is aroused. On whatever occasion tireless energy is aroused . . . on that occasion the energy enlightenment factor is aroused . . . ; and one develops it, and by development it comes to fulfillment.[1]

Energy (*viriya,* in Pali) is the root of all accomplishment, and in this way, it is in direct opposition to sloth and torpor. Although it seems obvious that energy is needed to bring any endeavor to completion, how we understand this quality of mind and how we apply it can determine whether it is the source of joyful interest, which is the next factor of awakening, or the source of frustration and discouragement.

In the Abhidhamma, energy is called a "variable mental factor," which means that it can be associated with either wholesome or unwholesome states. It's not difficult to see that people use their energy for many different ends, sometimes for good, sometimes for harm. But on a subtler level, even when there is a wholesome purpose, we need to investigate whether we are applying this factor of energy in a skillful or unskillful way.

ENERGY AS THE POWER TO DO

We can get a sense of the many nuances of *viriya* from the different ways this Pali term has been translated into English. It has been translated variously as "energy," "effort," "strength," "courage," "vigor," "perseverance," and "persistence." Each one of these words points to a different facet of the Pali term. In its most basic meaning of "energy," *viriya* is the capacity for activity, the power to do something. This energetic capacity, the power to do, manifests in a variety of ways.

Strength

One function of energy is to shore things up, like reinforcing a levee in times of flood. In *The Questions of King Milinda,* Nagasena describes *viriya* this way:

> Just as, Your Majesty, someone might shore up a house that
> was falling down with an extra piece of wood, and thus being
> shored up, that house would not fall down. Even so, Your
> Majesty, *viriya* has the characteristic of shoring up; shored up
> by *viriya*, no skillful dhammas are lost.[2]

The Buddha emphasized this aspect very clearly in the Dhammapada when he said that when we practice, wisdom grows; and when we don't practice, it wanes. It is precisely the factor of energy that keeps us on a trajectory of awakening, where no skillful dhammas are lost.

It is in this shoring up of wholesome states that *viriya* also manifests as strength.

> And what is the faculty of strength? Here, the noble dis-
> ciple dwells as one who has produced strength; for the sake
> of abandoning unskillful dhammas and arousing skillful

dhammas one is firm, of steady valor, un-relinquishing in purpose with regard to skillful dhammas.[3]

In both these teachings, there is a channeling of energy for the development of wholesome states of mind. The Buddha is highlighting the importance of this power, the capacity to act, and encouraging and exhorting us to use it in the service of freedom.

Courage

Another aspect of *viriya,* one that we might not immediately associate with energy and strength, is that of courage. This is a quality that powerfully energizes our heart as we walk on the path. While the nature of sloth and torpor is to retreat from difficulties, the nature of courage is the opposite. Courage is energized by challenges; it is inspired by difficult tasks and even seeks them out. When courage is present, we rise to meet different challenges for the sake of what we want to accomplish, and we're not discouraged by thought of hardship or by the length of the undertaking. When still a bodhisattva striving for Buddhahood, Siddhartha made the following well-known resolve:

> Let only my skin, and sinews, and bones remain, and let my flesh and blood in the body dry up, I shall not permit the course of my effort to stop until I win that which may be won by human ability, human effort and human exertion.[4]

We may read this and think, "Yes, that kind of courageous determination is fine for a Buddha-to-be, but it seems very far away from anything I could do." And although we may not yet have the Bodhisattva's level of resolve, still there are many examples of people exercising great valor and courage in pursuit of their goals.

Charles Stevenson, IT manager at the Insight Meditation Society, told me a story illustrating many of the facets of *viriya.* Before coming to the meditation center, he had served in the army and at one point volunteered to run a marathon with a full thirty-five-pound pack on his back. And much of the course was run in desert sands. When I asked him why he would ever want to volunteer for such an endeavor, he replied that he wanted to face and test his mind in extreme circumstances. In retelling the story, he said that at mile thirteen, he very much wanted to stop and take one of the accompanying all-terrain vehicles back to a rest area, and that there were many beguiling thoughts urging him to do that. But, somehow, he called on reserves of energy, strength, and courage, and finished the race. This is the quality of *viriya*. It shores up one's determination, gives strength to the mind, and faces difficulties with courage. And perhaps what was most remarkable to me, he signed up to run the race again the following year.

We also often see this factor of courageous energy in the work of people in the front lines of social action. Think back to the beginning of the civil rights movement in this country. I remember seeing film clips of Martin Luther King, Jr. leading freedom marches in both the North and the South, surrounded by people filled with hatred and violence. Yet in the face of all that, King inspired the nation with his commitment to nonviolence and love.

These stories inspire me because we don't often challenge ourselves to extend our limits, to really see what is possible, especially when doing so is uncomfortable or difficult. As the Burmese meditation master Sayadaw U Tejaniya remarked:

> Avoiding difficult situations or running away from them does not usually take much skill or effort. But doing so prevents you from testing your own limits and from growing. The ability to face difficulties can be crucial for your growth. However, if you are faced with a situation in which the difficulties are simply overwhelming, you should step back for the time being and wait until you have built up enough strength to deal with it skillfully.[5]

BALANCING THE QUALITY OF EFFORT

Understanding different nuances of *viriya*—energy, strength, courage—brings us to the thorny problem of understanding the relationship between all of these qualities and effort. What is effort? When is it balanced? When is it counterproductive? Effort is an expenditure of energy to accomplish some objective. But the word *effort* in English has so many connotations that we need to carefully examine its skillful application in practice. To do that, we will first look at its unskillful application.

Effort can become unskillful when there is a forcing of mind—what I call "efforting"—rather than a relaxation of mind. Effort becomes unskillful when there's some idea of gain and a mind full of expectations, rather than an openness and receptivity to what is already there.

I had a long and challenging experience with the misuse of effort early on in my practice. I had been meditating in India for several years, and at a certain point, the energy system in the body opened into an effortless flow of light. It was easy to sit for hours at a time, and I was thoroughly enjoying this time in practice. However, circumstances dictated my return to the States for several months, and during that time, I was often anticipating my return to India and my "body of light." But when I did get back to Bodh Gaya and resumed intensive meditation practice, what I experienced was not a body of light, but what felt like a body of twisted steel. Although clearly conditions had changed, for two years I struggled to get back that pleasant flow of energy. They were among the most difficult years of my practice, as I was always wanting something other than what was there.

Finally, after all that time, I let go of the wanting and settled back—with acceptance—into what was presenting itself. And although the body of light didn't return in the same way, there was an easeful flow of phenomena arising and passing in each moment. I realized that I had been dragging around the corpse of previous experience, trying to reclaim something that had changed and passed.

The lesson here is that we need to be mindful of *how* we're making effort. If there is a strong agenda—the "in-order-to" mind I've spoken of—being aware in order for something in particular to happen, or if we're holding on to the object too tightly, afraid that we'll lose it, then we need to open and relax the mind, softening the quality of our effort. On the other hand, if the mind is continually drifting off and there is no effort to investigate what is going on, then we need to strengthen this effort factor.

This doesn't mean that we somehow find the perfect balance and then always remain in it. The cultivation of *viriya* is a very refined art. We always need to see the present circumstance, then understand it with wisdom—"Is the mind too tight? Is it too loose?"—and then make the proper adjustment. In describing the art of right effort, the Buddha used the example of tuning the strings of a lute. If the strings are either too tight or too loose, we can't produce beautiful sounds. So from time to time we need to tune the instrument of our minds, paying attention to the quality of our efforts.

The Cycle of Effort and Energy in Our Practice

In exploring this energy factor of enlightenment, it is helpful to see how effort creates energy. Usually we think that we need energy in order to make effort, and that if we're feeling low energy, we simply need to rest. And at times that may be the case. But think of times when you're feeling low energy and then you make the effort to engage in some physical exercise or some mental challenge. It's surprising how often and how quickly this effort energizes and renews you.

On meditation retreats, we can experience these energy cycles many times a day. Once we understand the different aspects of *viriya,* we can work with them in a variety of skillful ways. At times, we might want to emphasize the courageous side of *viriya,* seeing where we limit ourselves and becoming inspired to play at the edges of our comfort zone. This might mean sitting a little longer than we're used to or resolving not to move or change posture while we're sitting. It might mean doing some longer walking periods or following the eight precepts, which includes not eating after noon, rather than the basic five. It is important that these be done with the qualities of interest, willingness, and the courage to explore. It is not a question of "should" or right and wrong.

On the other side, if the mind feels too tight, if there is too much efforting and we're filled with self-judgment, then the softer side of *viriya* can be cultivated. These are the aspects of perseverance and constancy. We understand that our minds are always with us and that we can train ourselves to be aware of whatever we're doing, paying attention to our minds as we go through the day. In this situation, we see that by opening and relaxing, we're making the space for a very natural energy to arise.

THE CAUSES FOR ENERGY TO ARISE

It's easy to understand the need to cultivate energy in order to accomplish any of our goals and aspirations. But what are the causes for energy to arise, and what inspires us to then channel energy as a factor of awakening—that is, to use our energy to abandon what is unwholesome and to develop and bring to perfection all the skillful states of mind?

Spiritual Urgency

The proximate cause for the arising of *viriya* as a factor of enlightenment is the feeling of spiritual urgency. The Buddha talked of attending to these awakening factors as a matter of vital concern and not simply as something to do in our off-hours.

There are some powerful reflections that remind us of this urgency. We can reflect on the preciousness of our present circumstances. Whether we think of it in the context of many lives or just in this life, we can see and appreciate how rare it is for all the conditions to come together in order for us to hear the Dharma, and, even more so, for us to have the interest, motivation, and opportunity to practice. We often think that conditions will always be favorable, but any look at the world around us reveals the truth of uncertainty—from war and violence to natural disasters, to our own ageing bodies. Wise reflection on the uncertainty of conditions heightens the appreciation of our present circumstances and thus becomes the cause for the arousal of energy.

Reflecting on death is another powerful reminder to use the time of our lives in a way that benefits ourselves and others. Each day, life just gets shorter; day-by-day, life is running out. Can we hold this truth in our awareness as a way of arousing spiritual urgency? Does it inspire us? Does it frighten us? The Buddha would often exhort the bhikkhus, "There are trees and the roots of trees. Meditate now lest you regret it later."

We can also reflect that the end of all accumulation is dispersion and look to see what we spend so much time accumulating. It might be wealth and possessions, or people and relationships, or projects and great works. Although all of these things might be of some benefit, the great Indian adept Shāntideva reminds us, "And fix this firmly in your understanding: all that may be wished for will by nature fade to nothing."[6]

This understanding leads to the powerful recollection that the only abiding possession is the fruit of our karma. By virtue of our past wholesome actions, we all have the amazing good fortune of being on a treasure island—that is, our precious human birth. It is an island of treasures because all the causes of happiness are present. It is a place where there is an opportunity to practice the Dharma. The Buddha summed up these possibilities in one short, pithy teaching: "Refrain from what is unwholesome, do good, purify the mind. This is the teaching of all the Buddhas."

Reflecting on Saṃsāra

We can further inspire *viriya* by reflecting on the defects of saṃsāra. One meaning of *saṃsāra* is "perpetual wandering." According to the Buddha's teaching, driven by the forces of our own karma, our wholesome and unwholesome actions, we wander through all the realms of experience, from the lowest to the highest, and back again, much like a bee buzzing around in a jar. We can see this process even within one day. How many different mind worlds have we lived in today, for shorter or longer periods of time? We might have imagined ourselves with friends or family or gotten lost in plans for the future. We might have inhabited worlds of happiness or sadness, anxiety or excitation, calm or restlessness. All of this is the play of the mind. When we're identified with the play, we are lost in the wanderings of saṃsāra.

Notice carefully the moments of coming out of long trains of thought. It's like coming out of a movie theater. When we're lost in the story, it all seems so real, yet all of it is just another transparent movie of the mind. What frees us from these endless cycles is the heroic power of *viriya*. We arouse the energy to be mindful of the flow of changing phenomena, rather than being lost in and carried away by it. We step out of our conditioned patterns to cut through, to see through, the fundamental knot of self. These reflections on our own precious human birth, on the uncertainty of conditions, on the inevitability of death, on the defects of saṃsāra, and on the possibilities of liberation all arouse the factor of courageous energy, and it, in turn, becomes the basis, the root, the foundation of all accomplishment.

28

Rapture

THE FOURTH OF THE SEVEN factors of awakening is called, in Pali, *pīti*. This word has been translated in many ways, including "rapture," "happiness," "joy," "delight," and "pleasurable or rapt interest." Reflect for a moment on your felt sense of what these words suggest. *Pīti* has the function of refreshing and delighting the mind and body, like a cool breeze on a hot day. Because rapture directly opposes ill will and is incompatible with it, when the mind is filled with *pīti,* there's no room for anger or ill will to arise.

In order to clarify our understanding of this factor of awakening, it's helpful to distinguish *pīti* from a state often associated with it—a state that, in Pali, is called *sukha. Sukha* is also often translated as "joy" or "happiness," which can be confusing. As our practice deepens, the distinctions between these two states of mind become clearer, but for now, I'll mention just a couple of features of each.

On the conceptual level, *sukha* belongs to the second aggregate of feelings—namely, pleasant ones—while *pīti* belongs to the fourth aggregate of mental formations. Rapture usually has an intense energetic quality of arousal and excited anticipation. It's the anticipation that arises when we're crossing a hot desert and suddenly see a cool and refreshing oasis. Sometimes, though, the energy of *pīti* can be so intense that if our bodies are not sufficiently open, it can become uncomfortable. *Sukha,* or happiness, on the other hand, is a softer and more refined experience of comfort and wellbeing. *Sukha* arises when we actually arrive at the oasis and feel the ease of relief.

Just as the Buddha distinguished between worldly and unworldly pleasant feelings in the second foundation of mindfulness, discussed in earlier chapters, here too, there is a distinction between rapture associated with sense pleasures and unworldly rapture born from seclusion and renunciation. Seclusion and renunciation here refer both to external conditions and, perhaps more importantly, to the seclusion of mind when the hindrances, those factors that trouble and disturb the mind, are overcome.

When we are considering rapture as a factor of enlightenment, it is the unworldly type of rapture that contributes to our awakening. The Buddha said in the Ānāpānasati Sutta (the discourse on mindfulness of breathing) that rapture is born from tireless energy, energy comes from investigation and inquiry, and this discerning wisdom arises from continuous mindfulness. Right here, we see the lawful progression of the factors of awakening.

THE FIVE GRADES OF RAPTURE

How do we recognize when rapture is present? How do we experience it, and how can it be cultivated?

The Buddha spoke of five grades or levels of rapture. The first is called "minor rapture." When this is present, there is a lifting of the spine, and we can hold the posture effortlessly. There might be feelings of goose bumps or a trembling of the body.

The second is called "momentary rapture," which is felt as a sudden jolt of energy, like a flash of lightning. It might feel like when an elevator we're in suddenly makes a short drop. At one point in my practice, I was doing lying-down meditation, and as a jolt of this momentary rapture became strong, I was suddenly thrust into an upright position.

The third kind of *pīti* is called "wavelike or showering rapture." This manifests as thrilling kinds of sensations coming over the body again and again, like waves lapping the shore. Sometimes, with each wave, the feeling of rapture becomes stronger and stronger.

The fourth kind is "uplifting rapture." When this kind of *pīti* is present, it feels like the whole body has risen up into the air and is no longer touching the ground. It's as if we are seated on a cushion of air or floating up and down. I reported one kind of experience like this to Sayadaw U Paṇḍita, saying that it felt like I was on a magic carpet. Because he likes meditation reports to be accurate descriptions of what is actually being felt in terms of the body elements, and not so interested in our poetic descriptions of it, his only comment to me was, "Have you ever been on a magic carpet?" His comment did help to deflate my unnoticed attachment to this pleasant state. Another manifestation of this kind of rapture can happen in walking meditation, when we might feel we are sinking into the earth or walking on an elastic rubber membrane.

In the Buddhist texts, there are many stories of people levitating in the air. Although this may be outside the range of our own experience, according to the teachings and from actual accounts of advanced yogis, this can happen either as a spontaneous manifestation or through mastery of this uplifting rapture. During a three-month retreat at the Insight Meditation Society, one meditator reported to me that as he was doing lying-down meditation in his room, he felt his body actually rise a couple of inches off the bed. I didn't know whether it was just a perception of floating or if it really happened, so in the end I just said, "Did you note it?"

The fifth kind of *pīti* is called "pervading rapture." Mahasi Sayadaw described it this way: "a sublime feeling of happiness and exhilaration filling the whole body with an exceedingly sweet and subtle thrill."

These different kinds of rapture and joy develop in our practice when there is a strong momentum of mindfulness and the five spiritual factors are all in balance. At that time, the practice seems to be going on by itself, and the mind is filled with tremendous confidence and energy. We are seeing and understanding how things arise and pass away very quickly, and this wisdom and effortless energy fills the mind with an intense, pleasurable interest. At these times, there is often a spreading luminosity in the mind, and some meditators can see things in the dark or remember things from long ago.

The Imperfections of Insight

When all of these wholesome states have been strengthened through practice and are now manifesting in our experience, they are working on their own, expressing their own nature. But there is also a hidden danger in these wonderful states of mind. Our mind can become so elated and excited by what it is seeing and how it feels that we can lose sight of right understanding. This is when we can get caught up in what are called the "corruptions" or "imperfections" of insight. Having been forewarned that this might happen, almost everyone thinks, "I won't get fooled by these states," and yet almost everyone does for a shorter or longer period of time. This vipassanā happiness can be so strong that we begin to think, "Now I've got it. Finally, I understand what this meditation is all about. This is how my practice will be from now on." Or we become convinced that no one else has ever experienced such states before—not our fellow meditators, not even our teachers.

We can become so exhilarated by the rapture and the other awakening factors that we take this experience to be nibbāna, the ultimate peace. One text describes it this way: "When insight is adorned with these qualities, attachment arises which is subtle and peaceful, and it clings to that insight and is not able to discern the attachment as being a defilement."

In one story, the arahant monk Dhammadinnā wondered whether his own teacher, the elder MahaNaga, had brought his work to completion or not. Through his eye of wisdom, he saw that his teacher was still an ordinary man, and he knew that if he did not go to him, his teacher would die an ordinary man. So Dhammadinnā rose up into the air with supernormal power and alighted near the elder, who was sitting in his daytime quarters. As the story goes, he paid homage to MahaNaga and sat down to one side.

> "Why have you come unexpectedly, friend Dhammadinnā?" . . .
> "I have come to ask a question, venerable sir." "Ask friend. If we know, we shall say." He [Dhammadinnā] asked a thousand questions.
>
> The Elder replied without hesitation to each one. To the remark "Your knowledge is very keen, venerable sir. When was this state attained by you?" he replied, "Sixty years ago, friend."—"Do you practice concentration, venerable sir?"—"That is not difficult, friend."—"Then make an elephant, venerable sir." The Elder made an elephant all white. "Now, venerable sir, make that elephant come straight at you with his ears outstretched, his tail extended, putting his trunk in his mouth and making a horrible trumpeting."

The Elder did so. Seeing the frightful aspect of the rapidly approaching elephant, he sprang up and made to run away. Then the Elder with cankers destroyed [Dhammadinnā] put out his hand, and catching him by the hem of his robe, said, "Venerable sir, is there any timidity in one whose cankers are destroyed?"

Then he recognized that he was still an ordinary man. He knelt at Dhammadinnā's feet and said, "Help me, friend Dhammadinnā."—"Venerable sir, I will help you; that is why I have come. Do not worry." Then he expounded a meditation subject to him. The Elder took the meditation subject and went up on to the walk, and with the third footstep he reached Arahantship.[1]

UNDERSTANDING AND WORKING WITH RAPTURE

So on the one hand, we need to cultivate rapture and all the other factors of awakening; on the other hand, we need to know how to work with them skillfully so we don't become attached to these pleasant meditative experiences, or we need to learn how to recognize the attachment itself. Here is where we need to bring right understanding and investigative wisdom into play. We understand that all these states are impermanent and selfless, that they don't belong to anyone. They are all conditioned by various causes and simply arise expressing their own nature. This wise understanding points us in the right direction at this very critical juncture in practice. This stage of insight is called "understanding what is the path and what is not."

How do we come to this understanding? Whenever we feel one of the manifestations of rapture, it is important to recognize it for what it is. We might feel it in the body, as momentary, wavelike, or pervading pleasurable feelings. Or we might experience it as a heightened interest and delight in the mind. Recognizing these experiences of rapture, we then look at the mind's relationship to them. Are we relating to them with wrong view: "This is mine; it has arisen in me"? Are we relating to them with conceit: "This is who I am"? Or are we relating through craving: "I like this. I want it to continue"? We might think we're not doing any of these things, yet one clue to their presence might be a sense of disappointment or longing when the rapture fades or disappears.

CAUSES FOR THE ARISING OF RAPTURE

Sometimes, in hearing the teachings, with all of the many lists and categories, we might feel them to be dry and analytical. But as we put them all into practice, the feelings of happiness, contentment, joy, and wellbeing begin to gradually pervade our lives. Suzuki Roshi, the founder of the San Francisco Zen Center, describes this development in his book *Zen Mind, Beginners Mind:*

> It is not like going out in a shower in which you know when you get wet. In a fog, you do not know you are getting wet, but as you keep walking you get wet little by little. If your mind has ideas of progress, you may say, "Oh, this pace is terrible!" But actually it is not. When you get wet in a fog it is very difficult to dry yourself.[2]

Rapture arises when there is a strong momentum of mindfulness. It arises out of a delight in clear seeing, a delight in knowing. There can be this dhamma delight even in an exploration of the hindrances or different defilements, as we come to a deeper understanding of them. Sayadaw U Tejaniya emphasizes this aspect in his teachings: "You should be happy when you know or understand anything."

For example, what happens when we investigate boredom or disinterest in the practice? These states seem the very opposite of *pīti*. But when we take interest in the boredom itself, we discover something of immense value. We see that boredom does not have anything to do with the object; it simply has to do with the quality of our attention. When our attention is half-hearted, when we're "more-or-less mindful," then there is disinterest, whatever the experience might be. As Fritz Perls, the founder of Gestalt psychology, said, "Boredom is lack of attention." So instead of seeing boredom or disinterest as a problem, we begin to take it as feedback. Instead of struggling with what is arising, we step back and simply ask ourselves, "What is the mind knowing?" and then bring our attention in close to whatever it is.

Suzuki Roshi described this process clearly:

> We say, "Pulling out the weeds we give nourishment to the plant." We pull the weeds and bury them near the plant to

give it nourishment. So even though you have some difficulty in your practice, even though you have some waves while you are sitting, those waves themselves will help you. So you should not be bothered by your mind. You should rather be grateful for the weeds, because eventually they will enrich your practice.[3]

WAYS TO STRENGTHEN RAPTURE

The Buddha spoke of different reflections that can strengthen the enlightenment factor of rapture.

Reflect on the Buddha, Dhamma, and Sangha

Reflecting on these three jewels with a mind that is concentrated has a tremendous power to uplift the mind and inspire our practice. There are many ways of practicing these reflections. In Buddhist cultures, whether in Asia or in the West, one of the most common chants heard in temples is the Homage to the Buddha, Dhamma, and Sangha. It's particularly beautiful to hear it in Pali, but this English translation will give some sense of the inspiration that can come from it:

> Such indeed is the Exalted One, worthy, perfectly enlight-
> ened, endowed with knowledge and conduct, well-gone,
> knower of the worlds, supreme trainer of persons to be
> tamed, teacher of gods and humans, enlightened and exalted.
>   Well expounded is the Dhamma by the Exalted One,
> directly visible, unaffected by time, calling one to come and
> see, leading onwards, to be realized by the wise.
>   The order of the Exalted One's disciples is practicing well;
> . . . is of upright conduct; . . . has entered the right path; . . .
> is practicing correctly . . . is worthy of gifts and salutation,
> supreme field of merit for the world.

Another kind of reflection can happen when we take refuge. When I take refuge before a meditation period, I express it in this way: "I take refuge in the Buddha and the awakened mind. I take refuge in the Dharma and the noble path. I take refuge in the Sangha of realized beings. By the merit of generosity and the other *paramitas* (perfections), may my heart and mind be purified of all defilements and may I quickly attain liberation for the welfare and benefit of all beings." Every time I do this, I am reminding myself of what each of the refuges actually means, of what is necessary for purification, of the actual goal of practice, and of the motivation of *bodhichitta*. And at the end of the sitting, I will dedicate the merit to the welfare, happiness, and awakening of all. We can each find for ourselves the words that inspire us and develop strength and rapture in our hearts and minds.

Contemplate Sīla

Another reflection that gives rise to rapture is the contemplation of our sīla, our moral virtue. We might call it a reflection on our commitment to nonharming. For laypeople, this commitment is usually expressed in terms of the five or eight precepts.

Reflecting on our sīla can take different forms. First, we recognize the beauty and power in those moments of restraint from unwholesome actions. What is the quality of our mind when we protect life rather than destroy it—when we take an insect outside rather than killing it? Can we pay attention to the feeling of empowerment that arises when we refrain from some kind of harmful or useless speech, or when we act with integrity in situations where that might be in conflict with our desires? At all these times, we can recognize the feeling in the mind as we make choices that are in accord with our values, feeling the qualities of great interest and joy in the Dhamma.

A second reflection on sīla is looking back over our lives, particularly from the time we consciously commit to wise action, and appreciating the fact that we are directing our lives in this way. In one verse of the Dhammapada, the Buddha says, "Happiness is virtue lasting through old age." Remember that the practice of sīla involves training, not commandments, and that even after lapses we can retake the precepts and begin again. This enables us to appreciate all the times we have lived by this commitment to nonharming, and it also allows us to learn from those times that we haven't.

Reflect on Acts of Generosity

Another reflection that brings joy and rapture to the mind is remembering and delighting in our acts of generosity. Sometimes this is not easy for Westerners to do, because we might confuse this wholesome recollection with pride or conceit. But just as it's possible to have a feeling of loving appreciation for the generosity of others, we can have this same feeling for our own generous actions. One striking example of this happens regularly at some of the meditation monasteries in Asia. Laypeople will often come to the monasteries to offer food to the meditators and then sit in the dining hall as the yogis are eating, delighting in the offering.

As an experiment, think back over particular generous acts you've done, remembering the initial thoughts of giving, how you felt in the moment of the offering, and the reflections afterwards. How did you feel then? How do you feel now in remembering? This recollection on generosity gladdens the heart and is the cause for rapture to arise. In remembering skillful actions of both sīla and generosity, we have the inner sense of and feeling expressed by the Pali word *sadhu*, which means "well done." *Sadhu* is often said three times after one has performed or witnessed a wholesome action.

Reflect on the Devas

Reflecting on devas, those beings in higher realms of existence, can also give rise to rapture in the mind. These are beings with bodies of light and who enjoy many kinds of heavenly delights. Remember that in the Buddhist understanding, these beings are not gods or angels who live in realms of eternal reward. Although they enjoy many kinds of bliss during their deva lifespan, they are still on the wheel of conditioned existence.

When the Buddha would first meet people, he would often give them a graduated discourse, beginning with the happiness of generosity and sīla, and then talking of the delights of the deva worlds as a way of brightening and uplifting the mind. Then, when people's minds were open, pliable, and receptive, he would give those teachings that liberate the mind from all conditioned existence.

While for some people starting with the highest teachings might free the mind, we shouldn't ignore the various skillful means that help us on the path of awakening. A traditional reflection on devas that can bring delight and joy to the mind is reflecting that these beings have been people who possessed those good qualities that brought them rebirth in the deva worlds, and that these same qualities are in all of us. Of course, many people in the West may not believe in other realms of existence, and so this particular reflection might not be effective for them. When I first went to practice in Bodh Gaya, Munindra-ji would delight in telling us about these realms, especially since he had trained Dipa Ma in the power to explore them herself. He would always end his descriptions by saying, "There's no need to believe this. It's true, but you don't have to believe it."

Reflect on Peace

The last of the reflections that can bring about *pīti*, or dhamma joy, is the reflection on peace, the subsiding of the mental defilements. Notice the quality of peace when the mind is free of the hindrances or defilements. This is particularly noticeable when the mind comes out of some mental drama. It might be a lustful fantasy, some bout of annoyance or ill will, or maybe just quick moments of desire or irritation. We can bring understanding to these states, how we get caught up in them and how release from them happens, and then begin to taste what is called "momentary freedom." Reflecting on this quality of peace inspires us with what's possible in our lives.

Reflection on peace also refers to nibbāna. Although we may not yet have realized nibbāna for ourselves, even reflecting on how the Buddha described it can arouse interest and joy in the mind. Some people have gotten enlightened just hearing the words the Buddha used to point to and remind us of this highest happiness: *the unborn, the undying, the peaceful, the deathless, the serene, the wonderful, the amazing, the unailing, the unafflicted, dispassion, purity, freedom.*

It is this fourth factor of awakening, rapture, that fills us with a joy in the Dhamma and inspires us to fulfill this great journey. Although there is the potential for rapture to become an imperfection of insight because of our attachment to it, this interest-arousing factor plays an important role both in the first two states of concentrated absorption and as one of the essential factors of awakening. As the Buddhist scholar Rupert Gethin points out, it is rapture, or dhamma happiness, and the next awakening factor of calm that are at the heart of the positive emotional effects of the path.

29

Calm

IN DISCUSSING THE SEVEN FACTORS of enlightenment, we might reflect on how rare it is in spiritual teachings to have such a clear understanding of the precise qualities that lead to awakening. This understanding takes our journey out of the realm of mysticism, unquestioning faith, or accident and into the realm of how the mind works: what conditions create suffering and what qualities lead to freedom.

The Buddha taught how each one of these enlightenment factors arises naturally out of the preceding one in a chain of sequential development. Recall how mindfulness is the underlying condition for all those to follow. When there is a continuity and momentum of awareness, a face-to-face encounter with experience, then we're present enough to investigate and understand what is going on. This is investigation of dhammas, the second factor of awakening.

Investigation of dhammas is the wisdom aspect of the mind, and it means both directly experiencing the nature of phenomena and seeing how this experience correlates with the broad scope of the Buddha's teaching. For example, through mindfulness and investigation, we begin to see and realize for ourselves what are skillful mind states and what are not. Here, we are no longer working from book knowledge, but rather the wisdom of our own experience.

As a result of this investigation and understanding, the enlightenment factors of energy and rapture naturally flow. Having seen clearly what is wholesome and what is not, we're motivated to arouse the energy, the strength and courage, to develop the former and abandon the latter. We can see a simple but powerful expression of this motivation in our own lives when we actively engage with the five precepts. Following the precepts is a decision, a commitment, to refrain from certain things we know to be harmful to others or ourselves. We arouse the energy to undertake this training based on our understanding. And contrary to possible apprehensions that this will be burdensome and difficult, we often find it to be just the opposite.

The strength and energy of our commitment to the precepts bring a feeling of joy and confidence. We're no longer so carried away by old habits, no longer continually wavering about actions we know are unskillful but still continue to do. Based on mindfulness and investigation, *viriya,* or energy, steadfastly plants the flag of sīla. As His Holiness the Sixteenth Gyalwa Karmapa said, "If you have one hundred per cent dedication and confidence in the teachings, then every living situation can be part of the practice. You can be living the practice, instead of just doing it."[1]

The enlightenment factor of rapture is born from the freedom from remorse that comes from practicing the precepts of nonharming, and the increasing momentum of awareness that comes from sustained, balanced energy. Rapture is the quality of intense interest, and it arises from a close and caring attention to whatever is arising. It is just the opposite of boredom, which is a lack of attention; so when we're feeling bored or disinterested, that feeling itself is a very useful feedback that our attention has become halfhearted. In *The Manuals of Buddhism,* Ledi Sayadaw, the great Burmese meditation master and scholar, wrote, "Rapture is the joy and happiness that appears when the power of seeing and knowing increases." At one time, Ānanda asked about the rewards and blessings of practice:

> "What, Venerable One, is the reward and blessing of wholesome morality?" "Freedom from remorse, Ānanda." "And of freedom from remorse?" "Joy, Ānanda." "And what is the reward and blessing of joy?" "Rapture, Ānanda." "And of rapture?" "Tranquility, Ānanda."[2]

The Buddha goes on to say that these states arise naturally, one from the other.

THE QUALITIES OF CALM

This brings us to the next factor in the unfolding sequence. It is one that plays a crucial and powerful role on the path of liberation, yet it is often overlooked or underemphasized in our practice. This is the enlightenment factor of calm or tranquility. The Pali word for this factor, *passaddhi,* can be translated as "calm," "tranquility," "serenity," or "composure." It is the soothing factor of mind that quiets the disturbances. It manifests as peacefulness or coolness in both the mind and body. It is what a tired worker feels upon sitting down in the cool shade of a tree on a sweltering day, or what a child feels when her mother lays a cool, soothing hand on her feverish forehead.

Passaddhi encompasses both physical composure and mental tranquility. It is this quality of calm that keeps the mind composed and unruffled in times of difficulty. Buddhist psychology describes how it brings along with it other wholesome states, such as lightness, wieldiness, proficiency, and sincerity. While the first three of these associated states seem obvious concomitants of calm, it is interesting to reflect on the last. Why does calm bring sincerity? When our minds are tranquil, a natural genuineness, honesty, and freedom from duplicity are also present.

In meditation teachings, we sometimes hear of the danger of becoming attached to this wonderfully calming, peaceful state of mind. When we first touch this space of tranquility in our meditation, there is a profound sense of relaxation, relief, and ease, especially as we contrast it with the speed and distractedness of our daily lives, and with the difficulties and struggles we sometimes experience in practice. The tranquility can be so enticing that we might start practicing only for the calm, becoming attached to it and identified with it, and forget that it, too, is a constructed state. We can easily sink into the enjoyment of it and forget to bring mindfulness to it.

Although this is an important caution, the Buddha clearly emphasized the importance of calm in the list of the awakening factors. The happiness of a tranquil mind plays a key role in the path of awakening. Here, the instructions on the factors of enlightenment, found in the Satipaṭṭhāna Sutta, provide crucial guidance:

If the tranquility awakening factor [or any of the others] is present [in him], one knows, "the tranquility awakening factor is present in me"; if the tranquility awakening factor is not present [in him], one knows "there is no tranquility awakening factor present in me." One knows how the unarisen tranquility factor can arise, and how the arisen tranquility factor can be perfected by development.[3]

It is mindfulness that knows whether tranquility is present or not. And investigation, energy, and interest—what we might call "meditative intelligence"—lead onward to its development and fullness, but without becoming identified with or ensnared by it.

WAYS TO DEVELOP CALM

How, then, do we develop and perfect this beautiful, peaceful state? The Buddha gave general instructions for the development of all the awakening factors and then specific ones for the cultivation of calm and each of the other factors:

"Bhikkhus, as to internal factors, I do not see any other factor that is so helpful for the arising of the seven factors of enlightenment as this: careful attention. When a bhikkhu is accomplished in careful attention, it is to be expected that the seven factors of enlightenment will be developed and cultivated.

"Bhikkhus, as to external factors, I do not see any other factor that is so helpful for the arising of the seven factors of enlightenment as this: good friendship. When a bhikkhu is accomplished in good friendship, it is to be expected that the seven factors of enlightenment will be developed and cultivated."[4]

We have good friends in the Buddha and his teachings. They point us first to the awareness of the enlightenment factors and then encourage us to frequently pay wise attention to them.

Mindfulness of Breathing

In one of the first set of instructions in the Satipaṭṭhāna Sutta discussed in chapter 7: Mindfulness of Breathing, the Buddha outlines a simple four-step progression. First, breathing in and out, one knows one is breathing in and out. Second, breathing in long or short breaths, one knows one is breathing in long or short breaths. Third, one trains breathing in and out, experiencing the whole body. And fourth, one trains breathing in and out, calming the bodily formations.

There are some different interpretations of whether "the whole body" and "bodily formations" refer just to the whole body of the breath felt at one place or the breath as it moves through the physical body. As one example, Ledi Sayadaw explains these instructions in this way:

> In the third stage, when the perception of the long and short out-breaths and in-breaths has been mastered, every breath occurring within the body must be experienced in its entirety, right from its starting point within the body through its middle to the point where it ends within the body, the extremities of the breath (start or end as the case may be) being at the tip of the nose and at the navel.
>
> In the fourth stage . . . the coarse or rough breaths must be calmed down and allayed by degrees, making them more and more gentle and delicate, until ultimately the stage is reached when one thinks that one's out-breaths and in-breaths have entirely disappeared.[5]

We can experiment for ourselves, finding what comes most easily and naturally. At the beginning of a sitting, it might be helpful to do a few body scans, relaxing each part of the body. Then, as we let the attention settle on either the breath or whole-body awareness, we can prompt the development of calm with these words in the mind: "Breathing in, calm the breath; breathing out, calm the breath," or, "Calm the bodily formations." Or we might simply use the word *calm* or *calming* with each breath. (Also see chapter 7: Mindfulness of Breathing.)

Settling Back into Experience

There is often a subtle, or not so subtle, striving or efforting even with something as simple as the breath. Repeatedly reminding ourselves to relax, to calm the formations of body and mind, actually brings about a letting go, a settling back into a more tranquil state, free of wanting, of getting. We can then give wise attention to this experience of calm. The Buddha said that frequently giving attention to calm is the nutriment for the arising and fulfillment of this factor of enlightenment.

We can also practice tranquility as we move about. Notice the feeling of rushing, which can happen even in moving slowly, and notice what characterizes that experience. We find that we're slightly ahead of ourselves, energetically toppling forward. Rushing is a kind of energetic excitability that doesn't allow for the ease and composure of a tranquil mind.

We can use the simple phrase "When walking, just walk" to remind us to settle back into the moment, without efforting or striving, without wanting some state or leaning into a destination. We can just feel the simplicity of each movement, moment after moment: when walking, just walk. This same reminder can be extended to any activity: When standing, just stand. When seeing, just see.

THE ROLE OF CALM ON THE PATH TO AWAKENING

As we recognize and pay attention to the experience of calm, we begin to understand the role this enlightenment factor of tranquility plays in the larger context of awakening. In one discourse, the Buddha said,

> "These two qualities have a share in clear knowing. Which two? Tranquility (*samatha*) and insight (*vipassanā*).
> "When tranquility is developed, what purpose does it serve? The mind is developed. And when the mind is developed, what purpose does it serve? Passion is abandoned.
> "When insight is developed, what purpose does it serve? Discernment is developed. And when discernment is developed, what purpose does it serve? Ignorance is abandoned."[6]

Observe how in moments of calm and composure, the mind is free of desire, of wanting, and free of the restlessness and subtle agitation that characterize those states.

When the mind is tranquil, free of desire, even temporarily, a kind of happiness and ease arise that are subtler and more refined than the joy of rapture, which can be a little excitable. And it is this happiness of tranquility that, in turn, becomes the conditioning factor for concentration and liberating wisdom.

"And what, Venerable One, is the reward and blessing of tranquility?" "Happiness, Ānanda." "And of happiness?" "Concentration, Ānanda." "What, Venerable One, is the reward and blessing of concentration?" "Vision and knowledge according to reality." "And of vision and knowledge according to reality?" "Turning away and detachment, Ānanda." "And of turning away and detachment?" "The vision and knowledge with regard to deliverance, Ānanda."[7]

Although the Buddha laid out this progression so clearly, the enlightenment factor of calm is frequently overshadowed by its jazzier neighbors, rapture and concentration. In looking back at my own practice, I have seen that I often give more emphasis to the development of concentration; however, this is sometimes accompanied by a kind of striving and efforting that actually get in the way. In my efforts to concentrate, I was sometimes unknowingly practicing desire and the wanting mind, which are exactly what hinder concentration. It is worth remembering that the quality of calm has the precise function of cooling out this desiring mind: as tranquility develops, desire is abandoned. And it is this tranquility that allows for concentration, the next factor of awakening, to naturally arise.

30

Concentration

IN THE PARINIBBĀNA SUTTA, THE discourse describing the last days of the Buddha's life, the Buddha lays out what are called "the thirty-seven principles of enlightenment." They are called that because, according to Ledi Sayadaw in his *Manual of Factors Leading to Enlightenment,* they are the proximate causes, the requisite ingredients, and the sufficing conditions for awakening. In the thirty-seven principles of enlightenment, concentration appears four different times—as a spiritual faculty, a spiritual power, a factor of awakening, and as the last step of the Noble Eightfold Path. Clearly, concentration is one of the key players on this path of awakening.

THE TWO ACTIVITIES OF THE MIND
The Pali word for concentration is *samādhi,* and it refers to two different but related activities of mind: the mental factor of one-pointedness and the meditative states of concentration.

The Mental Factor of One-Pointedness
One-pointedness serves to unify all the different factors of mind on a single object or on moment-to-moment changing objects. When one-pointedness is strong, we are undistracted, and we feel this nondistractedness as peace both in our meditation practice and in our lives.

It is interesting to note that in the Abhidhamma, one-pointedness is a common factor, which means that it arises, at least to some degree, in every moment of consciousness. If there were no concentration or one-pointedness at all, we would never be able to connect with an object. But even though some degree of one-pointedness is always present in order for us to know anything, this factor of mind is often weak and unstable. The Buddha described this familiar condition in one verse of the Dhammapada, saying, "The mind, hard to control, flighty, alighting where it wishes, one does well to tame. The well-trained mind brings happiness."

Most of us can probably relate to the flighty mind, alighting where it will. How often do we get caught up in trains of associated thought before we even realize that we're thinking? But it is important to remember that the mind can be trained, and the factor of concentration can be strengthened through skillful practice. The Pali word for meditation is *bhāvanā,* and it literally means "causing to be developed." Just as our bodies get stronger through physical training, concentration gets stronger through mental development.

Buddhist texts describe two types of concentration that help settle the flighty mind. The first is fixed-object concentration. This is when we keep the mind steady on a single subject. There are forty traditional subjects, including the breath, the *brahmavihāras, kasinas* or colored discs, thirty-two parts of the body, the Buddha, the Dharma, the Sangha, generosity, morality, peace, and so on. This type of single-subject meditation can lead to different levels of meditative absorption, known in Pali as the *jhānas.*

A strong one-pointedness directed to changing objects moment after moment leads to momentary concentration, the second type of samādhi. When there is continuity of mindfulness, this momentary samādhi remains steady, and as it strengthens over time, we begin to feel a natural, easeful momentum in practice. This kind of one-pointedness does not lead to absorption, but it is the basis for different vipassanā insights.

The Meditative States of Concentration

The second meaning of *samādhi* is more general and refers to the whole range of meditative states of concentration. This more general meaning is not limited simply to the factor of one-pointedness, but also includes other associated factors of deepening concentration—factors such as rapture or calm, happiness or equanimity.

JHĀNA AND THE FOUR DEVELOPMENTS OF CONCENTRATION

In understanding the enlightenment factor of concentration, there is one more term to explore: *jhāna*. The term literally means "to meditate," and it is used to describe different levels of samādhi. Buddhaghosa, the great Buddhist commentator of the fifth century, describes *jhāna* as having the characteristic of contemplation—contemplation of a single object, which leads to the states of absorption, and contemplation of the characteristics of phenomena, which is concentration leading to meditative insights. These stages of insight are sometimes called *vipassanā jhānas.*

Over the last years, there has been a growing interest in the West in the practice of absorption. Not surprisingly, though, different teachers have quite different views on what these states are and the best way to develop them. Some of the differences have to do with what depth of absorption actually constitutes *jhāna,* and whether one loses all awareness of the body and physical senses in these states, or there is still awareness of subtle body energies. Some teachers emphasize the development of a *nimitta,* a mental sign or image, as the object of jhanic concentration, others not. Some say insight can be developed while one is in *jhāna,* and others say that one needs to come out of the absorption to contemplate the changing nature of phenomena.

Although there are these varied views about what the Buddha meant when he repeatedly emphasized the development of *jhāna,* all agree that deepening states of concentration, of unification, of steadiness and nondistractedness of mind, are skillful in themselves and necessary supports for the development of wisdom. As the Buddha said in the Connected Discourses, "For one who is concentrated, one knows and sees things as they really are."

In one discourse, the Buddha described four developments of concentration, and each one, in turn, answers the question of why this factor is so important.

Pleasant Abiding

The first development of concentration, as the first *jhāna,* leads to a pleasant abiding here and now, what the Buddha called "a blameless kind of happiness." In the Bodhisattva's own quest for enlightenment, after spending six years practicing intense physical austerities and still not finding the way, he remembered sitting as a young boy in the shade of a rose-apple tree, watching a ploughing ceremony, and spontaneously entering into the first *jhāna*. He realized that this happy, concentrated state was not something to be feared, as it is secluded from the hindrances and can be the basis for awakening.

Knowledge and Vision

The second development of concentration leads to the attainment of what is called "knowledge and vision." This refers to the special power of the divine eye, which, along with the other supernormal powers, can be developed based on the fourth *jhāna*. Although this power may seem far away from our own experience, there are people in these times who have these attainments. Our teacher, Dipa Ma, was accomplished in both *jhāna* and vipassanā and demonstrated these abilities to her own teacher, Munindra-ji.

But we also need to recognize the danger of these powerful states when they arise without wisdom. In the Buddha's time, his cousin, Devadatta, was filled with pride about these attainments, and it led him to perform many unwholesome actions. And in Tibet, there is the famous story of Milarepa, who developed these powers to exact revenge on his relatives for stealing his inheritance and condemning his family to penury. Afterward, he regretted using his powers in this way and then went in search of his teacher, Marpa, thus embarking on his great journey of awakening.

Insight and Wisdom

The third development of concentration leads us into the realm of insight and wisdom. The Buddha here describes using the concentrated mind in the service of clear comprehension, so that "feelings are known as they arise, persist and pass away; perceptions are known as they arise, persist and pass away; thoughts are known as they arise, persist and pass away." Without the steadiness of concentration, it is easy to get caught up in the feelings, perceptions, and thoughts as they arise. We take them to be self and get carried away by trains of association and reactivity. Notice the profound difference between being aware of a thought and being lost in it. It is the power of concentration that keeps the defilements at bay, so that we can see clearly what it is that is going on.

Uprooting the Defilements

The fourth development of concentration leads to the ending and uprooting of the defilements, the culmination of the path, by remaining focused on the arising and falling away of all the aggregates. This is concentration in the service of wisdom.

MOMENTARY CONCENTRATION AND ABSORPTION

These last two developments of concentration express the meaning of *jhāna* as contemplating the characteristics of phenomena and not simply abiding in an absorbed state. These insight practices of seeing the rise and fall of all phenomena can be done either with strong momentary concentration (vipassanā) or by using the meditative absorption (*jhāna*) as the basis for deeper investigation. Sayadaw U Paṇḍita described the relative power of these two methods. Momentary concentration is like swimming across a lake; absorption is like being carried across in a motorboat. Although both methods serve to get us across, the journey is quicker and more enjoyable for those who have a boat.

Sometimes, however, depending on one's own particular background and affinity for deep absorption, it might take less time to swim to the other shore than to build the boat. As we become stronger swimmers, we can develop enough strength to bring us all the way to final liberation. In the texts, this is called "the path of dry insight"—that is, without jhanic attainment. At one point, someone came to a group of arahant monks, asking if they had attained the *jhāna* of the meditative absorptions. They replied, "We are contemplatives, dry insight meditators, liberated by wisdom alone." In this example, through the jhanic motorboat might be better called "dry insight," and the journey of the swimmers called "wet insight."

One Form Does Not Exclude the Other

As we hear about these different ways of practice and try to determine the methods best suited for ourselves, it's helpful to remember that it's not an either-or situation or that one way excludes the other. At different times, one or another approach might be appropriate.

When I first went to India and began practice with Munindra-ji, for the first couple of days, I had a little light appear in my mind. Since he had just come back from Burma, where he had trained Dipa Ma, he might have thought I had some potential for samādhi and so told me to just concentrate on the light. At that time, I had not meditated intensively at all, and I had no training in vipassanā or any idea of how to work with the hindrances. It was all pretty hopeless. As I tried to focus on the light, I just got more and more frustrated and discouraged. After a short time, Munindra-ji understood what was happening and switched me back to mindfulness practice.

As I started vipassanā, at first I had no concentration at all; I would sit and simply think for an hour. Although it wasn't really meditating, it was very pleasant, and the hour went by pretty quickly. Then, as I began to be more mindful and make a little more effort, slowly I came to understand the hindrances better, and the mind didn't wander quite as much. But it still felt like a struggle, always trying to bring the mind back. Although I had a strong commitment and no doubt in the practice, it wasn't all that much fun.

On my second trip to Bodh Gaya, about six months after my first time there, I asked Munindra-ji about doing mettā practice. I felt that lovingkindness was a quality that I could well strengthen in my life. Although the noisy conditions in India were not ideal for concentration practice, Munindra-ji gave me the instructions to begin. As it had been in vipassanā, the beginning was quite difficult. But after about a month, my mind settled more deeply into the mettā phrases, and I began to get my first taste of a somewhat concentrated mind. It wasn't any particularly high or exalted state, but it was enough for me to understand why people actually enjoy the practice. When the mind begins to settle, everything seems to flow along by itself, and the meditation becomes much easier.

It's important to remember that concentration, like all other mental and physical experiences, is a constructed, conditioned state, impermanent like everything else. This means that the strength of concentration can and will wax and wane at different times. This is natural. But the more we practice, whether it's the momentary concentration of vipassanā or the absorption *jhānas* of fixed-object concentration, we establish a base of steadiness and strength underneath all the changes.

WAYS TO AROUSE CONCENTRATION

What is so powerful about the Buddha's teachings is that he lays out the path of practice step-by-step. He doesn't just talk about some ultimate destination; he tells us how to actually get there.

Know When Concentration Is Present and When It Is Not

The first step in developing concentration is having the confidence that we can do it. Although a very few people, like Dipa Ma, have a naturally concentrated mind, for most of us, it is a question of patience and perseverance, taking one step, one breath, at a time. As we do this, concentration and the other awakening factors gradually grow and mature. The Buddha's instructions in the Satipaṭṭhāna Sutta point out the way:

> If the concentration awakening factor is present in one, he knows "There is the concentration awakening factor in me"; if the concentration awakening factor is not present in one, one knows "There is no concentration awakening factor in me"; one knows how the unarisen concentration awakening factor can arise, and how the arisen concentration awakening factor can be perfected by development.[1]

So we begin by simply being mindful of whether concentration is present or not. The Buddha, here, doesn't say anything about judging oneself or the practice. Rather, it is the clear discernment of the present condition of mind. Then, based on that assessment, we can practice arousing samādhi if it is not present and developing it further if it is.

Reflect on Your Sīla

In many places, the Buddha taught that the foundation for concentration is sīla, or ethical conduct, and that if there is no virtue, the basis for concentration is destroyed. We might read this, reflect that we're basically moral people, that we more or less follow the precepts, and then move on to great visions of absorption, supernormal powers, and full enlightenment.

But it is helpful to examine more fully how all of this works. Why is morality the basis for concentration, and how can we refine this understanding in our lives? As mentioned in earlier chapters, sīla is the cause for nonremorse, nonremorse the condition for happiness, happiness the cause for concentration, and concentration the condition for liberating wisdom. We can see how this cycle and its opposite play out in our practice. A common meditation experience is to relive memories of past wholesome and unwholesome actions. In remembering them, the former bring an ease and confidence of mind, a gladdening of the heart; the latter bring feelings of regret and remorse.

Of course, once we have established ourselves in the precepts, then even if memories of these unwholesome, unskillful past actions arise, we have the inner stability to be with them, learn from them, and let them go. If we are not established in sīla, this commitment to nonharming, then these thoughts and feelings continue to arise as we try to meditate, and concentration becomes very difficult.

Develop and Strengthen Concentration

Once we are established in sīla, we can employ different methods in developing and strengthening the factor of concentration. One of the most basic and easily applied methods is mindfulness of breathing. The breath is always with us and is intimately connected with our state of mind. Indeed, the opening set of instructions of the Satipaṭṭhāna Sutta has to do with mindfulness of breathing, as discussed in the opening chapters.

As we develop the art of concentration, we each need to find for ourselves the right balance of investigation, tranquility, and method. Having established a certain level of stability on the breath, or whatever other object of concentration we might be using, we can then take another step in strengthening concentration and wisdom. This was described very clearly by an unusual Thai teacher named Upasika Kee.

Born in 1901 and largely self-taught, Upasika Kee became one of the foremost dhamma teachers in Thailand. This is all the more remarkable within traditional Thai Buddhist culture, because she was not a monastic, but a laywoman. Her teachings, some of which are collected in the book *Pure and Simple,* are amazingly clear, direct, and uncompromising in their devotion to liberation. In this particular teaching, she leads us from awareness of the breath to awareness of the knowing mind:

Now, for how we *do* breath meditation: The texts say to breathe in long and out long—heavy or light—and then to breathe in short and out short, again heavy or light. Those are the first steps of the training. After that we don't have to focus on the length of the in-breath or out-breath. Instead, we simply gather our awareness at any one point of the breath, and keep this up until the mind settles down and is still. When the mind is still, you then focus on the stillness of the mind at the same time you're aware of the breath.

At this point you don't focus directly on the breath. You focus on the mind that is still and at normalcy. You focus continuously on the normalcy of the mind at the same time that you're aware of the breath coming in and out, without actually focusing on the breath. You simply stay with the mind, but you watch it with each in-and-out breath. . . .

This is when you focus on the mind instead of the breath. Let go of the breath and focus on the mind—but still be aware of the breath on the side. You don't have to make note of how long or short the breath is. Make note of the mind that stays at normalcy with each in-and-out breath. Remember this carefully so that you can put it into practice.[2]

"Normalcy" is the translation of the Thai word *pokati*. Its usual range of meanings includes "ordinary," "at equilibrium," and "unaffected by events." In this particular training, Upasika Kee is emphasizing the normalcy, or ordinariness, of the knowing mind. This mind is not some subtle, far-off state, but simple everyday awareness. One simply knows the breath and stays with the experience of knowing. As we learn to recognize and trust this simplicity, we can stabilize our awareness in the knowing itself, and we can more easily integrate this awareness, in a seamless way, into all the activities through the day. As the writer Wei Wu Wei expressed it, "What you are looking for is what is looking."

Becoming aware of the knowing mind itself leads naturally from a knowing of the breath to a knowing of the whole range of experience. Here, through the momentum of continuous mindfulness, the momentary concentration becomes strong and effortless. As Sayadaw U Tejaniya expressed it in *Awareness Alone Is Not Enough*,

"When mindfulness has gained momentum, 'we' don't need to do anything anymore. The mind knows what to do. At this stage there is no more personal effort. You could call it effortless awareness."[3] In this nondoing, we deepen our experience of *anattā,* of selflessness, understanding that this whole mind-body complex is simply empty phenomena rolling on.

WORKING WITH THOUGHTS THAT ARISE IN THE MIND

In any discussion of concentration, an important issue that arises is how to relate to the many thoughts that arise in the mind. There are different ways of working with thoughts, depending in part on whether we're practicing a fixed-object concentration, aiming for full absorption, or engaging in momentary concentration, which develops one-pointedness on changing objects. In the first, as the name implies, the idea is to keep the mind steady on a fixed object, so anything else that arises is seen as a distraction. Here we either ignore or simply let go of whatever arises and come back again and again to the object of meditation.

In insight practice, on the other hand, where we use momentary concentration to investigate changing objects, there is a different attitude of mind with regard to thoughts. Again, Sayadaw U Tejaniya has some wise words of advice:

> When the mind is thinking or wandering . . . just be aware
> of it. Thinking is a natural activity of the mind. . . . You are
> doing well if you are aware that the mind is thinking. . . . But
> if you feel disturbed by thoughts . . . , or if you have a reaction
> or judgment of them, there is a problem with your attitude.
> The wandering mind . . . is not the problem. Your attitude that
> "they should not be around" is the problem. So understand that
> you have just become aware of some functions of the mind.
> These too are just objects for your attention.
>
> Thinking is a mental activity. When you are new to this
> practice you should not try to watch thinking continu-
> ously. Neither should you try to avoid observing thoughts by
> immediately going to your primary meditation object. When
> you realize that you are thinking, always pay attention to the

thought first, and then remind yourself that a thought is just a thought. Do not think of it as "my thought." Now you can return to your primary meditation object.

When you feel disturbed by the thinking mind, remind yourself that you are not practicing to prevent thinking, but rather to recognize and acknowledge thinking whenever it arises. If you are not aware, you cannot know that you are thinking. The fact that you recognize that you are thinking means that you are aware. Remember that it does not matter how many times the mind thinks, wanders off, or gets annoyed about something—as long as you become aware of it.[4]

How the Factors of Enlightenment Work Together

In working with thoughts in the mind, we can see how different factors of enlightenment work together in the service of awakening. Mindfulness recognizes that a thought is present, and continuity of mindfulness strengthens and steadies the concentration of mind. Investigation of dhammas, which is the wisdom factor of mind, then explores the inherently impermanent and insubstantial nature of thought. If we're mindful as thoughts appear, and we see how they self-liberate in the moment of awareness, then there's nothing more we need to do. However, we often get involved with thoughts and are carried away by their story. In this case, it's helpful to look more carefully at their content, asking whether the thought is skillful or not, helpful or not.

Very often simply asking these questions is enough to let go of identification with the thoughts and see their changing, selfless nature. Regarding thoughts, the question "Is it necessary?" can also be a powerful reminder of our intentions, aligning our efforts with our highest aspirations. The Buddha compared the progressive refinement of the mind to the various stages of refining gold, so that in the end, all the impurities are entirely removed.

Impurities of Thought

It's interesting to reflect on what *impurities* means in terms of our practice. Some aspects of the word are obvious, like wrong actions of body and speech, and unwholesome thoughts of greed, ill will, and cruelty. But the Buddha also spoke of subtler impurities, such as being lost in worldly thoughts of family and friends, of reputation, of work. As laypeople living in the world, we do need to think about these things sometimes. But very often, we're simply lost in a kind of unnoticed reverie about them, drifting along in habits of thought that may not be particularly unwholesome, but may be inappropriate or unnecessary for the task at hand. Are they necessary? Probably not.

And an even subtler level of impurity is when we're lost in Dharma thoughts about our practice and different meditative states. These thoughts are so seductive precisely because they are about the Dharma. And as with worldly thoughts, there are times when conscious, mindful Dharma reflection can be a big help on the path. But when we're simply lost in Dharma reveries or in judgments about our practice, they are not particularly helpful.

As we become aware of these kinds of thoughts, understanding them for what they are and letting them go, the mind then becomes inwardly steadied, composed, and unified. This is the enlightenment factor of concentration that is calm and refined, achieving increasing levels of mental purification. As with all the factors of awakening, concentration, too, is developed gradually. The Buddha used the example of how the ocean floor gradually slopes away from the shore and how all kinds of mental development follow the same pattern of gradually increasing depth. Everything is possible if we proceed with patience and perseverance. We might take as an example the famous cellist Pablo Casals, who still practiced three hours a day at age ninety-three. When asked why he still practiced that long, he said, "I'm beginning to see some improvement."

31

Equanimity

THE PRACTICE AND DEVELOPMENT OF concentration leads to equanimity, the last of the seven factors of awakening. Equanimity has far-reaching implications, both for how we live our lives in the world and for the unfolding of insight on the path to liberation. From one perspective, one could say that the whole path rests on the maturing of this powerful enlightenment factor.

"Equanimity" is the translation of the Pali word *upekkhā*. Although *upekkhā* has several meanings, here it refers to one of what the Abhidhamma calls "the universal, beautiful factors of mind." These are a group of mental qualities that always arise together in every wholesome mind state; these qualities include faith or confidence, mindfulness, self-respect, nongreed, nonhatred, and pliancy. Equanimity, as one of these beautiful universals, is the mental factor called "neutrality of mind." Bhikkhu Bodhi said that the Pali term could literally be translated as "there in the middleness." Although this is an awkward construction in English, it does convey the balancing power of equanimity. Its characteristic is evenness, and when it is highly developed, it manifests as unshakeable balance of mind. It serves to prevent either deficiency or excess in the other mental factors.

Equanimity arises out of concentration in the sequential progression of the seven awakening factors, because concentration has the power to keep the mind secluded from the hindrances. This seclusion then allows for balance and neutrality to be established, and the mind to be unmoving in the face of pleasure or pain.

In English, when we speak of neutrality of mind, the phrase might suggest a feeling of indifference or being disconnected from experience. But as we explore the many ways equanimity actually manifests in our lives, we see that it is not indifference at all. We begin to understand why equanimity is called a "beautiful factor" and why it would be hard to overestimate its beneficial effects.

EQUANIMITY AS A QUALITY OF BALANCE

The first way we experience the cool, restful quality of equanimity is in the peace and balance it brings to our daily lives. Each of us is touched by what are called "the eight worldly vicissitudes." These are the endlessly changing conditions of gain and loss, praise and blame, fame and disrepute, and pleasure and pain. When equanimity is developed, we ride these waves with balance and ease. Without it, we're tossed about by the waves, often crashing into the changing circumstances of our lives.

Gain and Loss

We can see the play of gain and loss, and their effect on the mind, in so many different areas of experience. Often we think of them only in terms of material possessions, but we feel their effect whenever we're invested in or attached to a particular outcome, whenever we take something to be "I" or "mine." In the world of finances, gain and loss can be a mood-altering drug. For many people, whole days can be enjoyed or ruined just by the stock market going up or down.

We see the play of gain and loss in the complex world of tribal loyalties, whether local or global. If you happen to live in New England, you might see gain and loss in the intensity of feeling at a Red Sox–Yankees baseball game, in the fans' feeling of elation at a win and their dejection at a loss. We can see it in intense partisan political dramas, particularly those that occur in election years. If you follow the political news closely, do you notice all the ups and downs of your mental states as polls change or as events in the campaign influence the standings of the candidate you're invested in? And, of course, there is the gain and loss that are part of feelings of extreme nationalism, with all the attendant consequences.

Even on retreats, the concepts of gain and loss condition our practice and the assessment of ourselves as yogis. If we have a calm, concentrated sitting, the thought might come, "Now I've got it"; we experience gain and expect it to stay. The next sitting or the next day, maybe the mind is filled with restlessness or boredom: loss. The thought comes, "What did I do wrong? How did I lose it?" Gain and loss untempered by equanimity, by balance, by being in the middleness, keep us in servitude to the inevitably changing conditions of our lives.

Praise and Blame

We can also notice the reactions in the mind in the face of praise and blame. These reactions became very obvious to me after I wrote the book *One Dharma* and then read the different customer reviews on Amazon. To mention just a few: "Concise, enlightening, takes one to the core of Buddhism." "I love it." "A practical enlightening book that is a pleasure to read."

And then: "One Dharma not emerging in this book. Not as significant a book as the title might suggest."

And one of my blame favorites: "This is pretty silly stuff."

When the book first came out and I read the various postings, I could feel my heart and mind glowing or dimming depending on the comments. Fortunately, before too long, Dharma practice came to the rescue. I soon remembered the universal nature of praise and blame. Even the Buddha received both. I began to see the humor in the situation and to allow the mind to rest more easily in equilibrium. The Buddha expressed the unwavering capacity of equanimity in one of the verses of the Dhammapada:

> As a solid mass of rock
> Is not moved by the wind,
> So a sage is not moved
> by praise and blame.

Fame and Disrepute

The third pair of vicissitudes, the inevitable changes in our lives, has to do with fame and disrepute. These are just more generalized forms of praise and blame. The great lesson here is that even though we may hanker after fame or shrink from disrepute, they really only exist as ideas in other people's minds. If we are well established in the nonremorse of good sīla, we can remain quite unmoved and equanimous in the face of these external projections.

Pleasure and Pain

The last pair of changes is the alternation of pleasure and pain, or happiness and sorrow, in our lives. For most of us, there is a deep conditioning in the mind to try to hold on to what is pleasant and to push away or avoid what is unpleasant. But it is precisely this conditioning that powers the rollercoaster of hope and fear. With increasing clarity and wisdom, we see that these changes are inevitable and that they are not mistakes. It's not that pleasant feelings go away because we've done something wrong; it's simply the nature of all conditioned things to change.

Many years ago, I was teaching a retreat at a wilderness ranch in northern New Mexico. On the last afternoon, we all went for a walk along a river that wound its way through the canyons. It had recently rained, and I slipped on a wet rock, hyperextending my knee. I thought it would be okay as I made my way back to the lodge, but that evening, after giving a Dharma talk while sitting cross-legged on my cushion, I found that I could no longer put any weight at all on that leg. I had to be carried back to my room. For the rest of the night, I watched my mind go back and forth between self-blame and concern for how I would manage the rest of my summer schedule.

Finally, my mind just settled into the realization that accidents happen, and a mantra suddenly appeared in my mind, one that has served me well since: *anything can happen anytime.* This is not a mantra of despair or fear; it actually provided a great sense of relief. It is the simple recognition and reminder that yes, this is how things are. Conditions are always changing and often outside of our control. We don't have to live defensively in the fear of the unexpected if we accept that anything can happen anytime. I have found this reminder amazingly helpful in accepting change with a deepening and easeful equanimity. The Buddha, in talking of the vicissitudes, said, "Praise and blame, gain and loss, pleasure and sorrow come and go like the wind. To be happy, rest like a great tree in the midst of them all."

EQUANIMITY AS A DIVINE ABODE

The second type of equanimity manifests as the fourth of the *brahmavihāras,* those mind states called "the divine abodes": loving-kindness, compassion, appreciative joy, and equanimity.

It is impartiality, equanimity's ability to hold all equally, that gives the other *brahmavihāras* their boundless capacity. When we remain unmoved in the face of those who praise and those who blame, we remain able to seek the welfare of both. We can see this at work in watching how people like the Dalai Lama or Dipa Ma relate to the people they meet. The Dalai Lama has often said that he tries to meet everyone as if they are old friends. And someone once described being hugged by Dipa Ma "so thoroughly that all my six feet fit into her great, vast, empty heart, with room for the whole of creation."

THE WISDOM ASPECT OF EQUANIMITY

The third manifestation of equanimity takes us deep into the experience of meditative awareness. The wisdom aspect of equanimity is beautifully expressed in the famous opening lines of "On the Faith Mind," by the Third Zen Ancestor: "The great way is not difficult for those who have no preferences. When attachment and aversion are both absent, the way is clear and undisguised. Make the smallest distinction, however, and heaven and earth are set infinitely apart."

Practicing the great way, the equanimity of nonpreferential awareness, supports the development of all the awakening factors. As they become strong, we gain ever-deeper insights into the three characteristics. We know the truth of change, not only as a conceptual understanding, but also in the direct experience of things arising and passing away. Sometimes this experience of impermanence is on a macro level and then, increasingly, on a momentary micro level. At this point, our meditation is less involved with what it is that's arising than with the process of change itself.

We experience the truth of dukkha, the unreliability and unsatisfying nature of conditioned phenomena. We see the continual dissolution of everything that arises and, at times, even the momentary dissolution of consciousness itself. There are many stories in the Discourses of people getting enlightened by hearing just this one teaching: "Whatever has the nature to arise will also pass away." What would it be like if we really let this teaching in? If our understanding of it were complete, we wouldn't hold on to anything.

And we experience the truth of selflessness when we see nothing lasts long enough to be called "self." All phenomena arise out of appropriate causes and conditions, unsubstantial, empty of any inherent self-existence. Phenomena are like rainbows—colored light arising out of momentary changing conditions, both vivid and insubstantial at the same time.

As each of these insights matures within us, we pass through various stages. In some stages, the mind is filled with exhilarating rapture when we see clearly for the first time the very rapid rise and fall of phenomena. In other stages, there is a great clarity, when we understand more deeply what is the path and what is not. Here we learn not to cling even to the special meditative states of rapture and happiness. We also go through the dark night of the soul that St. John of the Cross described. There are periods of profound distress, where we see that nothing at all in conditioned existence can provide a true and lasting happiness.

But if we persevere on the path, we reach the culmination of mundane meditative insights, which is the powerful state of equanimity about all formations. This is a state of deep delight born of peace. Here the mind is not disturbed at all by the alteration of pleasant and unpleasant experience. We abide in a smooth current of awareness without even the slightest micromovements of reaction in the mind. At this point, the equanimity has balanced all the other factors of mind, and the practice is rolling along all by itself.

This stage of stable equanimity is likened to the mind of an arahant, which is unshakeable with regard to anything arising in the field of consciousness. It's useful to remember that one isn't actually an arahant yet, but stable equanimity is a taste of what the Buddha repeated many times in the Satipaṭṭhāna Sutta: "And one abides independent, not clinging to anything in the world."

EQUANIMITY AS A PARAMI

The fourth kind of equanimity to mention here is the last of the *paramis,* those qualities that a bodhisattva perfects over lifetimes of fulfilling the great aspiration of Buddhahood. They are also the same qualities, developed to a somewhat lesser extent, that bring about our own liberation. In the Theravāda teachings there are ten of these *paramis,* and many of the Jatāka Tales, those tales of the Buddha in his previous lives, recount stories of how they were developed.

The ten *paramis* are generosity, morality, renunciation, wisdom, diligence, patience, truthfulness, resolve, lovingkindness, and equanimity. Of these, patience and equanimity are considered the mainstays for all the others. Ledi Sayadaw wrote that only when we have set ourselves up with these two can we expect to fulfill the rest.

HOW TO DEVELOP AND STRENGTHEN EQUANIMITY

The remaining question, then, is how to develop and strengthen this amazingly beneficial quality of equanimity. There are a few succinct teachings that describe how we can develop it in the midst of our worldly activities.

Forego Attachment

At one point, the Thai master Ajahn Chaa held up a cup in front of a group of his students. He said that the best way to relate to the cup is as if it is already broken. We use it and take care of it, but we remain unattached because we know it is subject to change.

In the same way, there is a powerful teaching in the Bhagavad Gita, the great Hindu text, that says we should act without attachment to the fruit of the action. We can do what we do with full commitment, but the outcome is often beyond our control. When we act without attachment to the outcome, then our minds remain peaceful no matter how things unfold.

The last of these teachings that I have found helpful in my life is something the Dalai Lama emphasizes—namely, that the value of an action is measured not by its success or failure, but by the motivation behind it. When our motivations are skillful, then we can abide in equanimity regardless of whether we succeed or fail in our endeavors.

Associate with Wise, Equanimous People

The Buddha taught that associating with wise, equanimous people strengthens equanimity. As the texts say, "Avoid those people who go crazy." If you have ever watched some of the political news shows, you can understand the wisdom of this advice. Panelists are often shouting down other peoples' views, firmly attached to their own, hardly engaged in meaningful dialogue. Although it makes for good theater, just in watching these shows, much less participating, we can feel the energetic impact of such exchanges. They are hardly conducive to equanimity.

Practice Its Brahmavihāra Aspect

We can also develop equanimity as one of the *brahmavihāra* meditations. The classical phrase that is repeated in this practice is, "All beings are the heirs of their own karma. Their happiness or unhappiness depends on their actions, not upon my wishes." As we repeat these phrases, first in regard to someone we feel neutral about and then successively in regard to a benefactor, a friend, a difficult person, and all beings, we are reminded where happiness truly lies. Although we may wish for people to be happy and at peace, that outcome will ultimately rest on their own actions. The practice of equanimity in this way allows us to hold the wish for their wellbeing with proper balance, and each repetition of the phrases can be the offering of the gift of wisdom.

Practice Wise Attention and Continuous Mindfulness

Finally, we develop equanimity in our insight practice through wise attention and continuous mindfulness. We practice inclining the mind toward equanimity and not being seduced by the lesser happiness of excitement or the simple enjoyment of pleasant feelings. This is a mind that is imperturbable and balanced, with an impartiality that embraces all. The Buddha summed it up well when he said, "There is no higher happiness than peace."

MINDFULNESS OF DHAMMAS

The Four Noble Truths

32

The First Noble Truth

Dukkha

"Again, monks, in regard to dhammas, one abides contemplating dhammas in terms of the four noble truths. And how
does one, in regard to dhammas, abide contemplating dhammas in terms of the four noble truths?

"Here one knows as it really is, 'this is dukkha'; one knows
as it really is, 'this is the arising of dukkha'; one knows as
it really is, 'this is the cessation of dukkha'; one knows as it
really is, 'this is the way leading to the cessation of dukkha.'"[1]

It's not surprising that the Buddha concludes all of the teachings of
the Satipaṭṭhāna Sutta, the direct path to awakening, with the contemplation of the four noble truths. They express the very essence of the
Buddha's awakening, and despite the many differences among the various Buddhist traditions, all of them agree that the four noble truths are
the foundation of understanding and realization. Sāriputta, the chief
disciple of the Buddha, spoke with a group of monks about these truths:

"Friends, just as the footprint of any living being that walks
can be placed within an elephant's footprint, . . . so too, all
wholesome states can be included in the Four Noble Truths."[2]

Not only does this contemplation include all that is wholesome in our lives and practice, but it is also the indispensable foundation for realization. The Buddha spoke to this point very clearly:

> "Just as, bhikkhus, if anyone should speak thus, 'Without having built the lower storey of a peaked house, I will erect the upper storey,' this would be impossible; so too, if anyone should speak thus: 'Without having made the breakthrough to the noble truth of dukkha as it really is . . . [the origin of dukkha, the cessation of dukkha, the way leading to the cessation of dukkha], I will completely make an end to dukkha'—this is impossible.
>
> "Just as, bhikkhus, if anyone should speak thus: 'Having built the lower storey of a peaked house, I will then erect the upper storey,' this would be possible; so too, if anyone should speak thus: 'Having made the breakthrough to the noble truth of dukkha as it really is . . . [the origin of dukkha, the cessa-tion of dukkha, the way leading to the cessation of dukkha], I will completely make an end to dukkha'—this is possible."[3]

THE MEANING OF DUKKHA

The first challenge facing us as we read and apply these teachings is understanding what the Pali word *dukkha* means. In many ways, this term defines the entire spiritual path. The Buddha often said that all conditioned phenomena are dukkha and that out of his vast and limitless knowledge he teaches only this: dukkha and its end.

The problem is that there is no single word in English that fully cap-tures the range of its meanings. Most commonly, *dukkha* is translated as "suffering," and although in some contexts this translation works well, it is not a perfect fit. In one teaching the Buddha said, "Whatever is felt is included in dukkha." But as we know, some feelings are pleas-ant and enjoyable; we don't feel them as suffering. And to say that all things are suffering because of their changing nature also doesn't corre-spond to our experience when painful feelings change to pleasant ones. We are relieved in that experience rather than suffering because of it.

So while "suffering" as the often-used translation of *dukkha* might sometimes be appropriate, it can also be misleading. It doesn't always resonate with our own lived experience. We might begin to get a better sense of its meaning by remembering its etymological derivation. The word is made up of the prefix *du* and the root *kha*. *Du* means "bad" or "difficult." *Kha* means "empty." "Empty," here, refers to several things—some specific, others more general.

One of the specific meanings refers to the empty axle hole of a wheel. If the axle fits badly into the center hole, we get a very bumpy ride. This is a good analogy for our ride through saṃsāra. On my first trip to Burma, a group of friends and I went up-country to visit Mahāsi Sayadaw's home temple. We made part of the journey in an oxcart, and it was undoubtedly similar to modes of transportation in the Buddha's time. This extremely bumpy journey was a very visceral example of dukkha, the first noble truth.

In more general philosophical terms, "empty" means devoid of permanence and devoid of a self that can control or command phenomena. Here we begin to get a sense of other, more inclusive meanings of the term *dukkha*. Words like *unsatisfying, unreliable, uneaseful,* and *stressful* all convey universal aspects of our experience. Anālayo clarifies an important point regarding these various translations:

> Thus, "suffering," unlike "unsatisfactoriness," is not inherent
> in the phenomena of the world, only in the way in which the
> unawakened mind experiences them. This is indeed the under-
> lying theme of the four noble truths as a whole: the suffering
> caused by attachment and craving can be overcome by awaken-
> ing. For an *arahant,* the unsatisfactory nature of all conditioned
> phenomena is no longer capable of causing suffering.[4]

Now we can integrate the understanding that, indeed, all conditioned phenomena are dukkha—that is, unsatisfactory, incapable of giving lasting satisfaction, and at the same time, even in the midst of experience, able to bring the suffering of our minds to an end. Having a clearer sense of what *dukkha* means, we can return to the basic instruction the Buddha gave in the sutta: "And one knows as it really is, this is dukkha."

HOW WE EXPERIENCE DUKKHA

Here we're faced with the second challenge: what exactly is the "this" that is unsatisfactory, unreliable, uneaseful, and at times suffering?

Fortunately, in the first discourse he gave after his enlightenment, the Buddha elaborated on what it is that is dukkha. After his great awakening under the Bodhi tree in Bodh Gaya, the Buddha spent the next seven weeks contemplating various aspects of his realization. Then, as he considered whom he might teach this profound and subtle Dharma to, he thought of his five former companions, with whom he had practiced the various ascetic disciplines. They were living in a deer park in Sarnath, a small village across the Ganges River from the ancient city of Varanasi, sometimes called Benares. This was an eight-day journey on foot from Bodh Gaya.

This is the first discourse the Buddha gave, and it is called "Setting the Wheel of the Dharma in Motion." Over the centuries since the Buddha's time, it is a wheel that has rolled across continents and oceans, inspiring countless people to put the teachings into practice. In this discourse, the Buddha lays out the great middle way, between the extremes of self-indulgence and self-mortification, and the four noble truths as the wisdom framework for freedom.

> "Now this, bhikkhus, is the Noble Truth of dukkha: birth
> is dukkha, aging is dukkha, illness is dukkha, death is
> dukkha; union with what is displeasing is dukkha; separa-
> tion from what is pleasing is dukkha; not to get what one
> wants is dukkha; in brief, the five aggregates subject to
> clinging are dukkha."[5]

In these few lines, the Buddha points to the experience of dukkha both in terms of the ordinary experiences of our lives and, on a deeper and more comprehensive level, in terms of the five aggregates subject to clinging. But even with those aspects that are part of the ordinary flow of our lives, how often do we stop and reflect deeply on them? We're so often intent on the next hit of experience, the next thing we have to do, that we don't take time to step back and really look at what our lives are about.

The Buddha didn't say, "Believe." He said, "Come and see." His was an invitation, an exhortation, to stop and take a look at the nature of this body and mind, to investigate it for ourselves. As we begin this investigation, it's helpful to remember a line from the refrain from the Satipaṭṭhāna Sutta that has particular importance in our understanding of the first noble truth. The line reminds us, "One abides contemplating dhammas [here, the first noble truth] internally, externally, and both." So we investigate how we actually experience dukkha internally, in ourselves, and externally, in the world.

The Dukkha of Painful Experiences

Things are unsatisfying, unreliable, and sometimes suffering in three ways. First, there is the dukkha of experiences that are painful in themselves. This is where the translation of dukkha as "suffering" most frequently applies. There is the obvious suffering caused by war, violence, hunger, natural disasters, political and social oppression, and injustice. These are very real situations for hundreds of millions of people.

There is the inevitable pain of the body, starting with childbirth, and then sickness, injury, and ageing common to us all. And most likely, we won't be feeling our best at the time of death. All of this is not a mistake; it's just nature at work.

There's also the optional but deeply conditioned suffering in the mind: feelings of fear, jealousy, anger, hatred, anxiety, grief, envy, frustration, loneliness. There's a long list of what are called "afflictive emotions." Many times, in reporting states like this to Sayadaw U Paṇḍita, he would say, "Good. Now you're realizing the truth of dukkha." Each time we can open to the painful experiences of mind and body, we are investigating and realizing the first noble truth for ourselves. As the Buddha said, "Here one knows as it really is—this is dukkha."

The Dukkha of the Changing Nature of All Things

The second way we experience dukkha, the unsatisfying, unreliable nature of things, is through the direct and increasingly refined perception of their changing nature. As noted in chapter 31: Equanimity, many people have become enlightened by hearing just this one short teaching: "whatever has the nature to arise will also pass away." But because this statement is so glaringly obvious, we often ignore or overlook its deep implications. Although we may not always feel this flow of incessant change as suffering, we still come to realize that nothing can be counted on to bring lasting fulfillment, precisely because nothing lasts. This great truth of change inevitably leads us to times of association with what we don't want and separation from what we do. And these situations, in turn, often condition resistance to the unpleasant things that come and clinging to the pleasant ones.

On the conceptual level we understand all this quite easily, but in our lives, how often are we living in anticipation of what comes next, as if that will finally bring us to some sort of completion or fulfillment? When we look back over our lives, what has happened to all those things we were looking forward to? Where are they now? This doesn't mean that we should never enjoy ourselves or enjoy different pleasant experiences. It just means we need to realize and remember the very transitory nature of that happiness and to deeply consider what our highest aspirations really are.

Some powerful reflections and reminders in this regard are that all times of being together will end in separation, that all accumulation will end in dispersion, and that all life will end in death. And at the moment of death, what really belongs to us? Surprisingly, reflecting in this way on the truth of dukkha, which simply sees how things are free of hope and fear, brings a great lightness of heart and mind. It's a great relief to be out of the grip of deluded enchantment. There's a freshness and vivid clarity in seeing things as they are.

> "Bhikkhus, there are these five themes that should often
> be reflected upon by a woman or a man, by a householder
> or one gone forth. What five? (1) . . . 'I am subject to old
> age; I am not exempt from old age.' (2) . . . 'I am subject
> to illness; I am not exempt from illness.' (3) . . . 'I am
> subject to death; I am not exempt from death.' (4) . . .
> 'I must be parted from everyone and everything dear and
> agreeable to me.' (5) 'I am the owner of my kamma, the
> heir of my kamma; I have kamma as my origin, kamma
> as my relative, kamma as my resort; I will be the heir of
> whatever kamma, good or bad, that I do.'"[6]

These five reflections are practiced daily by people in many Buddhist traditions. They are reminders of what is true, and they free us from the delusion that we can somehow avoid these aspects of life. It would be helpful to make these reflections part of one's own daily practice and to see the effect that they have in our lives.

In an even more explicit way, the Buddha reminds us of events that will certainly happen, because, in fact, they happen to everyone.

> (1) "Bhikkhus, for the instructed noble disciple, what is subject to old age grows old. When this happens, one reflects thus: 'I am not the only one for whom what is subject to old age grows old' . . . (2) 'I am not the only one for whom what is subject to illness grows ill' . . . (3) 'I am not the only one for whom what is subject to death dies' . . . (4) 'I am not the only one for whom what is subject to destruction is destroyed' . . . (5) 'I am not the only one for whom what is subject to loss is lost.'"[7]

When we reflect in this way, we understand that we are all part of this great matrix of life and death, of creation and destruction, and that living with this understanding brings peace. There is a story of the great African-American tennis champion Arthur Ashe. In the late 1980s, Ashe contracted HIV from a blood transfusion he received during heart-bypass surgery. Ashe publicly announced his illness in April 1992, and began working to educate others about HIV and AIDS. When asked about his illness, he replied, "If I were to say, 'God, why me?' about the bad things, then I should have said, 'God, why me?' about the good things that happened in my life."

As a way of developing this heightened awareness of all that life brings, the Buddha spoke of the great benefit of mindfulness of death. On one occasion, he addressed a gathering of monks:

> "Bhikkhus, mindfulness of death, when developed and cultivated, is of great fruit and benefit, culminating in the deathless, having the deathless as its consummation. But do you, bhikkhus, develop mindfulness of death?"[8]

Six bhikkhus replied, each saying how he developed this mindfulness. Often in these situations, the Buddha would hear their replies and praise their different perspectives on practice. Here, though, there is a surprisingly different outcome.

The first bhikkhu said that he would think, "May I live just a night and day so that I may attend to the Blessed One's teaching." The second said, "May I live just a day so that I may attend to the teachings." The third, "May I live just the length of time it takes to eat a single alms meal so that I may attend to the Blessed One's teachings." The fourth, "May I live just the length of time it takes to chew and swallow four or five mouthfuls of food . . ." The fifth said, "May I live just the length of time it takes to chew and swallow a single mouthful of food . . ." And the last said, "May I live just the length of time it takes to breathe out after breathing in, or to breathe in after breathing out, so that I may attend to the Blessed One's teaching. I could then accomplish much. It is in this way that I develop mindfulness of death."[9]

With regard to the first four, the Buddha said, these are called "bhikkhus who dwell heedlessly." They develop mindfulness sluggishly for the destruction of the taints. But with regard to the last two, these are called "bhikkhus who dwell heedfully." They develop mindfulness of death keenly for the destruction of the taints.

> "Therefore, bhikkhus, you should train yourselves thus: 'We
> will dwell heedfully. We will develop mindfulness of death
> keenly for the destruction of the taints.' Thus should you
> train yourselves."[10]

In reading about this encounter between the Buddha and these six bhikkhus, at first I thought that all of them were doing pretty well regarding keeping death in the forefront of their awareness. But the Buddha's rejoinder helped me investigate a bit further about just how this practice works. Many of us may have the aspiration to die as consciously as possible, to be aware—and interested—in the whole process of leaving this life for whatever might happen next. But will we actually be able to maintain that state of awareness during such a momentous process?

The Buddha's instruction about training ourselves to dwell heedfully, to develop mindfulness of death keenly, has a surprising benefit. Not only does it keep this great truth of death front and center in our lives, but reflecting on it within the space of one in-breath or one out-breath, or within the time it takes to chew and swallow a single mouthful of food, also helps the mind completely settle back into that very moment. When James Joyce wrote of one of his characters,

"Mr. Duffy lived a short distance from his body," he could have been describing most of us. But knowing that death is possible while we're taking this very breath, the mind is no longer caught up in anticipation of either external sense pleasures or future plans or even of some better meditation experience. We are completely present for the process of our death, present even if in contemplating in this way, we feel some anxiety or unease. They, too, are fully accepted as being what is arising in that moment. Holding in the light of death whatever might arise, we can practice being compassionate toward it all. What may be surprising is that this exercise actually uplifts the mind; we feel more alive from our awareness of death.

On a recent retreat, when I was applying the Buddha's advice to keep awareness of death present within a single breath, I found that this reflection would also arise while walking as well: death may come within this very step. And each time, the reflection itself settled my mind effortlessly in the moment, in the words of the Satipaṭṭhāna Sutta, "free from desire and discontent with regard to the world."

The Dukkha of Conditioned Experience

The third experience of dukkha is as the burdensomeness of conditioned existence. Think of what we need to do simply to fulfill the basic needs of life. We work for food, for water, for shelter, for medicines. Sometimes these are easily obtained, but for many people they are not. There's the effort to care for the body, to keep it clean, to maintain health as best we can.

On the BBC special *Planet Earth,* there was one episode showing the extraordinary effort some male birds make to attract a mate. There were amazing mating dances, feather displays, and even nest-building competitions. All of this effort was simply to propagate the genes, and many times all these efforts were not enough, and another male won out. I call this kind of dukkha the Buddhist equivalent of the second law of thermodynamics, which says that all systems uninfluenced by outside forces tend to disorder. This means that in order to sustain life, we need to keep introducing energy into the system. And still, in the end, entropy always prevails.

In order to understand this first noble truth, we need to reflect on and investigate all of these different aspects in our lives. When we see the word *dukkha,* what meaning do we habitually ascribe to it? Is it limited to things obviously unpleasant, or can we expand our understanding and begin to get a sense of what the Buddha meant when he said all conditioned things are dukkha? The British Buddhist scholar Rupert Gethin wrote in *The Buddhist Path to Awakening,* "Understanding the first noble truth involves not so much the revelation that dukkha exists, as the realization of what dukkha is."

The Buddha helps us further with this realization in his concise summing up of the noble truth: "[I]t is, in short, the five aggregates subject to grasping." Contained in the meaning of this one line is the whole of samsaric conditioning and, by implication, an understanding of the remaining three noble truths that make possible our liberation.

> "Suppose, bhikkhus, a dog tied up on a leash was bound to a strong post or pillar: it would just keep on running and revolving around that same post or pillar. So too, uninstructed worldling[s], regard form as self . . . feeling as self . . . perception as self . . . volitional formations as self . . . consciousness as self. . . . They just keep running and revolving around form, around feelings, around perception, around volitional formations, around consciousness. As they keep on running and revolving around them, they are not free from them. They are not freed from birth, ageing and death; not freed from sorrow, lamentation, pain, displeasure, and despair; not freed from suffering.
>
> "But the instructed noble disciple[s] do not regard form as self, nor feeling as self . . . nor perception as self . . . nor volitional formations as self . . . nor consciousness as self. . . . They no longer keep running and revolving around them. As they no longer keep running around them, they are freed from them, freed from birth, ageing and death; freed from sorrow, lamentation, pain, displeasure, and despair; freed from suffering."[11]

THE GATEWAY TO AWAKENING AND COMPASSION

Practicing the instruction in the Satipaṭṭhāna Sutta, "Here one knows as it really is—this is dukkha," brings two great results. It is the gateway not only to awakening, but also to the arising and nourishing of compassion. Compassion is that feeling in the heart that wants to help others and ourselves be free of suffering. It's the feeling described by the Japanese Zen master and poet Ryokan, "O that my monk's robes / were wide enough / to gather up all the people / in this floating world." The first noble truth leads us to the practice of compassion, because it is the practice of letting things in, letting people in, letting all parts of ourselves in.

The Buddha concluded his teaching on the first noble truth with this recounting of his night under the Bodhi tree:

> "'This is the noble truth of dukkha': thus, bhikkhus, in regard to things unheard before, there arose in me vision, knowledge, wisdom, true knowledge, and light.
>
> "'This noble truth of dukkha is to be fully understood': thus, bhikkhus, in regard to things unheard before, there arose in me vision, knowledge, wisdom, true knowledge, and light.
>
> "'This noble truth of dukkha has been fully understood': thus, bhikkhus, in regard to things unheard before, there arose in me vision, knowledge, wisdom, true knowledge, and light."[12]

The Second Noble Truth

The Cause of Dukkha

IN THE CONTEMPLATION OF THE second noble truth, we explore the cause of dukkha, which is craving. It is striking that from the long list of unwholesome factors in the mind the Buddha singles out this one particular energy as being the condition for dukkha to arise. It is this powerful force in the mind that keeps the whole wheel of saṃsāra, of conditioned existence, rolling on.

> "Monks, I do not envision even one other fetter—fettered by which beings conjoined go wandering and transmigrating for a long, long time—like the fetter of craving."[1]

What exactly is craving, and how do we experience it in our lives and practice? Craving is the translation of the Pali word *taṇhā*, which means "thirst" or "fever of unsatisfied longing." These translations of *taṇhā* give a sense of its intensely compelling nature, this primal energy that seems to come from deep within our being. That fever of unsatisfied longing is just the opposite of peace.

We sometimes use the words *craving* and *desire* synonymously, but this can sometimes be confusing in a Dharma context, because the word *desire* in English has a wide range of meanings. Sometimes it is the thirst of craving that is rooted in greed. But sometimes desire simply means the motivation to do something, the desire to accomplish some aim, which could be skillful or unskillful depending on the motivation associated with it. In the context of this chapter on the origin of dukkha, I'll be using these two terms—*desire* and *craving*—interchangeably, understanding that in this case, *desire* refers to desire bound up with greed and leading to clinging and grasping.

THE FIRST DOMAIN OF CRAVING:
THE DESIRE FOR SENSE PLEASURES

The Buddha spoke of three domains of craving: desire for sense pleasures, desire for renewed existence or becoming, and desire for nonexistence or nonbecoming.

The first and most obvious of these is the familiar craving we have for sense pleasures. These are the sights, sounds, smells, tastes, and touch sensations that are wished for, desirable, and agreeable. We might also include here the agreeable, pleasant states of mind. In the Buddha's teachings, the mind is considered to be the sixth sense. All of these desires are just our usual engagement with life—enjoying and wanting what is pleasurable, avoiding as best we can what is disagreeable.

But here the Buddha begins a revealing analysis of our situation. He didn't condemn sense pleasures as being sinful. Rather, in his quest for enlightenment, his introspective, scientific method led him to ask some basic questions about life experience. The first question he asked was, "What is the gratification in the world?"

As a young prince, he himself had thoroughly enjoyed the various strands of sense pleasures. From the time of his birth until he left home at age twenty-nine, he was fully immersed in this world of pleasurable activities. They were not foreign to him. Then, as recounted in the suttas, the thought came to him that whatever pleasure and joy there are in the world, this is the gratification in the world—that if there were no gratification in the world, beings would not become enamored with it. So it is precisely because there *is* gratification that we desire or crave these sense pleasures.

Rather than simply read the Buddha's words, we can follow his lead and ask ourselves the same question: What is the gratification we find in our lives? What sense experiences are we enamored of? Our gratification and cravings come in a wide range of intensities and frequencies. At one extreme, there might be obsessive cravings that consume our lives—addictions to food, alcohol, drugs, sex, power, wealth, fame, even love. Or we may have these same kinds of desires, not necessarily on an obsessive level, but still as the driving force behind many of our actions. It would be worth examining the motivating forces in our lives, becoming more conscious of what it is we desire, what moves us to act.

We can also watch craving just as a passing thought of wanting in the mind. It's interesting to see the deep-rooted persistence of even small desires for sense pleasures. A thought might come, "a cup of tea," and, especially on retreat, we might simply note it. It comes again, and we note it. And again, until often, in the end, we are carried away and act on the desire. There is nothing wrong with a cup of tea; this is simply an exercise in learning about the power of desire in our minds and lives.

These different patterns of craving, desire, wanting are so familiar to us that they just seem like the ordinary fabric of life. They are so much a part of who we take ourselves to be that they often remain invisible until we bring the power of mindful awareness to them. During the day, notice the gratification that comes from different sense pleasures. It might be from very simple things like a hot shower, or the tastes of enjoyable food, or that moment when we first lie down at night after a busy day; or it might be the enjoyment of pleasant fantasies and the desire for them to continue. See what you become enamored of and the desire and craving that often follow. At some point of investigation and self-reflection, we might resonate with the Buddha's words, "Whatever gratification there is in the world, that I have found." Or are we still holding out hope for some new and unexpected gratification of the senses?

THE DRAWBACKS OF SENSE PLEASURES

The Bodhisattva did not stop with his understanding of gratification. He then asked the next probing question, "Bhikkhus, I set out seeking the drawbacks in the world." "Drawbacks" is one translation of the Pali word *ādīnava,* which is also often translated as "dangers," "defects," or "disadvantages." All of these are what we might colloquially call "the downside of things." And what the Buddha is here calling the drawbacks or dangers of the world are precisely the truth of dukkha talked about earlier: that the world is impermanent, bound up with dukkha, subject to change.

But how many of us, when times are good, when we're enjoying the various joys and pleasures of the world, have enough prescience or foresight to stop and consider, "What is the downside here?" For most of us, these joys and pleasures are just life as usual. It would be illuminating to see how and when occasional desires strengthen into deeper habit patterns of wanting. It's as if some new desire or craving becomes so habitual that we no longer even particularly notice it. Yet the Buddha is clearly trying to tell us something of import.

> "[P]eople who are not free from lust for sensual pleasures, who are devoured by craving for sensual pleasures, who burn with the fever of sensual pleasures, still indulge in sensual pleasures; the more they indulge in sensual pleasures, the more their craving for sensual pleasures increases and the more they are burned by the fever of sensual pleasures, yet they find a certain measure of satisfaction and enjoyment in dependence on the five cords of sensual pleasure."[2]

We don't usually feel burning in the fever of craving. We're more enamored of the gratification and don't necessarily consider what the downside might be. So how can we understand the drawbacks of craving for sensual pleasures that the Buddha refers to? There are several ways.

Craving Doesn't Deliver Lasting Happiness

First, sense pleasures don't, in the end, deliver on their promise of happiness. We believe the experience of sense pleasures will bring us happiness because of the pleasant feelings that arise. And they do bring some happiness for a time. The problem is that pleasant feelings are very impermanent, sometimes momentarily so. They continually change and disappear. So we go after another and another, and all too soon our lives are at an end. It's like trying to quench our thirst by drinking salt water; it only makes us thirstier. How many sense pleasures, pleasant feelings, have we already enjoyed in our lives? Countless ones. Yet we never come to a sense of completion. We're always waiting for, anticipating, the next one. How much of our lives and energy do we want to invest in this endless pursuit?

Although most of us are laypeople living in and engaged with the world of sense pleasures to some degree or other, some deep part of us knows that it is not the way to peace. Dharma practice opens us to possibilities of much greater happiness in our lives.

Craving Can Lead to Suffering

The second danger is that when craving becomes a strong and powerful force in the mind, it can lead us to many unwholesome actions, creating more unskillful karma, which results in suffering. Craving plays a pivotal role in the teaching of dependent origination. Based on contact and feeling, whether pleasant or unpleasant, craving arises. Because of craving, clinging; because of clinging, becoming. And so the whole cycle—old results (feelings) causing new actions, which, in turn, bring new results—goes on.

An idiomatic way of expressing these links might bring home just how common and familiar they are to us: "I want, I need, I must have." How many times have we gone from a simple wanting, a desire, to that convincing mind state of "needing"? Right there we have gone from craving to clinging. And as the felt need gets stronger, it turns into "must have." This is already on the cusp of action, of becoming. Pay attention during the day to this sequence. It could happen with very little things or with more major ones: "I want a cookie. I need a cookie. I must have a cookie." And off we go.

The Buddha talked of nine things rooted in craving: pursuit; acquisition; decision; desire and lust; selfish tenacity; possessiveness; avarice; concern for protection; and quarrels, strife, dissension, offensive talk, slander, and lies. We can see how craving gives rise to these things on both a personal level and also a national level, thus seeing how craving leads directly to different kinds of suffering. In the years leading up to the 2008 financial meltdown in the United States, one desire or another enticed people and institutions to assume huge, unmanageable debt, and millions of people lost their jobs and often their homes. They grasped at things beyond their means to pay for them, until eventually, the whole edifice came tumbling down. So this second noble truth—the origin of dukkha—is not a hypothetical proposition. It plays out in society and in our own lives.

Craving Can Lead to Agitation

We can experience a third disadvantage or drawback of craving in the immediacy of our own Dharma practice. Have you noticed any times of wanting and expectation in your meditation—wanting some new, imagined pleasurable experience to be happening, or a present one to remain, or an old one to return?

The danger here is that expectation, the wanting itself, inevitably brings agitation. What makes this particular danger so seductive is that it often comes disguised as dharma aspiration. But these are two very different mind states. Aspirations inspire us, while expectations simply lead us into cycles of hope and fear: hope that what we want will happen; fear that it won't.

There is a very illuminating dialogue in the suttas about these cycles:

> On one occasion, the Blessed One was dwelling at Rājāgaha, in the Bamboo Grove, the squirrel sanctuary. Now on that occasion the Venerable Assaji was dwelling in a potter's shed, sick, afflicted, gravely ill.
>
> Then the Blessed One dressed and, taking bowl and robe, approached the Venerable Assaji and said: "I hope you are bearing up, Assaji, I hope you are getting better, I hope that your painful feelings are subsiding and not increasing, and that their subsiding, not their increase, is to be discerned."
>
> "Venerable Sir, I am not bearing up, I am not getting better. Strong painful feelings are increasing in me, not subsiding, and their increase, not their subsiding, is to be discerned."
>
> "I hope then, Assaji, that you are not troubled by remorse and regret."
>
> "Indeed, venerable Sir, I have quite a lot of remorse and regret."
>
> "I hope, Assaji, that you have nothing for which to reproach yourself in regard to virtue."
>
> "I have nothing, venerable Sir, for which to reproach myself in regard to virtue."
>
> "Then, Assaji, if you have nothing for which to reproach yourself in regard to virtue, Assaji, why are you troubled by remorse and regret?"
>
> "Formerly, Venerable Sir, when I was ill I kept on tranquilizing the bodily formations, but now I do not obtain

concentration. As I do not obtain concentration, it occurs to me: 'Let me not fall away [from the path]!'"

"Those ascetics and brahmins, Assaji, who regard concentration as the essence and identify concentration asceticism, failing to obtain concentration, might think, 'Let us not fall away!'"[3]

So even when we are considering concentration, one factor of awakening, we should remember that the essence of the path is non-clinging—to anything. The next time you feel frustrated or agitated in your practice, look to see if expectation is operative, and notice the craving behind it. Here struggle can become useful feedback. It's telling us that something is arising in our experience that we're not accepting. If we were accepting it, we wouldn't be struggling. *Nonacceptance* is just another word for *wanting*—wanting something other than what is happening. And wanting, craving, is the cause of dukkha.

When we have the courage to see the world and our life experiences clearly, we can recognize both the gratification they offer and, at the same time, see the drawbacks, the downside that is there. When we go beyond the superficial and conventional understandings of our habitual patterns, when we look deeper and enlarge the scope of our vision, we develop a wiser relationship with all aspects of our experience.

THE SECOND DOMAIN OF CRAVING: THE DESIRE TO BE

The second kind of craving the Buddha spoke of goes even deeper than the craving for sense pleasures. It is called "craving for becoming, for renewed existence." This is the very basic urge or desire to be. It is the desire for continuing existence, particularly in pleasant realms. We may or may not believe in rebirth and different planes of existence, although they are mentioned often in the Buddha's teachings, but we don't have to believe in them in order to experience this powerful craving for becoming. We can see it in the planning mind, in the act of imagining ourselves in some future situation. We might be planning for something at work or perhaps for our next vacation. It all starts with just a thought, and then weeks or months or even years later, a whole chain of thoughts and actions has materialized in our lives.

Notice how often we get lost in mind fantasies of a future self: "I'll do this," "I'll go there." Losing ourselves in these projects is a manifestation of craving for becoming. In a sutta called "One Fortunate Attachment," the Buddha gave clear advice for freeing ourselves from this craving:

"Let not a person revive the past
Or on the future build his hopes;
For the past has been left behind
And the future has not been reached.
Instead with insight let him see
Each presently arisen state;
Let him know that and be sure of it,
Invincibly, unshakeably.

One who dwells thus ardently,
Relentlessly, by day, by night—
It is he, the Peaceful Sage has said,
Who has one fortunate attachment."[4]

What would it be like to live with that one fortunate attachment: not reviving the past, not hoping to be in the future?

On a more momentary level, we can see this craving for becoming in our relationship to the unfolding process itself. Even if we don't have expectations for some big, wonderful experience, how often do we seem to be leaning forward into the next moment, as if somehow the next step, the next breath, the next sensation or thought, will resolve everything, complete everything. We can see this leaning happen when we're feeling something unpleasant and watching for it to change. Or we see it when we're being with some emotion and wanting to feel it more deeply.

This sense of leaning forward, anticipating the next moment, is also a kind of craving for becoming. Here we're not seeing each of these experiences simply as insubstantial, empty phenomena arising and passing in each moment. We're living in a world of wanting. We forget that liberation is not about becoming or getting, not about holding on or craving or clinging, but about letting go, letting be. The great Indian saint Ramana Maharshi put it very simply: "Try to be less, not more."

THE THIRD DOMAIN OF CRAVING: THE DESIRE FOR NONEXISTENCE

The third kind of craving the Buddha talked about is desire for nonexistence: "This experience is so bad. If only I could not be." There are times in some people's lives when conditions feel unbearable and there is a strong desire to end it all.

On a more momentary level, we can notice the mind that wants to get rid of the present-moment experience because it is unpleasant. Here we can see how interrelated the three kinds of craving are. Because something is unpleasant, we desire its nonexistence, which leads to a craving for something pleasant, or wanting to experience a future existence different from what is happening.

The problem here is that this craving for nonexistence, no less than the other two types of cravings, is both sustained by and feeds the sense of self. And this is the fundamental wrong view that keeps the wheel of saṃsāra rolling along: a self to gratify, a self to clone in the future, a self to get rid of. The great discovery in our practice is that, on one level, birth and death, existence and nonexistence, self and other are the great defining themes of our lives. And on another level, it's all just a dance of insubstantial appearances, what the Buddha called "the magic show of consciousness."

The twentieth-century Taoist philosopher Wei Wu Wei (Terence Grey) described this dance in his book *Posthumous Pieces,* in which he wrote, "Destroy 'the ego,' hound it, beat it, snub it, tell it where it gets off. Great fun no doubt, but where is it? Must you not find it first? Isn't there a word about catching your goose before you can cook it? The great difficulty here is that there isn't one."

34

The Third Noble Truth

The Cessation of Dukkha

"Now this, bhikkhus, is the noble truth of the cessation of
dukkha: the remainderless fading and cessation, renunciation,
relinquishment, release, and letting go of that very craving."[1]

This statement from the Buddha is a very clear and unambiguous
declaration of what frees the mind. Can we even imagine a mind
free of craving? We might resonate more easily with St. Augustine's
famous prayer: "Dear Lord, please make me chaste, but not yet."

Some years ago, in reflecting on this third noble truth, I began to
understand the Buddha's words in a new and more immediate way.
Rather than understanding the end of craving only as some far-off
goal, as the end of the path in the distant future, or as some special
meditative state to try to sustain, I understood it as being a practice
to experience right now, in each moment.

When we explore directly, in our experience, the meaning of the
Buddha's declaration, we can see for ourselves how craving obscures
the natural ease and openness of mind, and how in moments free of
desire, wanting, and clinging, we can recognize the taste of happiness
and peace. As a simple experiment, the next time you have some
wanting or desire in the mind, investigate what the wanting feels like

and then notice how it feels when the wanting passes away. Given the great law of impermanence, it always will.

Tulku Urgyen Rinpoche, one of the great Tibetan Dzogchen masters of the last century, spoke frequently of recognizing the nature of mind—its empty, aware nature, free of any clinging to anything—for short moments many times. This can become a framework for understanding our own practice of letting go of craving: short moments, many times. As we do this, we learn to recognize and increasingly trust this place of ease.

Although there are different methods, vocabularies, and even metaphysical descriptions for the nature of ultimate freedom among the various Buddhist traditions, there is one common understanding of what frees the mind: liberation through nonclinging. This phrase is found throughout the Pali discourses and also in many of the teachings of the great Tibetan lamas and Chinese and Japanese Zen masters.

Patrul Rinpoche, a nineteenth-century wandering Dzogchen master of eastern Tibet, was much beloved by the ordinary Tibetans and known as "the Enlightened Vagabond." He had some useful words about nonclinging in a teaching called "Advice From Me to Myself":

> Listen up, old bad-karma Patrul,
> You dweller in distraction.
>
> For ages now you've been
> Beguiled, entranced, and fooled by appearances.
> Are you aware of that? Are you?
> Right this very instant, when you're
> Under the spell of mistaken perception
> You've got to watch out.
> Don't let yourself get carried away by this fake and empty life.
>
> Your mind is spinning around
> About carrying out a lot of useless projects:
> It's a waste! Give it up!
> Thinking about the hundred plans you want to accomplish,
> With never enough time to finish them,
> Just weighs down the mind.

You're completely distracted
By all these projects, which never come to an end,
But keep spreading out more, like ripples in water.
Don't be a fool: for once, just sit tight. . . .

If you let go of everything—
Everything, *everything*—
That's the real point![2]

WAYS TO ABANDON CRAVING

So the question for us is how to experience and practice this noncraving and nonclinging, first on a momentary level and then, in the end, as the unshakeable deliverance of mind, the cessation of craving without remainder. We can practice and accomplish this in various ways, and different Buddhist traditions highlight one or another of these methods.

Focus on the Drawbacks of Conditioned Experience

Regarding the end of craving, the Buddha made a very obvious but often overlooked observation: When we focus on the gratification that comes from sense pleasures, desire increases. When we focus on the drawbacks of sense pleasures, craving diminishes. But how often, in the midst of our involvement with the world of sense objects, do we pay attention to whether we are further conditioning or deconditioning craving? This would be an interesting practice to bring to the world and see what we could learn from it.

We can decondition, relinquish, and abandon craving through an increasingly refined awareness of the three characteristics. The more clearly we see the impermanence of all experience, the more we understand for ourselves the basic unreliability and ultimately unsatisfying nature of all phenomena. And through a sustained wise attention, we understand more deeply the selfless, impersonal nature of this whole unfolding process—that nothing lasts long enough to be considered "self." These universal characteristics are the drawbacks, the dangers, the downsides of conditioned experience.

Happily, though, there is also an upside. It is precisely because impermanent, conditioned phenomena are unsatisfying that we are motivated to awaken. Seeing these characteristics clearly becomes the cause of and condition for liberation. The Buddha pointed to this very directly:

> "If there were no danger, beings would not become disen-
> chanted with the world. But because there is danger in the
> world beings become disenchanted by it."[3]

It can be illuminating to watch our reactions to this teaching. How do we relate to words like *danger, drawback,* or *disenchantment?* Do they sound gloomy or fearful? Or, by helping us see things more completely, do they bring a sense of openness and relief? It's especially helpful to understand the word *disenchantment,* because the Buddha often speaks of this as the precursor to awakening. Remember, *disenchantment* means to wake up from the spell of enchantment, to wake up from the dreamlike state of ignorance.

On a recent retreat, I had a revealing experience of how easily we fall under the spell of ignorance and how, in a moment, we can wake up from that spell. You are probably familiar with the experience of waking up in the morning and then, perhaps, slipping back into a dream state for a few minutes before waking again. This might happen just once or maybe several times before we're fully alert. On this particular retreat, I was noticing that phenomenon very clearly. Then, later in the day, in times of walking meditation, I began to notice more clearly how often there is a thin layer of background thoughts, images, fragments of stories, floating like a thin layer of clouds across the mind. This stream of thoughts is really the hardly noticed but ongoing creation of the world we inhabit. And almost always the thoughts were self-referential in one way or another: memories, plans, likes and dislikes. What struck me forcibly at that time was that the experience of slipping into and out of these background thought worlds was the same experience of slipping back into a dream state after being awake. I realized that we are simply dreaming the self into existence. And I found that occasionally repeating that phrase during the day—"dreaming myself into existence"—reinforced the strong aspiration to stay awake and to notice more carefully the dream.

Notice How Impermanence Pervades Our Lives

An increasingly refined awareness of the three characteristics leads to a disenchantment that frees the mind. Sometimes we're aware of one or another of these characteristics on a macro level. For me, reading history has been a powerful reminder of the changing, insubstantial nature of all we take to be so vitally important in our lives. Recently, I read a biography of Genghis Khan, who created the Mongol Empire in the twelfth and thirteenth centuries. It was quite remarkable that this person who ruled most of Asia and even parts of Europe, whose word affected the lives of millions of people, is now just one more chapter in the rise and fall of empires, hardly thought about at all.

A deep reflection on this great truth of impermanence enlarges the context of our own experience and loosens the bonds of craving and attachment. It's the difference between the rollercoaster emotions of a child, with its many highs and lows in even just one day, and equanimity and wisdom that adults (ideally) develop about changing life circumstances. In the early years of my practice, when I would be going through a particularly difficult time, I would often imagine myself six months or a year in the future and know that at that time I would hardly remember what I was currently going through. It definitely helped to lessen the intensity of the dramas of the moment.

In meditation, we experience the disenchanting truths of change, unreliability, and selflessness on much more momentary levels. We can see so clearly that whatever arises also passes away, and that the whole cycle happens very quickly. At first this insight is exhilarating; there is a refined perception of what is happening and many of the factors of awakening are coming into balance for the first time. But then fear, and even despair, can arise, as we look deeper and see the continual dissolution of both consciousness and its object. Everything seems to be crumbling away, leaving us with no place to take a stand. If we can stay mindful and balanced in our experience of this phenomenon, even when dissolving objects are not clearly discernible, we come to a profound equanimity, at which point the practice is going on all by itself.

One metaphor describing this process is of a person jumping out of an airplane in free fall. At first, there is tremendous elation in the experience. Then the person realizes that there's no parachute and so feels intense fear and dread. But after some time, he realizes that there is also no ground. The fear dissolves, and then there is just the ease and balance of the ride.

Cut through Identification with the Knowing Mind

In the meditative process, sometimes all objects seem to disappear and all that's left is consciousness, the knowing mind. But care is needed here because there can be a subtle attachment to this state, an identification with awareness itself. This becomes an interesting place of investigation; we can notice how easy it is to make a home of awareness and have a sense of self settle right in. Andrew Olendzki, a Senior Scholar at the Barre Center for Buddhist Studies, expressed it this way: "Consciousness is not a thing that exists, but an event that occurs."

The question then arises, how can we cut through this subtle identification with knowing, with consciousness? Different traditions use different methods. As mentioned earlier, Mahasi Sayadaw describes this state very clearly and reminds meditators to keep noting the knowing mind, until one goes beyond even knowing.

In some Tibetan and Zen traditions, another approach is used to cut through any identification with knowing: looking for the mind itself. Tulku Urgyen Rinpoche would often instruct his students to look for the mind. Can you see it, taste it, touch it? When we look for it, there is nothing to find, and the not-finding *is* the finding. When we recognize that moment of not-finding, the mind's empty, selfless nature is revealed.

There is a powerful Zen dialogue that illuminates this point. The dialogue takes place between Bodhidharma, who is credited with bringing Buddhism to China in the fifth or sixth century, and Daizu Huike, who was to become his Dharma heir. Legend has it that Bodhidharma had meditated in a cave for nine years when Huike came to him for teachings.

> Huike said to Bodhidharma, "My mind is anxious. Please pacify it." To which Bodhidharma replied, "Bring me your mind, and I will pacify it." Huike said, "Although I've sought it, I cannot find it." Bodhidharma then said, "There, I have pacified your mind."[4]

When we look for the mind, there is nothing to find, and yet the capacity for knowing is there. In the not-finding, the mind is already pacified. This is more than a witty Zen story. We can apply this wisdom at any time during the day, and perhaps especially when our minds are anxious, seeing that the empty, aware nature is always there, already pacified.

NIBBĀNA: THE UNCONDITIONED

When the Buddha speaks of the end of dukkha, he is not simply talking about being in a good mood. The radical, uncompromising freedom of nibbāna is not dependent on conditions being favorable; it's not dependent on conditions at all. This deeper freedom, the end of craving, comes through a profound inner shift of understanding, in which the strongly held view of self is purified through the experience of what is unconditioned, unborn.

It's not surprising that different Buddhist traditions, even within Theravāda, express this experience in different ways. In many texts it is described as the cessation of conditioned consciousness. As practice matures, we reach a stage of perfect equanimity, where all the factors of enlightenment ripen. At this time, there are no cravings or yearnings, even for the next breath or the next moment of experience. There is not the slightest impulse toward either becoming or not becoming. As the mind settles into this perfect balance of non-craving, the flow of consciousness conditioned by changing objects suddenly stops. The mind then opens to and alights upon nibbāna, the unconditioned, the unborn.

> "There is, monks, an unborn, unbecome, unmade, uncon-
> ditioned. If, monks, there were no unborn, unbecome,
> unmade, unconditioned, no escape would be discerned
> from what is born, become, made, conditioned. But
> because there is an unborn, unbecome, unmade, uncondi-
> tioned, therefore an escape is discerned from what is born,
> become, made, conditioned."[5]

These moments of consciousness that take nibbāna as their object are called "path" and "fruition" (*magga phala,* in Pali). The path moment, likened to a sudden flash of lightning that illuminates the sky, has the power to completely uproot certain defilements from the mind, so that they don't arise again, and to weaken the defilements that remain. For this reason, the Buddha described nibbāna in this way: "And what, Bhikkhus, is the unconditioned? The destruction of lust, the destruction of hatred, the destruction of delusion. This is called the unconditioned."

The Mind Released

The Thai Forest tradition describes the experience of the unconditioned from another perspective, which has some strong resonance with Tibetan and Zen teachings as well. In the teachings of some of the Thai masters, a distinction is made between the consciousness that is included in the five aggregates and that arises dependent on one of the six sense objects, and another kind of consciousness called *citta,* heart-mind. This consciousness, in its pure and unmodified state, is beyond the aggregates. It is called "the signless," because it has no sign of impermanence or other signs by which it can be known. This is the mind free of any defilement.

Ajahn Maha Boowa teaches about this consciousness when he speaks of the conventional mind and the mind released. The conventional mind is ruled by the tides of proliferating thought and conditioned by ignorance and craving. When these defilements disappear through mindfulness and wisdom, then the true mind, or the mind released, appears to its full extent. All that remains is simple awareness, utterly pure. The aggregates, or conditioned phenomena, still function according to their own nature, but they do not in any way affect the mind released. This mind, this pure awareness, does not partake of any feeling apart from the ultimate ease, the highest peace, which is its own nature. Ajahn Maha Boowa, like the Buddha, emphasized that the defilements, the path, and enlightenment are all right in the heart.

In several suttas the Buddha describes this experience of the mind released:

> "'Consciousness without feature,
>   without end,
>   luminous all around:
> Here water, earth, fire, & wind
>   have no footing.
> Here long & short
>   coarse & fine
>   fair & foul
>   name & form

are all brought to an end.
With the cessation of [the activity of] consciousness
each is here brought to an end.'"6

This consciousness has no center or reference point of self; it is unsupported, unconditioned, unconstructed. It is described as the consciousness that makes no showing. The Buddha used a simple example to describe this unmanifest nature:

"Just as if there were a roofed house or a roofed hall having
windows on the north, the south or the east. When the sun rises,
and a ray has entered by way of the window, where does it land?"
"On the western wall, lord."
"And if there is no western wall, where does it land?"
"On the ground, lord."
"And if there is no ground, where does it land?"
"On the water lord."
"And if there is no water, where does it land?"
"It does not land, lord."
"In the same way, where there is no passion for nutriment
of physical food . . . contact . . . intention . . . consciousness,
where there is no delight, no craving, then consciousness
doesn't land there or grow. . . . That, I tell you, has no sorrow,
affliction, or despair."7

Think of how light lands on an object, even an object as insubstantial as air. Our ability to see the light, the radiance of it, depends on the object. But what happens when there is no object at all on which the light can land? The light then is unmanifest, unborn.

Beware the Conditioned Mind

In these most subtle realms of pure awareness and ultimate ease, we must remember that great care is needed. We can mistake wonderful and refined states of mind for the mind released. Ajahn Maha Boowa describes his process of understanding and awakening:

This radiance is the ultimate counterfeit, and at that moment
it's the most conspicuous point. You hardly want to touch it

at all, because you love it and cherish it more than anything else. In the entire body there is nothing more outstanding than this radiance, which is why you are amazed at it, love it, cherish it, dawdle over it, want nothing to touch it. But it's the enemy king: unawareness. . . .

Once when I went to practice at Wat Do Dammachedi, the problem of unawareness [ignorance] had me bewildered for quite some time. At that stage the mind was so radiant that I came to marvel at its radiance. Everything of every sort which could make me marvel seemed to have gathered there in the mind, to the point where I began to marvel at myself. "Why is it that my mind is so marvelous?" Looking at the body, I couldn't see it at all. It was all space—empty. The mind was radiant in full force. But luckily, as soon as I began to marvel at myself to the point of exclaiming deludedly in the heart without being conscious of it. . . . "Why has my mind come so far?"—at that moment, a statement of Dhamma spontaneously arose. This too I hadn't anticipated. It suddenly appeared, as if someone were speaking in the heart, although there was no one there speaking. It simply appeared as a statement: *"If there is a point or a center of the knower anywhere, that is an agent of birth."* That's what it said.[8]

This is a critical point worth repeating: as long as there is identification with anything, any sense of the knower, we are still bound by the conventional conditioned mind. Through our practice of mindfulness and wisdom, we keep deconstructing the sense of self, until only the ultimate ease remains. Although there are many different descriptions of the enlightened mind, there is one reference point of understanding that illuminates them all: the final uprooting of greed, hatred, and ignorance.

The third noble truth is the cessation of dukkha: "Realized is the unconditioned, achieved is the end of craving."

35

The Fourth Noble Truth

The Way Leading to the Cessation of Dukkha

IN THIS FINAL SECTION OF the teachings, the fourth of the noble truths, the Buddha summarizes all the instructions and essential elements of the path to realization:

> "And what, monks, is the Noble Truth of the Way of Practice Leading to the Cessation of Dukkha? It is just this Noble Eight-Fold Path, namely: - Right View, Right Thought, Right Speech, Right Action, Right Livelihood, Right Effort, Right Mindfulness, Right Concentration."[1]

This section of the text comes from the Mahāsatipaṭṭhāna Sutta, which is found in the Long Discourses of the Buddha. It is distinguished from the Satipaṭṭhāna Sutta of the Middle Length Discourses only by this further elaboration of the four noble truths.

When I first began reading and studying the teachings, this enumeration of the Eightfold Path seemed like an abstract philosophical list. It took me a long time to even remember what all the eight steps were. But as I continued my practice, and I explored more fully how to live the path rather than just read about it, this teaching took on an ever-expanding richness and depth. It began to reveal its own internal logic and consistency. Each step on the path leads to the next, culminating in the transformation of ignorance into liberating wisdom and awakening.

The eight steps on the path fall into three groups of training: the morality group of Right Speech, Right Action, and Right Livelihood; the concentration group of Right Effort, Right Mindfulness, and Right Concentration; and the wisdom group of Right View and Right Thought. In Pali, these groups are often referred to as the trainings in sīla, samādhi, and *paññā*.

If the training in sīla, or virtue, is the foundation for the others, why does the Buddha list the wisdom factors as the first two steps on the path? An interesting and unique aspect of the Buddha's teaching is that its starting point is not dogma or belief, but understanding. Even if this understanding is still conceptual, if we continue our practice, it leads us onward, culminating in direct, intuitive realization of the four noble truths. In this way, the wisdom factors are both the beginning and the end of this noble path.

It is not insignificant that the Buddha called this last of the noble truths "a path." The implication is that these eight successive steps lead somewhere, that there is a final goal. Although the notion of goal can sometimes lead to overstriving, to a kind of spiritual ambition that gets in the way of realization, this overstriving has more to do with *how* we are practicing rather than to the understanding that there is indeed an end of dukkha. René Daumal, in his book *Mount Analogue,* describes the crucial balance between living fully in the moment and, at the same time, keeping the vision of our final destination:

> Keep your eye fixed on the way to the top, but don't forget to look right in front of you. The last step depends on the first. Don't think you've arrived just because you see the summit. Watch your footing, be sure of the next step, but don't let that distract you from the *highest goal.* The first step depends on the last.[2]

STREAM-ENTRY

The first stage of awakening to which the path leads, the first actualization of this Noble Eightfold Path, is called "stream-entry." As mentioned in the last chapter, this is the path moment that uproots the first three of the ten fetters that bind us to conditioned existence: doubt, belief in rites and rituals as a path to freedom, and most fundamentally, the belief in self. Stream-entry has a couple of important implications. First, we have entered the stream toward enlightenment, and that stream flows in just one direction—toward full awakening. At this point, there is no going back.

Second, there is still a lot of work to do. Mahānāma was a layperson of the Buddha's Sakya clan who had attained stream-entry. But in one encounter with the Buddha, Mahānāma said that at times his mindfulness still got muddled. He asked the Buddha what his destination would be if he were distracted at the moment of death. The Buddha replied, "Don't be afraid, Mahānāma. Your death will not be a bad one. When a person's mind has been fortified for a long time by faith, virtue, learning, generosity and wisdom, his mind goes upward, goes to distinction."[3]

As a way of further highlighting the importance of the Eightfold Path, the Buddha once said to Sāriputta, his chief disciple and the one foremost in wisdom,

> "Sāriputta, this is said: 'The stream, the stream.' What, now, Sāriputta is the stream?"
>
> "This Noble Eightfold Path, venerable sir, is the stream; . . ."
>
> "Sāriputta, this is said: 'A stream-enterer, a stream-enterer.' What, now, Sāriputta, is a stream-enterer?"
>
> "One who possesses the Noble Eightfold Path, venerable sir, is called a stream-enterer: . . ."[4]

But for many of us the question arises, how can I know whether I truly possess the Noble Eightfold Path or not? The Buddha explained it in this way to two laypeople, the royal chamberlains of King Pasenadi:

> "The noble disciple, chamberlains, who possesses four things is a stream-enterer. . . .
>
> "What four? Here, chamberlains, a noble disciple possesses confirmed confidence in the Buddha . . . in the Dhamma . . . in the Sangha. He dwells at home with a mind devoid of the stain of stinginess, freely generous, open-handed, delighting in relinquishment, one devoted to charity, delighting in

giving and sharing. A noble disciple who possesses these four things is a stream-enterer."[5]

At other times, the Buddha includes in the qualities of a stream-enterer "possessing virtues dear to the noble ones—unbroken, untorn, unblemished, unmottled, freeing, praised by the wise, ungrasped, leading to concentration." The Buddha then goes on to say that the value of these qualities surpasses by far even sovereignty over the whole world.

Realization of Stream-Entry

Realization of the path can happen in different ways. Sometimes it is a spontaneous opening that can happen at any time in our lives. We might hear a short teaching, and the mind releases into what is unborn, unarisen. Realization could also happen outside the context of any specific teaching, simply as the result of our past practice and *paramis*. There are many stories of people attaining different stages of awakening in this way—in the moment of hearing a bird song or seeing a candle being snuffed out. Finally, it can happen—and most often does—as a progression through the classical stages of insight, which deepens our realization of the impermanent, unsatisfying, and selfless nature of all experience. Depending on our own particular background and conditioning, any one of these forms of realization can become the doorway to the unconditioned.

People's experience of stream-entry will vary greatly. The Abhidhamma, the Buddhist psychology, describes three different kinds of stream-enterers, the differences among which depend on the relative strength of the spiritual faculties of faith, energy, mindfulness, concentration, and wisdom. For some, it is a radical shift of perspective, like the shattering power of a massive earthquake or being struck by a bolt of lightning—or as if one has been turned inside out. For others, the moment may hardly be noticed.

There are both benefits and cautions in this mapping of the path. The benefit is that mapping provides signposts along the way to full enlightenment. It reminds us that many people have walked on what has been called "the ancient royal road to nibbāna," which is the ultimate good, and that they have passed through all the same difficulties and challenges that we encounter. The caution is that we can become attached to the idea of attainment, either before or after different experiences, and thus simply be strengthening the habit of self.

As a reference point for assessing different meditative experiences, we can always use the mirror of mindfulness to see whether the defilements have indeed been weakened and, at certain points, uprooted—or not. This, in the end, is what the path is all about. It's also helpful to know that although in different Buddhist traditions there are other maps of the path, different descriptions of how the mind is liberated, the Eightfold Path of practice enumerated in the very first discourse of the Buddha is the foundation of them all.

We often think of meditation as being at the heart of the path of awakening, and in many ways it is. The cultivation of mindfulness and concentration makes possible the wisdom that liberates the mind. But as we explore the different steps of the path in the following chapters, we will see that the Buddha's teaching of liberation includes more of life experience than simply the specialized circumstances of meditation practice. Walking the path transforms every aspect of our lives.

And, as Dzigar Kongtrul Rinpoche reminds us, we each need to walk the path by ourselves:

> The potential for realization is universal and present for all of us. True benefit will come from your own efforts and realization. For your efforts to bring benefit, you must take your life into your own hands and examine your mind and experience.
>
> From this point of view, nobody could be kinder to you than yourself. Nobody could have a greater effect on you or actually do more for you than yourself. The Buddha said, "I have shown you the path of liberation. Now liberation depends on you." This is really true. If you don't take your life into your own hands, not even the buddhas can make a difference. It's up to you.[6]

MINDFULNESS OF DHAMMAS

The Noble Eightfold Path:
Wisdom Factors

36

Right View

Worldly Ease

THE FIRST AND CRITICALLY IMPORTANT step of the Noble Eightfold Path is Right View or Right Understanding. Sometimes, when we hear the term *Right View,* we may associate it with an orthodox dogma that we need to subscribe to and that we then perhaps rebel against. But it becomes easier to understand its meaning if we see that the right view the Buddha enumerated is "right" in terms of understanding the first three noble truths. It is the view that helps us realize them for ourselves. Keep in mind that none of the Buddha's teaching requires blind belief. The invitation is always to "come and see"—to investigate and examine for ourselves whether the teachings accord with reality and are conducive to our welfare and happiness.

Right View is the important first step on the path because it sets the direction. No matter how long or difficult our journey may be, if we're heading in the right direction and we keep on going, we'll certainly reach the goal. If we don't know the right direction, then even with strong aspiration and efforts, we might wander for a long time and never reach our destination. The Buddha said that just as the dawn is the forerunner and precursor to the rising sun, so is Right View the forerunner and precursor of the breakthrough to the four noble truths.

In several discourses, the Buddha elaborates on Right View, making an interesting distinction between what we might call worldly or mundane right view—that is, the understandings that lead to worldly ease and happiness—and supramundane right view, those understandings that lead to liberation.

> "And what, bhikkhus, is right view? Right view, I say, is twofold: there is right view that is affected by taints, partaking of merit, ripening on the side of attachment; and there is right view that is noble, taintless, supramundane, a factor of the path."[1]

It is worth going into some detail about both of these aspects of understanding, because they have important consequences for our lives. (Note: I am using *Right View,* capitalized, to refer to the particular step of the Eightfold Path, but *right view,* lowercased, refers to the various understandings in the mind.)

Worldly right view very pragmatically acknowledges that for those of us who are not yet fully liberated, our wholesome actions are often in the realm of desire, of acquiring merit, of aiming for particular happy results in our lives. Even though these acts are wholesome (for example, acts of generosity), they may still be in the realm of acquisition—that is, making good karma for good results, rather than in the abandonment of desire. This aspect of right view is especially relevant for those of us who are laypeople, living our lives engaged with the world. It shows how we can live in the world in a way that brings happiness and ease rather than stress and difficulties.

There is a traditional expression of mundane right view found in the suttas, where in a few brief, sometimes cryptic phrases the Buddha points to a wealth of Dharma understanding. Some aspects will seem obvious, while others may be outside the realm of our immediate experience. But it is worth staying open to what might be different ways of understanding the world.

> "And what, bhikkhus, is right view that is affected by the taints, partaking of merit, ripening on the side of attachment? 'There is what is given and what is offered and what is sacrificed; there is fruit and result of good and bad actions; there is this world and the other world; there is

mother and father; there are beings who are reborn spontaneously; there are in the world good and virtuous recluses
and brahmins who have realized for themselves by direct
knowledge and declare this world and the other world.'
This is right view affected by taints, partaking of merit,
ripening on the side of attachment."[2]

MUNDANE RIGHT VIEW AND THE LAW OF KARMA

What does all this mean? All of these specific declarations rest on the
framework of understanding the law of karma, the understanding
that the only things that truly belong to us are our actions and their
results. According to the law of karma, the results of our actions
follow us like a shadow. When we integrate this realization into our
lives, we pay more attention to our choices and actions, and to where
they are leading.

The Practice of Generosity

In the Buddha's description of mundane right view, held in the
context of the law of karma, he elaborated a few particular areas
of investigation and practice. The first statement, "There is what is
given and what is offered and what is sacrificed," refers to the moral
and karmic significance of generosity. Acts of giving have power. The
Buddha emphasized this in his well-known teaching that said if we
knew as he did the fruits of giving, we wouldn't let a single meal pass
without sharing it.

A question for us then is how, in our fast-paced, individualistic
culture, can we actually make generosity a practice? One way that I've
found very helpful is to act on each of those moments of generous
impulse. If I have a thought to give, whether it is just a small gesture
or something big, I try to act on it at the appropriate time, rather
than letting the thought simply pass away or second-guessing myself
("Should I? Shouldn't I? Is it too much?"). Acts of generosity bring
obvious benefit to the recipient, but they also bring benefit to ourselves, both in the moment and also when these wholesome karmic
actions bear fruit. One of the immediate blessings of generosity is that
it feels good in the moment. Every time we give, we're strengthening
associated factors of mettā and renunciation; in those moments, we
have friendly, loving feelings toward the recipient at the same time

that we're letting go. And if we consciously reflect on the whole process, then the practice of generosity also fosters the growth of wisdom. The Buddha often began the sequence of his graduated teachings with talks on generosity because they gladden and brighten the heart, making it open and receptive for the further teachings of liberation.

Motivations and Their Consequences

The second phrase in the description of mundane right view, "there is fruit and result of good and bad actions," has already been discussed in terms of the law of karma. But there is no way to overestimate the importance of these teachings—that our actions bring results, that we are the heirs, the owners, of our actions. Putting this understanding into practice enables us to engage creatively with our lives, knowing that our choices, and more precisely, our motivations, shape how our lives unfold. We begin to take a much greater sense of responsibility for what we do, knowing that it has consequences both in the moment and for the future.

The Buddha was very helpful in pointing out quite specifically what actions are unwholesome and lead to suffering, and what actions are wholesome and lead to happiness. These ten unwholesome actions are killing, stealing, committing sexual misconduct, lying, speaking harshly, backbiting, engaging in useless speech, covetousness, ill will, and wrong view. The ten wholesome actions are the refraining from these. Both the wholesome and unwholesome aspects are woven into the other seven steps of the Eightfold Path, which we will discuss in the following chapters.

Rebirth and Other Planes of Existence

The next aspect of mundane right view says, "there is this world and the other world." This is a statement about rebirth and the other planes of existence. For many of us, this concept is probably outside the realm of our own direct experience, and it is also outside the mainstream of Western thought. So it may be difficult to resonate with this part of the teachings.

For me, there was a very gradual process in opening to these possibilities. I came to Dharma practice from a study of Western philosophy, and I had no belief at all in past and future lives or other realms of existence. Over time, though, several things began to open my mind.

First, the more I practiced and studied the Dharma, because so much of what the Buddha taught did resonate with what I was experiencing, I began to think that if he was right about so much, maybe I should keep an open mind about what is still beyond my immediate experience. I began practicing poet Samuel Taylor Coleridge's "willing suspension of disbelief." I saw that just as we can become attached to our belief systems, we can also become attached to our disbeliefs.

Second, I met teachers such as Dipa Ma who could say from their own experience, "Yes, this is true." Such statements are not at all proofs of rebirth, but my great trust in Dipa Ma, specifically, opened my mind to further consider these possibilities. In this same vein, in our first teacher-training program at the Insight Meditation Society, we had a young Sri Lankan man whom I had first met in Sri Lanka when he was a child. At age two or three, before he could even read or write, he started spontaneously chanting long, complex Buddhist suttas and chanting them in an ancient melody no longer heard in Sri Lanka. As he got a little older and started meditating, he began remembering some of his past lives, and in one he was one of a group of chanting monks in the entourage of the fifth-century great Buddhist commentator Buddhaghosa. He said that the spontaneous chants he'd experienced as a very young boy came from the practices of that life. Again, while this story in no way constitutes scientific proof of past lives and rebirth, experiences like this certainly raise interesting questions and possibilities.

The last part of this opening to potentials beyond my own field of experience was the growing meditative insights into the nonmaterial nature of awareness. As we become mindful of the experience of awareness itself, it's possible to intuit it without any physical limitations.

Each of us has our own relationship to these teachings on rebirth and other realms, and it is important to emphasize that awakening doesn't depend on any belief. But as the great transmission of buddhadharma from East to West unfolds, it's helpful not to immediately dismiss what is beyond our limited personal experience, but to simply keep an open mind regarding this and other possibilities.

Karmic Relationships with Our Parents and Children

The next phrase in mundane right view, "there is mother and father," highlights not the obvious fact that we're all born of parents, but the fact that there is also a special karmic relationship to them, with attendant responsibilities. Here in the West, and perhaps in the East as well, there are sometimes complications and difficulties in the relationships we have with our parents. The Dalai Lama's often repeated teaching that at some point all beings have been our mothers doesn't necessarily evoke the same feelings in us as it does in him.

Regardless, though, of our present relationship with our parents, the Buddha is pointing out that there is a karmic debt for the great gift of our precious human birth. He said that the best possible repayment of that debt is to somehow connect our parents with the Dharma or at least to try and plant a few seeds of these understandings within them. Great skill and sensitivity is needed in doing this, and how each of us goes about it will vary depending on the particular relationship we have.

Almost certainly, though, proselytizing won't work. The greatest communication is usually how we are rather than what we say. If there is already an open, loving communication, then there are real possibilities for dharma discussion and maybe even an encouragement to practice. If communication is difficult, the first steps might simply be to cultivate less judgment and more acceptance of our parents just as they are.

Over the years of teaching, I know of many instances where there was tremendous conflict, and sometimes even trauma, in these relationships, but over time, with years of practice and much patience, the relationships transformed into ones of genuine mettā and openness.

These difficulties are not limited to this modern age. Even Sāriputta, the chief disciple of the Buddha and second only to the Buddha in his wisdom, had mother problems. Sāriputta was born into a brahmin family and had three brothers and three sisters. All of them eventually ordained as monks and nuns, and all became arahants. But his mother was a staunch brahmin, and she remained hostile to the Buddha and his teaching. There is a story about Sāriputta going to visit his mother in her home village:

> [O]nce, when the Ven. Sāriputta was in his own village
> of Nālaka with a large retinue of monks, he came to his
> mother's house in the course of his alms round. His mother
> gave him a seat and served him with food, but while she
> did so she uttered abusive words: "Oh, you eater of others'

leavings!" she said. "When you fail to get leavings of sour rice gruel, you go from house to house among strangers, licking the leavings off the backs of ladles! And so it was for this that you gave up eighty crores of wealth and became a monk! You have ruined me! Now, go on and eat!" Likewise, when she was serving food to the monks, she said: "So! You are the men who have made my son your page boy! Go on, eat now!"

Thus she continued reviling them, but Sāriputta spoke not a word. He took his food, ate it, and in silence returned to the monastery. The Buddha learned of the incident from his son Rāhula, who had been among the monks at the time. All the bhikkhus who heard of it wondered at the elder's great forbearance, and in the midst of the assembly the Buddha praised him.[3]

Many years later, as Sāriputta was contemplating his own passing away, he reflected on his mother who, although she was the mother of seven arahants, still had no faith in the Buddha, Dharma, or Sangha. Through his eye of wisdom, he also saw that she had the necessary supportive conditions for stream-entry, but that only he would be able to bring this about.

So Sāriputta returned to his mother's home, to his own birth chamber, and it's said that on the last evening of his life, gods from all the heavenly realms appeared in order to pay homage to this great enlightened being. This finally seemed to impress his mother: "[I]f all these celestial beings are paying homage to my son, what great virtues must the Buddha have." Her heart softened, and Sāriputta gave a final discourse establishing his mother in the fruit of stream-entry, bound for full awakening.

Although we may not have celestial beings appear as we visit our parents, this story does point to the importance the Buddha placed on this fundamental relationship. It may be an easy one, or one that takes great patience and forbearance, but it's worth reflecting on how we might help establish in our parents some seeds of dharma understanding. And even if they have already passed away, it's possible to share our merit with them, dedicating it to their welfare and happiness and awakening. Depending on circumstances, this can have a very beneficial effect.

Although it is not mentioned specifically in the suttas about right view, there is the same level of responsibility, care, and love toward one's own children. One intriguing story in the texts tells about Anāthapiṇḍika, the very wealthy householder who was the chief male lay supporter of the Buddha. He had four children: three daughters, who were all steeped in the Dharma and had attained various stages of enlightenment, and one son, who was not at all interested and simply liked to immerse himself in worldly pleasures.

Anāthapiṇḍika, out of concern for his son's welfare, began bribing his son with gold pieces to go hear the Buddha speak. When the boy did, the Buddha, through the power of his mind, kept Anāthapiṇḍika's son from getting a clear understanding of what he was saying, so that the young man kept asking questions to clarify the meaning. And in the very process of questioning and clarifying the meaning, he, too, became a stream-winner.

Sometimes our efforts to share the Dharma with our family members bring discernible results, and sometimes they do not. There were people in the Buddha's time who, for whatever karmic reason, even the Buddha couldn't help. But we may be able to plant Dharma seeds that will ripen at some future time. What is important is our intention and motivation for sharing the Dharma.

Realization through Direct Experience

The last two statements in worldly right view affirm that there are beings who are reborn spontaneously in other realms, and that there are wise and virtuous people in the world who have realized the truth through their own experience. Regarding the first of these, I've already mentioned the importance of staying open to possibilities beyond our present experience. In the Buddha's teaching we're not enjoined to blind belief in anything; at the same time, it's helpful to let go of attachment to blind disbelief. We can simply recognize that rebirth and other realms of existence are part of the teachings and that we may not yet have personal experience of them.

It is the last aspect of mundane right view that I find particularly relevant now in our Western culture: "there are in the world wise and virtuous recluses and brahmins who have realized for themselves by direct knowledge"—in other words, wise and virtuous people who have realized the truth through their own direct experience. As a society, we don't generally recognize wisdom as a cultural value. We more frequently value talent, wealth, looks, and even, to some extent, intelligence. But I haven't yet seen any magazine cover dedicated to the wisest person of the year.

Our egalitarian values can sometimes diminish the understanding that there actually are people wiser than ourselves, people from whom we can genuinely learn about the Dharma, the truth, the way things are. Acknowledging this also keeps us open to wisdom from unexpected sources. We learn to listen for that voice of genuine experience, rather than being influenced, positively or negatively, by personality or position. Recognizing that there are genuinely wise and awakened beings in the world helps us reaffirm the understanding that wisdom and awakening are possible for us as well.

We can practice applying various aspects of mundane right view in different ways. Some may be obvious to us, like the practice of generosity, which bears wholesome fruit, or investigating our motivations and acting on the wholesome and letting go of the unwholesome. Other aspects of this right view may not be immediately apparent. We may want to experiment to see how they affect the quality of our lives.

For example, if we consider the possibility of rebirth and other planes of existence, would it change in any way how we live, the choices we make, the stress or ease in our lives? In one simple way, I've found that being open to this teaching of rebirth has taken a certain pressure off my life. Within the realm of the mundane, of worldly happiness, I no longer feel the need to fulfill every desire or accomplish every goal this time around. Life increasingly feels like a long weekend going by too fast. If I don't become an expert skier in this life, or whatever the desire might be, maybe I'll accomplish it in the next. This way of seeing allows me to prioritize what seems most important without thinking that I'm missing out on the other things I don't get to do. Everything gets a bit more relaxed.

Of course, as we begin to explore the noble or supramundane right view, we see that real freedom lies in letting go of all craving, all desire for acquisition, for becoming, and cutting through the great Gordian knot of self.

37

Right View

Liberation

NOBLE RIGHT VIEW, WHICH LEADS onward to nibbāna, is described in two ways in the suttas. First, it is described as the wisdom factor of mind. It illuminates what arises so that we can know and understand things as they really are. The arising of wisdom is like turning on a light in a darkened room. In the Abhidhamma, the Buddhist psychology, wisdom is one of the twenty-five beautiful mental factors.

Second, noble right view is described in terms of its objective content—that is, *what* wisdom discovers as it illuminates our experience. And in the Mahāsatipaṭṭhāna Sutta, the Buddha equates this liberating right view specifically to the understanding of the four noble truths:

> "And what, monks, is Right View? It is, monks, the knowl-
> edge of dukkha, the knowledge of the origin of dukkha, the
> knowledge of the cessation of dukkha, and the knowledge of
> the way of practice leading to the cessation of dukkha. This
> is called Right View."[1]

The Buddha is so clear about emphasizing the importance of right view in promoting the welfare of beings:

"Bhikkhus, I do not see even a single thing on account of which unarisen wholesome qualities arise and arisen wholesome qualities increase and expand so much as right view."[2]

Mindfulness of the four noble truths is, in fact, the last set of instructions in the Satipaṭṭhāna Sutta. We've already discussed the first three of them in previous chapters, but it might be helpful to review and highlight a few of their key elements as they pertain to the right view of the awakened mind.

THE SUBTLETY OF WRONG VIEW

All of us have directly experienced the truth of dukkha—that is, the unsatisfying, unreliable, sometimes suffering nature of experience. The body gets sick, ages, and finally dies. The mind suffers through various afflictive emotions: fear, anger, jealousy, despair, envy, greed, restlessness. There's a long list of them. As the sutta reminds us, association with the unpleasant is suffering. Separation from the pleasant is suffering. Not getting what we want is suffering. We're all familiar with these experiences.

The Buddha then summed up this first noble truth even more fundamentally and comprehensively, in a way that brings the extent and subtlety of our wrong view into stark relief. He said, "[I]n brief, the five aggregates of clinging are dukkha." Why is this? Because these five aggregates, which constitute what we claim as self, as "I"—material elements, feelings, perceptions, mental formations, and consciousness—are in constant change and flux. There is nothing in their nature that can provide a place of peace, of rest, of security. And the more we cling to that which in its very nature is subject to change, the greater unease there is in our lives.

A simple example of aggregates of clinging: If we're attached to looking and feeling young, how do we feel as the body ages? How much advertising and production of material goods in our society is devoted to the body looking a particular way? This is attachment to the aggregate of physical form, attachment to the aggregate of pleasant feeling associated with it, attachment to the aggregate of the perception of youth, identified with all the volitions and mental states to accomplish it, and attachment to identification with the one knowing all of this. Right here, in this not-uncommon pattern, we see the clinging to the five aggregates at work.

What is quite amazing is that even in the face of recognizing impermanence, which is not an esoteric, hidden truth, even in the face of something so obvious as the truth of change, the habit of clinging is so strong. What feeds and nourishes this habit of grasping is one particular kind of wrong view, a view that keeps us bound to saṃsāra. In Pali, it is called *sakkāyadiṭṭhi,* or wrong view of self. This term is also sometimes translated as "personality view" or "personality belief."

It's easy to think about this as a Buddhist philosophical principle and miss the critical importance of it in our lives. The Buddha highlights just how important it is:

> "Bhikkhus, I do not see even a single thing so blameworthy
> as wrong view. Wrong view is the worst of things that are
> blameworthy."[3]

How Delusion Strengthens Wrong View

Why does the Buddha make such a strong declaration about this wrong view of self? It is because so many of our unwholesome actions, with their attendant karmic results, are born from it. As long as this view is the central understanding of our lives, and it is for most people, we spend energy and effort gratifying the self, defending it, holding on to it. And yet all of this potent karmic activity is revolving around something that isn't even there. This is the obscuring power of delusion.

A few examples show how our ordinary way of viewing experience is unknowingly strengthening wrong view. "I feel happy," "I feel miserable," and "I am delighted" are all wrong views about mental feelings. We take what is impersonal, the feeling tones, to be "I" or "mine." "I want to do this, to see this, to hear this, to go there" are all delusions about the mental factor of desire to do. We add the "I" and "mine" to the working of an impersonal factor. "I make an effort" or "I have concentration" is wrong view about those two qualities. We can analyze almost every aspect of our daily life and see how we are continually identifying with the different mind states, moods, and emotions that arise, and creating and strengthening the sense of self in the process.

ENHANCING RIGHT VIEW OF NON-SELF

The underlying context for whatever practice we're doing is seeing whether it serves and enhances the right view of non-self. It is this foundation that brings us from conceptual and worldly right view to what the Buddha called "the right view that is noble, taintless, supramundane, a factor of the path." The instructions are so clear, although as we know, a great deal of patience and perseverance is required in order to integrate them into our understanding and fulfill them in our lives.

Observe the Changing Nature of the Aggregates

We can approach the understanding of selflessness most easily by refining our awareness of impermanence, particularly noticing the changing nature of the five aggregates. In fact, these aggregates are a clarifying shorthand for everything we experience. We begin to deconstruct the concept of self first by seeing what is actually there and then by seeing the very momentary, fleeting, insubstantial nature of those experiences. There are different ways we can go about seeing this way.

We might spend some sustained periods of time focusing on a particular aggregate, such as being as continuously aware as possible of the body. This might entail maintaining awareness of the breath, or of changing postures, or of the arising and passing of different sensations.

We might focus for some time on the impermanent nature of feelings, recognizing that we experience whatever arises, moment after moment, as being pleasant, unpleasant, or neutral. The more we attend to the impermanence of these experiences, the less we cling to them as being "I" or "mine" or self. We can pay particular attention to perceptions, the recognition and interpretation of objects of the senses. How we perceive things strongly conditions both feelings and mental formations.

I had one experience that particularly highlighted these patterns of conditioning. Quite a few years ago, I was teaching a retreat in Mendocino, California, with my colleague Sharon Salzberg. We were sitting in my room, talking before the morning meditation. All of a sudden, and quite spontaneously, I burped a cloud of sweet-smelling smoke and ash from my mouth. It was exceedingly strange, and neither of us knew what to make of it. We simply went on with the retreat, but I was definitely wondering what that was all about.

About a month later, as we were beginning to teach our first three-month retreat in Bucksport, Maine, I was in a bank, standing before the teller's window. Again, quite without warning, the same thing happened. The teller looked at me quite strangely. At this point, I felt I should try and find some explanation for this very strange occurrence.

At the time, Ram Dass was teaching in New York with a woman named Joya, who reputedly had psychic abilities. I asked a friend to tell Joya about the smoke and ash and to see if she had any ideas about it. Her response was that it was the holy *verbuti* of the Indian saint Sai Baba. *Verbuti* was the ash that he would spontaneously manifest and give to his disciples. Well, I felt pretty good after hearing that.

Some time later, I met up with Munindra-ji, my first Dharma teacher, and asked him. He said in his usual matter-of-fact manner, "Oh, it is the fire element." That was a little less impressive. Finally, I had the opportunity to ask Dipa Ma, our wonderful teacher from Calcutta, who had great meditative and psychic attainments. She just looked at me and said, "You must have some disease!" Different concepts, different feelings about them, and yet the experience was the same.

We get lost in this world of perception and interpretation about more ordinary experiences, in the endless stories we create about ourselves and the world. How much of the time are we living in the dreamlike nature of thoughts and perceptions, even while we're awake? It's tremendously freeing to highlight those moments when we awaken from being lost and to recognize the impermanent, selfless nature of this particular aggregate of perception.

We can practice a sustained mindfulness of the fourth aggregate, mental formations, as well. This is becoming aware of all the moods, emotions, reactions, and even refined meditative states that arise. All of them are not self, not "I," not "mine." All are arising out of conditions, and all pass away when conditions change. Although they seem so important when we're lost in them, they are as ephemeral as clouds forming and dissolving in the sky. Based on right view, we can practice not identifying with either the wholesome or unwholesome formations as self.

And on the subtlest level, we need to cut through the identification with consciousness, not creating a haven for wrong view by taking consciousness, the knowing faculty, as being "I" or "mine."

"Any kind of form whatsoever, Rāhula, whether past, future,
or present, internal or external, gross or subtle, inferior or

superior, far or near—having seen all form [feeling, perception, formations, consciousness] as it really is with correct wisdom thus: 'This is not mine, this I am not, this is not myself,' one is liberated through nonclinging. . . .

"When one knows and sees thus . . . the mind is rid of I-making, mine-making and conceit, has transcended discrimination, and is peaceful and well liberated."[4]

See Which Aggregate Is Predominant in the Moment

Besides focusing on a particular aggregate for some time, we can also strengthen this aspect of right view by recognizing which of the aggregates is predominant in the moment, and by seeing the interplay and changing nature of them all. For example, you might be walking outside and feeling the sensation of the movement of walking. This is mindfulness of the material elements. Then you feel the warmth of the sun or a cold blast of wind. The warmth and cold are also physical elements. But then the feeling of pleasant or unpleasant may become predominant. We recognize that as the feeling aggregate, arising in the moment and passing away.

You hear a sound and recognize it as that of a bird, or see something and recognize it as a tree or a building or a person. That moment of recognition and perhaps subliminal naming is the aggregate of perception. Then you might be gladdened by the sun's warmth or a birdsong, or be reactive to a person walking by. These mind states are all part of the aggregate of mental formations coming into the foreground. And sometimes you might be walking, simply resting in awareness, with mindfulness predominantly on this knowing faculty. There is no particular order in which the different aggregates come into the foreground. Right view, as the wisdom factor of mind, simply investigates what is predominant and sees its impermanent, selfless nature.

THE THREE DISTORTIONS OF EXPERIENCE

There are three distortions of experience that can occur. The first is distortion of perception; the second, distortion of mind; and the third, distortion of view. The first is when we simply mistake one thing for another. We might be walking in the woods, see a stick lying on the path, and mistake it for a snake. This kind of distortion is easily remedied by a closer investigation of the experience. Distortions of mind occur when we think and ruminate about our mistaken perceptions. We see the stick, take it to be a snake, and then, thinking about all the stories we've heard about poisonous snakes, we become afraid. This is the distortion of mind. It's a little deeper than the first distortion, but it's still quite possible to see through it as we examine the situation more closely.

It is distortion of view that is the deepest and most difficult to remedy. This is the case when we become so convinced of the truth of something that no matter what evidence is presented to the contrary, we hold tenaciously to that belief. There are many examples of this at work in our lives and in our society. There are many people today in America who completely dismiss the theory of evolution in spite of overwhelming scientific evidence supporting it, because it doesn't fit with their particular view of the world. In the political arena, there are members of the "birther movement," people who don't believe that President Barack Obama was born in the United States. It's certainly legitimate to question and then to examine the evidence. Distortion of view takes place when we hold so deeply to our viewpoint that not even known facts can sway our beliefs.

The Buddha talked about these different distortions in terms of seeing what is impermanent as permanent, what is unsatisfying as satisfying, what is non-self as self, and what is non-beautiful as beautiful. These four hallucinations, discussed in detail in chapter 24: The Wheel of Saṃsāra, happen every time we become attached to or cling to some experience. We hold on because we forget that there is nothing that lasts or is ultimately satisfying. We become attached because we claim things as being "I" or "mine," and in our attraction to the beautiful, we usually don't perceive its decaying nature.

Until we're fully enlightened, we will all experience these distortions to a greater or lesser extent. From the perspective of the spiritual path, what is essential is that we establish ourselves in right view, so that even as we continue to fall under the sway of distortions of perception and of mind, we understand that they are temporary and, therefore, no longer set the direction of our lives. As Ledi Sayadaw pointed out, once we have established right view within ourselves, we no longer will commit any weighty, unwholesome actions that lead to misfortune. And the two remaining distortions, of perception and mind, merely enable such beings to enjoy those worldly pleasures that they have lawfully earned.

In one discourse the Buddha said there are two conditions for the arising of right view: the voice of another and wise attention. We have heard the voice—or the words—of the Buddha. The rest is now up to us.

38

Right Thought

Renunciation

THE SECOND STEP OF THE Noble Eightfold Path, following on Right Understanding, is Right Thought, sometimes called Right Intention or Right Resolve. In the context of this chapter, I'll be using these terms interchangeably. The importance of this step on the Path is highlighted by one obvious but often-overlooked truth: the great power of habit and habitual tendencies in the unfolding of our lives. The more often a particular thought arises in the mind, the more likely that it will arise again:

> "Bhikkhus, whatever a bhikkhu frequently thinks and pon-
> ders upon, that will become the inclination of the mind."[1]

Given that our actions are conditioned by how we think about ourselves and the world, and that wholesome and unwholesome actions bring their respective results, we can begin to recognize the pivotal role right thought plays on our path. And all the different elements of right view, the first step, lead us to cultivate those thoughts and intentions that result in both worldly happiness and a more ultimate freedom.

"And what, monks, is Right Thought? The thought of renunciation, the thought of non-ill-will, the thought of harmlessness. This, monks, is called Right Thought."[2]

The question for us is how to put this step on the Path into practice. In one discourse of the Middle Length Discourses called "The Two Kinds of Thoughts" (mentioned in chapter 3: Mindfulness: The Gateway to Wisdom), the Buddha suggests one way to begin: cultivate a clear discernment of the kinds of thoughts that arise in our minds. We can notice which thoughts are rooted in desire, ill will, or cruelty, consciously reflect on the karma that they cause, and then abandon them, letting them go. And we can notice those thoughts inclining toward renunciation, goodwill, and compassion, reflect on their value, and then strengthen them in our lives. All of this is wise reflection in the service of the Path.

As we become more mindful of these two classes of thoughts, we also become more aware of the strength and seductive powers of the unwholesome patterns. Ill will and aversion are said to be more dangerous than greed and desire, but easier to uproot; whereas desire is less dangerous, but harder to uproot. Why is this? Ill will has more harmful consequences, but it is always unpleasant, and the suffering of it is obvious. Sense desires, on the other hand, are usually associated with pleasure, and it's not always apparent why renouncing them is a good idea.

At one time, a householder named Tapussa went to see Ānanda and said,

> "Venerable Ānanda, sir, we are householders who indulge in sensuality, delight in sensuality, enjoy sensuality, rejoice in sensuality. For us—indulging in sensuality, delighting in sensuality, enjoying sensuality, rejoicing in sensuality—renunciation seems like a sheer drop-off. Yet I've heard that in this doctrine and discipline the hearts of the very young monks leap up at renunciation, grow confident, steadfast, and firm, seeing it as peace. So right here is where this doctrine and discipline is contrary to the great mass of people: i.e., [this issue of] renunciation."[3]

After hearing these householders, Ānanda said, "Let's go ask the Buddha about this." So they went off to where the Buddha was staying, and Ānanda repeated their conversation. The Buddha replied:

> "So it is, Ānanda. So it is. Even I myself, before my Awakening, when I was still an unawakened Bodhisatta, thought: 'Renunciation is good. Seclusion is good.' But my heart didn't leap up at renunciation, didn't grow confident, steadfast, or firm, seeing it as peace. The thought occurred to me: 'What is the cause, what is the reason, why my heart doesn't leap up at renunciation, doesn't grow confident, steadfast, or firm, seeing it as peace?' Then the thought occurred to me: 'I haven't seen the drawback of sensual pleasures; I haven't pursued [that theme]. I haven't understood the reward of renunciation; I haven't familiarized myself with it. That's why my heart doesn't leap up at renunciation, doesn't grow confident, steadfast, or firm, seeing it as peace.'"[4]

The Buddha went on to say that by reflecting on the drawbacks of sense pleasures and familiarizing himself with the rewards of renunciation, there arose the possibility of his heart leaping up at renunciation, growing confident, steadfast, and firm, seeing it as peace.

RECOGNIZING OUR OWN ADDICTIONS

As we reflect on the drawbacks of sense pleasures and the rewards of renunciation, we often find difficulty even when we just hear the word *renunciation*. It can set off alarm bells within us, perhaps because we associate it with the repression of desires, with deprivation, with a rather bleak and austere lifestyle. So it's no wonder that our hearts don't leap up at the thought of it.

But a more accurate and liberating understanding of renunciation would be as the experience of nonaddiction. We all know the suffering bound up with addictions, whatever they might be. We might be addicted, in one way or another, to food, drugs, sex, alcohol, or perhaps more unnoticed, to work, power, recognition, wealth, or even comfort. We can become addicted to and entranced by certain mind states and emotions, like excitement or intensity or fear—witness the very big audience for terrifying horror movies.

We become addicted not only to the gratification of our wants, but also to the mental habit of wanting itself. There's a phenomenon I call "catalogue consciousness." Have you ever found yourself casually opening a catalogue that comes in the mail and turning the pages, just waiting for something to want. It's rare that we put down the catalogue halfway through. We love to want, and we love the anticipation of fulfilling a want.

Meditators can also get addicted to different meditative states, like rapture or calm. How often in our practice are we trying to recreate some experience we've had before? We can get addicted to investigation; we can become overly fascinated with everything we're discovering. At one point in my practice in Burma, when I had been there for several months, the mindfulness had become very sharp, and I was seeing extremely minute details about what was arising. When I reported this to Sayadaw U Paṇḍita, thinking that things were going very well, all he said to me was, "You're too attached to subtlety." It was such a powerful reminder that the practice is about renunciation, about letting go; everything in our practice is in the service of that. It is best summed up in one line of the Diamond Sutra: "Develop a mind that clings to naught." Or, rather than "clings to naught," perhaps we should say, "doesn't cling to anything."

What's so beguiling about our addictions, whether great or small, is that in the moment of gratification, they do give us pleasure. But then we grasp at them, feel the lack when they change, and reach for them again and again, or we look for another source of momentary satisfaction, and then another and another, until we're totally immersed in the wanting and grasping states of mind. We become quite firmly enmeshed in the force field of our desires, usually not even suspecting that we're entrapped. We might look at all our habitual actions during the day. Although we probably don't think of them as addictions, how easy would it be to let go of a strong habit?

WISE RESTRAINT

It's possible, though, to relate to desire in an altogether different way, a way of much greater freedom. We can practice developing a wise restraint, where we settle back and allow the desires to arise and pass away without feeling the need or compulsion to act on them. In this practice of renunciation, we can taste for ourselves that there is greater ease in not wanting than in wanting. Here we get a glimpse of the third noble truth, the end of craving, even if, at first, it's just for a few moments.

As an experiment, pay careful attention to those moments when you go from being lost in wanting, lost in some enjoyment of sensual pleasures, including your mental fantasies, to being free of the wanting. Or notice the transition from moments of being lost in and identified with pleasant feelings to being mindful of them.

My experience is that when I'm aware of those moments of transition, it always feels like I'm being released from the grip of something, no matter how pleasant it might have been. It feels like I'm opening to a larger, wider, more expansive state of heart and mind. A verse in the Dhammapada expresses this clearly: "If by giving up a lesser happiness a greater happiness could be found, a wise person would renounce the lesser for the sake of the greater."

In these moments, we might understand the possibility of our "hearts leaping up at renunciation, growing confident, steadfast, and firm, seeing it as peace."

Renunciation Is a Gradual Process

But even when we've had this experience in our practice and in our lives, developing the *parami* of renunciation is still a gradual process. There's often fear or anxiety in the thought of giving something up, of letting go, until we've seen for ourselves, repeatedly, that doing so leads to greater happiness and wellbeing. Just before going to Burma for the first time, I had anxiety dreams about arriving at the monastery and having to give up my *zafu*, my meditation cushion. That didn't happen, but the dreams were indicative of the deep-seated fear of going into the unknown, to a place where renunciation was more the norm.

In all the monasteries in Burma, lay meditators follow what are called "the eight precepts," rather than the basic five followed by householders. The main addition is the practice of not taking any solid food after noon. What I've found interesting, in watching my own mind, is seeing how easy and unproblematic it is in those situations to observe this precept and how conducive doing so is to lightness of body and mind. And yet, when left to my own devices, I see a reluctance to play at that edge. This points to the depth of our conditioning and the value of repeating practices of renunciation until the rewards and happiness from them become the default understanding of our lives.

The Buddha often referred to the blessing of renunciation as "the cleansing of the mind." I feel this blessing frequently when I'm with monks or nuns who are well established in the monastic lifestyle, where renunciation is a way of life. There is a certain purity, clarity, simplicity, and contentment that stands in rather stark contrast to the busyness, clutter, and ordinary desires of our worldly life. There's a delight in just being with such people, a kind of contact high of peace and ease.

WAYS TO PRACTICE RENUNCIATION

Although most of us are not living as monks or nuns, we can still find ways to practice renunciation in our lives and experience the contentment that it brings.

Change Habit Patterns

We can examine various habits and simply change the routine. See what it's like to drink green tea instead of black, to get up fifteen minutes earlier than usual, to check email one time less a day. We can practice renouncing complexity. We so often create very complicated lives for ourselves, getting lost again and again in the drama of our stories and emotions, in some way relishing them.

And yet, when we investigate our experiences in the moment more carefully, we see that it's really only six things that ever happen: sights and sounds, smells and tastes, sensations in the body, and objects of mind. So when things seem too stressful, too complex, or confused, remember the possibility of renouncing the habit of proliferating thoughts, particularly the "I-me-mine" story, and come back to the simple experience of the moment. Stephen Mitchell, in his wonderful book *Parables and Portraits,* clearly depicts these possibilities in his lines about Sisyphus:

> We tend to think of Sisyphus as a tragic hero, condemned by the gods to shoulder his rock sweatily up the mountain, and again up the mountain, forever.
>
> The truth is that Sisyphus is in love with the rock. He cherishes every roughness and every ounce of it. He talks to

it, sings to it. It has become the mysterious Other. He even dreams of it as he sleepwalks upward. Life is unimaginable without it, looming always above him like a huge gray moon.

He doesn't realize that at any moment he is permitted to step aside, let the rock hurtle to the bottom, and go home.

Tragedy is the inertial force of the mind.[5]

Practice the Wisdom of No

There's also a practice of renunciation I call "the wisdom of no." So often in spiritual practice we emphasize yes—the yes of acceptance, openness, richness, fullness of experience. And this yes is an effective antidote to the patterns of self-judgment, contraction, and limitation. But there is also the wisdom of no, when we recognize that some things are not skillful, not helpful, not leading to happiness. At those times, we can practice saying, "No thanks, I'll pass."

It's important to understand what this restraint means, because it lies at the heart of our practice. Practicing the wisdom of no is a great art, and we need to learn how to do it in a loving and wise way. Restraint is not repression or avoidance. Restraint doesn't mean pushing things away or denying their presence. It does not mean being judgmental or having aversion toward certain aspects of our experience.

With wise restraint, we are open to everything that arises, but we see it all with discriminating wisdom. We see the skillful thoughts and activities that are conducive to greater happiness, and we see the unskillful ones that lead to further suffering and conflict. It's like a parent saying no to a child who is about to do something harmful. It's a no of concern and care for the welfare and happiness of the child. Imagine what a child would be like if every behavior were allowed. You have probably noticed by now that most of us have an inner two-year-old. We also need to be the wise and loving parent who says, "No, that's not a good idea."

As we watch our minds through the day, we can practice the wisdom of no even in small things. One of the practices that Sayadaw U Tejaniya suggests with regard to thoughts and desires is asking the questions, "Is this necessary?" and "Is this helpful?" Often something is not, and we can practice letting it go. "No, I don't need to do this." "No, I don't need to carry on with this thought."

We can see the power of this wisdom in our practice of the precepts. We might have an impulse to kill an insect or take something not offered, but our commitment to the precepts can stop the impulse before it leads to action. This is the practice of renunciation. Here, the power of no becomes the expression of a free mind. This restraint leads to strength of mind, conservation of energy, and steadfastness and stillness that is not so easily shaken.

Cultivate an Unshakeable Mind

In his book *The Hero with A Thousand Faces,* Joseph Campbell wrote of the Buddha's life as the great archetypal journey of awakening. He described the eve of the Buddha's enlightenment, when, still a bodhisattva, he came face-to-face with Māra, all the forces of desire and aversion. Campbell describes in one line the unshakeable steadfastness of the Bodhisattva's mind in the face of all these powerful forces: "And the mind of the great being was not moved." This line can become a polestar for us, as we practice the renunciation of identifying with whatever arises, so that our own minds are not moved in the face of desire, longing, or fear.

Ajahn Chaa, the great Thai master of the twentieth century, expressed it very succinctly:

> If you let go a little, you will have a little peace. If you let go
> a lot, you will have a lot of peace. If you let go completely,
> you will have complete peace. Your struggles with the world
> will have come to an end.[6]

39

Right Thought

Lovingkindness

THE SECOND ASPECT OF RIGHT thought—namely, those thoughts that lead to our own wellbeing and the wellbeing of others—is lovingkindness or goodwill, thoughts free of ill will. The poet Rilke captured the richness of this possibility:

> Once the realization is accepted that even between the closest people infinite distances exist, a marvelous living side-by-side can grow up for them, if they succeed in loving the expanse between them, which gives them the possibility of always seeing each other as a whole and before an immense sky.[1]

In our lives, we sometimes meet people who can see us whole and before an immense sky, who don't judge or discriminate, and who seem to radiate feelings of genuine caring and love and kindness toward everyone they meet. They may be well-known people like the Dalai Lama, Mother Teresa, Martin Luther King, Jr., or Gandhi. They may be different teachers that we've been with or ordinary people in our lives. With all these people, they give their love not because of who we are, because of our position or title or wealth, but simply because we're fellow human beings. When the Dalai

Lama greets you, you feel like you're the most important person in the world because his attention is undivided. He has said that one of his great practices of lovingkindness is trying to treat whoever he meets as an old friend.

This very special quality is the feeling of mettā, the Pali word for lovingkindness. It's the generosity and openness of heart that simply wishes well for all beings. Although we derive great benefit from the feeling and practice of lovingkindness, it does not seek any self-benefit. Mettā is not given with the expectation of getting anything in return. Even when we direct mettā toward ourselves, it is simply the gateway to an open heart.

Because there is no expectation, mettā is not dependent on external conditions, on people, on ourselves, being a certain way. For this reason, mettā doesn't easily turn into disappointment, ill will, or jealousy, as love with desire and attachment so often does. What gives lovingkindness its great expansive power is that in the end, when developed and practiced, it makes no distinction between beings. It's not a feeling limited to those closest to us. We might feel close to one, two, five, twenty, even a hundred people, but certainly not to everyone in the world. Mettā, though, has this power to embrace all beings with the simple wish "May you be happy." For this reason, it is called one of "the boundless states of heart and mind," one of "the immeasurables."

A story about the Dalai Lama highlights this all-embracing quality of metta. After a large conference at a hotel in Arizona, he wanted to meet all the hotel employees. As they lined up near the hotel entrance, His Holiness went down the line, greeting each person in turn. Although hotel management might not so easily grant such a request from one of us, this story can remind us to examine the attitudes in our own minds as we meet people, even in passing. One practice that I've found helpful is to practice metta while walking down a street. When wishing well to every passing person, it's amazing to feel the level of silent connection that arises from this simple wish: *be happy.*

THE PRACTICE OF METTĀ

The first time I did intensive mettā practice I was in Bodh Gaya, India, staying at the Burmese Vihāra. Munindra-ji was giving me the progressive instructions, starting with sending loving wishes to myself, then to a benefactor, and then to a friend. Then he said to start sending mettā to a neutral person. At first, I didn't quite register who that would be, but he explained that it is someone that we don't have any particular feelings for one way or another. At that time, there was an old Indian gardener at the Vihāra, someone I passed many times a day. It was a bit shocking for me to realize that he was, indeed, a neutral person, in that I never really gave him any thought at all.

I started sending mettā to this gardener, "May you be happy," spending many hours a day in this practice. Something quite amazing began to happen. My heart would light up every time I saw him, and I had such warm, loving feelings for this "neutral person." He was no longer neutral. This was a real turning point in my practice, realizing that our feelings do not ultimately depend on the other person or even on their behavior. How we feel about someone is up to us.

There is great purity and a quiet happiness in moments of genuine mettā, because those moments are not mixed with anything harmful, either to oneself or others. The only wish is for all to be happy, to be free of enmity and hatred, to be at peace. A moment of mettā is a moment of pure gold. Some lines from the Buddha's discourse on mettā highlight this feeling of goodwill:

> In gladness and in safety, may all beings be at ease. Whatever living beings there may be, whether they are weak or strong, omitting none, the great or the mighty, medium, short or small, the seen and the unseen, those living near and far away, those born and to be born—may all beings be at ease. Let none deceive another, or despise any being in any state. Let none through anger or ill will wish harm upon another. Even as a mother protects with her life her child, her only child, so with a boundless heart should one cherish all living beings, radiating kindness over the entire world, spreading upwards to the skies, and downward to the depths, outwards and unbounded, freed from hatred and ill will. Whether standing or walking, seated or lying down, free from drowsiness, one should sustain this recollection. This is said to be the sublime abiding.[2]

The Benefits of Mettā Practice

As these feelings of goodwill and kindness soften us, our minds and hearts become smooth, gentle, more pliable. Because of this softening, there is a lessening of our many reactive judgments and comments, about ourselves as well as others. We become more patient and caring with difficulties and disturbances. As we're less reactive, not so caught up in immediate likes and dislikes, there is more space for discerning wisdom. We can then see more clearly what is truly skillful and unskillful in our lives, and so we make wiser choices. This, in turn, leads to more happiness, more joy, and more mettā. It's an upward spiral. As an experiment, the next time you're walking down a street, start practicing mettā for all the people you pass. It might be expressed as the simple wish "Be happy." Then notice the difference between these times of sending mettā and times of not sending, when we're most likely lost in the wanderings of our minds.

As mettā grows stronger and steadier, we feel more tolerant of ourselves and others, a little less judgmental. Gradually we start to live in a growing field of goodwill and good humor, holding ourselves and others with a lighter heart. The poet W. H. Auden captured this possibility when he wrote, "You shall love your crooked neighbour / With all your crooked heart." The beauty and power of the Buddha's teachings are that they are not something to simply admire in others, but to practice and develop in ourselves.

DESIRE: THE NEAR ENEMY OF LOVINGKINDNESS

Although it's easy to recognize the value and benevolence of this feeling of lovingkindness, still there are many times when we find it lacking in our lives, when our hearts are not soft and open, when our minds are not pliable. It's helpful to understand why.

There is a powerful force in the mind that comes masquerading as love, but that actually obstructs and obscures it. It is called "the near enemy of mettā" because it looks like lovingkindness, but in fact is quite different. This near enemy is the mind state of desire, attachment, longing, and craving. The confusion of these two states, love and desire, has enormous implications for our relationships and our lives.

Think for a moment of when you feel most loving. It is a generosity of the heart, the offering of a simple wish: "Be happy." Now think of when you have felt strong desire for or attachment to another person.

There is a feeling of wanting or holding something for ourselves. It could be the wanting of pleasure, of fulfillment, of acceptance, even the wanting to be loved. The energy movements in our heart of these two states are really opposite to one another. One is an offering; the other is a taking, a holding on. As we pay close attention to our experience, both in formal meditation and in our lives, the distinction between mettā and desire becomes increasingly clear.

Recognizing When Desire Is at Play

Sometimes even in the practice of lovingkindness itself we can see these two forces intertwined. As we repeat each mettā phrase—"May you be happy, may you be peaceful"—is it a simple expression of goodwill, a simple gift of loving attention in the moment? Or are we practicing with one eye on what we're getting from it? At times in my practice I would be repeating the phrases, but always watching, checking, "Am I getting more concentrated? Am I getting more loving?" At these times, I was concerned with how I was feeling and forgetting the simplicity and purity of the wish for someone's happiness.

In yet another way, we can mingle various motivations. We might be saying the mettā phrases, but the underlying motivation is, "May you be free of all those annoying qualities that make me feel aversion," again forgetting that how we feel is up to us. There are also situations in our lives when we think we're sending love, but really are sending a desire for something else. Many years ago, I was visiting a friend in the countryside of Western Massachusetts. As I was walking along a dirt road through a forest, I passed one house with a dog barking, somewhat aggressively, in the yard. I started sending mettā to the dog: "Be happy, be happy." After a few minutes of this, the dog came over and bit me. There couldn't have been more immediate feedback; although the words in my mind were those of lovingkindness, the energy feeling was much more fear and aversion.

It is insightful and freeing when we see clearly the difference in our own experience between lovingkindness and desire. It then becomes possible to slowly disentangle them in our lives. We understand more deeply, for ourselves, the consequences of each of these mind states. In our close relationships, do fear, insecurity, possessiveness, projections come from mettā or from wanting and desire? Which of these feelings bring us happiness, completion, and contentment?

CULTIVATING LOVINGKINDNESS

As we learn to distinguish these two feelings and their consequences, we can then make some wiser choices about which thoughts and feelings we practice and cultivate, and which we see and let go of. This is taking to heart the Buddha's words "what we frequently think and ponder upon, that will become the inclination of the mind." This doesn't mean, however, that as soon as we say the first mettā phrase, all our desires and attachments fall away. But as we become more familiar with the unique characteristics of lovingkindness, we recognize when it is present, we practice it, and over time it becomes more the way we are rather than something we do. All of this is part of the practice of Right Thought, the second step of the Noble Eightfold Path.

In the understanding and practice of lovingkindness, I find it is sometimes easier to connect with the kindness aspect than with the aspect of love. *Love* is a very grand word, subtle and complex in its meaning. And our understanding of it has been so conditioned by movies, books, and advertising, as well as by our own fantasies. In light of all this conditioning, people often feel that they are not loving enough or do not have the capacity for love. Maybe we think it should be some great ecstatic feeling that carries us away on waves of bliss, and then we feel disappointed or discouraged when this doesn't happen. *Kindness* is a much more humble word, down to earth, pragmatic. It's a friendly and spontaneous responsiveness to people and situations around us. Kindness is a basic and natural openness of heart that lets the world in.

How, then, do we strengthen the feeling of mettā within ourselves? Nyoshul Khen Rinpoche, one of the great Dzogchen masters of the last century, expressed it very simply:

> I would like to pass on one little bit of advice I give to
> everyone. Relax, just relax. Be nice to each other. As you
> go through life, simply be kind to people. Try to help them
> rather than hurt them. Try to get along with them, rather
> than fall out with them. With that, I will leave you, and with
> all my very best wishes.[3]

Focus on the Good Qualities in People

The proximate cause for lovingkindness to arise is focusing on the good qualities in people, whether others or ourselves. We're all a package of different qualities, some desirable, some not. When we don't see the good in people and focus instead on their annoying, irritating qualities, it's easy for ill will, judgments, anger, and even hatred to arise. But if we make it a practice to seek out and relate to the good in each person, then the feeling of lovingkindness grows quite naturally.

At first, this practice might require some effort, a change of mental habits. We all have an inner remote control. When we're lost in some aversive state, or even just a neutral one, we can practice changing channels. The mettā channel is always available. We simply need to avail ourselves of it. As we develop the habit of seeing the good in people, even while recognizing the complexity of the whole person, we begin to respond in more generous and loving ways.

A great gift comes to us as we see the good in others, and that is the feeling of gratitude for the good people have done for us. The Buddha called gratitude one of the most beautiful and rare qualities in the world. We can so easily take for granted or forget the kindnesses people show us, the help that they have offered. When we feel gratitude, whether to particular people or to life itself, mettā flows forth naturally.

There is also an interesting connection between mindfulness and mettā. In the silence of meditation, we sometimes think of people we haven't thought of in years, often with a tenderness that might not have been there in the original encounter. As our minds become more open and less defensive, we begin to experience mettā as a basic quality of awareness. Someone once asked Dipa Ma whether she should be practicing mindfulness or lovingkindness. Dipa Ma answered, "From my experience there is no difference. When you are fully loving, aren't you also mindful? When you are fully mindful, is this not also the essence of love?" For Dipa Ma, love and awareness were one.

All this doesn't mean that we'll never get angry or annoyed. Rather, as the Dalai Lama said, "Sometimes I do get angry, but deep in my heart I don't hold a grudge against anyone." By focusing on the good in ourselves and others and feeling gratitude for the good others have done for us, we can more easily open to a place of forgiveness, not holding on to old grudges and hurts. Sometimes we let go of these in a moment; sometimes letting go of them is part of a longer process.

At the beginning of a meditation period, it can be helpful to ask for and extend forgiveness. And even with people we find difficult, we can reflect on our basic intention of goodwill.

In reading one issue of *The New Yorker* magazine, I came across an article about the French essayist Michel de Montaigne. In it, they quoted one of his writings in which he refers to one of the great friendships of his life. The passage perfectly captures the beauty and power of lovingkindness:

> In a truly loving relationship—which I have experi-
> enced—rather than drawing the one I love to me I give
> myself to him . . . Not merely do I prefer to do him good
> than to have him do good to me, I would even prefer that
> he did good to himself rather than to me: it is when he does
> good to himself that he does most good to me. If his absence
> is either pleasant or useful to him, then it delights me far
> more than his presence.[4]

The willingness to train our hearts, whether in mettā or anything else, requires great patience, which the Buddha called "the highest devotion." The recollection of the attitude of mettā in all aspects of our lives gradually transforms how we are in the world, with ourselves and with all others.

40

Right Thought

Compassion

RIGHT THOUGHT INCLUDES ALL THE intentions and aspirations that lead to wholesome actions, which result in the welfare and happiness of ourselves and others. These are thoughts of renunciation, free of sense desire; thoughts of goodwill and lovingkindness, free of ill will; and lastly, thoughts of compassion, free of cruelty.

The dichotomy of skillful and unskillful is here very clear. Cruelty wishes to cause harm to people; it is the disposition to give unnecessary pain and suffering. Cruelty is a feeling of extreme heartlessness. We see the manifestation of this mind state in the many situations of violence throughout the world. Sometimes this quality of cruelty seems contagious, with whole populations involved in killing fields of destruction. We have seen this in Cambodia, Rwanda, Darfur, and many other places around the world. We can see the heartlessness of actions in the decimation of many native cultures, in the violence of slavery and its legacy of racism, in the targeted cruelty of homophobia, in violence against women. The range and force of this state of mind is extensive and far-reaching.

Compassion is the antidote to this great destructive power. Compassion is the strong wish of the mind and heart to alleviate all suffering. It opens our hearts to the suffering that is there, and it overcomes our indifference. It is the strong and deep feeling that is moved to act. As Thich Nhat Hanh so aptly put it, "Compassion is a verb." And it was this very feeling that motivated the Bodhisattva on his long journey to Buddhahood.

In our times, the Dalai Lama is an inspiring exemplar of this ennobling mind state. He expressed the challenge for us very clearly: "Compassion and love are precious things in life—they are not complicated. They are simple, but difficult to practice."[1]

It's worth investigating why such a beautiful and wholesome state is so difficult to practice; a careful examination might reveal even small and unnoticed moments of cruelty within ourselves.

AWAKENING COMPASSION IN OURSELVES

Compassion arises out of our willingness to come close to suffering. The problem is that even though we may want to be compassionate, and perhaps often are, it is not always easy to open to the suffering that is present. And just as there are many times when we don't want to acknowledge and open to our own pain, we don't necessarily want to be with the pain of others.

There are strong tendencies in the mind that keep us defended, withdrawn, indifferent, or apathetic in the face of suffering. This indifference is often unacknowledged and is a great barrier to a compassionate response.

As an experiment, watch your mind the next time you approach a situation of suffering. It might be some pain in the body or some emotional distress, like discontent, fear, unworthiness, jealousy, or loneliness. It might be an interaction with a difficult person, or a situation of suffering in the world—situations of racial injustice, political or religious violence, or of natural disasters. What happens as we face these situations, either in person or through the vivid images of the media? Do we feel uneasy? Do we withdraw? Do we numb ourselves? Do we let it in?

The question for us is, how can our hearts stay open given the magnitude of suffering that exists in the world? Is it even possible to open to it all with compassion, diminishing the subtle cruelty of indifference? The challenge is not a theoretical one. It is not enough to admire from afar the qualities of kindness and compassion as being noble ideas, but somewhat removed from our daily lives. It is not enough to cultivate them only in the solitude of a meditation retreat. Our practice is about the transformation of consciousness that makes compassionate responsiveness the default setting of our lives.

Compassion requires both openness and equanimity. It requires learning to let things in without drowning in the difficulties and without being overcome by sorrow. It means learning to simply be with the truth of things as they are. This is the great gift of mindfulness that opens us to compassion. Being with the truth of what is present is what we do every time we open to our own pain or difficulty. As we practice opening to and coming close to the suffering in our own lives with compassion, we then have greater strength and courage to be with the suffering of others.

Empathy Is the First Step

Empathy is the beginning of compassion. Empathy happens when we take a moment to stop and feel what is really going on with another person before we rush on with our lives. This is its own practice, because many times we might be cognizant of another's pain, but we don't take the time, even a few moments, to come close to it, to really open to it.

We can practice this openness in different kinds of situations. When we're on retreat, we might feel the distress of the restless person sitting next to us instead of getting lost in aversion and reactivity because they are disturbing our meditation. It might be opening to the difficulties and suffering of someone we're very close to or opening to a stressful situation in the world. Or there might be situations where people really are behaving very badly, causing a great deal of harm either to themselves or others. Our usual reaction is some judgment about how bad they are coupled with a righteous feeling. But it's also possible to stop and feel what is going on in a larger context of understanding.

Dr. Tenzin Choedrak, who at one time was the physician to the Dalai Lama, was imprisoned and tortured by the Chinese authorities for more than seventeen years. He described what made it possible for him to survive not only physically, but also with an open and compassionate heart. He saw that his torturers, his enemies, were human beings like himself, that his guards and tormentors were people who were also in adverse conditions, creating the unwholesome karma that would bring about their own future suffering. He never forgot the commonality of the human condition or the understanding that all actions bring consequences. And he saw the law of karma not as a vehicle of revenge—"they'll get theirs"—but as a vehicle of compassion. Claude Levenson, the Dalai Lama's biographer, says that Choedrak had "a gaze filled with the perception of one who has seen so much that he has seen everything, seeing beyond the suffering he has experienced, beyond all the evil and the abuses he has witnessed, yet expressing boundless compassion for his fellow human beings."

Cultivating Wholesome Responses to Suffering

It is important to understand that in situations where it is possible to stop the harmful behavior, we need to take appropriate actions, set proper boundaries, and do whatever is necessary to prevent further harm. But can we do this with a wise attention to our own motivations? Is our motivation anger or resentment? Is it compassion? The great lesson here is that how we feel and respond to the situation is up to us.

Being willing to come close to suffering takes empathy a step further. Compassion is not only feeling what others are going through, but also being motivated to act on that feeling. As compassion grows in us, we begin to actively engage with the suffering in the world, responding to the various needs of beings in whatever way is appropriate and possible.

Sometimes we act in small, disregarded ways, making small gestures of friendliness or generosity or forgiveness toward the people around us. Or our response to suffering might come as a spontaneous action of real heroism. Some years ago, there was an incident in the New York subways that made national news. Someone had fallen on to the tracks as a train was pulling into the station. Wesley Autrey was standing on the platform, saw what had happened, and jumped down, laying flat on top of the person so that the train just passed over them—barely. He became known as "the Subway Hero." His response to all of the attention was quite remarkable: "I don't feel like I did something spectacular; I just saw someone who needed help. I did what I felt was right."[2] Sometimes compassion manifests as acts of tremendous determination. In the book *Mountains Beyond*

Mountains, Tracy Kidder describes the humanitarian work of Dr. Paul Farmer, who devoted his life to serving people in Haiti and other underserved places in the world. There was one story in the book that highlighted for me an essential quality of compassion. Farmer had set up a clinic where many people were coming for treatment, but on a couple of days, he had gone off to help some families living in a remote area. Some of his colleagues criticized his decision, saying he could have helped more people had he stayed at the clinic. Farmer replied, "If you say that seven hours walk is too long to walk for two families of patients, you're saying that their lives matter less than some others. And the idea that some lives matter less is the root of all that's wrong with the world."³

Sometimes compassion shows itself through great courage. Videos of Martin Luther King, Jr. on some of his marches, both in the North and in the South, surrounded by people filled with hate and an ever-present threat of violence, show the amazing power of his love and compassion in those situations. Somehow, he was able to stay connected with those feelings even in the most difficult circumstances. And while the effect of those marches was not always immediate, when we look at the powerful legacy of his life on our culture, we can appreciate the Buddha's words even more: "Hatred never ceases by hatred; it only ceases by love."

The Field of Compassion Is Limitless

There is no particular prescription for what we should do. There's no hierarchy of compassionate action. The field of compassion is limitless—it is the field of suffering beings. We can each find our own way. It can take the form of an active engagement with the world. It can take the form of living in a mountain cave, with the motivation to awaken for the benefit of all beings.

In the Buddhist tradition, the Bodhisattva, the Buddha before his awakening, spent countless lifetimes practicing as a renunciate before the great energy of his enlightened compassion flowered in the world. His aspiration was not just to alleviate the suffering of a particular situation, but to understand the root causes of all suffering—the forces of greed, hatred, and delusion—and how to be free of them. Twenty-six hundred years later, we are still benefiting from the power of his compassion and wisdom.

THE PRACTICE AND EXPRESSION OF COMPASSION

We can practice compassion from two sides. First, we purify our own hearts and minds as a way of more effectively taking care of others. If two people are stuck in quicksand, neither can really help the other. But if one person is on solid ground, then it's possible for lifesaving help to be given. This understanding is applied every time we're on an airplane and hear the announcement about the oxygen masks: "In the event of a loss of cabin pressure, the air masks will automatically descend. Please put on your own mask first, and then assist the people around you." If we jump into situations without proper understanding and motivation, we often only add to the confusion.

The second way we develop compassion is the practice of putting others before ourselves. This way of practice is beautifully expressed by Shāntideva in his great classic "Guide to a Bodhisattva's Way of Life." A few stanzas from this work convey the possibilities inherent in this understanding:

> For all those ailing in the world,
> Until their every sickness has been healed,
> May I myself become for them
> The doctor, nurse, the medicine itself.
>
> Raining down a flood of food and drink,
> May I dispel the ills of thirst and famine.
> And in the ages marked by scarcity and want,
> May I myself appear as drink and sustenance.
>
> For sentient beings, poor and destitute,
> May I become a treasure ever plentiful,
> And lie before them closely in their reach,
> A varied source of all that they might need.
>
> My body, thus, and all my goods besides,
> And all my merits gained and to be gained,
> I give them all away withholding nothing,
> To bring about the benefit of beings.
>
> . . .

Like the earth and the pervading elements,
Enduring like the sky itself endures,
For boundless multitudes of living beings,
May I be their ground and sustenance.

Thus, for everything that lives,
As far as the limits of the sky,
May I provide their livelihood and nourishment
Until they pass beyond the bonds of suffering.[4]

It's possible to read these stanzas and become inspired, but also, perhaps, a bit daunted. Would we ever be able to live with this degree of
compassion, this great generosity of spirit? We need great humility in
nourishing this aspiration. We can simply plant the seeds of this great
motivation of *bodhichitta,* that our lives and our practice be for the
benefit of all, and water and nurture those seeds until they gradually
become a force for great good in the world. Henry David Thoreau
beautifully expressed this possibility: "Though I do not believe that
a plant will spring up where no seed has been, I have great faith in a
seed. Convince me that you have a seed there, and I am prepared to
expect wonders."[5]

One of the great turning points in my practice, one that for
me gave strength to this aspiration, was realizing that wisdom and
compassion were expressions of each other. Compassion is the very
activity of emptiness of self. This is compassion not as a stance of
the ego, or even as a particular practice, but as the spontaneous
expression of a heart and mind free of self-reference. Dilgo Khyentse
Rinpoche, a great Dzogchen master of the last century, pointed to
this directly when he reminds us that when we recognize the empty,
selfless nature of phenomena, "the energy to bring about the good
of others dawns uncontrived and effortless."

So each of us, in our own way, can plant and water the seeds
of right thought and a kind heart, and slowly they will grow and
become the guiding principles of our lives. And even at those times
when we're not acting from this place of wisdom and compassion, it
can still be the reference point that reminds us of other choices.

Mingyur Rinpoche, in his book *The Joy of Living,* highlights this
connection between our practice of awareness and compassion:

But the best part of all is that no matter how long you meditate, or what technique you use, every technique of Buddhist meditation ultimately generates compassion, whether we're aware of it or not. Whenever you look at your mind, you can't help but recognize your similarity to those around you. When you see your own desire to be happy, you can't avoid seeing the same desire in others, and when you look clearly at your own fear, anger, or aversion, you can't help but see that everyone around you feels the same fear, anger, and aversion. When you look at your own mind, all the imaginary differences between yourself and others automatically dissolve and the ancient prayer of the Four Immeasurables becomes as natural and persistent as your own heartbeat:

May all sentient beings have happiness and the causes of happiness.

May all sentient beings be free from suffering and the causes of suffering.

My all sentient beings have joy and the causes of joy.

May all sentient beings remain in great equanimity, free from attachment and aversion.[6]

MINDFULNESS OF DHAMMAS

The Noble Eightfold Path:
Morality Factors

41

Right Speech

HAVING ESTABLISHED OURSELVES TO SOME degree in Right View, and having cultivated the discernment and practice of Right Thought, we can explore what the Buddha lays out as the consequences of these in how we live our lives. These are the next three steps of the Eightfold Path: Right Speech, Right Action, and Right Livelihood.

As we examine our commitment to awakening, we might notice a tendency to make these steps lesser endeavors, not quite on the same level as our meditation practice. But if we hold these steps in this way, we are fragmenting our lives and weakening essential elements of the Path. Seven of the ten unwholesome actions the Buddha said to avoid are purified by these three steps of the Path. Each one requires mindful attention, and together they become the foundation for deepening concentration and wisdom.

Bhikkhu Bodhi emphasizes this point in his book *The Noble Eightfold Path:*

> Though the principles laid down in this section restrain
> immoral actions and promote good conduct, their ultimate
> purpose is not so much ethical as spiritual. They are not
> prescribed merely as guides to action, but primarily as aids to
> mental purification. As a necessary measure for human well

being, ethics has its own justification in the Buddha's teaching, and its importance cannot be underrated. But in the special context of the Noble Eightfold Path ethical principles are subordinate to the path's governing goal, final deliverance from suffering.[1]

The first of this triad of path factors is Right Speech. Speech is such a powerful influence in our lives because we speak a lot. Speech conditions our relationships, conditions our minds and hearts, and conditions karmic consequences in the future.

TRUTHFULNESS

The most basic aspect of Right Speech is truthfulness, refraining from saying that which is untrue. Although this principle seems so obvious and straightforward, it may not be as easy to practice as we assume. There are many kinds of false speech, from slight exaggerations and humorous untruths to falsehoods whose motivation might be self-protection or the protection of others. Sometimes deliberate lies are spoken with the malicious intent of causing divisiveness and harm. It's interesting that during political elections, we now have programs devoted to fact-checking, to noting when candidates are saying things that are patently false.

In any situation where we say what is untrue, what is the motivation? Is it greed for something, a desire for recognition or self-aggrandizement? Is it a fear of rejection or jealousy? Telling untruths becomes very complicated. After we tell one lie, we then need to tell other lies to bolster the first, and then we need to remember them all. Mark Twain pointed this out when he said, "If you tell the truth you don't have to remember anything."

Lying is a great corrosive force both in our relationships and in society. It undermines our ability to trust. The German philosopher Nietzsche highlighted this when he wrote, "I'm not upset that you lied to me. I'm upset that from now on I can't believe you." The Buddha spoke very bluntly against lying:

> Thus one should never knowingly speak a lie, either for the sake of one's own advantage, or for the sake of another person's advantage, or for the sake of any advantage whatsoever.[2]

In the Bodhisattva's long journey to Buddhahood, he committed many misdeeds, at different times breaking one or another of the precepts. But it's said that in all that time he never knowingly spoke an untruth, so central is truthfulness to the path of awakening. We can reflect on this as an inspiration for our own commitment to truthfulness in our lives.

But what seems so simple can be surprisingly difficult. Sometimes little lies just seem to tumble out. During one three-month retreat at the Insight Meditation Society, a staff member was getting something out of the big walk-in refrigerator. On opening the door, he saw a meditator inside the walk-in taking a handful of dates. When the staff person asked if he could help, the meditator said, "Oh, I'm just looking for the maintenance person."

There might also be lies of omission, where we cover or withhold something of critical importance. As the poet Adrienne Rich wrote, "Lying is done with words and also with silence." We might also operate under the illusion that we would never lie, in any form, and this could make it harder to see or acknowledge lying when we do.

I had one very powerful, painful, and ultimately freeing experience in my practice with Sayadaw U Paṇḍita. In one interview during my first retreat with him, in 1984, I was caught up in some idea of where my practice was, and I presented my experience in the light of this idea. When I finished my report, Sayadaw just looked at me and said, "That isn't true." I was devastated by the truth of his comment, and it took me many days to recover my equilibrium. When I finally worked through all the feelings of shame and self-judgment, I came to the place of recognizing, "Yes, my mind *can* dissemble." There was a great freedom in that recognition, a letting go of the previously unnoticed pretense that I would never tell a lie, particularly to my teacher. When we're willing to see ourselves more honestly, it becomes much easier to recognize those impulses, which gives us more opportunity to refrain from them.

Truthfulness as the first aspect of Right Speech has profound implications. Our goal in practice is to see what is true and to live in accordance with it. As Bhikkhu Bodhi observes in *The Noble Eightfold Path*, "Truthful speech establishes a correspondence between our inner being and the real nature of phenomena. . . . Thus, much more than an ethical principle, devotion to truthful speech is a matter of taking our stand on reality rather than illusion . . ."[3]

The Buddha expressed the overriding importance of truthful speech in a conversation he had with his young son, Rāhula, who was a novice monk at the time. The Buddha pointed to a bowl with a little water at the bottom of it, saying so little is the spiritual achievement of one who is not afraid to tell a deliberate lie. The Buddha then spoke in a similar way about the water being thrown away and the bowl empty. Finally, the Buddha turned the bowl upside down and said, "Do you see, Rāhula, how this bowl has been turned upside down? In the same way, one who tells a deliberate lie turns his spiritual achievements upside down and becomes incapable of progress. Therefore one should not speak a deliberate lie, even in jest."

Given this emphasis on truthfulness of speech, it's helpful to sensitize ourselves to even small falsehoods. Mindfulness can be like a warning bell that goes off to remind us "this isn't true," and in that moment we can then realign ourselves with Right Speech.

SLANDER AND GOSSIP

The second aspect of this step of the Eightfold Path is refraining from speech that is slander, gossip, and backbiting. These types of speech cause disharmony and loss of friends. The Buddha gave very explicit advice in this regard:

> What he has heard here he does not repeat there, so as to
> cause dissension there; and what he has heard there he does
> not repeat here, so as to cause dissension here. Thus he unites
> those who are divided; and those who are united he encour-
> ages. Concord gladdens him, he delights and rejoices in
> concord; and it is concord that he spreads by his words.[4]

But given the strong tendency to gossip about others, a question arises about why we find it so enjoyable. When we're gossiping, does it reaffirm some sense of self? Is there some ego gratification? Soon after I began teaching, someone interviewed me for a book about spiritual practices in the West. He was a very skillful interviewer, and I was somewhat flattered that he was interested to know what I thought about various teachers. Fortunately, mindfulness came to the fore, and I remembered these teachings on Right Speech. When the book came out with everything I had said in the interview, I was so grateful that I had refrained from this kind of gossip.

I first became interested in Buddhism when, as a Peace Corps volunteer in Thailand, I conducted an experiment that proved very revealing. I decided that for a period of some months, I would not speak about a third person; I would not speak to someone about someone else. There were some striking results. First, a large percentage of my speech was eliminated. I was surprised to realize how much of my speech revolved around this kind of talk. Second, as I stopped verbalizing my various thoughts, comments, and judgments of other people, I saw that my mind became much less judgmental, even about myself. This care with speech resulted in a much more peaceful mind.

But even if we loosen the parameters a bit, we can still take great care when we're speaking of other people. Is it our intention to divide or to bring people together? Just paying attention to this one question would change our lives.

On another level, our speech may also be a kind of gossip about ourselves. Is our talk overly self-referential, always bringing the conversation back to ourselves? If this is the case, it would be insightful to explore the motivation. Or we might have the opposite conditioning; rather than always taking center stage, we might obsessively stay behind the scenes, hardly ever giving voice to our thoughts and feelings. In a less obvious way, this type of speech too is a manifestation of conceit. Speech can be such a powerful mirror for our motivations, both wholesome and unwholesome. When we have the interest and alertness to look at it, we see that speech is a mirror of our minds.

EMOTIONAL TONE

The third aspect of Right Speech has to do with the emotional tone in our minds and hearts, and how it conditions and flavors the words we use. The practice of this step on the Path is refraining from harsh, angry, and abusive speech. As the Buddha said, "One should speak such words as are gentle, soothing to the ear, loving, such words as go to the heart, are courteous, friendly, and agreeable to many."

We need to be conscious of the energy behind our words. How do we feel when angry words are directed at us? We probably would feel hurt or defensive, and often our own anger arises in response. Anger is not the best environment for open communication, and at its most basic level, open communication is what Right Speech is all about. The intent here is not to suppress whatever feelings we may have, but to communicate them in a way that fosters connection rather than divisiveness.

MINDFUL LISTENING

Right Speech also has implications for how we listen. The Buddha outlined a practice for staying mindful of how another person is addressing us, without getting caught up in our own reactivity. And even more than that, he enjoins us to abide compassionate for their welfare, with a mind of lovingkindness:

> "Bhikkhus, there are five courses of speech that others may use when they address you: their speech may be timely or untimely, true or untrue, gentle or harsh, connected with good or with harm, or spoken with a mind of lovingkindness or with inner hate. . . . Herein, Bhikkhus, you should train yourself thus: 'Our minds will remain unaffected, and we shall utter no evil words; we shall abide compassionate for their welfare, with a mind of lovingkindness. . . . We shall abide pervading that person with a mind imbued with lovingkindness; and starting with him, we shall abide pervading the all-encompassing world with a mind . . . abundant, exalted, immeasurable, without hostility, without ill will.'"[5]

Listening with compassion and lovingkindness even when harsh or untrue words are addressed to us is a tremendously challenging aspect of mindfulness, and it is a good example of what it means to be mindful externally as well as internally. Although such listening may seem very difficult to accomplish, in fact, many parents demonstrate it easily with their young children. Children, in moments of frustration or upset, will yell at their parents, "I hate you." And yet, for many parents, at least much of the time, the response remains loving. This practice would transform the world if people would begin to apply it throughout their lives.

USELESS AND FRIVOLOUS TALK

The last aspect of Right Speech is refraining from useless or frivolous talk. The Pali word for this type of speech is a good example of onomatopoeia—that is, it sounds just like what it is—*samphappalāpa*. We see this kind of speech very often in social situations, where we say things just to be heard, rather than for any meaningful purpose. When we pay attention to this tendency, we find that these rather useless words are enervating and worthless. Over time, this kind of speech often results in an unspoken loss of respect from others. When we stop to consider these social interactions, don't we find that we hold in high regard those people whose speech is both kind and useful?

The Buddha expressed it this way:

> One speaks at the right time, in accordance with facts, speaks
> what is useful, speaks of the Dhamma . . . one's speech is
> like a treasure, uttered at the right moment, accompanied by
> reason, moderate and full of sense.[6]

Here, the Buddha is speaking to the monastic community and so suggests guidelines appropriate to that situation.

Bhikkhu Bodhi, in *The Noble Eightfold Path,* expands on these suggestions with regard to laypeople, acknowledging that laypeople will have more need for affectionate small talk with friends and family, polite conversation with acquaintances, and talk in connection with their work. But even with this more-expanded understanding of Right Speech, there is great room for the restraint of *samphappalāpa.* As a practice, when I'm with friends or family and I see the impulse to say something completely useless, I've found it tremendously helpful and strengthening for mindfulness and wise attention to refrain from doing so. Such restraint feels like a little victory over Māra.

Because Right Speech is such a powerful part of our practice, we can understand why the Buddha gave so much emphasis to it. Right Speech, as the third step of the Noble Eightfold Path, cultivates abstinence from unwholesome mind states; gives expression to the beautiful motivations of lovingkindness, compassion, and altruistic joy; and, most importantly, aligns us with what is true.

"Bhikkhus, possessing five factors, speech is well spoken, not badly spoken; it is blameless and beyond reproach by the wise. What five? It is spoken at the proper time; what is said is true; it is spoken gently; what is said is beneficial; it is spoken with a mind of lovingkindness."[7]

42

Right Action
and Right Livelihood

RIGHT ACTION AND RIGHT LIVELIHOOD complete the morality section of the Noble Eightfold Path. As with Right Speech, we cultivate these steps not only for their ethical value, but also as essential means of awakening. It's impossible to separate meditative wisdom from the moral understanding that makes it possible.

The Buddha expresses this integrated path of practice in one famous verse of the Dhammapada: "Avoid what is unskillful, do what is good, purify the mind." Especially in times of great cultural changes, when there is often a useful questioning of old norms and values, it's helpful to rearticulate the importance of personal integrity and responsibility, so that we don't simply get lost in the confusion of our desires and impulses.

It's said that what most moved the Buddha after his enlightenment was seeing people seeking happiness, yet doing the very things that brought about suffering. As Shāntideva said, "We're like senseless children who shrink from suffering but love its causes."

RIGHT ACTION

Although all these steps of Right Speech, Action, and Livelihood revolve around abstinence from unskillful acts, avoiding what is unskillful, each one also contains its positive expression—doing what is good. Right Action is cultivating the clarity and strength of mind to abstain from those actions of the body causing harm to oneself or others:

> "And what, monks, is Right Action? Refraining from taking
> life, refraining from taking what is not given, refraining from
> sexual misconduct. This is called Right Action."[1]

So much of what the Buddha taught seems so obvious—don't kill, don't steal, don't harm. Still, as we try to apply and practice this in our lives, we can come to the forward edge of our understanding and commitment. And this edge can be a challenging place to be. One teacher commented that if practicing the precepts doesn't make us uncomfortable, it's probably a sign that we should investigate them more deeply.

I appreciate this comment because it points to these steps on the Path as actual practices, things to understand and investigate in our lives, rather than taking it for granted that we're basically good people and then looking no further.

Abstaining from Physical Harm

The first part of Right Action is abstaining from killing or physically harming others or ourselves. This includes people not killing other people, not killing animals for sport or pleasure, and not killing living beings because we don't like the way they look. In my early years of practicing in India, during the hot summer months, I would rent a cabin in the Himalayan hill station of Dalhousie. It was at seven thousand feet, with beautiful views of the Himalayan peaks. The cabin was quite primitive, with no electricity or running water, and on the inside there were some huge, hairy spiders that hung out on the ceiling of the bedroom.

At first, it seemed like an impossible situation. Thinking of them being overhead as I slept was not very agreeable. But I was trying to follow the precepts and so didn't want to kill them. I also didn't see any effective way of both removing them and keeping them out. In the end, I simply surrendered, allowing them their space on the ceiling and claiming the rest of the space as my own. Surprisingly, it didn't take long at all before they ceased to be a problem. I didn't bother them, and they didn't bother me. Peaceful coexistence reigned.

The Buddha's words on Right Action point to the possibility of realigning our priorities:

> Here someone avoids the taking of life and abstains from it.
> Without stick or sword, conscientious, full of sympathy, he is
> desirous of the welfare of all sentient beings.[2]

There are important consequences in those moments when we are conscientious and mindful, refraining from taking life, even when it is the life of something as small as an ant or mosquito. In those moments of restraint, we are considering the welfare of that being. It always feels better, more connected, more loving, to remove an insect from the house than to kill it. And so we find the feelings of loving-kindness and compassion grow as we practice this abstinence.

But living in the world, we laypeople sometimes face some compelling situations. When we're faced with malaria-carrying mosquitoes, or carpenter ants destroying our house, or deer ticks that might be carrying Lyme disease, do we just say, "Be happy," or does killing in those circumstances secure a greater good? A lot of care and awareness is needed here, as the idea of a greater good has often been used to rationalize very harmful actions. And yet at times it may indicate an appropriate response.

Keep in mind that this step on the Path, abstinence from killing, refers to our volitional actions, where there is an intention to take life. There are times when we inadvertently take a life without any intention to kill—for example, when we unknowingly step on some insects or when a surgeon loses a patient—and these occurrences are not considered breaking this precept.

Abstaining from Taking What Is Not Given

The second aspect of Right Action is abstaining from stealing, from taking what is not given. This precept is important in society and in our interpersonal relationships because it creates real refuges of safety. One of the most striking experiences at meditation retreats, or other situations where groups of people are committed to following the precepts, is that even if large amounts of money or valuables are left lying around, they are not misappropriated. When we first opened the Insight Meditation Society, people would sometimes ask for keys to their rooms. We didn't even have any, and it was an education in Right Action to realize that they weren't needed.

We can see the tremendous impact and power of this step on the Path when we look at the economic and social harm caused by the actions of people who are not committed to it. The Enron scandal, the Madoff scheme, and the banking crisis all had devastating consequences to so many people, and all are based on excessive greed and deception. Although we may not be grand thieves, it would still be instructive to look at our lives and see if there are times when, in some way, we are taking things not freely offered.

Just as the positive side of nonkilling is cultivating loving care for all living beings, the positive expression of nonstealing is contentment, which the Buddha called "our greatest wealth." And in this time of overconsumption of resources, this expression of nonstealing might mean not taking or using more than we need. Of course, what we need is always a subjective evaluation, but we can at least begin to examine our lives from this reference point: do I really need this?

Abstaining from Sexual Misconduct

The last aspect of Right Action is abstaining from sexual misconduct. This can mean different things depending on the context of our lives. For monks and nuns or meditators on retreat, it means refraining from any sexual activity. But what does this step on the Path mean for laypeople living in the world? Thich Nhat Hanh describes it well in his discussion of the third precept:

> Aware of the suffering caused by sexual misconduct, I vow to
> cultivate responsibility and learn ways to protect the safety
> and integrity of individuals, couples, families, and society. . . .
> To preserve the happiness of myself and others, I am deter-
> mined to respect my commitments and the commitments of
> others. I will do everything in my power to protect children
> from sexual abuse and to prevent couples and families from
> being broken by sexual misconduct.[3]

It's important to become conscious and mindful in this area, because, as we all know, sexual energy is a tremendously powerful force.

Crimes of passion fill not only the news cycles, but also works of great literature throughout the ages. I heard one of the best and pithiest descriptions of the harmful consequences of unmindful sexual activity in a meditation retreat with Sayadaw U Paṇḍita. He was speaking about this precept in Burmese and went on at some length about it. The translator then expressed everything Sayadaw had said in just four words: *lust cracks the brain.*

When we pay careful attention to the energy of sexual desire, we can learn a lot about the nature of desire itself and the energy systems of the body. Meditation retreats are a particularly helpful time to see and understand its transient, impermanent nature. When we're in the throes of this strong feeling, we usually think that the choice is either to express or suppress it. But with mindful awareness, we can feel the force of desire, open to it, and then see that it arises and passes away by itself.

When sexual desire arises, how does the mind relate to it? Do we indulge the fantasies because they're pleasant, because there's not much sloth and torpor at those times? Is there fear of this desire or aversion to the idea of it arising and disturbing our practice? Or can we see it with equanimity and wisdom, as simply being part of the passing show of phenomena? In meditation, we begin to feel the whole body as an energy field, and this field is felt and expressed in different ways depending on where we focus our attention.

The more we understand the experience of sexual desire when we're on retreat and not acting on it, the more mindfulness and wisdom we can then bring to this area of our lives. We understand what is skillful and what is not, and integrate them as part of our path of awakening.

The Karmic Consequences of Actions

Examining the deeper implications of this step on the Path leads us to subtler understandings of the Buddha's teachings. For example, Bhikkhu Bodhi points out that acts of killing can be driven by greed, hatred, or delusion and that killing driven by hatred is the most serious, particularly if it is premeditated, because there have been many intense mind moments that have gone into planning and thinking about it. Always, the unwholesome karma is proportional to the force and strength and duration of the defilements.

Later teachings also explain that the consequences or results of an action are conditioned by the moral qualities of both the actor and the recipient of the act. This is true of both negative and positive actions. For example, on the positive side, gifts are purified both by the motivation of the giver and also the purity of the recipient. In this light, it was considered of inestimable merit to make an offering to the Buddha or to other enlightened beings. And at the same time, in the perfection of generosity, we give without discrimination, whenever the opportunity is there.

It's not that an act of generosity or an act of harm has some absolute karmic consequence. Rather, the karmic fruits of these actions are conditioned by various factors, including the intensity and duration of the defilements or wholesome motivations and the purity of both the actor and the recipient of the action.

The reason for elaborating these considerations, even in brief, is not to engender a particular belief, but rather to lay out some of the ethical nuances of Right Action and have them be a condition for our own active investigation. As the Buddha said in the Kalama Sutta to a group of people who were perplexed by the various views expounded by different teachers:

> "It is fitting for you to be perplexed, Kalamas, fitting for you to be in doubt. . . . Come, Kalamas, do not go by oral tradition, by lineage of teaching, by hearsay, by a collection of scriptures, by logical reasoning, by inferential reasoning. . . . But when, Kalamas, you know for yourselves: 'These things are unwholesome; these things are blameworthy; these things are censured by the wise; these things, if accepted and undertaken, lead to harm and suffering,' then you should abandon them. . . .
>
> "[W]hen you know for yourselves: 'These things are wholesome; these things are blameless; these things are praised by the wise; these things, if accepted and undertaken, lead to welfare and happiness,' then you should live in accordance with them."[4]

The Buddha's teaching is never about blind belief, but about the wisdom of our own inquiry.

Sudden Awakening, Gradual Cultivation

It's also helpful to investigate what keeps us complacent about the choices we make. Some time ago, I was asked to contribute an article to a book about global warming. Although I was aware of the magnitude of the problem, I hadn't really spent much time reflecting about it or seriously considering what actions I might take. What then piqued my interest was *why* I hadn't spent time considering one of the major problems confronting our planet.

As I reflected on this question, one particular teaching began to shed some light on this pattern of inaction; this teaching can be a light that illuminates many other important issues in our lives as well. The great twelfth-century Korean Zen master Chinul framed his teachings in terms of what he called "sudden awakening, gradual cultivation":

> Although he has awakened to the fact that his original nature is no different from that of the Buddhas, beginningless habit energies are extremely difficult to remove suddenly.[5]

> Hindrances are formidable and habits are deeply ingrained.[6]

> So how could you neglect gradual cultivation simply because of one moment of awakening? After awakening you must be constantly on your guard. If deluded thoughts suddenly appear, do not follow after them. . . . Then and only then will your practice reach completion.[7]

We have probably all had moments of what we might call a sudden awakening to the truth of global warming or racial injustice or the vast inequalities of wealth or any other issue in which simply being part of society involves us. Yet these moments of awakening and understanding can quickly pass, and the beginningless habit energies of forgetfulness, of other desires, of basic ignorance, resurface once again.

Here is where Chinul's emphasis on gradual cultivation can become a template not only for this step of Right Action, but also for the entire journey of awakening. We need to repeatedly remind ourselves, whatever the situation may be, of what Right Action is appropriate, making some effort to keep ourselves informed over and over again, so that we don't fall back into deluded thinking. As

Chinul says, "How could you neglect gradual cultivation simply because of one moment of awakening?"

What motivates and energizes us to make this effort are precisely the previous steps on the Path. As we understand through Right View the selfless, interconnected aspect of all things, and as we cultivate Right Thoughts of renunciation, lovingkindness, and compassion, then we are moved to speak and act in such a way that minimizes harm and is conducive to the welfare of all.

RIGHT LIVELIHOOD

The next step on the Path is Right Livelihood. So often we separate our work from our spiritual practice, yet the Buddha puts this part of our lives in a central place on our journey of awakening. The work we do as laypeople may occupy more time than anything else in our lives, so it's essential that we relate to it in the context of our highest aspirations.

With Right View, we have an understanding of the law of karma, of what is wholesome and what is unwholesome, and when we refrain from those actions of body and speech that cause harm, we naturally avoid those livelihoods that likewise cause suffering. In this regard, the Buddha specifically mentions five kinds of livelihood to avoid: trading in weapons and instruments for killing; trading in human beings—buying and selling children and adults (although this may seem very foreign to most of us, unfortunately it goes on in many places in the world, even our local U.S. communities); avoiding livelihoods involving meat production and the killing of animals; manufacturing or selling of intoxicants or addictive drugs; and producing or trading in any kind of poison. In addition, the Buddha talks of abstaining from any livelihood involving deceit.

All of these livelihoods seem like obvious ones to avoid, since they actively cause harm to other beings and have negative karmic consequences for ourselves. But how can we understand Right Livelihood in its positive aspect? We might hold some ideal of a life of service, but then feel that we don't live up to it and, consequently, ignore the cultivation of this step on the Path. How can we approach Right Livelihood on a subtler and more integrated level?

It's possible to develop the attitude of service in whatever work we might do. Are we simply doing a job to support ourselves and our families, or are we watching the attitudes in our minds as we work? Do we work with care, with attentiveness to others, with a genuine desire to be helpful? Right Livelihood is not only about what we do, but also how we do it.

We've all had interactions with people who go out of their way to be of service, and we experience the good feelings generated by those interactions. And we've probably had the opposite experience as well. If we're not engaged in a harmful occupation, then whatever work we do can be an arena for cultivating generosity and lovingkindness. As the meditation master S. N. Goenka expressed it, "If the intention is to play a useful role in society in order to support oneself and to help others, then the work one does is Right Livelihood."

In an exploration of Right Livelihood, there are also implications for our relationship to money and wealth. In some spiritual traditions, money is seen as either an evil to be avoided or as something quite apart from a spiritual life. In the Buddha's teachings, wealth rightfully gained is seen as a blessing that can be used for the benefit and welfare of others. Two of the most prominent laypeople mentioned in the suttas are Visakha and Anāthapiṇḍika, the chief female and male lay supporters of the Buddha. They were both stream-enterers, well established on the Path, who used their vast wealth to both support the Sangha and the spread of the Dharma, as well as to take care of those in need.

Right Livelihood, in its broadest application, can be seen as the expression of *bodhichitta*. The Dalai Lama captured this truth when he said, "To take responsibility for others gives us the power of a radiant heart, a responsive and heroic heart."[8]

Whatever work we do can be performed with the noble aspiration of benefitting other beings. The practice of Right Livelihood, the fifth step of the Noble Eightfold Path, takes this aspiration and puts it into practice.

MINDFULNESS OF DHAMMAS

The Noble Eightfold Path:
Concentration Factors

Right Effort, Right Mindfulness, Right Concentration

THE LAST THREE STEPS OF the Noble Eightfold Path are Right Effort, Right Mindfulness, and Right Concentration. Together, these three steps are called "the samādhi" or "concentration part" of the Path. Although it is the wisdom factor that cuts through delusion and ignorance, this blade of wisdom is sharpened and finely honed by these three supporting factors.

RIGHT EFFORT

It's important that we understand Right Effort, the sixth step on the Path, in the context of awakening. The mental factor underlying effort is *viriya,* or energy, one of the factors of enlightenment. But as we all know, energy can be used for many different goals, both wholesome and unwholesome. And even when we use our energy in the service of what is wholesome, is it simply for the accumulation of merit and worldly happiness or is it associated with the Right View that liberates the mind?

Prevent the Arising of Latent Defilements

The Buddha spoke of Right Effort as the application of energy to four great endeavors. The first is to prevent the arising of unwholesome states not yet arisen. This aspect of Right Effort points to a fundamental understanding of how our minds work. In the suttas, the most pragmatic description of nibbāna is the mind that is free from the root defilements of greed, hatred, and delusion. We've all experienced many wholesome mind moments when these defilements are not present, yet have also had unwholesome factors frequently reemerge as conditions change. This is the functioning of what are called "latent defilements," mind states that are not present in the moment, but that have the potential to arise whenever the conditions for them to reappear are present.

It is just this understanding that can inspire a feeling of spiritual urgency. When we're leading basically good and wholesome lives, it is easy to become complacent about our present circumstances. But even under these favorable conditions, we still have many moments when greed, hatred, or delusion arises. We see something beautiful and we want it; our minds are pulled toward it. Or perhaps we see somebody doing something we don't like, and the mind is suddenly filled with judgment and aversion. Or we may be tired, and the mind simply dulls out in delusion. So the first of the four great endeavors is recognizing the enduring power of these latent defilements, understanding what gives rise to them, and preventing them from arising and taking hold.

In the Tibetan tradition, one of the powerful mind-changing reflections (mentioned in earlier chapters) is the reflection on the preciousness of our human birth. It's precious because now we have the opportunity to weaken and eventually uproot these latent defilements that have been with us throughout our lives.

How, then, do we practice this first aspect of Right Effort? The previous steps on the Path, Right Speech, Action, and Livelihood, provide the foundation, through abstinence from unwholesome activities. We then need to exercise wise attention on the different objects of experience arising through the senses. If our attention is casual, careless, and unwise, then we simply fall into old habits of reactivity. For me, one of the most radical, far-reaching, and challenging statements of the Buddha is his statement that as long as there is attachment to the pleasant and aversion to the unpleasant, liberation is impossible. Clearly, we need a wise and sustained attention to weaken these deeply conditioned habits of mind.

Abandon Unwholesome States That Have Arisen

The second great endeavor is to abandon those unwholesome states that have already arisen. We've discussed in detail the many ways of working with the five hindrances (see Mindfulness of Dhammas—The Five Hindrances). Mindfulness of them is always the first strategy; if we're not even aware that they are present, there's not much possibility of abandoning them. Sometimes mindfulness itself is enough. We see the unwholesome states, and, in an expression from Tibetan teachings, they self-liberate.

"At present the natural clarity of your mind is obscured by delusions," says Dilgo Khyentse Rinpoche in the book *Journey to Enlightenment.* "But as the obscuration clears you will begin to uncover the radiance of awareness, until you reach a point where, just as a line traced on water disappears the moment it is made, your thoughts are liberated the moment they arise."[1]

At times, though, the hindrances may be tenacious, and we need additional strategies for abandoning them. In one sutta, the Buddha describes five techniques for dispelling distracting thoughts and unwholesome mind states. The first is using its opposite as an antidote. For example, if ill will has arisen, we can refocus the mind on mettā. Or if restlessness is present, calming the mind through calming the breath can be helpful. If envy or jealousy is strong, we can turn the mind to the feeling of *muditā,* empathetic joy. All of these remedies come from understanding that we have an inner remote control with an ability to change channels.

The second means for removing unwholesome states already arisen is through the factors of *hiri* and *ottappa,* often translated respectively as "self-respect" and "respect for the wise." These wholesome factors of mind bring a heightened sense of conscience and responsibility. Reflecting on how the wise might view an unwholesome mind state or activity is often a powerful ally in this endeavor to abandon what is unwholesome; for this reason, these factors are called "the guardians of the world." Care is also needed here so that this review of our actions is done from a place of wise understanding and is not simply feeding into patterns of self-judgment or guilt. But used wisely, *hiri* and *ottappa* can awaken us from the power of deluded thinking.

The third method for dispelling unwholesome mind states already arisen is a deliberate diversion of attention. If we're really lost in a quagmire of hindrances, we can deliberately divert our attention to some other object. There has been some research done on the value of this strategy of diversion—namely, the well-known marshmallow experiment. This was an experiment on deferred gratification conducted in 1972 by psychologist Walter Mischel of Stanford University. Mischel offered children a tray with marshmallows, cookies, and other treats; he told them that they could take one and eat it right away, or, if they waited for a few minutes as he left the room, they could have a second one when he returned. The experimenters filmed the reactions of various children. Some immediately ate the first treat. Others tried different strategies to help themselves delay gratification. Jonah Lehrer, in his *The New Yorker* article "Don't! The Secret of Self-Control," describes what happened:

> Footage of these experiments, which were conducted over several years, is poignant, as the kids struggle to delay gratification for just a little bit longer. Some cover their eyes with their hands or turn around so that they can't see the tray. Others start kicking the desk, or tug on their pigtails, or stroke the marshmallow as if it were a tiny stuffed animal. One child, a boy with neatly parted hair, looks carefully around the room to make sure that nobody can see him. Then he picks up an Oreo, delicately twists it apart, and licks off the white cream filling before returning the cookie to the tray, a satisfied look on his face.[2]

The experiment found that those children who were able to divert their attention to something other than the treat were better able to resist the immediate temptation and wait for a greater good (in this case, a second treat). We can use this same strategy to let go of various hindrances and unwholesome mind states: we can shift our attention to some other object until those mind states have weakened or passed away.

The fourth method of dispelling distracting thoughts is just the opposite: looking directly at them, investigating their source and their hold on the mind. Here, we might be a little more engaged in seeing what thoughts or emotions are underneath or associated with the unwholesome states; for example, fear often underlies anger, or boredom often underlies desire.

And in the fifth method, when all else fails, the Buddha suggests forcibly suppressing the unwholesome thought. One way of doing this is imagining oneself shooting down these thoughts as soon as they arise, like shooting down targets at an amusement-park shooting-gallery game. I've found this method particularly helpful with recurrent unwholesome thoughts that have already been seen so many times that it's not a question of denial or suppression of feeling. Here, it's an attitude that takes no quarter, but involves a sense of humor. I call this method "cowboy dharma."

All these teachings remind us that meditation is an art. On this step of the Path, Right Effort, it's not a question of simply following any one technique or thinking there is only one correct approach. Rather, we understand the mind as a vital, vibrant, ever-changing interplay of different mental qualities. If we have a strong commitment to awakening, then we investigate, experiment, and test different ways of abandoning that which is unskillful. The Buddha was the ultimate pragmatist. The teachings are not about dogma, but about skillful means, about understanding what works.

Arouse Wholesome States Not Yet Arisen
The third great endeavor is to arouse wholesome states that have not yet arisen. There are many ways of categorizing these wholesome states of mind, but perhaps we can understand them most succinctly as the seven factors of awakening. In *The Noble Eightfold Path*, Bhikkhu Bodhi says,

> The seven states are grouped together as "enlightenment factors" both because they lead to enlightenment and because they constitute enlightenment. In the preliminary stages of the path they prepare the way for the great realization; in the end they remain as its components. The experience of enlightenment, perfect and complete understanding, is just these seven components working in unison to break all shackles and bring final release from sorrow.[3]

Maintain and Strengthen Wholesome States Already Arisen
The fourth and last of the great endeavors is to maintain and strengthen those wholesome states that have already arisen. This is

the effort to nurture and sustain what the Abhidhamma calls "the beautiful mental factors." So often we focus on our shortcomings and mistakes, and overlook the many wholesome mind states that arise during the day.

I had an interesting experience of this in my early days in India. At that time, there were just a few of us staying at the Burmese Vihāra in Bodh Gaya. One evening, we had a little gathering, and one of the women said she had written a song about our group. My first thought was that it would be a humorous roast, gently poking fun at our various foibles. Surprisingly, it turned out to be quite the contrary. She had written verses about what she saw as each of our good qualities, and there was this wonderful feeling of mettā that pervaded the entire evening.

It is a good practice to recollect the factors of enlightenment, or any other wholesome state, and become familiar with them. In this way we can recognize them when they arise and cultivate their growth. Recognizing these beautiful mind factors in ourselves strengthens our confidence and inspires even further Right Effort. It puts us on the glide path of awakening.

There is some good news here. In his book *Outliers,* Malcolm Gladwell references many studies showing that the mastery of any given discipline depends less on some innate talent and genius and more on the number of hours devoted to practice. We don't have to be a spiritual genius; we just have to put in the time.

The last two steps of the Noble Eightfold Path are Right Mindfulness and Right Concentration. These have already been discussed in some detail in Mindfulness of Dhammas—The Seven Factors of Awakening, so here I will highlight just a few important aspects of each of them.

RIGHT MINDFULNESS

Right Mindfulness is the essential key to practice. It is the first of the factors of enlightenment, and it gives rise to all the others. As we have seen, in the Satipaṭṭhāna Sutta, the Buddha elaborates comprehensively the many ways we practice and cultivate this state.

Mindfulness is the presence of mind, the quality of awareness often described as "bare attention." Bhikkhu Bodhi describes it very well:

In the practice of right mindfulness the mind is trained to remain in the present, open, quiet, and alert, contemplating the present event. All judgments and interpretations have to be suspended, or if they occur, just registered and dropped. The task is simply to note whatever comes up just as it is occurring, riding the changes of events in the way a surfer rides the waves on the sea. The whole process is a way of coming back into the present, of standing in the here and now without slipping away, without getting swept away by the tides of distracting thoughts. . . . To practice mindfulness is thus a matter not so much of doing but of undoing.[4]

Although the practice of mindfulness is very simple, it is not always easy to do. As we know, our minds often get lost in mental proliferation of overlaying concepts, evaluations, and likes and dislikes regarding the bare experience of what is happening. And there can be also a nonconceptual identification with experience, the creation of a sense of self, that hinders mindful bare attention.

To help clarify the difference between ordinary, conventional knowing and mindful knowing, I use the example of "black Lab consciousness." Have you ever watched the playful antics of Labrador retrievers? The black Labs clearly recognize sights and sounds and particularly smells. But when they play, the Labs just run from one sense impression to the next, literally being led around by the nose. There is no apparent mindfulness about what they are doing.

As a way of understanding the difference between this black Lab consciousness and mindfulness, pay careful attention to the moments of awakening after being lost in a thought. Just in that moment of transition, we can get a very clear, immediate experience of what mindfulness means. In one moment, we're lost, carried away by a thought, and in the next, we've become aware that we're thinking. We are waking up from the dream of our lives.

RIGHT CONCENTRATION

Through the power and continuity of mindfulness, we then develop the next and last step on the Noble Eightfold Path—Right Concentration. When mindfulness is directed toward stabilizing the attention on a single object, it leads to deepening states of calm and tranquility, culminating in what are called the *jhānas,* or meditative absorptions.

When mindfulness is directed to a precise noting/noticing of changing objects, the concentration brings increasing clarity of the three characteristics: impermanence, unsatisfactoriness, and selflessness.

The characteristic of concentration in both these ways of practice is undistractedness, and it is this steadiness of mind that makes it possible for wisdom to arise. It is concentration that makes the mind pliable and pervades it with a happiness much greater than the happiness of sense pleasures. Without concentration, the Buddha said, our minds are like fish flopping about on dry land, and that dwelling without reverence and deference toward concentration leads to the decay and disappearance of the teachings.

The Buddha was very clear about the importance of this last step on the Path:

> "Bhikkhus, develop concentration. A bhikkhu who is concentrated understands things as they really are. And what does he understand. . . . the arising and passing away of the aggregates."[5]

In the Buddha's words, "A bhikkhu who is concentrated understands things as they really are," we see that this last step of the Path, Right Concentration, leads us back to the first step, Right View. With ever-deepening levels of understanding, we see that the Noble Eightfold Path comes full circle again and again, spiraling upward toward liberation.

THE REFRAIN: ON DHAMMAS

As he does after each set of instructions in the first three satipaṭṭhānas, the Buddha returns to the refrain after each of the dhamma instructions, emphasizing the particular ways of developing the contemplation of them:

> "In this way, in regard to dhammas, one abides contemplating dhammas internally . . . externally . . . internally and externally. One abides contemplating the nature of arising . . . of passing away . . . of both arising and passing away in dhammas."[6]

As you reflect on different aspects of your own practice and everyday experience, consider for yourself how the refrain applies to each of them. For example, when you notice the presence of a hindrance or a sound or a particular thought, what is your general attitude toward it? Are you aware in the moment of the arising and passing away of these phenomena? What thoughts and feelings arise when you notice someone else's energy or concentration? How does this noticing, or lack of it, inform your own practice? Are you able to view your experience and theirs objectively and free of clinging?

To further exemplify the importance of the refrain in our practice of dhammas, we will look at how it applies to the four noble truths. When we put the four noble truths into practice, we can notice how they operate in ourselves, in others, and in both ourselves and others. This emphasis on seeing the universal aspects of our personal experience helps us keep both an equanimous and compassionate mind in our interactions with others. The more we understand ourselves, the more we understand each other. When we investigate the nature of suffering in our own lives, the more compassionate we are in seeing the suffering of others. And as we understand more deeply the possibility of freedom in ourselves, the more we understand that all beings share in this possibility.

The refrain reminds us to also contemplate the arising and passing away of all elements of our experience. When we experience the impermanence of phenomena, internally, externally, or both, we also understand their unsatisfying and selfless nature. We can then see for ourselves the obvious truth that when we cling or hold on to that which changes, we suffer.

The Buddha then concludes the refrain:

> "Mindfulness that 'there are dhammas' is established in one to the extent necessary for bare knowledge and continuous mindfulness. And one abides independent, not clinging to anything in the world.
>
> "That is how in regard to dhammas one abides contemplating dhammas in terms of the four noble truths."[7]

44

The Realization of Nibbāna

ALTHOUGH RIGHT CONCENTRATION IS THE last step on the Noble Eightfold Path, it is not the end of the Path itself. We use the refined power of concentration to explore the nature of phenomena—the mind, the body, the world—and concentration has as its final goal the uprooting of defilements, the coming to the end of suffering.

> "And what, bhikkhus, is the unconditioned? The destruction of lust, the destruction of hatred, the destruction of delusion: this is called the unconditioned. . . ."[1]

> "And what, bhikkhus, is the path leading to the unconditioned? The emptiness concentration, the signless concentration, the undirected concentration: this is called the path leading to the unconditioned. . . ."[2]

Emptiness concentration is when we see and understand all things as being empty of self. Signless concentration, sometimes called *vipassanā samādhi,* abandons the sign of permanence through the contemplation of change. And undirected concentration arises when we contemplate the unsatisfying nature of conditioned phenomena and so no longer lean toward that which is impermanent, unreliable, and selfless.

As these insights are brought to maturity, at a certain point the mind opens to the experience of nibbāna, the unconditioned, uprooting, by stages, all the defilements that keep us bound. The Buddha described this experience in different ways: "the perfection of wisdom," "the highest happiness," "unsurpassable freedom," "a state of peace," "the sublime," "the auspicious," "the wonderful," "the marvelous," "an island," "a shelter," and "a refuge." At the same time, as a caution against reifying nibbāna in some way, he also describes it as unborn, unmade, unbecome, unconditioned. The realization of nibbāna is the great fruition of our practice, the accomplishment that has been voiced by so many awakened beings: *done is what had to be done.*

The Buddha concludes the Satipaṭṭhāna Sutta with a prediction that has important implications for how we understand practice:

> "Monks, if anyone should develop these four satipaṭṭhānas in such a way for seven years . . . Let alone seven years . . . six years . . . five years . . . four years . . . three years . . . two years . . . one year . . . seven months . . . six months . . . five months . . . four months . . . three months . . . two months . . . one month . . . half a month . . . if anyone should develop these four satipaṭṭhānas in such a way for seven days, one of two fruits could be expected . . . : either final knowledge here and now, or, if there is a trace of clinging left, non-returning. So it was with reference to this that it was said:
>
> "'Monks, this is the direct path for the purification of beings, for the surmounting of sorrow and lamentation, for the disappearance of dukkha and discontent, for acquiring the true method, for the realization of Nibbāna, namely, the four satipaṭṭhānas,'"[3]

One important implication of this very direct statement is that awakening is really possible. It's something that all of us can achieve because it is the potential of the mind itself. Even the first few moments of genuine mindfulness are a turning point in our lives, because we realize, perhaps for the first time, that the mind can be trained, can be understood, can be liberated. We get glimpses of something beyond our ordinary, conventional reality, touching a space that transforms our vision of who we are and what the world is. And we understand that there is a direct and clearly articulated path to this end. These intimations give passionate meaning to questions of ultimate truth, because although we may not always be living in that space, we understand it to be the source of everything we value.

The second implication of the Buddha's prophetic statement is that there is a variable timeframe for awakening. Given the Buddha's understanding that the development of mind occurs over lifetimes, perhaps we are just at the beginning of the journey, or perhaps we are nearing the end. Each of us has different backgrounds and conditionings. But as Bhikkhu Bodhi points out,

> Liberation is the inevitable fruit of the path and is bound to blossom forth when there is steady and persistent practice. The only requisites for reaching the final goal are two: to start and to continue. If these requirements are met, there is no doubt the goal will be attained.[4]

The great gift of this amazing discourse, the Satipaṭṭhāna Sutta, is that it shows us the way.

APPENDIX A

Translation of the Satipaṭṭhāna Sutta by Anālayo[1]

ANĀLAYO WAS BORN IN 1962 in Germany, and was ordained as a Buddhist monk in 1995 in Sri Lanka. He completed his PhD on satipaṭṭhāna at the University of Peradeniya and is currently engaged in writing, teaching, and the practice of meditation.

Thus have I heard. On one occasion the Blessed One was living in the Kuru country at a town of the Kurus named Kammāsadhamma. There he addressed the monks thus: "Monks." "Venerable sir," they replied. The Blessed One said this:

[DIRECT PATH]

"Monks, this is the direct path for the purification of beings, for the surmounting of sorrow and lamentation, for the disappearance of dukkha and discontent, for acquiring the true method, for the realization of nibbāna, namely, the four satipaṭṭhānas.

[DEFINITION]

"What are the four? Here, monks, in regard to the body a monk abides contemplating the body, diligent, clearly knowing, and mindful, free from desires and discontent in regard to the world. In regard to feelings he abides contemplating feelings, diligent, clearly knowing, and mindful, free from desires and discontent in regard to the world. In regard to the mind he abides contemplating the mind, diligent, clearly knowing, and mindful, free from desires and discontent in regard to the world. In regard to dhammas he abides contemplating dhammas, diligent, clearly knowing, and mindful, free from desires and discontent in regard to the world.

[BREATHING]

"And how, monks, does he in regard to the body abide contemplating the body? Here, gone to the forest, or to the root of a tree, or to an empty hut, he sits down; having folded his legs crosswise, set his body erect, and established mindfulness in front of him, mindful he breathes in, mindful he breathes out.

"Breathing in long, he knows 'I breathe in long,' breathing out long, he knows 'I breathe out long.' Breathing in short, he knows 'I breathe in short,' breathing out short, he knows 'I breathe out short.' He trains thus: 'I shall breathe in experiencing the whole body,' he trains thus: 'I shall breathe out experiencing the whole body.' He trains thus: 'I shall breathe in calming the bodily formation,' he trains thus: 'I shall breathe out calming the bodily formation.'

"Just as a skilled turner or his apprentice, when making a long turn, knows 'I make a long turn,' or when making a short turn knows 'I make a short turn' so too, breathing in long, he knows 'I breathe in long,' . . . (continue as above).

[REFRAIN]

"In this way, in regard to the body he abides contemplating the body internally, or he abides contemplating the body externally, or he abides contemplating the body both internally and externally. Or, he abides contemplating the nature of arising in the body, or he abides contemplating the nature of passing away in the body, or he abides contemplating the nature of both arising and passing away in the body. Or, mindfulness that 'There is a body' is established in him to the extent necessary for bare knowledge and continuous mindfulness. And he abides independent, not clinging to anything in the world.

"That is how in regard to the body he abides contemplating the body.

[POSTURES]

"Again, monks, when walking, he knows 'I am walking'; when standing, he knows 'I am standing'; when sitting, he knows 'I am sitting'; when lying down, he knows 'I am lying down'; or he knows accordingly however his body is disposed.

[REFRAIN]

"In this way, in regard to the body he abides contemplating the body internally . . . externally . . . both internally and externally. He abides contemplating the nature of arising . . . of passing away . . . of both arising and passing away in the body. Mindfulness that 'There is body' is established in him to the extent necessary for bare knowledge and continuous mindfulness. And he abides independent, not clinging to anything in the world. That too is how in regard to the body he abides contemplating the body.

[ACTIVITIES]

"Again, monks, when going forward and returning he acts clearly knowing; when looking ahead and looking away he acts clearly knowing; when flexing and extending his limbs he acts clearly knowing; when wearing his robes and carrying his outer robe and bowl he acts clearly knowing; when eating, drinking, consuming food, and tasting he acts clearly knowing; when defecating and urinating he acts clearly knowing; when walking, standing, sitting, falling asleep, waking up, talking, and keeping silent he acts clearly knowing.

[REFRAIN]

"In this way, in regard to the body he abides contemplating the body internally . . . externally . . . both internally and externally. He abides contemplating the nature of arising . . . of passing away . . . of both arising and passing away in the body. Mindfulness that 'There is a body' is established in him to the extent necessary for bare knowledge and continuous mindfulness. And he abides independent, not clinging to anything in the world. That too is how in regard to the body he abides contemplating the body.

[ANATOMICAL PARTS]

"Again, monks, he reviews this same body up from the soles of the feet and down from the top of the hair, enclosed by skin, as full of many kinds of impurity thus: 'In this body there are head-hairs, body-hairs, nails, teeth, skin, flesh, sinews, bones, bone-marrow, kidneys, heart, liver, diaphragm, spleen, lungs, bowels, mesentery, contents of the stomach, feces, bile, phlegm, pus, blood, sweat, fat, tears, grease, spittle, snot, oil of the joints, and urine.'

"Just as though there were a bag with an opening at both ends full of many sorts of grain, such as hill rice, red rice, beans, peas, millet, and white rice, and a man with good eyes were to open it and review it thus: 'This is hill rice, this is red rice, these are beans, these are peas, this is millet, this is white rice'; so too he reviews this same body . . . (continue as above).

[REFRAIN]

"In this way, in regard to the body he abides contemplating the body internally . . . externally . . . both internally and externally. He abides contemplating the nature of arising . . . of passing away . . . of both arising and passing away in the body. Mindfulness that 'There is a body' is established in him to the extent necessary for bare knowledge and continuous mindfulness. And he abides independent, not clinging to anything in the world. That too is how in regard to the body he abides contemplating the body.

[ELEMENTS]

"Again, monks, he reviews this same body, however it is placed, however disposed, as consisting of elements thus: 'In this body there are the earth element, the water element, the fire element, and the air element.'

"Just as though a skilled butcher or his apprentice had killed a cow and was seated at a crossroads with it cut up into pieces, so too he reviews this same body . . . (continue as above).

[REFRAIN]

"In this way, in regard to the body he abides contemplating the body internally . . . externally . . . both internally and externally. He abides contemplating the nature of arising . . . of passing away . . . of both arising and passing away in the body. Mindfulness that 'There is a body' is established in him to the extent necessary for bare knowledge and continuous mindfulness. And he abides independent, not clinging to anything in the world. That too is how in regard to the body he abides contemplating the body.

[CORPSE IN DECAY]

"Again, monks, as though he were to see a corpse thrown aside in a charnel ground—one, two, or three days dead, bloated, livid, and oozing matter . . . being devoured by crows, hawks, vultures, dogs, jackals, or various kinds of worms . . . a skeleton with flesh and blood, held together with sinews . . . a fleshless skeleton smeared with blood, held together with sinews . . . a skeleton without flesh and blood, held together with sinews . . . disconnected bones scattered in all directions . . . bones bleached white, the color of shells

. . . bones heaped up, more than a year old . . . bones rotten and crumbling to dust—he compares this same body with it thus: 'This body too is of the same nature, it will be like that, it is not exempt from that fate.'[2]

[REFRAIN]

"In this way, in regard to the body he abides contemplating the body internally . . . externally . . . both internally and externally. He abides contemplating the nature of arising . . . of passing away . . . of both arising and passing away in the body. Mindfulness that 'There is a body' is established in him to the extent necessary for bare knowledge and continuous mindfulness. And he abides independent, not clinging to anything in the world. That too is how in regard to the body he abides contemplating the body.

[FEELINGS]

"And how, monks, does he in regard to feelings abide contemplating feelings?

"Here, when feeling a pleasant feeling, he knows 'I feel a pleasant feeling'; when feeling an unpleasant feeling, he knows 'I feel an unpleasant feeling'; when feeling a neutral feeling, he knows 'I feel a neutral feeling.'

"When feeling a worldly pleasant feeling, he knows 'I feel a worldly pleasant feeling'; when feeling an unworldly pleasant feeling, he knows 'I feel an unworldly pleasant feeling'; when feeling a worldly unpleasant feeling, he knows 'I feel a worldly unpleasant feeling'; when feeling an unworldly unpleasant feeling, he knows 'I feel an unworldly unpleasant feeling'; when feeling a worldly neutral feeling, he knows 'I feel a worldly neutral feeling'; when feeling an unworldly neutral feeling, he knows 'I feel an unworldly neutral feeling.'

[REFRAIN]

"In this way, in regard to feelings he abides contemplating feelings internally . . . externally . . . internally and externally. He abides contemplating the nature of arising . . . of passing away . . . of both arising and passing away in feelings. Mindfulness that 'There is feeling' is established in him to the extent necessary for bare knowledge and continuous mindfulness. And he abides independent, not clinging to anything in the world.

"That is how in regard to feelings he abides contemplating feelings.

[MIND]

"And how, monks, does he in regard to the mind abide contemplating the mind?

"Here he knows a lustful mind to be 'lustful,' and a mind without lust to be 'without lust'; he knows an angry mind to be 'angry,' and a mind without anger to be 'without anger'; he knows a deluded mind to be 'deluded,' and a mind without delusion to be 'without delusion'; he knows a contracted mind to be 'contracted,' and a distracted mind to be 'distracted'; he knows a great mind to be 'great,' and a narrow mind to be 'narrow'; he knows a surpassable mind to be 'surpassable,' and an unsurpassable mind to be 'unsurpassable'; he knows a concentrated mind to be 'concentrated,' and an unconcentrated mind to be 'unconcentrated'; he knows a liberated mind to be 'liberated,' and an unliberated mind to be 'unliberated.'

[REFRAIN]

"In this way, in regard to the mind he abides contemplating the mind internally . . . externally . . . internally and externally. He abides contemplating the nature of arising . . . of passing away . . . of both arising and passing away in regard to the mind. Mindfulness that 'There is a mind' is established in him to the extent necessary for bare knowledge and continuous mindfulness. And he abides independent, not clinging to anything in the world.

"That is how in regard to the mind he abides contemplating the mind.

[HINDRANCES]

"And how, monks, does he in regard to dhammas abide contemplating dhammas? Here in regard to dhammas he abides contemplating dhammas in terms of five hindrances. And how does he in regard to dhammas abide contemplating dhammas in terms of the five hindrances?

"If sensual desire is present in him, he knows 'There is sensual desire in me'; if sensual desire is not present in him, he knows 'There is no sensual desire in me'; and he knows how unarisen sensual desire can arise, how arisen sensual desire can be removed, and how a future arising of the removed sensual desire can be prevented.

"If aversion is present in him, he knows 'There is aversion in me'; if aversion is not present in him, he knows 'There is no aversion in me'; and he knows how unarisen aversion can arise, how arisen aversion can be removed, and how a future arising of the removed aversion can be prevented.

Free Gifts!

Visit **SoundsTrue.com/Free** to download these **3 free gifts**

The Self-Acceptance Project

Twenty-three respected authors and spiritual teachers discuss the power of self-compassion, especially during challenging times.

The Practice of Mindfulness

Guided practices from six leading teachers to open us to the depths of the present moment.

Meditation Music

Nine inspiring tracks for healing, relaxation, and releasing stress.

Free Gifts!

Visit **SoundsTrue.com/Free**
to download these **3 free gifts**

The Self-Acceptance Project
Twenty-three respected authors and
spiritual teachers discuss the power
of self-compassion, especially during
challenging times.

The Practice of Mindfulness
Guided practices from six leading
teachers to open us to the depths of
the present moment.

Meditation Music
Nine inspiring tracks for healing,
relaxation, and releasing stress.

SOUNDS TRUE
many voices, one journey   800.333.9185

ST298

"If sloth-and-torpor is present in him, he knows 'There is sloth-and-torpor in me'; if sloth-and-torpor is not present in him, he knows 'There is no sloth-and-torpor in me'; and he knows how unarisen sloth-and-torpor can arise, how arisen sloth-and-torpor can be removed, and how a future arising of the removed sloth-and-torpor can be prevented.

"If restlessness-and-worry is present in him, he knows 'There is restlessness-and-worry in me'; if restlessness-and-worry is not present in him, he knows 'There is no restlessness-and-worry in me'; and he knows how unarisen restlessness-and-worry can arise, how arisen restlessness-and-worry can be removed, and how a future arising of the removed restlessness-and-worry can be prevented.

"If doubt is present in him, he knows 'There is doubt in me'; if doubt is not present in him, he knows 'There is no doubt in me'; and he knows how unarisen doubt can arise, how arisen doubt can be removed, and how a future arising of the removed doubt can be prevented.

[REFRAIN]

"In this way, in regard to dhammas he abides contemplating dhammas internally . . . externally . . . internally and externally. He abides contemplating the nature of arising . . . of passing away . . . of both arising and passing away in dhammas. Mindfulness that 'There are dhammas' is established in him to the extent necessary for bare knowledge and continuous mindfulness. And he abides independent, not clinging to anything in the world.

"That is how in regard to dhammas he abides contemplating dhammas in terms of the five hindrances.

[AGGREGATES]

"Again, monks, in regard to dhammas he abides contemplating dhammas in terms of the five aggregates of clinging. And how does he in regard to dhammas abide contemplating dhammas in terms of the five aggregates of clinging?

"Here he knows, 'Such is material form, such its arising, such its passing away; such is feeling, such its arising, such its passing away; such is cognition, such its arising, such its passing away; such are volitions, such their arising, such their passing away; such is consciousness, such its arising, such its passing away.'

[REFRAIN]

"In this way, in regard to dhammas he abides contemplating dhammas internally . . . externally . . . internally and externally. He abides contemplating the nature of arising . . . of passing away . . . of both arising and passing away in dhammas. Mindfulness that 'There are dhammas' is established in him to the extent necessary for bare knowledge and continuous mindfulness. And he abides independent, not clinging to anything in the world.

"That is how in regard to dhammas he abides contemplating dhammas in terms of the five aggregates of clinging.

[SENSE-SPHERES]

"Again, monks, in regard to dhammas he abides contemplating dhammas in terms of the six internal and external sense-spheres. And how does he in regard to dhammas abide contemplating dhammas in terms of the six internal and external sense-spheres?

"Here he knows the eye, he knows forms, and he knows the fetter that arises dependent on both, and he also knows how an unarisen fetter can arise, how an arisen fetter can be removed, and how a future arising of the removed fetter can be prevented.

"He knows the ear, he knows sounds, and he knows the fetter that arises dependent on both, and he also knows how an unarisen fetter can arise, how an arisen fetter can be removed, and how a future arising of the removed fetter can be prevented.

"He knows the nose, he knows odors, and he knows the fetter that arises dependent on both, and he also knows how an unarisen fetter can arise, how an arisen fetter can be removed, and how a future arising of the removed fetter can be prevented.

"He knows the tongue, he knows flavors, and he knows the fetter that arises dependent on both, and he also knows how an unarisen fetter can arise, how an arisen fetter can be removed, and how a future arising of the removed fetter can be prevented.

"He knows the body, he knows tangibles, and he knows the fetter that arises dependent on both, and he also knows how an unarisen fetter can arise, how an arisen fetter can be removed, and how a future arising of the removed fetter can be prevented.

"He knows the mind, he knows mind-objects, and he knows the fetter that arises dependent on both, and he also knows how an unarisen fetter can arise, how an arisen fetter can be removed, and how a future arising of the removed fetter can be prevented.

[REFRAIN]

"In this way, in regard to dhammas he abides contemplating dhammas internally . . . externally . . . internally and externally. He abides contemplating the nature of arising . . . of passing away . . . of both arising and passing away in dhammas. Mindfulness that 'There are dhammas' is established in him to the extent necessary for bare knowledge and continuous mindfulness. And he abides independent, not clinging to anything in the world.

"That is how in regard to dhammas he abides contemplating dhammas in terms of the six internal and external sense-spheres.

[AWAKENING FACTORS]

"Again, monks, in regard to dhammas he abides contemplating dhammas in terms of the seven awakening factors. And how does he in regard to dhammas abide contemplating dhammas in terms of the seven awakening factors?

"Here, if the mindfulness awakening factor is present in him, he knows 'There is the mindfulness awakening factor in me'; if the mindfulness awakening factor is not present in him, he knows 'There is no mindfulness awakening factor in me'; he knows how the unarisen mindfulness awakening factor can arise, and how the arisen mindfulness awakening factor can be perfected by development.

"If the investigation-of-dhammas awakening factor is present in him, he knows 'There is the investigation-of-dhammas awakening factor in me'; if the investigation-of-dhammas awakening factor is not present in him, he knows 'There is no investigation-of-dhammas awakening factor in me'; he knows how the unarisen investigation-of-dhammas awakening factor can arise, and how the arisen investigation-of-dhammas awakening factor can be perfected by development.

"If the energy awakening factor is present in him, he knows 'There is the energy awakening factor in me'; if the energy awakening factor is not present in him, he knows 'There is no energy awakening factor in me'; he knows how the unarisen energy awakening factor can arise, and how the arisen energy awakening factor can be perfected by development.

"If the joy awakening factor is present in him, he knows 'There is the joy awakening factor in me'; if the joy awakening factor is not present in him, he knows 'There is no joy awakening factor in me'; he knows how the unarisen joy awakening factor can arise, and how the arisen joy awakening factor can be perfected by development.

"If the tranquility awakening factor is present in him, he knows 'There is the tranquility awakening factor in me'; if the tranquility awakening factor is not present in him, he knows 'There is no tranquility awakening factor in me'; he knows how the unarisen tranquility awakening factor can arise, and how the arisen tranquility awakening factor can be perfected by development.

"If the concentration awakening factor is present in him, he knows 'There is the concentration awakening factor in me'; if the concentration awakening factor is not present in him, he knows 'There is no concentration awakening factor in me'; he knows how the unarisen concentration awakening factor can arise, and how the arisen concentration awakening factor can be perfected by development.

"If the equanimity awakening factor is present in him, he knows 'There is the equanimity awakening factor in me'; if the equanimity awakening factor is not present in him, he knows 'There is no equanimity awakening factor in me'; he knows how the unarisen equanimity awakening factor can arise, and how the arisen equanimity awakening factor can be perfected by development.

[REFRAIN]

"In this way, in regard to dhammas he abides contemplating dhammas internally . . . externally . . . internally and externally. He abides contemplating the nature of arising . . . of passing away . . . of both arising and passing away in dhammas. Mindfulness that 'There are dhammas' is established in him to the extent necessary for bare knowledge and continuous mindfulness. And he abides independent, not clinging to anything in the world.

"That is how in regard to dhammas he abides contemplating dhammas in terms of the seven awakening factors.

[NOBLE TRUTHS]

"Again, monks, in regard to dhammas he abides contemplating dhammas in terms of the four noble truths. And how does he in regard to dhammas abide contemplating dhammas in terms of the four noble truths?

"Here he knows as it really is, 'This is dukkha'; he knows as it really is, 'This is the arising of dukkha'; he knows as it really is, 'This is the cessation of dukkha'; he knows as it really is, 'This is the way leading to the cessation of dukkha.'

[REFRAIN]

"In this way, in regard to dhammas he abides contemplating dhammas internally . . . externally . . . internally and externally. He abides contemplating the nature of arising . . . of passing away . . . of both arising and passing away in dhammas. Mindfulness that 'There are dhammas' is established in him to the extent necessary for bare knowledge and continuous mindfulness. And he abides independent, not clinging to anything in the world.

"That is how in regard to dhammas he abides contemplating dhammas in terms of the four noble truths.

[PREDICTION]

"Monks, if anyone should develop these four satipaṭṭhānas in such a way for seven years, one of two fruits could be expected for him: either final knowledge here and now, or, if there is a trace of clinging left, non-returning. Let alone seven years . . . six years . . . five years . . . four years . . . three years . . . two years . . . one year . . . seven months . . . six months . . . five months . . . four months . . . three months . . . two months . . . one month . . . half a month . . . if anyone should develop these four satipaṭṭhānas in such a way for seven days, one of two fruits could be expected for him: either final knowledge here and now, or, if there is a trace of clinging left, non-returning. So it was with reference to this that it was said:

[DIRECT PATH]

"Monks, this is the direct path for the purification of beings, for the surmounting of sorrow and lamentation, for the disappearance of dukkha and discontent, for acquiring the true method, for the realization of nibbāna, namely, the four satipaṭṭhānas."

That is what the Blessed One said. The monks were satisfied and delighted in the Blessed One's words.

Glossary

All of the following are Pali terms unless otherwise noted.

Abhidhamma System of Buddhist psychology; one of the three "baskets" of the Buddha's teachings, along with the Suttas (discourses) and the Vinaya (monastic discipline).

ādīnava Dangers

anattā Selflessness

anicca Impermanence

arahant Fully enlightened individual

asubha Nonbeautiful aspect of the body

bhāvanā Meditation

bhikkhu Monk

bhikkhunī Nun

bodhichitta (Sanskrit) The awakened heart-mind; the aspiration to awaken in order to benefit all beings

bodhisattva (Sanskrit) A being on the path to Buddhahood; colloquially, a being with altruistic motivations

brahmavihāra Divine abodes

buddhadhamma Teachings of the Buddha

cetanā Intention or volition

citta Heart-mind

devas Heavenly beings

dhamma (Pali), dharma (Sanskrit) The law; the truth; the teachings of the Buddha. Also appears in this book as "the Dhamma" or "the Dharma."

Dhammapada A collection of verses of the Buddha

dhammavicaya "Investigation of states" factor of enlightenment

diṭṭhi View (sometimes refers to wrong view)

dosa Anger, hatred, ill will, aversion

dukkha Suffering, unsatisfactoriness, stress

Dzogchen Tibetan practice of the Natural Great Perfection

gocara Pasture; can refer to the four fields of mindfulness

hiri Moral shame, self-respect, conscience

jhāna Concentration absorption

kamma Volitional action; often refers to actions and their results (*kamma-vipāka*)

khandha 1. Aggregate, a collection of things, a heap of things, a grouping of things, all the elements that make up the substance of something; 2. Elements or substratum of existence that gives rise to the appearance of self

kilesas Defilements

kukkucca Worry, anxiety, guilt

lobha Greed

magga phala Path and fruition knowledge

Māra The embodiment of delusion and ignorance

mettā Lovingkindness

moha Delusion, ignorance, illusion, bewilderment

mudita Empathetic joy; happiness in the happiness of others

nāmarūpa Mind-body

nibbāna The unconditioned state; the highest peace

nimitta Mental image as a sign of concentration

ottappa Fear of wrongdoing, respect for the wise

paññā Wisdom

paramis Past wholesome actions, those qualities that need to be brought to perfection for awakening

paramitas perfections

Parinibbāna The passing away of an arahant

Parinibbāna Sutta A discourse on the last days of the Buddha's life

passaddhi Tranquility, calm

paṭigha Aversion; ill will

pīti Rapture, joy

pokati (Thai) Nature, ordinariness

puñña Merit

rāga Lust

rūpa Material form, materiality, physical element

sakkāyadiṭṭhi Wrong view of self

samādhi Concentration

samatha Calm; concentration practice

sammādiṭṭhi Right view

sammāsankappa Right thought, right intention

sampajañña Clear comprehension

samphappalāpa Useless talk

saṃsāra 1. Wheel of life and death; 2. Perpetual wandering, continuing on

Samyutta Nikāya Connected Discourses of the Buddha

Sangha Assembly of monks and nuns; in contemporary Western usage, any community of Buddhist practitioners

sankārā 1. All conditioned things; 2. Volitional activities; 3. As one of the five aggregates, all the mental factors besides feeling and perception

saññā Perception

sati Mindfulness

satipaṭṭhāna Foundations of mindfulness

sīla Ethical conduct

skandha (Sanskrit) Aggregate

sukha Happiness, pleasure

suttas Discourses of the Buddha

taṇhā Thirst, craving, or desire

Tathāgata A synonym for Buddha meaning "Thus Come" or "Thus Gone"

Theravāda "School of the Elders"—Buddhist tradition found predominantly in Sri Lanka, Burma, Thailand, Laos, and Cambodia. It is also one of the Buddhist traditions now practiced in the West.

uddacca Restlessness, agitation, excitement, distraction, "shaking above," without rest

upekkhā Equanimity

vedanā Feeling

vicāra Sustained application; a factor of the first jhāna

vihāra Dwelling place, abode

viññāna Consciousness

vipassanā Insight meditation

viriya Energy

vitakka Initial application; a factor of the first jhāna

Acknowledgments

A DEEP BOW OF GRATITUDE to all my teachers, in particular, Anāgārika Munindra and Sayadaw U Paṇḍita, both of whom fostered in me a deep love of the satipaṭṭhāna teachings. Munindra's open-minded approach to Dharma practice laid the foundation for my ongoing interest in exploring different ways of developing mindfulness. And Sayadaw's great learning and mastery of the teachings set a very high bar of aspiration and endeavor.

I'm grateful to Anālayo and his own inspiring work on the Satipaṭṭhāna Sutta and to Bhikkhu Bodhi (and Wisdom Publications), whose masterful translations of the Buddha's teachings have made them eminently accessible to non-Pali scholars.

For a writer, a good editor is gold, and I've had the good fortune to work with two of the best. This book owes a great deal to Nancy Burnett and Amy Rost, both of whom contributed immeasurably to the organization and clarity of the work. Their skill and insight have refined and improved every page of this manuscript.

I would also like to thank Jill Shepherd for her efforts in tracking down the source of many of the quotations, and Dennis Holmes and Lloyd Williams for their initial encouragement to make these teachings on satipaṭṭhāna more widely available.

Finally, much appreciation to Reid Boates, my agent, and Tami Simon and the Sounds True team, all of whose interest and enthusiasm helped fuel the many hours of work necessary to bring this book to completion.

While many people have contributed to this work, whatever errors there may be are strictly my own.

May the merit of this Dharma offering be shared
by all beings everywhere. May it be dedicated to the welfare,
happiness, and awakening of all.

Notes

INTRODUCTION

1. Kelly McGonigal, "Healing the Whole Person," *Shambhala Sun,* January 2011, 60.

2. Bhikkhu Ñāṇamoli and Bhikkhu Bodhi, trans., *The Middle Length Discourses of the Buddha* (Somerville, MA: Wisdom Publications, 1995), 145.

3. Ibid., 1189n137.

CHAPTER 1

1. I drew on two translations for this rendition of a quote from the Satipaṭṭhāna Sutta number 10: Ñāṇamoli and Bodhi, *The Middle Length Discourses,* and Bhikkhu Anālayo, *Satipaṭṭhāna: The Direct Path to Realization* (Cambridge, UK: Windhorse Publications, 2003), 3–4.

2. Quoted in Dilgo Khyentse Rinpoche, "Teachings on Nature of Mind and Practice," *Tricycle: The Buddhist Review,* winter 1991. Reprinted in that article with permission from Editions Padmakara (St. Leon sur Vezere, France, 1990).

3. Shabkar Tsogdruk Rangdrol, *The Life of Shabkar,* trans. Matthieu Ricard (Albany, NY: State University of New York Press, 1994), 56–57.

4. From the Dhammapada. There are innumerable translations of the Dhammapada. This is my own rendition based on different readings over the years.

CHAPTER 2

1. Nārada Thera, *The Buddha Dhamma or The Life and Teachings of the Buddha* (New Delhi, India: Asian Educational Services, 1999), 69.

CHAPTER 3

1. Stephen Carter, *Civility* (New York: Harper Perennial, 1999).

2. Ñāṇamoli and Bodhi, *The Middle Length Discourses,* 207.

3. Ibid., 209.

4. Ajahn Chaa, *A Taste of Freedom* (Ubolrajadhani, Thailand: The Sangha Bung Wai Forest Monastery, 1991). Ebook available through the eBook Library at BuddhaNet: Buddhist Education and Information Network (buddhanet.net), website of the Buddha Dharma Education Association Inc.

CHAPTER 4

1. Ajahn Sucitto, from a talk given at the Insight Meditation Society on March 10, 1999.

CHAPTER 5

1. Bhikkhu Bodhi, trans., *The Connected Discourses of the Buddha* (Somerville, MA: Wisdom Publications, 2000), 961.

2. Gil Fronsdal, trans., *The Dhammapada* (Boston: Shambhala Publications, 2005), 29.

3. Ñāṇamoli and Bodhi, *The Middle Length Discourses,* 983.

4. Bodhi, *The Connected Discourses,* 1825.

CHAPTER 6

1. Walter Harding, *The Days of Henry David Thoreau* (Princeton, NJ: Princeton University Press, 1983), 464–465.

2. Quoted in Aldous Huxley, *The Perennial Philosophy* (New York: HarperPerennial, 2009), 285.

3. Quoted in Anālayo, 114.

4. "The Udana: Inspired Utterances of the Buddha, 1.10," quoted in Ajahn Pasanno and Ajahn Amaro, *The Island* (Redwood Valley, CA: Abhayagiri Monastic Foundation, 2009), 62–63.

CHAPTER 7

1. Ñāṇamoli and Bodhi, *The Middle Length Discourses,* 955.

2. Ibid., 956–58.

3. Ibid., 145.

4. Anālayo, 129n50.

5. Ibid., 128n45.

6. Ñāṇamoli and Bodhi, *The Middle Length Discourses,* 748.

7. Ibid., 943.

8. Ibid., 944.

9. Bodhi, *The Connected Discourses,* 1778.

CHAPTER 8

1. Anālayo, 4–5.

2. Ñāṇamoli and Bodhi, *The Middle Length Discourses,* 104.

3. Jack Kornfield and Paul Breiter, eds., *A Still Forest Pool: The Insight Meditation of Achaan Chaa* (Wheaton, IL: Quest Books, 1984, 2004), 162.

CHAPTER 9

1. Anālayo, 5.

CHAPTER 10

1. Anālayo, 5–6.

2. Ibid., 6.

3. Ibid.

4. Ñāṇamoli and Bodhi, *The Middle Length Discourses,* 281.

5. Ibid., 148.

6. Buddhaghosa, *The Path of Purification,* trans. Bhikkhu Ñāṇamoli (Kandy, Sri Lanka: Buddhist Publication Society, 2010), 366.

7. John D. Ireland, trans., "Attadanda Sutta: The Training (Sn 4.15)," Access to Insight, accessed August 20, 2012, accesstoinsight.org.

8. Nārgārjuna, quoted in trans. Lama Surya Das, *Natural Great Perfection* (Ithaca, NY: Snow Lion Publications, 1995), 61.

9. Nyoshul Khen Rinpoche, quoted in trans. Lama Surya Das, *Natural Great Perfection* (Ithaca, NY: Snow Lion Publications, 1995), 61.

10. The Dalai Lama, *A Flash of Lightning in the Dark of Night* (Boston: Shambhala Publications, 1994), 97.

11. Anālayo, 6–7.

CHAPTER 11

1. Bodhi, *The Connected Discourses,* 1265.

2. Ibid.

3. Ibid.

4. Ñāṇamoli and Bodhi, *The Middle Length Discourses,* 1134–35.

5. Anālayo, 7.

6. Bodhi, *The Connected Discourses,* 1272.

7. Amaro Bhikkhu, *Small Boat, Great Mountain* (Redwood Valley, CA: Abhayagiri Buddhist Monastery, 2003), 67.

8. Ñāṇamoli and Bodhi, *The Middle Length Discourses,* 347.

CHAPTER 12

1. Ñāṇamoli and Bodhi, *The Middle Length Discourses,* 1134.

2. Ibid., 340.

3. Ibid., 730.

4. Ibid., 401.

5. Ibid.

6. Maurice Walshe, trans., *The Long Discourses of the Buddha* (Somerville, MA: Wisdom Publications, 1987, 1995), 167.

7. Anālayo, 8.

CHAPTER 13

1. Anālayo, 8.

2. Bhikkhu Bodhi, *The Numerical Discourses of the Buddha* (Somerville, MA: Wisdom Publications, 2012), 97.

3. Anālayo, 8.

4. Ajahn Chaa, *A Taste of Freedom* (Kandy, Sri Lanka: Buddhist Publication Society Wheel Publications, 1988), 1.

5. Anālayo, 179n27.

6. Sayadaw U Tejaniya, *Don't Look Down on the Defilements, They Will Laugh at You,* 1st U.S. ed. (Kula, HI: Vipassana Metta Foundation, n.d.), 76.

CHAPTER 14

1. Anne Lamott, quoted in Anne Cushman, "The Wellspring of Joy," *Yoga Journal* (Jan/Feb 2004).

2. Fronsdal, 29.

CHAPTER 15

1. Michael Carrithers, *The Forest Monks of Sri Lanka* (Delhi: Oxford University Press, 1983), quoted in Anālayo, 183.

2. Anālayo, 8.

3. Ñāṇamoli and Bodhi, *The Middle Length Discourses,* 366.

4. Bodhi, *The Connected Discourses,* 1594.

5. Anālayo, 8–9.

6. Ñāṇamoli and Bodhi, *The Middle Length Discourses,* 208.

7. Bhikkhu Bodhi, ed., *In the Buddha's Words* (Somerville, MA: Wisdom Publications, 2005), 203–4.

CHAPTER 16

1. Carl Gustav Jung, "The Philosophical Tree," paragraph 335, in R. F. C. Hull, trans., *Alchemical Studies: Collected Works of C. G. Jung,* Volume 13 (Princeton, NJ: Princeton University Press, 1967), 265.

2. Thich Nhat Hanh, quoted in "Psychology—Seeding the Unconscious," excerpted from *Common Boundary* magazine on the website LifePositive, lifepositive.com, accessed April 1999.

3. Shāntideva, *A Guide to the Bodhisattva's Way of Life,* Stephen Batchelor, trans. (Dharamsala, India: Library of Tibetan Works and Archives, 1988), 58.

CHAPTER 17

1. Bodhi, *The Connected Discourses,* 1597.

2. Ibid., 1600.

3. Kornfield and Breiter, *A Still Forest Pool: The Insight Meditation of Achaan Chaa.*

CHAPTER 18

1. Nyanaponika Thera and Hellmuth Hecker, *Great Disciples of the Buddha: Their Lives, Their Works, Their Legacy* (Somerville, MA: Wisdom Publications, 1997), 189.

2. Anālayo, 9.

CHAPTER 19

1. Anālayo, 9.

2. Bodhi, *The Connected Discourses,* 1568.

CHAPTER 20

1. The phrase "cloudless, stainless vision of the Dhamma" appears frequently in different suttas. "'[T]urning upright what had been overthrown, revealing what was hidden, showing the way to one who was lost, or holding up a lamp in the dark for those with eyes to see,'" Bodhi, *The Numerical Discourses,* 1502.

2. Bodhi, *The Connected Discourses,* 230.

3. Fernando Pessoa, "Live, You Say, in the Present," *Poems of Fernando Pessoa,* Edwin Honig, trans. (San Francisco: City Lights Books, 2001), 31.

4. Acharya Buddharakkhita, trans., *Dhammapada: The Buddha's Path of Wisdom* (Kandy, Sri Lanka: Buddhist Publication Society, 1985), 76.

5. Christine Cox, "The Groucho Moment: Horsing Around with His Holiness," *Tricycle: The Buddhist Review,* spring 2004. Reprinted with permission from Christine Cox.

6. Wislawa Symborska, "View with a Grain of Sand," *View with a Grain of Sand: Selected Poems* (New York: Harcourt Brace and Company, 1995).

CHAPTER 21

1. Ñāṇamoli and Bodhi, *The Middle Length Discourses,* 350.

2. Bhikkhu Bodhi, ed., *A Comprehensive Manual of Abhidhamma* (Kandy, Sri Lanka: Buddhist Publication Society, 2003), 156.

3. Bodhi, *The Connected Discourses,* 952.

4. Victor S. Johnston, *Why We Feel: The Science of Human Emotions* (New York: Basic Books, 1999), 19–20.

5. Ajahn Jumnien, quoted in Anālayo, 94n7.

6. Mahāsi Sayadaw, from the translation of a taped talk "The Purification and Progress of Insight" (Malaysia, 1988), given to meditators at a certain stage of their practice.

CHAPTER 22

1. Anālayo, 9–10.

2. Bodhi, *The Connected Discourses,* 955–56.

3. Ibid., 877.

4. Dilgo Khyentse Rinpoche, "Teachings on the Nature of Mind and Practice," *Tricycle: The Buddhist Review,* winter 1991.

5. Bodhi, *The Connected Discourses,* 973.

6. Adapted from Bodhi, *The Connected Discourses,* 936–37.

7. Ibid.

8. Ibid.

9. Dilgo Khyentse, *The Collected Works of Dilgo Khyentse: Volume One* (Boston: Shambala Publications, 2010), 292–93.

CHAPTER 23

1. Bodhi, *The Connected Discourses*, 1140.

2. Anālayo, 10–11.

3. Bodhi, *The Connected Discourses*, 1232–33.

4. Sallie Tisdale, *Women of the Way: Discovering 2500 Years of Buddhist Wisdom* (San Francisco: Harper San Francisco, 2006).

5. Bodhi, *In the Buddha's Words*, 346.

6. Bodhi, *The Connected Discourses*, 207.

CHAPTER 24

1. Anālayo, 10.

2. Bodhi, *In the Buddha's Words*, 358.

3. Rune E. A. Johansson, *The Psychology of Nirvana* (London: Allen and Unwin, 1985), 96.

4. Anālayo, 229.

5. Anālayo, 11.

CHAPTER 25

1. Walshe, 418.

2. Bodhi, *The Connected Discourses*, 1587.

3. Ibid., 1583.

4. Ibid., 1595.

5. Anālayo, 11.

CHAPTER 26

1. Ānāpānasati Sutta, from Rupert Gethin, trans., *The Buddhist Path to Awakening* (Oxford, England: Oneworld Publications, 2001), 147.

2. "Early Buddhist Philosophy 9: The Questions of King Milinda," an online collection of "passages from Henry Clark Warren, *Buddhism in Translation, and Edward Conze, Buddhist Scriptures,* with modifications," Department of Philosophy, University of

Miami College of Arts and Sciences, as.miami.edu/phi/bio/
buddha/milinda.htm.

3. Gethin, 185.

4. Ñāṇamoli and Bodhi, *The Middle Length Discourses,* 1900–1901.

5. Dilgo Khyentse Rinpoche, "Teachings on Nature of Mind and Practice," *Tricycle: The Buddhist Review,* winter 1991.

6. Bodhi, *The Numerical Discourses,* 1250.

CHAPTER 27

1. Ñāṇamoli and Bodhi, *The Middle Length Discourses,* 947.

2. Quoted in Gethin, 78

3. Quoted in Gethin, 117.

4. Ledi Sayadaw, *The Manuals of Buddhism* (Yangon, Myanmar: Mother Ayeyarwaddy Publishing House, 2004), 316.

5. Tejaniya, *Don't Look Down on the Defilements,* 57.

6. Shāntideva, *The Way of the Bodhisattva,* trans. Padmakara Translation Group (Boston: Shambhala Publications, 1997), 112.

CHAPTER 28

1. Buddhaghosa, *The Path of Purification,* 740–41.

2. Suzuki Roshi, *Zen Mind, Beginners Mind* (New York: John Weatherhill, 1973), 46.

3. Ibid., 36.

CHAPTER 29

1. His Holiness the Sixteenth Gyalwa Karmapa, "On Confidence in Dharma: An Interview," Karma Triyana Dharmacharkra: North American Seat of His Holiness the Gyalwa Karmapa, kagyu.org, accessed 1998.

2. Nyanatiloka, *Path to Deliverance,* 4th ed. (Kandy, Sri Lanka: Buddhist Publication Society, 1982), 65–66.

3. Anālayo, 12.

4. Bodhi, *The Connected Discourses,* 1596.

5. Sayadaw, *The Manuals of Buddhism*, 666.

6. Thanissaro Bhikkhu, trans., "Viija-bhagiya Sutta: A Share in Clear Knowing (AN 2.30)," Access to Insight: Readings in Theravāda Buddhism, accesstoinsight.org.

7. Nyanatiloka, *Path to Deliverance*, 65–66.

CHAPTER 30

1. Anālayo, 12.

2. Upasika Kee, *Pure and Simple*, trans. Thanissaro Bhikkhu (Somerville, MA: Wisdom Publications, 2005), 49–50.

3. Tejaniya, *Awareness Alone Is Not Enough*, 1st U.S. ed. (Maui, HI: Vipassana Metta Foundation), 84. This book is available for free download.

4. Tejaniya, *Don't Look Down on the Defilements*, 23–24.

CHAPTER 32

1. Anālayo, 13.

2. Ñāṇamoli and Bodhi, *The Middle Length Discourses*, 278.

3. Bodhi, *The Connected Discourses*, 1868–69. For quotes throughout chapters 33 through 43, the original Pali term "dukkha" has been used instead of its usual English translation, "suffering," with the translator's/publisher's blessing. Bhikkhu Bodhi himself has pointed out that "suffering" captures only one nuance of "dukkha." I prefer to use the Pali term, so that readers can consider all shades of meaning in the context of the Buddha's words.

4. Anālayo, 245.

5. Bodhi, *The Connected Discourses*, 1844.

6. Bodhi, *The Numerical Discourses*, 686.

7. Ibid., 675.

8. Ibid., 876–78.

9. Ibid.

10. Ibid.

11. Bodhi, *The Connected Discourses,* 957. Throughout this quotation, the singular masculine pronoun *he* has been changed to the gender-neutral plural *they.*

12. Ibid., 1844–45

CHAPTER 33

1. Thanissaro Bhikkhu, trans., *Itivuttaka: This Was Said by the Buddha* (Barre, MA: Dhamma Dana Publications, 2001), 13.

2. Bodhi, *In the Buddha's Words,* 205.

3. Bodhi, *The Connected Discourses,* 941.

4. Ñāṇamoli and Bodhi, *The Middle Length Discourses,* 131.

CHAPTER 34

1. This quotation comes from the first discourse of the Buddha and is widely translated. This is an adapted version based on two translations: Bodhi, *The Connected Discourses,* 1844, and Thanissaro Bhikkhu, "The Four Noble Truths: Excerpts from the Pali Cannon," DharmaNet, dharmanet.org/4nobletruthssutras.htm.

2. Constance Wilkinson, trans., "Patrul Rimpoche (1808–1887): 'Advice from Me to Myself'," sealevel.ns.ca/patrul/.

3. Bodhi, *In the Buddha's Words,* 193.

4. Andre E. Ferguson, *Zen's Chinese Heritage: The Masters and Their Teachings* (Somerville, MA: Wisdom Publications), 20.

5. Bodhi, *In the Buddha's Words,* 366.

6. Thanissaro Bhikkhu, *A Handful of Leaves, Volume One* (Redwood City, CA: The Sati Center for Buddhist Studies; and Valley Center, CA: Metta Forest Monastery, 2002), 75.

7. Thanissaro Bhikkhu, *A Handful of Leaves, Volume Two* (Redwood City, CA: The Sati Center for Buddhist Studies; and Valley Center, CA: Metta Forest Monastery, 2003), 111.

8. Ajahn Maha Boowa, *Straight from the Heart* (Udorn Thani, Thailand: Wat Pa Baan Taad, 1987), 110, 132–33. Author's note: In *Straight from the Heart,* the twelfth sentence of the second paragraph reads, "If there is a point or a center of the knower

anywhere, that is the essence of a level of being." But when I was getting permission to use this quotation for my book *One Dharma*, the monk from the monastery in Thailand said that that was a mistranslation; he said it should instead read, "If there is a point or a center of the knower anywhere, that is an agent of birth."

CHAPTER 35

1. Walshe, 348.

2. René Daumal, *Mount Analogue* (New York: King Penguin, 1986), 11.

3. Bodhi, *The Connected Discourses*, 1808.

4. Ibid., 1792–93.

5. Ibid., 1795.

6. Dzigar Kongtrül, *It's Up to You* (Boston: Shambhala Publications, 2005), 128–29.

CHAPTER 36

1. Ñāṇamoli and Bodhi, *The Middle Length Discourses*, 934.

2. Ibid.

3. Nyanaponika Thera and Hellmuth Hecker, *Great Disciples of the Buddha: Their Lives, Their Works, Their Legacy* (Somerville, MA: Wisdom Publications; Kandy, Sri Lanka: Buddhist Publication Society, 1997), 34.

CHAPTER 37

1. Walshe, 348.

2. Bodhi, *The Numerical Discourses*, 117.

3. Ibid., 119.

4. Bodhi, *The Connected Discourses*, 698–99.

CHAPTER 38

1. Ñāṇamoli and Bodhi, *The Middle Length Discourses*, 208.

2. Walshe, 348.

3. Thanissaro Bhikkhu, trans., "Tapussa Sutta: To Tapussa (AN 9.41)," Access to Insight: Readings in Theravāda Buddhism, accesstoinsight.org.

4. Ibid.

5. Stephen Mitchell, *Parables and Portraits* (New York: Harper and Row, 1990), 48.

6. Ajahn Sumedho, *The Mind and the Way: Buddhist Reflections on Life,* (Somerville, MA: Wisdom Publications, 1995), xix.

CHAPTER 39

1. Rainer Maria Rilke, *Rilke on Love and Other Difficulties: Translations and Considerations,* trans. John J. L. Mood (New York: WW Norton and Co., 1975), 10.

2. The Amaravati Sangha, trans., "Karaniya Metta Sutta: The Buddha's Words on Loving-Kindness (Sn 1.8)" Access to Insight: Readings in Theravāda Buddhism, accesstoinsight.org.

3. His Holiness the Dalai Lama, *Dzogchen: The Heart Essence of the Great Perfection,* trans. Thupten Jinpa and Richard Barron (Ithaca, NY: Snow Lion, 2004), 211.

4. Jane Kramer, "Me, Myself, and I: What Made Michel de Montaigne the First Modern Man," *The New Yorker,* September 7, 2009, 40.

CHAPTER 40

1. His Holiness the Dalai Lama, *Tibetan Portrait: The Power of Compassion,* Phil Borges, photographer (New York: Rizzoli International Publications, 1996).

2. Wesley Autrey, quoted in Cara Buckley, "Man Is Rescued by Stranger on Subway Tracks," *The New York Times,* January 3, 2007.

3. Paul Farmer, quoted in Tracy Kidder, *Mountains Beyond Mountains: Quest of Dr. Paul Farmer, A Man Who Would Cure the World* (New York: Random House, 2003).

4. Shāntideva, *The Way of the Bodhisattva,* trans. Padmakara Translation Group (Boston: Shambhala Publications, 1997), 50–52.

5. Henry David Thoreau, *Faith in a Seed: The Dispersion of Seeds and Other Late Natural History Writings,* ed. Bradley P. Dean (Washington, DC: Island Press, 1993), xviii.

6. Yongey Mingyur Rinpoche, *The Joy of Living: Unlocking the Secret and Science of Happiness* (New York: Harmony Books, 2007), 251–52.

CHAPTER 41

1. Bhikkhu Bodhi, *The Noble Eightfold Path* (Seattle: BPS, Pariyatti Editions, 1984, 1994), 43.

2. Ibid., 47. Bodhi is quoting the Buddha's words found in the Anguttura Nikaya from another book, *The Word of the Buddha,* by Nyanaponika Thera (his own teacher).

3. Ibid., 49–50.

4. Nyanaponika Thera, via Bodhi, *The Noble Eightfold Path,* 50.

5. Ñāṇamoli and Bodhi, *The Middle Length Discourses,* 21.

6. Nyanaponika Thera, via Bodhi, *The Noble Eightfold Path,* 52.

7. Bodhi, *The Numerical Discourses,* 816.

CHAPTER 42

1. Walshe, 348.

2. Bodhi, *The Noble Eightfold Path,* 54.

3. Thich Nhat Hanh, *For a Future to Be Possible: Commentaries on the Five Wonderful Precepts* (Berkeley, CA: Parallax Press, 1993).

4. Walshe, 280–81.

5. Robert E. Buswell, Jr., *Tracing Back the Radiance: Chinul's Korean Way of Zen* (Honolulu, HI: University of Hawaii Press, 1991), 102.

6. Ibid., 109.

7. Ibid., 106.

8. His Holiness the Dalai Lama, *Essential Teachings* (Berkeley, CA: North Atlantic Books, 1995), 50.

CHAPTER 43

1. Matthieu Ricard, *Journey to Enlightenment: The Life and World of Khyentse Rinpoche, Spiritual Teacher from Tibet* (New York: Aperture Foundation, 1996), 104.

2. Jonah Lehrer, "Don't! The Secret of Self-Control," *The New Yorker*, May 18, 2009.

3. Bodhi, *The Noble Eightfold Path*, 72.

4. Ibid., 76.

5. Ñāṇamoli and Bodhi, *The Middle Length Discourses*, 1838.

6. Anālayo, 13.

7. Ibid., 13.

CHAPTER 44

1. Bodhi, *The Connected Discourses*, 1372.

2. Ibid., 1373.

3. Anālayo, 13.

4. Bodhi, *The Noble Eightfold Path*, 120.

APPENDIX A

1. For my rendering of the Satipaṭṭhāna Sutta, I have mostly adopted the translation given in Ñāṇamoli (1995): p.145–55. In a few instances, however, I have ventured to introduce my own renderings, based on the understanding gained in the progress of my research. In order to facilitate references to particular passages of the discourse, I have inserted a short headline above each section—Trans.

2. In the actual discourse, each of the individual stages of the corpse in decay is followed by a full version of the "refrain," which, for the sake of convenience, I have abbreviated here—Trans.

Index

A

Abbey of Gethsemani, 113–114
Abhidhamma, 131, 189, 227, 229,
  240
  beautiful factors of mind, 184–185,
    229, 396
  categories of mental factors,
    183–184, 266
  perception in, 37–38
abiding independent, 40–41, 118
absorption, 269–270
actions, 28
  consequences of (karma), 330,
    383–384
  motivations behind, 62–63, 102,
    186, 235, 283
  Right Action, 320, 379–386
  sense and, 206
  skillful vs. unskillful, 102–103
  suitability of, 63–64
  ten unwholesome actions, 158, 330
  unskillful, dwelling on past,
    157–158
activities, mindfulness of, 61–65
addictions, 347–348
ādīnava, 301–305
"Advice From Me to Myself," 310–311
aggregates. *See* five aggregates of
  clinging
agitation, 304–305
air element, 70
Ajahn Chaa, 39, 51, 60, 87–88, 107,
  151, 236, 283

Ajahn Dhammadaro, 49
Ajahn Jumnien, 193
Ajahn Maha Boowa, 49, 316–318
Ajahn Mun, 4
Ajahn Sucitto, 21, 23
Ajahn Sumedho, 15, 39
"already aware," 161–162
Anagarika Munindra, xi, 64
Anālayo, xii, xvi, 29, 48, 114
  biography of, 405
  on conditioned progression, 215
  on dhammas, 121
  on knowing, 35, 52
  on mindfulness, 150, 219–220
Ānanda, 30, 59–60, 97, 207–208,
  258, 263
  Tapussa and, 346–347
Ānāpānasati Sutta, 248
Anāthapiṇḍika, 334
anattā, 58, 114, 192, 274
anger, 103. *See also* aversion
anicca, 57. *See also* impermanence
Anna Karenina, 126
Anurādha, 200–202
Anuruddha, 12, 154–155
anxiety, 155
application, 147, 184
arahant(s), 41, 59
ardency, 3–9
arising and passing away, 29–31,
  115–116, 212–215, 221

Ashe, Arthur, 293
Assaji, 304–305
asubha, 68
attachment, 283, 392
attention, 184, 227, 258
    diversion of, 393–394
    lack of, 126, 252
    precision in, 159–160
    unwise, 157, 167–168, 212
    wise, 284, 344, 392
Auden, W. H., 356
Autrey, Wesley, 364
avarice, 184
aversion, 131–139
    attachment to, 392
    causes of, 132–134
    conditions underlying the removal
        of, 134–138
    practicing mindfulness for,
        134–135
    preventing future arising of,
        138–139
awakening. *See* realization; seven
    factors of awakening
awareness
    as already present, 161–162
    compassion and, 367–368
    continuity of, 231
    naked/bare, 230, 396–397
    pure, 316
    stability of, 227–228
Awareness Alone Is Not Enough,
    273–274

B
Bahiya, 41–42
Bahiya Sutta, 41–42
balance, 15–16, 278–280
Bankei, 216
bare knowing, 35–42, 116–117, 188,
    396–397
Barre Center for Buddhist Studies,
    xii, 314
Basho, 230
beautiful factors of mind, 184–185,
    229, 396
*Benedict's Dharma: Buddhists Reflect on
    the Rule of Saint Benedict,* 443

Bhagavad Gita, 283
bhāvanā, 266
bhikkhu(s), xv-xvi, 4, 12
Bhikkhu Bodhi, 168, 186, 189, 235,
    277
    on liberation, 403
    Noble Eightfold Path, The, 371–372,
        373, 377, 395
    on right mindfulness, 396–397
Bodh Gaya, xi, 47, 64, 149, 243, 256,
    270, 355, 396
Bodhi tree, 14, 214, 297
bodhichitta, 76, 219, 254, 367, 387
Bodhidharma, 314
bodhisattva, 56, 282
Bodhisattva, the, 57, 91, 362, 365,
    373
body, 3, 45–46, 198. *See also*
    mindfulness of the body
    anatomical parts, 67–69
    composite nature of, 198
    contemplation of, 28–29
    corpses, 76–77, 220
    elements, the, 69–76
    impermanence of, 68, 76–77
    mindfulness of, 28–29, 43–77
    sense of self and, 198
    wrong attitude, 68–69
boredom, 143–144
brahmavihāra(s), 108, 266, 281, 284
Brahmayu, 49
Brantley, Jeffrey, MD, xiii
breath/breathing, 29, 45–54, 191,
    272–273
    awareness of, 50–52
    calming the formations, 53–54
    experience of whole body, 52
    mindfulness of, 50–54, 260–261
    practicing with, 46–50, 260–261
    specific instructions on, 50–54
Buddha, the
    charge to his first enlightened
        disciples, 12
    on concentration, 398
    on contingent nature of
        consciousness, 189
    direct path of, xv, 402
    enlightenment of, 91

"Fire Sermon" of, 208–209
first discourse of, 290
on the first noble truth, 297
on the foundation for realization, 288
as "the Great Physician," 211
on impermanence, 201–202
on livelihoods to avoid, 386
on longevity of the Dharma, 23
on lying, 372, 374
nibbana, description of, 402
Pali language used by, xv
range of instructions by, xiv–xv, 45
reflecting on, 14–15
on senses, 206, 209–210
on seven factors of awakening, 225–227
song of enlightenment, 214
"thirty-seven principles of enlightenment" of, 265
on true happiness, 219
on truthfulness, 372, 374
Buddha, Dhamma, and Sangha, 253–254
Buddhadasa, 103
buddhadharma, 331
Buddhaghosa, 267, 331
Buddhist Path to Awakening, The, 296
Burmese Vihara, 47, 149, 355, 396

C
calm, 257–263
qualities of, 259–260
role/importance of, 259–260, 262–263
ways to develop, 260–262
Campbell, Joseph, 352
Carrithers, Michael, 121–122
Casals, Pablo, 276
"catalogue consciousness," 348
categories
of mental factors, 183–185
mindfulness of, 121–122
cetanā, 186
Ch'an, 192
change, 5–8, 173, 280, 291–295. *See also* impermanence
children, karmic relationship with, 334

Chinul, 385
Choedrak, Dr. Tenzin, 363–364
citta, 189, 316
clarity of cognition, 146–147
clear comprehension, 11–12, 61–65, 231
clear recognition, 236–237
clear seeing, 35, 95–96, 257–258
clearly knowing, 11–12, 61, 146–147
clinging, 69, 169–202, 303, 338–339. *See also* five aggregates of clinging
clinging to naught, 348
five aggregates of, 169–202
freeing the mind from, 71, 195–202
material elements and, 173
versus desire, 215
Coleridge, Samuel Taylor, 164, 331
commonality of human condition, 12
comparison (comparing mind), 155–156
compassion, 94, 296–297, 361–368
awakening in ourselves, 362–365
empathy and, 363–364
as limitless, 365
practice and expression of, 366–368
comprehension, clear, 11–12, 61–65, 231
conceit, 184, 236
concentration, 21–23, 95, 265–276
absorption, 269–270
arousing, 271–274
concentration factors of the Eightfold Path, 320, 389–403
as constructed and conditioned, 270
developing and strengthening, 272–274
emptiness concentration, 401
as factor of awakening, 265–276
four developments of, 267–269
imbalance with energy, 145, 156–157
importance of, 265, 267–269
jhana and, 267–269
meditative states of, 266–267
momentary, 269–270
one-pointedness, 265–266

qualities of, 107–108
Right Concentration, 320,
   397–398
two aspects of, 265–267
working with thoughts, 274–276
concepts, 173, 176–181
conditioned experience
cessation of conditioned consciousness,
   315
   drawbacks of, 311–312
   dukkha of, 295–296
   the unconditioned (nibbana),
      315–318
conditioned mind, 317–318
conditioned nature of consciousness,
   188–191, 206–208
conditioned nature of perception,
   215–220
conditioned response, 82–84, 175,
   212–214
conditioned thoughts and emotions,
   185–186
Connected Discourses of the Buddha,
   195, 207–208, 225, 267
consciousness, 18–19, 188–193
conditioned nature of, 188–191,
   206–208
   investigating, 191
contact, 184
continuity of mindfulness, 22–23,
   35–42, 117–118, 231, 283
   posture and, 55–56
contraction, 105–107
corpses, contemplation of, 76–77, 220
courage, 56–57, 241–242
Cox, Christine, 178–179
craving, 214, 299–300, 309–310
   drawbacks of, 301–305
   first domain of (desire for sense
      pleasures), 300–301
   leading to suffering, 303
   nine things rooted in, 303
   second domain of (desire to be),
      305–306
   third domain of (desire for
      nonexistence), 307
   ways to abandon, 311–315

Cunningham, Michael, 104
cycles of hope and fear, 304–305

D
Daizu Huike, 314
Dalai Lama, the, 76, 113–114, 281,
   332
   on anger, 360
   on compassion, 362
   Groucho Marx mask and, 178–179
   on honoring one's enemies, 138
   on karma, 8–9
   lovingkindness of, 353–354
   on motivations, 102, 283
Dalhousie, 380–381
dangers, 301–302
   of insight, 249–251, 259
dark night of the soul, 93, 282
Daumal, René, 320
death, 74–75, 245
   corpses, contemplation of, 76–77,
      220
   distraction at moment of, 321
   mindfulness of, 293–295
decision, 184
defilements, 208–210, 211, 215, 384
   latent, preventing the arousal of,
      391–392
   uprooting, 269, 315, 320–321, 401
delusion, 103, 184, 339, 393. See also
   Mara
dependent arising, 212–215
   breaking the chain of, 212–213
   of defilements, 208–210, 212
desire, 121–129, 214–215
   avoiding future arisings of, 128
   conditions underlying, 125–127
   conditions underlying the removal
      of, 127–128
desire to do, 184
distinguished from craving, 299–300
   as enemy of lovingkindness,
      356–358
   freedom from, 21
   happiness and, 126, 302–303
   knowing when it's absent, 125
   mindfulness of, 214–215

questioning if necessary and helpful, 351

recognizing, 124–125, 357

for sense pleasures, 300–301

sexual misconduct, abstaining from, 382

steps to working with, 124–128

versus clinging, 215

Devadatta, 268

devas, 255–256

dhamma(s), 1, 3, 119–168, 398–399. *See also* mindfulness of dhammas

basic organizing principles, 121–122

Buddha, Dhamma, and Sangha, 253–254

contemplation of, 124

dhamma/dharma, meanings of, 121

five aggregates of clinging, 169–202

four noble truths, 285–323

hindrances, effect on the mind, 122–124

hindrances, the five, 119–168

investigation of, 233–238, 257–258

seven factors of awakening, 233–284

steps to working with, 124–128

Dhamma, the, 126, 201

Dhammadinnā, 92, 93, 250–251

Dhammapada, 103, 116, 137, 230, 240, 266

on happiness, 254, 349

on karma, 8

path of practice, 379

dhammavicaya, 233

dharma. *See* dhamma(s)

Dharma, the, 168, 276

longevity of, 23

preciousness of, 4–5

qualities of, 211–212

reflecting on, 14–15

"Setting the Wheel of the Dharma in Motion," 290

Diamond Sutra, 238, 348

difficult emotions, 144

Dilgo Khyentse Rinpoche, 4–5, 76, 199–200, 202, 237–238, 367, 393

diligence, 283

Dipa Ma, 95, 146, 256, 268, 281, 331, 359

direct experience, 30, 173, 238

realization through, 334–335

direct path, xv, 402. *See also* Satipatthana

direct perception, 121–122

discernment, 16–17, 233–238, 346

lack of wise, 167–168

discontent, 21, 143–144

Discourse to Bahiya, 41–42

disenchantment, 312

distortions of experience, 342–344

diṭṭhi. *See* wrong view

divine abodes, 281

Dogen (Zen master), 65

dosa, 131

doubt, 163–168

knowing the cause and how to remove it, 167–168

knowing when present and absent, 166

manifestations of, 164–167

as most dangerous of hindrances, 164

in practice(s), 165–166

in the teachings, 164

drowsiness, 143–144

Duke Integrative Medicine, xiii

dukkha, 57–58, 281, 287–297. *See also* craving; suffering

cause of (second noble truth), 299–307

cessation of (third noble truth), 309–318

cessation of, way leading to (fourth noble truth), 319–323

of changing nature of all things, 291–295

of conditioned experience, 295–296

experience of, 289–296

as first noble truth, 287–297

five aggregates of clinging as, 338–339

as gateway to awakening and compassion, 296–297

meaning of, 288–289

of painful experiences, 291
wholesome responses to, 364–365
dukkhakhanda, 172
Dzigar Kongtrul Rinpoche, 323
Dzogchen masters, 65, 74, 310, 316, 358, 367
Dzogchen tradition, 4–5, 161, 165–166, 314
fabricated mindfulness in, 18–19

E

earth element, 70
effort, 4, 242–244, 391–396
balancing the quality of, 242–244
cycle of energy and, 244
effortless, 40
in mindfulness, 18, 36
repeated, 36
Right Effort, 320, 391–396
eight worldly vicissitudes, 278–280
Eightfold Path (The Noble Eightfold Path), 319–320, 325–403
concentration factors, 320, 389–403
importance of, 321–322
morality factors, 320, 369–387
Noble Eightfold Path, The (Bhikkhu Bodi), 371–372, 373, 377, 395
Right Action, 320, 379–386
Right Concentration, 320, 397–398
Right Effort, 320, 391–396
Right Livelihood, 320, 386–387
Right Mindfulness, 320, 396–397
Right Speech, 320, 371–378
Right Thought, 345–368
Right View, 327–344
stream-entry, 320–323
wisdom factors, 320, 325–368
elementary schools, teaching mindfulness in, xiii–xiv
elements, 69–76
contemplation of, 71
material elements, 173
emotions. *See* feelings
empathy, 363–364
emptiness concentration, 401
energy, 184, 239–246

arousing, 244–246, 258
causes for arising of, 244–246
effort and, 242–244
imbalance with concentration, 145, 156–157
meanings of viriya, 240
as power to do, 240–242
"Enlightened Vagabond, the," 310
enlightenment
as a real possibility, 402–403
factors. *See* seven factors of awakening
four noble truths and, 285–323
of laypeople, 32–33
realization of, 401–403
"thirty-seven principles of enlightenment," 265
Enron scandal, 382
envy, 184
equanimity, 277–284
as a divine abode, 281
as a parami, 282–283
balance and, 278–280
developing and strengthening, 283–284
eight worldly vicissitudes, 278–280
wisdom aspect of, 281–282
ethical conduct (sila), 15, 22, 160, 254, 271–272
experience, distortions of, 342–344.
See also direct experience
external practice, 28–29, 111–114
eyes, opening, 148, 160

F

fabricated mindfulness, 18–19
faith, 168, 185
fame and disrepute, 279–280
family members, 331–334
Farmer, Dr. Paul, 365
fear, 56–57, 304–305
of wrongdoing, 185, 228, 229
feelings, 3, 79–97, 103, 184
as aggregate of clinging, 173–175
awareness of, 106–107
changing nature of, 86–87
conditioned response and, 82–84

difficult, 144
distinguishing, 89–90
feeling tone, 174
  identification with, 199–200
  impermanence of, 174, 340
  liberation through, 81–88
  mindfulness of, 79–97, 173–175
  moment-to-moment awareness of,
    85–87, 96
  pleasant, unworldly, practice with,
    96
  pleasure, beneficial and unbeneficial,
    92
  relationship to mind, 135–136
  Satipatthana Refrain and, 96–97,
    111–118
  unworldly, 91–96
  *Why We Feel: The Science of Human
    Emotions,* 190–191
  worldly and unworldly, 89–98
  worldly, dangers of, 90
fetters. *See* defilements
fire element, 70, 341
"Fire Sermon (the)," 208–209
five aggregates of clinging, 169–202,
  296, 316, 338–339
  changing nature of, 340–342
  consciousness, 188–193
  contemplating, 195–202
feelings, 173–175
formations, 183–188
  material elements, 173
  particular aggregate predominant at
    the moment, 342
  perception, 175–181
  viewing as non-self, 197–200
five hindrances, the, 119–168
  aversion, 131–139
  desire, 121–129
  doubt, 163–168
  restlessness and worry, 153–162
  sloth and torpor, 141–151
focus, 22–23, 159–160, 397–398. *See
  also* attention; concentration
  of attention, 48–49
  on good qualities in people,
    359–360
Forest Refuge, xii
formations, 183–188

four categories of mental factors,
  183–185
four divine abodes, 75
four foundations of mindfulness, xv
Four Immeasurables, 368
four noble truths, 285–323, 338
  first: dukkha, 287–297
  second: cause of dukkha, 299–307
  third: cessation of dukkha,
    309–318
  fourth: the way leading to cessation of
    dukkha, 319–323
four qualities of mind, 1–23
  ardency, 3–9
  clearly knowing, 11–12
  concentration, 21–23
  mindfulness, 13–19
fruition, 315

G
gain and loss, 278–279
Gandhi, 353
generosity, 94, 254–255, 283
  practice of, 329–330
Genghis Khan, 313
Genjo Koan, 65, 228
Gestalt psychology, 252
Gethin, Rupert, 227, 256, 296
Gladwell, Malcolm, 396
gocara, 418
Goenka, S. N., 387
good friends/company, 149, 227,
  283–284
gossip, 374–375
gradual cultivation, 385–386
"Grain of Sand, View with a" (poem),
  179–180
"Great Physician, the," 211
greed, 184
Grey, Terence. *See* Wei Wu Wei
"guardians of the world," 228, 229
Guide to the Bodhisattva's Way of Life, A,
  138, 366–367
guilt, 161

H

habit patterns, 385, 392
  changing, 350–351
hallucinations of perception, 217–218, 343
happiness, 247, 254, 256, 262–263. See also rapture
  desire and, 126, 302–303
  pleasant abiding, 267–268
  taking what is unsatisfactory to be, 218–219
harm, abstaining from, 94, 343–344, 380–381
hatred, 131, 184
heart-mind, 316
Hero with a Thousand Faces, The, 352
hindrances, 119–168, 385. See also dhamma(s)
  "antihindrances," 225
  aversion, 131–139
  basic organizing principles, 121–122
  desire, 121–129
  doubt, 163–168
  the five hindrances, 119–168
how hindrances impact the mind, 122–124
  mindfulness of, 393
  restlessness and worry, 153–162
  sloth and torpor, 141–151
  steps to working with, 124–128
hiri, 228–230, 393
His Holiness the Dalai Lama. See Dalai Lama, the
His Holiness the Sixteenth Gyalwa Karmapa, 75, 258
Homer, 125
Hours, The, 104
Hsu Yun, 4
human birth, preciousness of, 148, 332, 392
humility, 367

I

"I" and "mine", false sense of, 41, 71–73, 191, 192, 197, 208, 219, 338. See also self; selflessness
identification, 314–315, 318

ignorance, 71
Iliad, The, 125
ill will, 17, 59, 101–102, 117
immeasurables, 354, 368
impermanence, 57, 74, 185, 195–196, 238, 280, 281. See also arising and passing away
  awareness of, 312–313
  of the body, 68, 76–77
  contemplation of, 29–33
  direct experience of, 30
  dukkha and, 291–295, 338
  of feelings, 86–87, 88, 340
  of five aggregates of clinging, 340–342
  insight into, 195–196
  of material elements, 173
  reflection on, 5–8
  of sense feelings, 302–303
  taking to be permanence, 217
  of thoughts, 237–238
  true knowledge of, 200
independence (abiding independent), 40–41, 118
insight, 262, 268–269
  imperfections/"danger" of, 249–251, 259
Insight Meditation Society, xii, 22, 68–69, 154, 241, 249, 373, 382
insight practice, 35, 274–275
intention, 52, 186–188
internal practice, 28–29, 111–114
investigation of dhammas, 233–238
  cultivating investigation, 234–238

J

Jataka Tales, 283
jhana(s), 70, 108, 266, 267–270, 397–398
  vipassana jhanas, 267
Johansson, Rune, 216
Johnston, Victor S., 190–191
Journey to Enlightenment, 393
joy, 93–96. See also rapture
Joy of Living, The, 367–368
Joya, 341

Joyce, James, 294–295
judgment (self-judgment), 158, 161
Jung, C. G., 131–132

K

Kalama Sutta, 384
Kali (maid), 137
Kalu Rinpoche, 176
Kalupahana, David, 40
karma
    consequences of actions, 330,
        383–384
    karmic debt, 332
    law of, 8, 329–335, 386
    reflection on, 8–9, 245–246
    relationship with children, 334
    relationship with parents, 331–333
Karmapa, His Holiness the Sixteenth
    Gyalwa, 75, 258
kasinas, 266
Kazantzakis, Nikos, 149
khanda, 172
Kidder, Tracy, 365
kilesas, 104
killing, 94, 380–381, 383
kindness, 358. See also lovingkindness
King, Martin Luther, Jr., 242, 353,
    365
Kinnell, Galway, 160
knowing mind, 314–315
knowledge, 268
    bare knowing, 35–42, 116–117
    pairwise progression of knowing
        and object, 36, 192
    true knowledge, 200
Krishnamurti, 234
kukkucca, 153

L

Lamott, Anne, 113
latent defilements, 391–392
laziness, 143–144. See also sloth and
    torpor
Ledi Sayadaw, 29, 205, 258, 265, 283,
    343
Lehrer, Jonah, 394

"less, not more," 306
Levenson, Claude, 364
liberation, 337–344, 401–403. See
    also nibbana
    as a real possibility, 402–403
    noticing liberated mind, 108–109
    perception and, 175
    "short moments many times," 108
    through feelings, 81–88
life faculty, 184
Life of Pi, 164
The Life of Shabkar, 5–8
light, focusing on, 147
listening, 376
Long Discourses of the Buddha, 319
long-enduring mind (ardency), 3–9
love, 94, 356, 358
lovingkindness, 138–139, 283,
    353–360
    benefits of practicing, 356
    cultivating, 358–360
    desire as "near enemy" of, 356–357
    focus on good qualities in people,
        358–360
    practice of, 354–355
lust, 382–383
lying, 372–374

M

Madoff scandal, 382
magga phala, 315
Maha Ghosananda, 68–69
MahaNaga, 250–251
Mahānāma, 32–33, 321
Mahāsatipaṭṭhāna Sutta, 337
Mahasi Sayadaw, 49, 95–96, 192, 249,
    289, 314
Mahasi tradition, 51
Mahayana, 238
Manual of Factors Leading to
    Enlightenment, 265
Manuals of Buddhism, The, 258
Mara, 14, 45–46, 62–63
Marpa, 268
Martel, Yann, 164

Marx, Groucho, 178–179
material elements, 173
meditation, 87–88
 different experiences of, 322–323
 proper fields for, 64
 sloth and torpor in, 142–143
 states of absorption (jhanas), 70,
  108, 266, 267–270, 397–398
meditation retreats, xiii, 115, 221,
 244, 249
mental clarity, 146–147
mental factors, 183–186, 265–266
 contemplation of, 185–186
mental noting, 39–40
Merton, Thomas, 113
mettā, 138–139, 353–360. *See also*
 lovingkindness
 benefits of, 356
 practice of, 354–355
Middle Length Discourses, 49, 319,
 346
Milarepa, 268
Milinda, Questions of, 233–234, 240
mind. *See also* mind states
 beautiful factors of, 184–185, 229,
  396
 contemplation of, 101
 contracted and distracted, 105–107
 ease of, 103
 emotions and, 135–136
 four categories of mental factors,
  183–185
 four qualities of, 1–23
 great and narrow, surpassable and
  unsurpassable, 107–109
 hindrances effect on, 122–124
 liberated, 108–109
mindfulness of, 99–118
monitoring, 108–109
 presence of mind, 228
 protecting, 16–18
 purification of, 59
 reactivity in, 114
 released, 316–318
 as sixth sense, 206
 training, 87–88
 unshakeable, 352
 wholesome and unwholesome states

 of, 16–18, 101–109, 167–168,
  184
 wholesome states of, arousing,
  113–114
 wisdom aspect of, 257, 337
mind, four qualities of, 1–23
 ardency, 3–9
 clearly knowing, 11–12
 concentration, 21–23
 mindfulness, 13–19
mind-body, 12, 36
 as resonating energy system, 12
 Satipatthana Sutta instructions on,
  xiv–xv
mind states, 16–18, 101–109, 131,
 393–395
 wholesome, 16–18, 113–114, 240
mindfulness, 13–19, 185, 393
 balancing the spiritual faculties,
  15–16
 "Be more mindful" instruction, 159
 continuity of, 22–23, 35–42,
  117–118, 231, 283
 establishment of, 32
 fabricated and unfabricated, 18–19
 as first factor of awakening,
  225–231
 focus "in front," 48–49
 four foundations/qualities of, xiv–xv,
  1–23, 227–231
 importance of, 108–109, 127–128,
  219–220
 momentum of, 36–37
 "more-or-less mindful," 167
 practicing internally and externally,
  28–29, 111–114, 221
 precision in, 159–160
 present-moment awareness, 13–14
 protecting the mind, 16–18
 remembering, 14–15, 228–230
 Right Mindfulness, 320, 396–397
 Satipatthana Refrain on, 35–42,
  117–118, 398–399
Mindfulness: A Practical Guide to
 Awakening, xii
Mindfulness-Based Cognitive Therapy,
 xiii
Mindfulness-Based Stress Reduction,
 xiii

mindfulness of categories of
phenomena, 121–122
mindfulness of dhammas, 119–169.
See also specific topics
aversion, 131–139
concepts, 176–181
consciousness, 188–193
desire, 121–129
doubt, 163–168
feelings, 173–175
five aggregates of clinging, 169–202
five hindrances, 119–168
formations, 183–188
four noble truths, 285–323
material elements, 173
noble eightfold path, 325–403
perception, 175–181
restlessness and worry, 153–162
seven factors of awakening,
233–284
six sense spheres, 203–222
sloth and torpor, 141–151
mindfulness of feelings, 79–97,
173–175. *See also* feelings
mindfulness of mental objects,
121–122
mindfulness of mind, 99–118
Satipatthana Refrain and, 111–118
wholesome and unwholesome roots
of mind, 101–109
mindfulness of seeing, 16
mindfulness of the body, 43–77
activities, 61–65
breathing, 45–54, 260–261
internal and external, 28–29
physical characteristics, 67–77
postures, 55–60
Mingyur Rinpoche, 367–368
mirrorlike, mindfulness as, 19, 117
Mischel, Walter, 394
Mitchell, Stephen, 350–351
Mogallāna, 149–150
moha. *See* delusion
moment-to-moment awareness,
85–87, 96
momentary freedom, 256
momentum of mindfulness, 36–37, 39

Mongol Empire, 313
monk. *See* bhikkhu
Montaigne, Michel de, 360
morality, 22, 102, 254, 283. *See also*
ethical conduct
morality factors of the Eightfold Path,
320, 369–387
"more-or-less mindful," 167
Mother Teresa, 14, 353
motivation(s), 15, 102, 186, 235, 283
awareness of, 12
consequences of, 330
recognizing, 62–63
Mount Analogue, 320
Mountains Beyond Mountains,
364–365
muditā, 393
mundane right view, 328–335
Munindra-ji, 22, 256, 268, 270, 341,
354
on meditation practice, 230
on observing the breath, 49
on unsatisfying nature of experience,
196

N
Nagasena, 234, 240
nāmarūpa, 58
Ñāṇananda, 38–39, 72
Nargarjuna, 74
Nazruddin, 35, 218
New York Times, The, 198, 211
New Yorker, The, 360, 394
nibbāna, xv, 315–318, 401–403
"ancient royal road to," 322
Buddha's description of, 402
descriptions of, 392
as possible in this lifetime, 402–403
realization of, 401–403
unconditioned, the, 315–318
Nietzsche, 372
nimitta, 267
nirvāna ("pseudo-nirvana"), 15
Noble Eightfold Path. *See* Eightfold
Path
Noble Eightfold Path, The (Bhikkhu
Bodhi), 371–372, 373, 377, 395

noble supernormal powers, 219–220

noble truths. *See* four noble truths

non-self. *See* selflessness

nonacceptance, 305

nondelusion, 64–65, 231

nonexistence, desire for, 307

nonharming, 94, 380–381, 383–384

nonreactivity, 82–84

not forgetting, 227–228

noting, mental, 39–40

Nyoshul Khen Rinpoche, 74, 358–359

O

Obama, President Barack, 343

occasionals, the, 184

O'Keeffe, Georgia, 57

Olendzki, Andrew, 314

One Dharma, 279

"One Fortunate Attachment," 306

one-pointedness, 184, 265–266

opposite, as antidote, 393

ottappa, 228–230, 393

Outliers, 396

overeating, 144–145

ownership, concept of, 177

P

Padmasambhava, 8

pain
   dukkha of painful experiences, 291

physical, 132

pleasure and pain, 280

pairwise progression of knowing and object, 36, 192

Pali, xv-xvi

paññā, trainings in, 320

Parables and Portraits, 350–351

paramis, 282–283, 322, 349

paramitas, 253

parents, karmic relationship with, 331–333

Parinibbāna Sutta, 265

Pasenadi, King, 92, 95, 321–322

passaddhi, 259

passive voice, 191

past, dwelling on, 157–158

path, 315, 320. *See also* Eightfold Path
   to realization, 319–323

Path of Purification, The, 73

patience, 283

paṭigha, 131

Patrul, 310–311

peace, 256, 282

perception, 37–39, 40–41, 175–181, 184
   attachment to perceptions, 216
   bias of, 216
   conditioned nature of, 215–220
   distortion of, 342–343
   four hallucinations of, 217–218, 343
   inaccuracy of, 175–176, 180–181
   limiting potential of, 38, 175
   role in conditioning and liberation, 175
   of solidity, 176
   superficial, 198
   as third aggregate, 175–181
   training our perceptions, 220

Perls, Fritz, 252

personality, as Not Self, 237, 339

personalizing difficulties, 134

Pessoa, Fernando, 177–178

physical characteristics, 67–77

physical sensation, 173

pīti, 247–256

place, concept of, 177

planes of existence, 330–331

Planet Earth, 295

pleasant abiding, 267–268

pleasure, 174, 186, 213
   attachment to, 392
   beneficial and unbeneficial types of, 92

pain and, 280
   sense pleasures, desire for, 300–301
   sense pleasures, drawbacks of, 301–305

pokati, 273

Pollock, Jackson, 159
Posthumous Pieces, 307
postures, 55–60
    changing, 148
    sitting posture, 47–48
practice(s)
    doubt in, 165–166
    focusing attention, 48–49
    fruition of, 402–403
    internal and external, 28–29,
        111–114, 221
    locations/fields for, 46–47, 64
    postures for, 47–48
    rewards of, 258
praise and blame, 279
preciousness of human birth, 148,
    332, 392
preciousness of the Dharma, 4–5
presence of mind, 228
present-moment awareness, 13–14
prompted consciousness, 18–19
pseudo-nirvana, 15
puñña, 419
Pure and Simple, 272–273
pure awareness, 316
Purification of View, 58, 192–193

Q

Questions of King Milinda, The,
    233–234, 240

R

radiant mind, 147
Rāhula, 59, 175, 374
Ram Dass, 341
Ramana Maharshi, 306
rapture, 184, 247–256, 258
    causes for arising of, 252–253
    five grades of, 248–251
    imperfections of insight, 249–251
    understanding and working with,
        251
    ways to strengthen, 253–255
reactivity, 114
realization, 337–344, 401–403. *See
    also* nibbana

foundation for, 288
    path to, 319–323
    of stream-entry, 322–323
    through direct experience, 334–335
rebirth, 211, 212, 330–331, 335
recognition, 38, 236–237
recollection, 14–15
Red Sox, 278
reflection
    on impermanence, 5–8
    on karma, 8–9, 245–246
    on preciousness of the Dharma, 4–5
    on samsara, 246
    use to weaken aversion, 136–138
    wise, 148–149, 160–161
refrain. *See* Satipaṭṭhāna Refrain
remembering, 14–15, 228–230
renunciation, 94–95, 219, 283,
    345–368
    blessings of, 350
    as gradual process, 349–350
    recognizing our addictions, 347–348
    ways to practice, 350–352
    wisdom of no, 351–352
    wise restraint, 348–350, 351
repetition, xvi, 27, 60, 96–97, 111
respect for the wise, 393
rest, 149–150
restlessness and worry, 153–162, 184
    causes of, 156–158
    conditions for removal of, 158–162
    manifestations of, 153–156
    mindfulness and, 158–159
restraint of the senses, 64, 128, 219,
    348–350
Rich, Adrienne, 373
Right Action, 320, 379–386
Right Concentration, 320, 397–398
Right Effort, 320, 391–396
Right Intention. *See* Right Thought
Right Livelihood, 320, 386–387
Right Mindfulness, 320, 396–397
Right Resolve. *See* Right Thought
Right Speech, 320, 371–378
    emotional tone, 375–376
    mindful listening, 376

slander and gossip, 374–375
truthfulness, 372–374
useless and frivolous talk, 377–378
Right Thought, 320, 345–368
compassion, 361–368
lovingkindness, 353–360
recognizing addictions, 347–348
renunciation, 345–368
wise restraint, 348–350
Right Understanding. *See* Right View
Right View, 320, 327–344
enhancing right view of non-self,
339–342
importance of, 337–338
law of karma and, 329–335
liberation, 337–344
subtlety of wrong view, 338–339
three distortions of experience,
342–344
worldly ease, 327–344
right view, 328
Rilke, 353
rūpa, 173
Ryokan, 40, 94, 297

S
sādhu, 255
Sai Baba, 341
St. Augustine, 309
St. Frances de Sales, 37
"St. Francis and the Sow" (poem), 160
St. John of the Cross, 93, 157, 282
sakkāyadiṭṭhi, 339
Sakya clan, 321
Salzberg, Sharon, 62, 340
samādhi, 21–22, 265–267, 391
"momentary samadhi," 23
trainings in, 320
vipassana samadhi, 401
samatha, 108, 262
sammādiṭṭhi. *See* Right View
sammāsankappa, 420
sampajañña, 11–12, 61
samphappalāpa, 377
saṃsāra, 5, 211–222
definition of, 115

reflection on, 246
wheel of, 211–222, 299, 307
wrong view and, 339
Samyutta Nikāya, 195, 225
San Francisco Zen Center, 252
Sangha, 14–15, 168, 253–254
saṅkārā(s), 183, 185
saññā. *See* perception
Sanskrit, xv-xvi
Sāriputta, 72, 287, 321, 332–333
sathi Sati, 189
sati, 13–19, 219–220, 227–231. *See
also* mindfulness
*Satipaṭṭhāna: The Direct Path to
Realization,* xii, xvi, 121, 215
Satipaṭṭhāna Discourse, 48
Satipaṭṭhāna Refrain, 27–42, 60,
96–97
abiding independent, 40–41, 118
arising and passing away, 29–31,
115–116, 221
bare knowing, 35–42, 116–117
conclusion of, 399
continuity of mindfulness, 35–42,
117–118
on dhammas, 398–399
on feelings and mind, 111–118
four foundations and, 27–33
importance of, 399
repetition of, 27, 60, 96–97, 111
sense spheres and, 221–222
Satipaṭṭhāna Sutta, xi, 195–196,
405–415. *See also mindfulness of
various aspects;* Satipaṭṭhāna Refrain
on calm, 259–260
conclusion of, 402
definition of the path, 3
as direct path to awakening, xv, 287,
402
on fetters/defilements, 215
on impermanence, 200
on mindfulness of feelings, 92
on mindfulness of four noble truths,
338
on mindfulness of mental objects,
121–122
range of instructions in, xiv-xv
repetition in, 27, 60, 111

on the senses, 206, 220
on seven factors of awakening,
223–284
translation of, 405–415
Sayadaw U Pandita, 15, 51, 142–143,
145, 291, 348
"Be more mindful" statement, 159
on sexual misconduct, 383
teaching techniques, 71, 136, 196,
249
on truth and lying, 373
on vipassana vs. jhana, 269
Sayadaw U Tejaniya, 108–109, 231,
242, 252, 273–275
on thoughts and desires, 351
seeing clearly, 35, 95–96, 257–258
self, 178–179, 197–201, 311
deconstructing the concept of,
200–201
forgetting, 65
"I" and "mine", false sense of, 41,
71–73, 185, 191, 192, 197, 208,
219, 338
passive voice and, 191
senses and, 206–207
taking what is non-self to be,
219–220
wrong view of, 339
self-control, 394
self-judgment, 158, 161
self-respect, 393
selflessness, 36, 58, 74–76, 114, 282
enhancing right view of, 339–342
five aggregates of clinging and,
197–200
mindfulness of dhammas and,
128–129
sense pleasures
desire for, 300–301
drawbacks of, 301–305
senses, 203–222. *See also* perception
conditioning and, 206–208,
215–220
defilements and, 208–210
experience of world through,
205–210
importance of, 205–206, 210
restraint of, 64, 128, 219, 348–350

Satipaṭṭhāna Refrain on, 221–222
sense objects, 205, 206
wheel of samsara and, 211–222
"Setting the Wheel of the Dharma in
Motion," 290
Seung Sahn Sunim, 9, 158
seven factors of awakening, 233–284
Buddha on importance of, 225–227
calm, 257–263
concentration, 265–276
contemplation of, 226–227
energy, 239–246
equanimity, 277–284
as "guardians of the world," 228,
229
how the factors work together, 275
investigation of dhammas, 233–238
mindfulness, 225–231
progression of, 227, 248, 257, 263,
277
rapture, 247–256
sexual misconduct, 382–383
shame, wise, 230
shamelessness, 184
Shāntideva, 138, 366
Siddhartha Gotama, xi, 91
sight, mindfulness and, 16
signless, the, 316
sīla, 15, 22, 160, 254, 271–272
trainings in, 320
sincerity, 259
Sisyphus, 350–351
sitting posture, 47–48
six sense spheres, 203–222
skillful actions, 102–103, 235–236,
361
slander, 374–375
sloth and torpor, 141–151, 184
causes of, 143–145
conditions underlying the removal
of, 145–148
description of, 141–142
in meditation practice, 142–143
mindfulness of, 145–146, 150
preventing future arising of,
150–151
solidity, perception of, 176

speech. *See* Right Speech
spiritual urgency, 245–246
Stanford University, 394
stealing, 381–382
stream-entry, 320–323
strength, 240–241
"Subway Hero," 364
suffering, 57, 82, 202, 287–297. *See also* dukkha
    avoidable, 102
    concept of self and, 180–181
    freeing the mind from, 81–88
    habit patterns of, 236–237
    terminology/word meanings, 288–289
    wholesome responses to, 364–365
sukha, 247–248
supernormal powers, 219–220
suttas. *See specific suttas by name*
Sutta Nipata, 74
Suzuki Roshi, 252–253
Symborska, Wislawa, 179–180

T
Ta Hui, 192
talking, too much, 157
taṇhā, 214, 299–300
Tao, 210
Tapussa, 346
Tathāgata, 30, 200–201, 202, 225
Teachings of the Buddha, xvi
Teijitsu, 208
ten unwholesome actions, 158, 330
Thai Forest masters/tradition, 4, 15, 21, 49, 151
Theravāda, 315
Thich Nhat Hanh, 63, 135–136, 362, 382
Third Zen Ancestor, 281
"thirty-seven principles of enlightenment," 265
Thoreau, Henry David, 36–37, 367
thoughts
    conditioned, 185–186
    emotions triggered by, 185

forcibly suppressing, 394
identification with, 199–200
impurities of, 275–276
nature of, 237–238
questioning if necessary and helpful, 351
two kinds of, 17, 346
unpleasant, 132–133
unwholesome, techniques for dispelling, 393–395
working with, 274–276
three characteristics of existence, 57–59
Tibetan Dzogchen. *See* Dzogchen masters; Dzogchen tradition
Tibetan tradition, 4–5, 161, 165–166, 314, 392
time, concept of, 177–178
Tolstoy, 126
torpor. *See* sloth and torpor
trainings in sila, samadhi, and panna, 320
tranquility, 185, 259–260, 262. *See also* calm
translation, notes on, xv-xvi
true knowledge, 200
truth, 372–374
    about desires, 126
    relative and ultimate, 73–76
truthfulness, 283, 372–374
Tsoknyi Rinpoche, 65
Tulku Urgyen Rinpoche, 310, 314
Twain, Mark, 372
"Two Kinds of Thoughts, The," 17, 346

U
Udāyi, 207–208
uddacca, 153
unconditioned, the, 315–318
unfabricated mindfulness, 19
universals, the, 184
unpleasant thoughts, situations, and experiences, 132–134, 174
unsatisfying nature of experience, 196–197

unshakeable mind, 352
unskillful actions, 102–103, 235–236, 361
  abstinence from, 379–380
  dwelling on past, 157–158
unwholesome actions, 158, 392
unwholesome factors of mind, 184
unwholesome states/patterns, 101–109
  abandoning, 393–395
  distinguishing wholesome states from, 167–168
  seductive powers of, 346
  techniques for dispelling, 393–395
unwise attention, 157, 167–168, 212
Upasika Kee, 272–273
upekkhā, 277–284
urgency, spiritual, 245–246

V
Varanasi, 290
vedanā, 81, 82, 85, 174
verbuti, 341
vicāra, 147
Videhika, 137
vihāra, 47
viññāna, 188
vipassanā, xi, 35, 108, 262, 269, 270
vipassanā jhānas, 267
vipassanā samādhi, 401
"vipassanā vendetta," 133
Virgin Mary, 113–114
viriya, 239–246
  Right Effort and, 391
Visakha, 92, 93, 387
vision, 268
vitakka, 147
volition, 186–188

W
walking, experience/contemplation of, 71
walking meditation, 23, 56
"When walking, just walk," 56, 262
water element, 70

Wei Wu Wei, 273, 307
wheel of samsara, 211–222, 299, 307. See also samsara
wholesome factors of mind, 184–185, 229, 393
wholesome states of mind, 16–18, 101–109, 113–114, 240
  arousal of, 395
  distinguishing from unwholesome, 167–168
  maintaining and strengthening, 395–396
willing suspension of disbelief, 164
wisdom, 268–269, 283, 323
  aspect of the mind, 257
  close association with, 230–231
  equanimity and, 281–282
wisdom factors of the Eightfold Path, 320, 325–368
wisdom of no, 351–352
Wisdom Publications, xvi
wise attention, 284, 344, 392
wise restraint, 348–350
Wittgenstein, Ludwig, 191
worldly right view, 328–335
worry. See restlessness and worry
wrong view, 184, 338–339
  of self (sakkayaditthi), 339
wrongdoing, fear of, 185, 228, 229

Y
Yankees, 278
yogi, 154
yogi mind, 154

Z
zafu, 349
Zen masters, 40, 65, 94, 158, 216, 297, 385
Zen Mind, Beginner's Mind, 252
Zen tradition, 228, 314, 316
Zorba the Greek, 149

About the Author

JOSEPH GOLDSTEIN HAS STUDIED AND practiced meditation since 1967. He is a cofounder of the Insight Meditation Society in Barre, Massachusetts, where he is one of the resident guiding teachers. In 1989 he helped establish the Barre Center for Buddhist Studies, a center for the integration of scholarly understanding and meditative insight, and in 1999 he helped envision and design the Forest Refuge, a center for long-term meditation practice. (For further information, please contact: Insight Meditation Society, 1230 Pleasant Street, Barre, Massachusetts 01005; dharma.org. For more information about Joseph's teaching schedule, visit onedharma.org.)

Joseph graduated from Columbia University in 1965 with a bachelor's degree in philosophy. He then spent two years teaching English as a Peace Corps volunteer in Thailand, where he first became interested in Buddhist meditation. After the Peace Corps, he spent most of the next seven years in India, studying and practicing with Anagārika Munindra, S. N. Goenka, and Dipa Ma, three renowned teachers of vipassanā meditation.

He began teaching in this country in 1974, and since that time has been leading intensive meditation retreats around the world, including an annual three-month retreat at the Insight Meditation Society. Since 1984, he has been a student of Sayadaw U Paṇḍita of Burma; and beginning in the early 1990s, Joseph also meditated under the guidance of Tulku Urgyen Rinpoche and Nyoshul Khen Rinpoche, two eminent Dzogchen masters.

The author of several books, he is also one of the contributors to *Benedict's Dharma: Buddhists Reflect on the Rule of Saint Benedict.*

About Sounds True

SOUNDS TRUE IS A MULTIMEDIA publisher whose mission is to inspire and support personal transformation and spiritual awakening. Founded in 1985 and located in Boulder, Colorado, we work with many of the leading spiritual teachers, thinkers, healers, and visionary artists of our time. We strive with every title to preserve the essential "living wisdom" of the author or artist. It is our goal to create products that not only provide information to a reader or listener, but that also embody the quality of a wisdom transmission.

For those seeking genuine transformation, Sounds True is your trusted partner. At SoundsTrue.com you will find a wealth of free resources to support your journey, including exclusive weekly audio interviews, free downloads, interactive learning tools, and other special savings on all our titles.

To learn more, please visit SoundsTrue.com/bonus/free_gifts or call us toll free at 800-333-9185.

SOUNDS TRUE
many voices, one journey